Sport, Culture, Society

D1643647

306 3388619?

Sport, Culture, Society

International historical and sociological perspectives

Edited by

J.A. Mangan and R.B. Small

Proceedings of the
VIII Commonwealth and International
Conference on Sport, Physical Education,
Dance, Recreation and Health

Conference '86 Glasgow
18–23 July

LETTERKENNY
306.
483
R.T.C. LIBRARY

PATRON
H.R.H. THE PRINCESS ANNE

LONDON   NEW YORK
E. & F.N. SPON

First published in 1986 by E. & F.N. Spon Ltd
11 New Fetter Lane, London EC4P 4EE
Published in the USA by E. & F.N. Spon
29 West 35th Street, New York NY 10001

© 1986 This collection: The Management Committee,
VIII Commonwealth and International
Conference on Sport, Physical Education,
Dance, Recreation and Health

Printed in Great Britain
at the University Press, Cambridge

ISBN 0 419 13920 6

All rights reserved. No part of this book may
be reprinted, or reproduced or utilized in any
form or by any electronic, mechanical or other
means, now known or hereafter invented,
including photocopying and recording, or in
any information storage and retrieval system,
without permission in writing from the
publisher.

British Library Cataloguing in Publication Data

Commonwealth and International Conference on Sport,
Physical Education, Dance, Recreation and Health (8th: 1986:
Glasgow)
Sport, culture, society – international historical and
sociological perspectives.
1. Sports — Social aspects — History
I. Title
306'.483   GV706.5
ISBN 0 419 13920 6

Contents

v

SECTION II SOCIOLOGICAL THEMES

Preface

The Conference Management Committee wish to express their sincere appreciation to H.R.H. The Princess Anne, Mrs Mark Phillips, a sportswoman of international renown, for her kindness in agreeing to become Patron to the VIII Commonwealth and International Conference.

Conference '86 has been a combined undertaking and credit for its success must be shared among the Conference Organising Committees, Professional Associations, The Scottish Sports Council, The Scottish Health Education Group, Glasgow District Council and Strathclyde Regional Council. The Conference has also benefitted from generous financial support provided by the Bank of Scotland and Guinness PLC.

The Management Committee has taken responsibility for all major decisions and guided the Conference administration from its inception. Membership of the Management Committee was as follows: Mr Telfer Blacklock (Scottish Education Department), Mr Derek Casey (Scottish Sports Council), Mr Graeme Donald (Adviser Borders Region), Mr Ben Fryer (Scottish Education Department), Mr Stanley Mitchell (Scottish Health Education Group), Mr Robin Smeaton (Coach to Scottish Squash Rackets Association), Mr David Wilkie (Jordanhill College of Education). The Management Committee also enjoyed the support of His Excellency Mr George Mamba (High Commissioner for Swaziland) and His Excellency Mr Ben Kipkulei (High Commissioner for Kenya).

The Programme Committee has worked with unswerving application and enthusiasm to create an interesting and attractive programme. The seven volumes of Conference Proceedings, published and available to delegates on the opening day of the Conference, are a fitting testimony to their skill and commitment.

The Programme Committee was formed with representatives drawn from the following associations: The Scottish Council for Physical Education, The British Society for Sports History, The International Association for the History of Sport and Physical Education (HISPA), The Scottish Sports Council and the Association of Scottish National Coaches, The British Association of Sports Sciences, The Scottish Council for Dance and the British Association for Sport and Medicine. The Programme Committee included the following members: Mr Graeme Donald, Mrs Sheena Good, Dr J.A. Mangan, Mr Roy Small, Dr Thomas Reilly, Dr James Watkins, Ms Peggy Woodeson, Mr Edwin Liddell, Mr Brian Porteous, Mr Robin Smeaton, Dr James Moncur and Dr James MacGregor.

The Finance and General Purposes Committee, a Subcommittee formed from the Management Committee controlled all financial matters and undertook responsibility for general administration. This Committee made a significant contribution to the success of the

Conference. Members of this Committee were as follows: Mr Ian Craik, Mr Derek Casey and Mr David Wilkie.

The co-operation and support of Jordanhill College of Education has been greatly appreciated. The Principal, Dr T.R. Bone, kindly made all the facilities and resources of the College available to the Conference.

Special mention must be made of the invaluable contribution made by the Conference Secretary, Ms Alison Maxwell, her assistant Ms Marie McCunn, Mrs Anne McLaren and Mrs Helen Smith for additional administrative support.

We are grateful to the speakers and participants for allowing us to publish their papers and hope that the Conference Proceedings will provide a valuable source of information and reference.

Bernard Wright
Director, Conference '86

Introduction

In his introduction to the Socio-Historical Section in the Proceedings of the VIIth Commonwealth and International Conference held in Brisbane in 1982, Dr James McKay suggested that the Conference was characterised by academic division and distance: historians were polarised into 'social historians' and 'descriptive and chronological' historians; sociologists split into 'critical sociologists' and in the absence of a label, we must suppose 'uncritical sociologists'; both historians and sociologists were internally divided regarding the appropriate conceptual and methodological approaches to their inquiries; cross-disciplinary exchanges were few and far between; 'pan-disciplinary' prospects were judged to be remote.

Disciplinary clouds seemingly dark and continuous, McKay looked for a silver lining. He urged both sociologists and historians to blend their studies into the wider mix of sport, leisure and recreation and eschew exclusivity. The fate of the conservative, he warned, would be to be passé and peripheral.

Four years have gone by. What of Glasgow '86? Perhaps it is a fortunate position for this editor to be in, due to printing deadlines, to have to write the editorial prior to the conference (and before all the papers are available). In the light of the comments on Conference '82 it might be better to travel than to arrive.

Several things are clear, however, from an initial consideration of available submissions. History and sociology remain self-absorbed. In history chronographers will share the lecture rostrum with interpreters; in sociology ideologists will mingle in the bar with empiricists. There is little evidence of a departure from exclusivity. Sport remains the central concern of most contributors. Plus ça change . . .

Perhaps conservatism is to be deprecated, possibly radicalism is to be espoused but it is arguable that more important than both is scholarship. Academic quality of contributions rather than the extent of their insularity ensures their acceptance among both 'marginalists' and 'mainstreamers'. Quality not integration should be the watchword for the next four years. Attention, acceptance and absorption stem directly from it.

J.A. Mangan
Editor, Socio-Historical Theme Committee
Glasgow, 1986

Section I

Historical Themes

SPORT AND SOCIETY: EMPIRE INTO COMMONWEALTH

HAROLD PERKIN
Department of History, Northwestern University

R.T.C. LIBRARY LETTERKENNY

Abstract of Keynote Address
"Let not England forget her precedence of teaching nations how to
live." - John Milton. The Doctrine and Discipline of Divorce.

The history of societies is reflected more vividly in the way they
spend their leisure than in their politics or their work. Sport in
particular is much more than a pastime or a recreation. It is an
integral part of a society's culture, an expression of its ideal of
man - and womanhood, a pursuit of the ends of life rather than the
means, an activity one really wants to do with one's whole self
unforced by the constraints of nature or the state. As such the
history of sport gives a unique insight into the way a society
changes and impacts on other societies it comes into contact with
and, conversely, the way those societies react back upon it. In
the case of Britain and its Empire in the last hundred years or so,
sport played a part both in holding the Empire together and,
paradoxically, in emancipating the subject nations from tutelage.
Thus it helped the Empire to decolonize on a friendlier basis than
any other in the world's history, and so contributed to the
transformation of the British Empire into the Commonwealth of
Nations.
   Every nation thinks itself superior in the important things of
life to all the others. In a marginal note to Areopagitica, his
unsurpassed argument for freedom of speech, John Milton casually
remarked that "God is English." For that reason God would naturally "reveal Himself to His servants, and as His manner is, first
to His Englishmen." It is not surprising therefore that in a later
work, concerned significantly to advocate divorce, Milton should
naively urge: "Let not England forget her precedence of teaching
nations how to live." He would have been more prophetic, perhaps,
if he had urged his fellow countrymen to teach the nations how to
play. Although sports and games are as old as the hills, few would
deny that most of the games the world now plays were first organized
in their present forms by the British in the nineteenth century:
association football, rugby, cricket, tennis, golf, rowing, track
and field athletics, and, most surprisingly for a country blessed
with a mild climate, skiing, which British sportsmen turned from a
Scandinavian peasant form of transport into an Alpine winter sport.

3

This precedence in competitive team games is all the more surprising
because the British had only just learned it themselves. Until the
early nineteenth century the British were renowned for their dis-
organized games: rowdy, bloodthirsty, cruel sports like bull and beer
baiting, dog and cock fighting, bare-fisted prize fighting, and games
of football for any number of players fought, literally, between
whole villages at risk of life and limb. The development of team
games was a reaction in the more orderly, civilized world of
Victorian Britain, if not from the bloodier sports themselves, then
from their suppression in the 1830s and 1840s.

All classes took part in the new organized games, though different classes tended to prefer different ones, but the class which
mattered most to the emerging Empire was the class educated at the
public schools. During the Victorian age organized games became
almost a religion in the private boarding schools which the British
absurdly call public. They were an antidote to the savage, boisterous free-for-all of an older society in which the playing fields
of Eton were a squalid battleground of hooligans and bullies.
Organized games in the reformed public schools of the new, reluctant-
ly industrial society were the cradle of leadership, team spirit,
altruistic self-reliance and loyalty to comrades - all the qualities
needed for the chief goal of upper middle-class education, the public
service. And the hardest and most challenging work in the public
service was governing the Empire.

When the public school boys and Oxbridge graduates went out to
rule the colonies they took with them the gospel of muscular
Christianity and organized games. There it helped to unite them, a
tiny minority in a hostile environment, around the values of home
and class. It also gave a self-confident class with little sympathy
for or understanding of non-European cultures something to offer the
natives more acceptable than Anglican Christianity alone. Cricket
and football, rugby and boxing were, of course, more acceptable to
the white settlers than to non-Europeans, but even the latter in the
long term, notably in India, Ceylon and the West Indies, took to
British games, especially cricket. In due course, beginning with the
white dominions, visiting cricket, rugby, soccer and other teams from
and return visits to Britain became symbols of the family relationship which held the Empire together.

The social cohesion symbolized by organized sport, however, can
cut both ways. It was not long before the visiting teams came to
stand for the cohesion of the colonial societies over against the
mother country, and sporting victory for jubilant escape from the
maternal apron strings. The triumph of taking "the Ashes of English
cricket" back to Australia was only one of many symbols of a growing
nationalism in the white colonies which would lead on to a mature
independence.

In the non-white colonies the story is more complex. Given the
segregated aloofness of the white ruling elite, it was not easy for
the races to mix on the playing field any more than off it, except
at the very highest level where the polo ponies of the Raj rode
against those of the Rajahs. For the subject races, however, the
mixture of love and hate, or at least admiration and dislike, they

4

felt for the conquerors led to a determination to outdo them at something, and the most convenient something was a competition harmless, non-political, and guaranteed to put the overlords' boasted sense of fair play to the test. This was perhaps most marked in the West Indies, where a love-hatred for the Anglicized upper class and its cricket became ritualized in a carnival version of the game at which the West Indians triumphantly excelled. In the end, cricket even survived the break-up of the Federation which the departing British left behind.

Although the British never like losing, they do it (or did before the advent of modern football hooliganism) more gracefully than most. At the finish, nothing became the largest empire the world has ever seen better than the leaving of it. Losing at organized games prepared the British psychologically, just as winning prepared the colonists, for decolonization and for the mutual acceptance of imperialists and former subject peoples on more or less equal terms - the more or less equal terms, perhaps, allowed to the "professionals" who regularly beat the "gentlemen" at cricket down to the Second World War, though it must be added that the professionals are now firmly on top and the gentlemen supperannuated. Thus organized sport paved the road from Empire to Commonwealth. Despite the family quarrels and, for some, loss by disenchantment and divorce, the spirit of organized sport continues to thrive and to symbolize both the independence of the parts and the cohesion of the whole of these Commonwealth Games.

ATHLETIC ALIENS IN ACADEME

JOHN BALE
Department of Education, University of Keele

Abstract
The international migration of sports personnel is a widespread
but under-researched phenomenon. The recruitment of student-
athletes by American universities is described historically and
geographically. A sample of European student-athletes is
analysed in order to discover their educational backgrounds and
achievements and their reactions to the overall experience of
being a foreign student-athlete in the USA.
Key words: Migration, American Universities, Student-athletes,
Recruitment, Education, Exploitation.

1. Introduction

The international migration of sports talent is analogous to
the "brain drain" yet it remains academically neglected.
Compared with the substantial literature on academic talent
migration (see, for example, Spaulding and Flack 1976) and
studies of students in foreign universities (e.g. Barber et al
1984, Klineberg and Hull 1979), published work on the
international movement of sports personnel is scant (Olin 1984),
though unpublished dissertations (e.g. Lay 1984, Hollander 1980)
illustrate the potential scope for scholarly studies of such a
global phenomenon.

The present study focuses on one type of international sports
talent migration, namely the recruitment by American universities
and colleges of foreign student-athletes. Initially, the
background and extent of such movement is described. The
educational backgrounds and achievements of such recruits are then
analysed since it is frequently asserted that student-athletes
are of relatively inferior academic calibre. In addition, the
overall experience of life as a foreign student-athlete is
assessed in view of the frequently held opinion that the
relationship between college and student-athlete is an
exploitive one.

2. The International Recruiting Game

The recruiting of sports talent by American universities and colleges is not a recent phenomenon (Cady 1978). The need for college sports teams to recruit talent from outside the immediate locality grew out of the American spirits of competition and boosterism. As Rooney (1980, 12) puts it,

> "the decision to adopt serious intercollegiate athletic programs was in large part prompted by what might be termed a 'glory of the place', place-boosting philosophy, combined with the growing commercial drive that in general character-ised American society .... The 'team' became a vehicle of community and school pride."

By the early 1950s national recruiting and the subsequent provision of "athletic scholarships" were the norm among the major sport-oriented universities. Today about 12,000 such scholarships are awarded annually and the national recruitment of high school talent has become a highly systematised affair.

A logical extension of national recruiting, the patterns of which have been described in detail by Rooney (1980, 1985), is recruitment at the international level of scale. Foreign student-athletes were initially attracted to the USA in the mid-1950s but the numbers remained relatively small until the 1970s. Many institutions and several sports are involved in the international recruiting game. The principal sport is track and field athletics but swimming, golf, tennis, ice hockey, skiing and gymnastics are also of significance. National statistics revealing the total number of foreign recruits are unavailable but the patterns shown by the information in Tables 1 and 2 for institutions in the Big 8 athletic conference are probably typical.

Table 1. Sports in which foreign student-athletes were recruited to Big 8 institutions, 1979-83

Sport	Number of foreign recruits
Track and field	42
Golf	10
Tennis	8
Skiing	5
Swimming	3
Others	4
Total	72

Source: Gautt 1983

Table 2.   Numbers of foreign recruits to Big 8 institutions
           1979-83

Year	Number of foreign recruits	Number of sports
1979	1	1
1980	8	3
1981	27	8
1982	18	5
1983	18	5

Source: Gautt 1983

The mid 1980s are witnessing a decline in the numbers of
foreigners being recruited, the result of legislation enacted
by the National Collegiate Athletic Association (NCAA) to reduce
the number of "over-age" student-athletes attending college.
This has had the de facto impact of reducing the number of
foreigners, many of whom had traditionally been over the age
of 20.

The spatial bounds from which student-athletes have been
recruited have expanded over time. Table 3 illustrates the
pattern for track and field athletics based on the number of
foreigners at college who have been included in the annual US
ranking lists published in Track and Field News. Whereas in the
mid 1950s virtually all such student-athletes came from Canada,
the Caribbean and north-west Europe, by the mid 70s the focus
had shifted much more to Africa. By the mid 1980s Kenya alone
supplied over 13% of such athletes, more than Canada (12%) or
the UK (9%).

Table 3.   Continental origins of superior male
           student-athletes; track and field athletics

	1955		1965		1975	
	n	%	n	%	n	%
Europe	8	53	13	37	29	30
North America	5	33	13	37	28	29
Oceania	2	13	3	9	5	8
Africa	0	0	3	9	24	25
South America	0	0	3	9	8	8
Asia	0	0	0	0	1	1
Total	15	100	35	100	95	100

(percentages may not add up to 100 due to rounding)

A number of questions arise from the brief background to international recruiting outlined above. For example, what kind of evaluation do foreign students make of alternative scholarship offers? What problems are posed by a period of sojourn in an alien environment? How many student-athletes remain in the USA when their life at college is over? These and other questions are addressed in the broader research project of which the present paper is but a small part. Space permits consideration of two particular aspects of such foreign recruits; first, the educational calibre of such foreign student-athletes and secondly the extent to which they are "exploited" by the system into which they are inducted. Having elaborated upon each of these reference can then be made to the findings of a questionnaire survey of European student-athletes undertaken by the author in 1985.

3. The "Dumb Jock" Hypothesis

A stereotype of American sporting life is the athletically able but intellectually inept student-athlete. For example, Shapiro (1984) indicated that over a 30 year period, 50% of students on athletic scholarship at Michigan State University were admitted with special considerations whereas the respective figure for the rest of the student body was only 3-4%. The same study showed that between 1950 and 1980 only 28% of student-athletes gaining a degree did so within 4 years of entry. At the University of Utah the overall graduation rate for student-athletes between 1973 and 1982 was 49% but this ranged from 62% for women's basketball to 34% for men's basketball (Henschen and Fry 1984). It is suggested by Nixon (1982) that those least likely to obtain degrees are in the major college sports of basketball and football but graduation rates obviously vary greatly between universities. For example, the graduation rates for football players in 1975/6 for seven universities quoted in Henschen and Fry (1984) ranged from 69% for Nebraska to 25% for Brigham Young University. Although it is difficult to generalise, it does seem that a substantial number of student-athletes from the USA is below the normal academic standard expected of a university undergraduate.

4. The Exploitation Hypothesis

The charge that student-athletes are exploited has been made by a number of observers of the American college sports scene. Evans (1979) states that "college athletes are recruited to work for their respective schools" while Sack (1977) asserts that student-athletes are a "proletarian class", ranking among the most exploited workers in American society. Snyder and Spritzer (1981, 337) summarise sport in the major university as having winning as a primary goal while individual development

9

is secondary and Ziegler (1979, 161) avers that the student-athlete is "pressurized inordinately". Sometimes exploitation is explicitly recognised by students themselves. Allen Bloomingdale, one-time college footballer, stated that "football used to be fun, but college has changed my mind over that. This university has stripped any love of football I ever had" (quoted in Isaacs 1978, 185).

If college sport is so exploitive why do students continue to accept athletic scholarships? According to Sack (1978) it is because they are victims of "false consciousness" or mystification, i.e. "Young athletes allow themselves to be exploited (because) they have often been conditioned from early childhood to value athletic accomplishment above all else" (Sack 1977, 96).

Although it is virtually impossible to empirically test whether false consciousness exists or not we can at least ask individuals if they feel themselves to be exploited by the system in which they find themselves. This is attempted in the second part of the section which follows.

5. Evidence from Europe

In the spring and summer of 1985 nearly 200 present or former European athletes who had at some time attended American universities were circulated with a questionnaire designed to elicit their backgrounds and experiences. A response rate of 50% included swimmers and track and field athletes, the majority from Britain but a small number from Sweden, Belgium and the Netherlands.

5.1 Academic Quality
The academic quality of the European student-athletes was assessed on three indicators. For British students their Ordinary and Advanced level General Certificate of Education (GCE) results were considered while for all respondents their intention with regard to higher education in their own countries and their subsequent rates of graduation in USA were taken into account.

In an attempt to establish international comparability of high school qualifications, the NCAA identifies 5 Ordinary level passes as minimal qualification commensurate with the grade point average of 2.0 "required" by American student-athletes for university entrance. British student-athletes were found to possess a substantially higher number of passes than this minimum standard, the average number of 'O' level passes being 6.5. Indeed over 80% had obtained at least 5 passes. What is more, 61.2% of the British student-athletes had obtained at least one 'A' level pass, the average being 1.5.

Of the European (including UK) student-athletes responding to the questionnaire 50% had been sufficiently serious about undertaking study in higher education to apply for entry to

institutions in their own countries. In several cases places had
been offered, only to have been subsequently rejected in favour
of American offers.

While at college in the USA few foreign students appeared to
experience problems with courses, only 15% so indicating. While
20.4% claimed to lack motivation in their studies over 80%
regarded the teaching as satisfactory or better. Only 20%
majored in PE or cognate subjects, the majority of European
student-athletes majoring in the Social Sciences.

In terms of graduation, 60.2% had either obtained or
expected to obtain a degree during their four years of athletic
eligibility. This is a high figure by American standards.

The evidence provided here suggests that European student-
athletes in American universities are, in an academic sense,
at least as good and on average almost certainly better than
their American counterparts.

5.2 Exploitation

Evidence of exploitation might most obviously be said to exist
if foreign student-athletes reacted negatively to their period
of sojourn in American universities. The questionnaire
respondents were asked to score their general feelings towards
the experience of being a student-athlete in the USA on a
"feeling thermometer" (Sudman and Bradburn 1982) on which
values ranged from 0 to 100, 50 being a neutral response and
scores over 50 indicating a "warm" feeling towards the
experience.

The modal value ascribed to the experience was 100 - a very
warm or favourable feeling, with the average being 87. Only
4 of the 93 respondents indicated a value of 50 or less and
none gave a value of less than 40. Such an overwhelmingly
favourable attitude towards the college experience is confirmed
by Hollander's (1980) survey in which he found that 77.6% of
respondent foreign track and field athletes in the USA
affirmed that they would encourage athletes from their own
countries to attend US colleges on the basis of their own
experiences.

Although such findings indicate that students do not feel
exploited in the way Allan Bloomingdale expressed his feelings,
the "feeling thermometer" obscures some indicators of possible
exploitation on the part of the universities concerned. For
example, when asked whether they thought their American degrees
would be of value in obtaining a job in their own country,
66% believed that they would, despite the fact that many
British professional bodies are known not to recognize American
degrees (Mellor 1961). This suggests that they had not been
fully informed about the value of their American qualifications.

Some of the problems cited by the European students also
hint at the possibility of an exploitive relationship. Although
59% rated the quality of the athletic coaching as satisfactory
or better, 31% claimed that problems existed in dealing with
the sports coach. There was also the suggestion in discussing

the factors influencing the final choice of university, that the coach may have exerted subtle pressure during the recruiting process.

However, on the available evidence claims of exploitation of foreign student-athletes are hardly proven and the most explicit evidence in fact tends to point in the opposite direction.

6. Conclusion

This paper has focussed on three aspects of the international recruitment of sports talent by American universities. First, such recruitment has grown steadily during recent decades and has gradually expanded over geographic space. Secondly, the academic quality of foreign student-athletes is high, probably higher than many of the American student-athletes with whom they mix. Thirdly, little evidence exists to suggest that foreign student-athletes feel themselves to be exploited by the college sports-set-up. Indeed some evidence (Sojka 1983) exists to suggest that it is the athletes who actually exploit the system.

The implications of this paper are that we should pause before making generalisations about the American college sports system. Sports are a heterogeneous collection of activities and what might apply to American students in football and basketball may not apply to foreign student-athletes in, say, track and field and swimming. Sportsworld is becoming a global arena; our knowledge of it will be enhanced with further studies of the international movement of sports talent.

References

Barber, E.G., Altbach, P.G. and Myers, R.G. (eds), (1980) Bridges to Knowledge: Foreign Students in Comparative Perspective. Chicago U.P., Chicago
Cady, E. (1978) The Big Game, University of Tennessee Press, Knoxville
Dunleavy, A., Miracle, A. and Rees, L. (eds) (1984) Studies in the Sociology of Sport, Texas Christian University Press, Fort Worth
Evans, A.S. (1979) Differences in the recruitment of black and white football players by a Big Eight university, Journal of Sport and Social Issues, 3, 2, pp 1-10
Gautt, P. (1983) personal communication.
Henschen, K. and Fry, D. (1984) An archival study of the relationship of intercollegiate athletic participation and graduation, Sociology of Sport Journal, 1, 1, pp 52-56
Hollander, T. (1980) A Geographic Analysis of Intercollegiate Foreign Track and Field Athletes in the United States, unpublished MA dissertation, Eastern Michigan University

Isaacs, N. (1978) <u>Jock Culture USA</u>, Norton, New York.

Lay, D. (1984) <u>The Migration of Scottish Footballers to the English Football League</u>, unpublished BA dissertation, University of Southampton

Mellor, B. (1961) <u>The American Degree</u>, Hong Kong University Press, Hong Kong

Nixon, H.C. (1982) The athlete as scholar in college: an exploratory test of four models, in Dunleavy, <u>et al</u>, (1982) pp 239-256

Olin, K. (1984) Attitudes towards professional foreign players in Finnish amateur basketball, <u>International Review for the Sociology of Sport</u>, 19, 3/4, pp 273-281

Rooney, J. (1980) <u>The Recruiting Game</u>, University of Nebraska Press, Lincoln

Rooney, J. (1985) America needs a new intercollegiate sports system, <u>Journal of Geography</u>, 84, 4, pp 139-143

Sack, A. (1977) Big time college football: whose free ride? <u>Quest</u>, 27, pp 87-96

Shapiro, B.J. (1984) Intercollegiate athletic participation and academic achievement, <u>Sociology of Sport Journal</u>, 1, 1, pp 45-51

Sojka, G. (1983) Evolution of the student athlete in America, <u>Journal of Popular Culture</u>, 16, 4, pp 54-67

Sudman, S., and Bradburn, N. (1982) <u>Asking Questions</u>, Jossey Bass, San Francisco

Ziegler, E. (1979) <u>Issues in North American Sport and Physical Education</u>, AAHPER, Washington

THE EFFECTS OF ACCULTURATION ON THE ABORIGINE: A CASE STUDY OF THE
SPORT OF CRICKET

MAXWELL L. HOWELL and R. A. HOWELL
Department of Human Movement Studies, University of Queensland

Abstract
Sport was viewed in Australia in the early years as a vehicle for
inculcating British norms and values into the Aboriginal culture.
Cricket in particular was seen as encouraging the adoption of
appropriate and acceptable behaviour characteristics and social
values. Although the first cricket team from Australia to tour
overseas was an Aboriginal team in 1867-8, the team had no official
status and their overseas successes did not lead to their acceptance
in cricket circles in Australia. This study discusses the first
Aboriginal team and analyses the careers of the three most
outstanding Aboriginal cricketers in Australia: Albert Henry, Jack
Marsh and Eddie Gilbert. Each one played for his State, but none was
selected to represent Australia. No male Aborigine has ever played
for Australia in cricket. The three State players were all fast
bowlers, who were "no balled" frequently and accused of "chucking".
After their playing careers ended, all three returned to their own
society, and each of their lives ended tragically. Their cricket
successes in the white community were only transitory experiences as
sport did not prove to be a "way out" for the Aboriginal cricketer.
They had learned the white man's game, but they did not acquire
social prestige or upward social mobility. Their expertise in the
physical skills of cricket did not lead to an acceptance or an
assimilation into the dominant white culture.
Key Words: Australia, Cricket, Aborigines, Social Prestige, Upward
Mobility, Assimilation.

1. Introduction

The Aborigines were virtually the sole occupants of the country which
we now know of as Australia for some 35-40,000 years. At the time of
white settlement in 1788, it has been estimated that there were some
300,000 plus Aborigines, coming from 200 separate tribes. Their
society was described by Fitzgerald (1982) as a "dynamic, balanced
and interdependent natural environment and a thriving human culture
composed of prosperous aboriginal nomads". Their society underwent
radical changes after 1788. In one state alone, Queensland, there
was only one-sixth of the population alive after sixty years of white
settlement.

The white settlers destroyed a lifestyle that had evolved over thousands of years, ignoring tribal territoriality and the husbanding of natural resources. There was cultural and sexual domination by the whites, and exploitation of the Aborigines as a labour source.

It was believed that sport might have a "civilizing effect" on the Aborigines. When reserves were set aside for their "protection", the sport of cricket was encouraged. It was argued that the British value system would accrue through the playing of games, particularly that of cricket, the game of Empire.

The Aboriginal Cricketers on Tour 1867-8

Mulvaney (1967) has researched extensively the Australian Aboriginal cricketers who toured England in 1867-8. They basically came from two tribes in western Victoria, where they had been playing cricket from about 1862 onwards, aided by white settlers who encouraged their participation. One of their early coaches was Australian-born but Rugby school educated T.W.Wills. Most of his family were annihilated by Aborigines in Queensland in 1861. Wills became a cricketer of note, playing for Victoria, and is one of those who pioneered Australian Rules football. He died of suicide in 1880.

In 1866, with Wills as captain, the Aborigines played at the Melbourne Cricket Ground. One player, Sugar, died before the match. The same year two of the Aborigines, namely Bullocky and Cuzens, played for their State, Victoria, in an inter-colonial match against Tasmania.

The Aborigines toured Sydney in 1867, but Watty died on the way home, and Jellico and Paddy soon after arriving back. The others - Tarpot and Dick-a-Dick - became seriously ill shortly thereafter. The Central Board for the Protection of Aborigines was asked to intervene to stop such tours, and they in turn appealed to the Chief Secretary and the Attorney-General to prevent a projected tour to England.

The team, however, secretly boarded a vessel on the way to England under the guise of going on a fishing trip. It was an unauthorised tour, it did not and still does not carry Australian status. It was, however, reasonably successful from the playing viewpoint, the highlights being games at the Oval against Surrey and at Lord's versus the M.C.C., won by the latter by a mere 35 runs. They played 47 matches from May 25 to October 17. Mullagh averaged 23.65 in batting in 45 matches and got 245 wickets for a 10 average. One player, King Cole, died on the trip. Mulvaney (1972) concluded that on their return the team went on to "obscurity and premature death". The game of cricket did not aid the assimilation and social mobility of these pioneers.

Albert Henry, Jack Marsh and Eddie Gilbert

The enforced movement of Aborigines to reserves, led by zealots such as the "Protectors" Archibald Meston and Walter Roth, caused a temporary cessation of Aborigines playing the game of cricket, particularly against white players.

However, by 1893 in Queensland, at the Deebing Creek Reserve, Aborigines such as Curtis, Coolwool, Brown and Thompson began playing cricket (Blades, 1985). Curtis in particular was outstanding, but he did not play for his State.

By 1901, there was an Aboriginal fast bowler, Larry Marsh, playing for New South Wales. His brother, Jack Marsh, also played in that year. In his first inter-colonial match he was no-balled fourteen times (Blades, 1985), and questions were increasingly raised about his bowling action. M. A. Noble, the sole N.S.W. selector, ruled that Marsh threw, and in 1902 the England captain refused to play against him. Despite this, Marsh played in 1902 against Queensland, which also had an Aboriginal fast bowler, Albert Henry, Queensland's first Aboriginal State representative in that sport.

Cricket historian Hutcheon (1949) was not impressed with Henry's initial State experience, though he took 2 for 63 and 1 for 38, stating he was "a real speed merchant but lacking in heart". Henry's performance in the return match was not rated any better.

Henry was rather a disappointment. He fielded well and in the first innings bowled fast and fairly well too, but in the second inning he 'dropped his bundle' as one of the Queensland players put it and elected to bowl a lot of slow stuff, which the batsmen were very severe on ... If we are to make a great bowler of him he needs taking in hand at once.

Interestingly, Albert Henry won the best bowling average in Queensland for the 1902-3 season, as did Marsh in the Sydney Club Competition of that year. However, neither was selected to play for Australia.

Henry increasingly came in conflict with the authorities, and his professional running did not endear him to the cricket administration. Hutcheon went on to say that

Henry was at times rather temperamental. A well-known umpire, A. L. Crossart, was officiating in a match between Toombul-Nundah and South Brisbane. The umpire (standing at square-leg) no-balled Henry on several occasions, considering his deliveries doubtful. The report of the matter subsequently delivered to the Q.C.A. read as follows:- "Mr. Henry, when the over was completed, deliberately went over to Umpire Crossart and said words to this effect, viz.: "You ... ..., you no-ball my good balls and the ones I did throw, you never. You know nothing about cricket." - at the same time shaking his hand in Umpire Crossart's face.

Henry was banned from playing cricket for a month over this outburst, and his "attitude" apparently got progressively worse. He was "removed from Deebing Creek [reserve] to Barambah, where he was imprisoned for one month 'for loafing, malingering and defying authority' " (Blades, 1985). He was sent to another reserve as his expressed and non-expressed attitudes continued to conflict with authority.

The other Aborigine to play for Queensland was the fast bowler Eddie Gilbert. Eddie was born in 1908 at Woodford and died at 69 years of age of congenital syphilis at Wacol where he had been a patient for 29 years at the Goodna Mental Asylum.

Gilbert was quiet, modest, unassuming and did not drink or smoke.

The remarkable thing about Gilbert was that he was a mere 5 ft. 8 inches and weighed approximately 9 stone. He had exceedingly long arms and used only a five yards run-up in his delivery.

Eddie Gilbert first came to public attention in the year 1930, when he was brought in to Brisbane to show his prowess at the nets. The impression was a favourable one, and in October, 1930, he was selected to play for Queensland Country against the Metropolitan Colts, and then for the Queensland Colts against N.S.W. Colts. He got six wickets for 82 in these games.

His form in these initial matches earned him his Queensland colours in the same season, 1930-31. In his first representative game, against South Australia, at the Brisbane Exhibition Grounds, Queensland was victorious, and Gilbert got 2 for 22 off 11 overs (4 maidens) in the first innings, and 2 for 76 in the second innings. His distinctively good performances earned him a spot on the Queensland team on its southern tour against N.S.W., Victoria and South Australia.

The 1931-32 season, his second, was Gilbert's high point. In his Sheffield Shield matches that year Gilbert got 21 wickets for 26.42 runs Thurlow, Queensland's other fast bowler, got only 17 wickets for 39.64 runs, and yet Thurlow represented Australia in that year, whereas Gilbert did not.

The first Sheffield Shield match of the 1931-32 season was against N.S.W. Following a disastrous first innings score by Queensland of 109, N.S.W. scored 432, with Gilbert getting 4 wickets for 84. Statistics are meaningless in analysing the sensation that occurred during N.S.W.'s first innings (Hutcheon, 1949).

> The innings will long be remembered in Queensland because of its sensational commencement. W. Bill was caught by Waterman off Gilbert before he had scored. The aborigine was sending them down at a tremendous pace. Then came the greatest achievement of Gilbert's career, which took the crowd at the Brisbane Cricket Ground by storm. The aborigine found a weak spot in the armour of Don Bradman. One was not prepared for Bradman's weak showing on this occasion. Gilbert at his fastest was yards faster than any other contemporary Australian fast bowler. After all, it is the extra bit of pace that counts, and on this occasion it caught Bradman napping. Result - a triumph for Queensland's aborigine bowler.

Years later Sir Donald said that while Gilbert was fresh that day his bowling was the fastest he had ever faced. It was the only time the bat was knocked from his hands (Robinson, 1978).

> "He classed this short burst as faster than anything seen from Larwood or anyone else" (Robinson, 1978).

The dismissal of Bradman was an incredible performance. Australia's cricketing super-hero was dismissed for a "duck" by an Aborigine.

> Six weeks after the Bradman incident Melbourne umpire Andrew Barlow let it be known that he intended to no-ball Gilbert.

When Victoria began batting late in the first day he called the Queenslander from square-leg four times in succession and eight times in two overs.

Queensland manager J. Holdsworth said Gilbert's action had been passed as fair on his previous visit to Sydney, Melbourne, and Adelaide. Queensland players could not understand why some balls were passed and others banned when they could see no difference in his action.

Before this match, his ninth, Gilbert had bowled 1694 balls for 31 wickets without an umpire questioning the fairness of any delivery (Robinson, 1978).

Mr. Crawford, the school teacher at the Cherbourg Reserve, who knew Gilbert well, asserted that not only did Gilbert not throw, but that the Queensland manager who looked after Gilbert when he went to Brisbane informed them that he would be no-balled when he went south, that the southern umpires would "get him". The Crawfords claimed they received a telegram from the manager informing them that he had been unfairly no-balled in Victoria (Crawford, 1985).

The assertion that he threw undoubtedly damaged his career. It seems more than a coincidence that two previous Aboriginal bowlers, Jack Marsh and Albert Henry, who many felt should have attained higher representation were also subjected to similar assertions that they "chucked".

Gilbert was obviously an outstanding athlete. Though Aborigines in the early years might have been encouraged into the game by white people in the hope that it would have a civilizing effect on them, it would appear that those who did play did so of their own free will, with no coercion. Gilbert, in particular, simply liked to play, and his success at cricket not only had a socializing effect on the settlement but had a significant effect on its morale. It was a significant psychological boost to beat a surrounding town at cricket or any other sport, to have Eddie Gilbert represent his state, and to reflect in his accomplishments as he bowled out Wendell Bill and particularly Don Bradman.

Gilbert died of congenital syphilis, Henry died prematurely of tuberculosis, and Marsh was kicked to death in a pub brawl.

The ethnocentric ideology prevalent in Australia that extolled European, but particularly English, values, the national fervour that surrounded cricket, and the racial stereotype that existed of the Aborigine, all argued for exclusion of the Aborigine from the "white man's sport", at least at the very top level of the game. Although it was not openly verbalised, it is highly possible that when it came to playing cricket for Australia, Aboriginal athletes had to contend with unspoken racial prejudice at the highest levels.

A central issue is whether cricket has acted as an agent of social mobility and assimilation for the Australian Aborigine. The evidence is very clear that while there may have been momentary fame with limited social acceptance, these experiences were not lasting for the Aborigine.

Broome (1980), in his study of Aborigines in boxing, concluded that: 3 3886 192

> Overall, boxing aided the repression of the Aboriginal minority ..
> ....
> The fight game siphoned off many of the toughest, gamest, most
> aggressive Aborigines and placed them in a white controlled
> sub-culture far from their country communities. Therefore, boxing
> attracted many of those with the most initiative and chanelled
> their energies into an activity which proved not only fruitless
> for social change, but exposed those potential leaders of change,
> to personal physical damage in the ring and dissipation from the
> temptation of white urban life. Many a promising mission lad
> ended up a decade later on the heap or on the grog after a
> vainglorious fisticuffs career.
> ... Boxing has done more to reinforce the basic oppression of
> Aborigines, than to overcome it!

The same may be said of the Aborigines' experience with cricket.
The pity is that, in their own society, before the arrival of the
white man, the culture of the Aborigines was rich in games which
complemented their societal values. The imposition of the white
culture generally caused a cessation of their indigenous activities
and an adoption of white sports inherent with white values. Their
own culture lost much of its richness in the transition.

The overall effect of acculturation had been to impose the culture
of the white community on the Aborigines. However, it became
apparent that if the Aborigines learned the culture too well then
they stood the risk of outright rejection by the white community.

References

Blades, Genevieve Clare (1985) Australian Aborigines, Cricket and
    Pedestrianism: Culture and Conflict, 1880-1900. B.H.M.S.
    (Honours) Degree. Univ. of Queensland.
Broome, R. (1980) Professional Aboriginal Boxers in Eastern
    Australia 1930-1979. Aboriginal History, Vol.4, No.1-2, pp.22-23.
Crawford, Mr. & Mrs. (1985) Personal interview.
Fitzgerald, Ross (1982) From the Dreaming to 1915: A History of
    Queensland. University of Queensland Press, St. Lucia, Queensland,
    p.3.
Hutcheon, E. H. (1949) A History of Queensland Cricket. V.E.Marten,
    Brisbane, p.71.
Lord, Stan (1983) Personal interview, December 1.
Mullins, Pat (1985) Interview by Edmond Scott.
Mullins, Patrick & Derriman, Phillip (1984) Bat and Pad, Oxford
    University Press, Melbourne, pp.213-215.
Ibid., pp.91-99.
Mulvaney, D.J. (1967) Cricket Walkabout: The Australian Aboriginal
    Cricketers on Tour 1867-8. Melbourne University Press, Melbourne.
Robinson, Ray (1978) Eddie Gilbert: Death of a Legend. Cricketer,
    Feb., p.19.
Torrens, Warwick (ed) (1982) Queensland Cricket and Cricketers
    1862-1981. Bayfield Printers, Brisbane.

306 .483

DIFFUSION OF SPORT: THE QUEENSLAND PATTERN 1850-1900

REET A. HOWELL and MAXWELL L. HOWELL
Department of Human Movement Studies, University of Queensland

Abstract
From 1850 to 1900 the colony of Queensland experienced significant
growth resulting from the opening up of the rich inland pastoral
lands, and the discoveries of gold and other minerals in the central
and northern parts of the colony. Towns, industries, roads,
railways, ports and communication networks followed the pastoral
advance, the mining frontiers and later the sugar cane plantations.
Railway developments were not concentric but linear, emanating from
the coast inland or from inland to the coast. Rather than a
north-south direction they ran east-west. The diffusion of sport
followed the spatial patterns established by the economic and social
development pattern of the colony. As the modes of transport
improved and as population numbers increased, clubs developed and
inter-town competitions emerged. Such regional competitions created
a need for standardisation of rules and organizational control in the
form of centralized bodies. The lack of north-south railway
development, in particular, affected the evolution and organizational
pattern of sport in Queensland.
Key Words: Queensland, Pastoral Advance, Mining Frontiers,
Transportation, Sport, Organization.

1. Introduction

From 1850 to 1890 all social institutions, including sport,
underwent remarkable transformation in Queensland. These changes
were stimulated by the economic developments, of which the main ones
were (Wilson, 1980):
- (a) Successive stages of pastoral advance, retreat and
  re-occupation;
- (b) Differentiation into a sheep region in the centre and a
  cattle region round the rim;
- (c) A chain of gold and other mineral discoveries up the Eastern
  Highlands;
- (d) Evolution of a coastal sugar plantation economy worked by
  black (and blackbirded) labour;
- (e) Testing of numerous (often competitive) town/port sites;
- (f) Rapid growth of the capital to 1890, but low urbanisation;
- (g) Transition from unmade tracks in the 1860s to railway
  penetration.

Queensland was opened up in this period, first by squatters who
kept leap-frogging over others who had preceded them. More
significant effects resulted from the various mineral discoveries,
which motivated people to go north and swelled the population of
previously virtually uninhabited areas.

Queensland's first discovery of gold was in 1858 at Canoona, and
although the find was disappointing the town of Rockhampton developed
as a consequence. In the early 1860s small finds were made at Peak
Downs in 1851 and Calliope in 1863. The first major find was on the
Mary River in 1867 and immediately the rush was on. The gold fever
continued northward, and in the late 1860s various discoveries were
made, with the find in 1868 at Ravenswood being the most significant.
This was subsequently overshadowed by a nearby find in 1871 at
Charters Towers which was to become one of Australia's greatest gold
producers. Other finds both north and south came later, but only the
Mount Morgan mine in 1880 was of a significant proportion.

At these sites stable communities evolved and roads, railways and
communication networks, as well as nearby ports, were quickly
established to link the gold centres with Brisbane and other parts of
Australia. The result was the development of towns such as
Townsville, Cairns, Port Douglas, Cooktown and Rockhampton.

Railway lines in most countries radiate from the capital or main
city outward, however, this did not occur in Queensland in these
early years. The railway system did not diffuse out from Brisbane,
but from Ipswich to Brisbane, not reaching the capital city until
1876. Ipswich was called the "home of the locomotive", and the
beginning of Queensland's railway system was at North Ipswich on
February 25, 1864.

Even Toowoomba, in 1867, was linked earlier than Brisbane with
Ipswich, while Dalby was linked with Toowoomba in 1868. As
Fitzgerald put it (1982): "All roads and rails did not, and were
never to lead to, Brisbane". This was markedly different from the
southern colonies.

Until Brisbane was linked with Ipswich, steamers plied the river
route. Ships such as the "Ipswich", "Brisbane", "Emu", "The Kate"
and so on carried trade and passengers. Linkage with northern and
southern coastal ports were also by steam, as there was no
south-north railway connection. In the north railway lines linked
the emerging coastal towns with the major inland mineral discoveries,
and hence routes were linear, east to west generally.

Sport

As towns reached a certain stage of growth and organization the need
for increased social intercourse became apparent. Sport was one of
the first social institutions to evolve meeting the needs of
entertainment and diversion as well as providing physical and
emotional outlets. Also sport was part of the "cultural baggage"
that was brought from the British Isles and it helped to replicate
the English way of life.

Horse racing was the first sporting industry to emerge in
Queensland and the sport went through a considerable transition, from
local races to regional and then to intercolonial races by the 1860s.
Regional and intercolonial competitions in all sports came about

through population and transportation changes. This transition is
shown in Table 1.

Table 1. Transition from Local to Regional to Intercolonial
Competition in Horse Racing

Classification	Meetings	Dates
Intercolonial	Queensland Champion Sweep-Stakes	1860s
Regional	Brisbane, Ipswich, Drayton Warwick, Gayndah	1840s & 1850s
Local	Local Race-Courses Challenge Races	1840s

    As for the diffusion of horse-racing throughout the colony, the
sport began in Brisbane in the 1830s and 1840s, spread to Drayton and
Ipswich in 1848, Warwick in 1850, thence to Gayndah (1852),
Maryborough (1859), Nanango (1860), Gladstone and Rockhampton (1861),
Peak Downs (1864), Townsville (1866), Stanthorpe and Mount Perry
(1872), Charters Towers (1874), and so on. No self-respecting town
was without organised horse-racing for long. As the frontier opened
up the sport of horse-racing was not far behind. Activities related
to the horse were fundamental to the way of life in the colony.
    Cricket's organisational progression was even more marked, though
its following and popularity nowhere approximated that of
horse-racing. However, cricket, during this period, developed from
only local matches to top level international contests.

Table 2. Transition of Cricket from 1840s to 1890s

Classification	Matches	Dates
International	Visit of English Teams	1880s
National	Queensland v Australia	1877
Intercolonial	Queensland v N.S.W.	1860s
Regional	Ipswich v Brisbane, etc.	1840s & 1850s
Local	Local Challenges and Local Clubs	1840s

    From 1850 to 1890 cricket became the main competitive sport in
this northern colony. The highlights were: the formation of the
Queensland Cricket Association in 1876; the inauguration of inter-
colonial cricket in 1864; Queensland playing Australia in 1877
(although it was 18 Queensland players against 11); international
matches against England in 1883, 1885 and 1887; and the graduation in
1893 towards playing 11-aside in intercolonial matches.
    The diffusion of cricket in Queensland paralleled the economic
developments of the colony and the evolution of towns as is evident
in Table 3.

Table 3. Diffusion of Cricket Throughout Queensland, 1840s to 1890s

Period	Town	Date
1890s	Kingaroy	1890
	Mackay	1890
	Charters Towers	1890
1870s	Laidley	1870s
	Mount Perry	1876
	Gatton	1870s
	Bundaberg	1872
	Stanthorpe	1872
	Townsville	1872
1860s	Gympie	1869
	Roma	1864
	Gayndah	1864
	Rockhampton	1862
	Maryborough	1861
	Toowoomba	1860
	Dalby	1860
1850s	Drayton	
1840s	Ipswich	1848
	Moreton Bay Cricket Club (Brisbane)	1847
	Local Challenges in Brisbane area	

The diffusion of the sport was such that by the 1840s cricket was only played in the first settled areas, those of Ipswich and Brisbane, but by the 1850s the game had developed adherents in Drayton. It was in the 1860s that a major expansion took place, and as towns developed throughout the colony, teams were quickly formed in these centres.

In Brisbane a further development took place with numerous clubs developing in the city such as the Brisbane Cricket Club, North Brisbane, South Brisbane, Albert, Victoria and National. Inter-club competition within Brisbane was inaugurated.

The first games were often haphazard and primitive, the grounds being uneven and equipment occasionally improvised.

An example of the types of matches in these early years could be when Maryborough, in 1869, played Gympie.

The Maryborough cricketers arrived in Gympie by Cobb's coach and six horses, at about 5 o'clock yesterday evening, escorted into town by several Gympie cricketers and their friends on horseback; our guests put up at Farley's, where they will stay during their visit ... The wickets, on Commissioner's Flat, where the match will be played, have been improved as far as practicable within the past three days. (Gympie Times, Feb.11, 1869).

The match received extensive daily coverage in the Gympie Times (Feb.13, 1869).

The most important cricket match that has taken place in Gympie was played on Thursday, and we have no hesitation in saying that it afforded a great deal of amusement and pleasurable excitement

not only to the players, but also to the public, and that it was
on the whole highly successful ... Although the cricket ground is
not so clear of trees, stumps, and other obstructions as could be
wished by the local players, when inviting their antagonists to
test their ability here, still it has been greatly improved. The
turf is naturally good, and could be made still better in time,
and the locality is in many respects an excellent one.

Gympie won the match, but the result was incidental to the social
interaction between the two towns that otherwise would not have been
possible. Cricket, indeed, was more than a game in such
circumstances - it brought people together from different locales, it
enhanced and facilitated social intercourse.
    The Queensland Cricket Association was formed in 1876 (Brisbane
Courier, Feb. 26, 1876): "cricket is undergoing a revolution in
Brisbane just now ... and the game is receiving a great impetus from
the extent to which the Cricket Fever has spread ...". Seven teams
were immediately affiliated to the new state body in 1876, while
there were 8 in 1878 and 14 in 1884.
    Rowing was another early sport that diffused rapidly and gained a
popular following. The sport began in Brisbane in the 1840s, but it
was not practised in Rockhampton until the 1860s. Maryborough
(1870s) and Bundaberg (1880s) became other rowing centres. The most
significant event was the race held in Rockhampton between Edward
Trickett, Australia's first world champion sculler, and Ned Hanlan,
who had taken his crown. Trickett was the host at the Oxford Hotel
at Rockhampton.
    The biggest rowing carnival ever held in the new colony was
organised at Rockhampton in 1890 by Thomas Skarratt Hall, a Director
of Mount Morgan Mine. The highlight was the race between Peter Kemp,
reigning world champion sculler, and James Stanbury. There were both
professional and amateur races.
    Rowing not only diffused in a satisfactory manner in the time
period, but it progressed from local competitions, in the 1840s, to
inter-club competitions in the 1860s, to regional contests in the
1880s, to intercolonial matches in 1885 and international matches in
the late 1880s.
    The increasing number of inter-town and inter-region competitions
forced the formation of local and state organisation in order to
standardise rules and provide equity in the competitions. Some of
the centralised bodies that emerged were:

1852   North Australia Jockey Club (Ipswich)
1863   Queensland Turf Club
1885   Central Queensland Racing Association (Rockhampton)
1876   Queensland Cricket Association
1889   Queensland Rowing Association
1894   Queensland Amateur Athletic Association (Rockhampton)
1895   North Queensland Amateur Athletic Association (Rockhampton)
1895   Southern Queensland Amateur Athletic Association (Brisbane)
1899   Queensland Amateur Athletic Association (Brisbane)

These early years witnessed the initial attempts to take over control of a particular sport. Ipswich formed the North Australian Jockey Club in 1852 in an attempt to wrest horse racing out of the hands of mainly Brisbane gentlemen riders. There was confusion in the colony as to which rules should be followed: Gayndah followed Newmarket Rules, whereas Maryborough followed Homebush Rules.

The North Australia Jockey Club went against the Newmarket Rules (England) and the Homebush Rules (Australia), setting up its own rules and regulations.

Years later The Queensland Turf Club was formed in Brisbane in 1863, and it adopted English Jockey Club Rules in 1885. However, the Central Queensland Racing Association was formed in protest. So there was a power struggle in the colony over the control of horse-racing. It was eventually won by the Queensland Turf Club.

The only other major sport where an administrative power struggle emerged was in athletics, in which sport Rockhampton endeavoured to exert its authority, forming the Queensland Amateur Athletic Association in 1894. This power seizure was short-lived, as northern and southern associations were formed in 1895, and the power base switched to Brisbane in 1899.

Summary
From 1850 to 1890 sport underwent a considerable transformation in the colony. In the 1840s sport was organised locally, with variable rules and a minimum of equipment and facilities. As roads, railway lines and sea-lanes were expanded, inter-town challenges and competitions became possible. The social side was emphasised in these early matches, and the ladies added to the spectacle by their presence. It was customary to follow the matches with dinners or have lunches during the contests where speeches a-plenty were given. As the visits increased in frequency, the necessity for rule consistency between towns became apparent. As some towns went further afield in search of a sporting contest, there arose a further need for a colony-wide organisation, not only to formulate rule consistencies within the colony, but to act as a coordinating body for inter-region, inter-colonial and, for that matter, international contests. Local pride and prestige caused a few problems as one town would vie with another for control over that sport, but this was understandable in this formative period of the colony when there were few traditions to fall back on.

The lack of a north-south rail system, in particular, limited somewhat the development of sport, for sport was often confined to those towns on the railway line, or within easy access by roads. However the enthusiasts were not to be denied in searching out the sporting experience. They came by foot, ship, horse, coach, horse-tram, and rail because of their love of sport, desire for friendly competition, and the physical and social outlets that it offered. Sport was eagerly sought after as a respite from the long hours of labour, offering welcome relief from, for most, an arduous life. From 1850 to 1890 sport had established itself in the colony, its sudden accession spurred on by the technological and economic changes within the state occasioned principally by pastoral expansion and mineral discoveries. Sport in the time period reflected those societal changes.

References

Brisbane Courier, Feb.26, 1876.

Fitzgerald, Ross (1982) *From the Dreaming to 1915: A History of Queensland*. University of Queensland Press, St. Lucia, p.266.

Gympie Times, Feb.11, 1869.

Gympie Times, Feb.13, 1869.

The Courier, May 27, 1861.

Wilson, R.K. (1980) *Australia's Resources and Their Development*. University of Sydney, Department of Education, p.45.

THE INTRODUCTION OF WESTERN SPORTS TO THE INDIAN PEOPLE OF CANADA'S
PRAIRIE WEST

JOHN DEWAR
College of Physical Education, University of Saskatchewan

Abstract
The effect of the Indian Treaties 6 and 7 between Her Majesty Queen
Victoria and the Cree and Blackfoot Confederacies of Canada's
plains have had a lasting effect on the Indian peoples and the
regions in which they live. The reservations established as a
result of these Treaties and the residential school system are
examined in relationship to the contribution athleticism made to
the programs both within and outside the schools. The team games
of western civilization have been well accepted by the Cree and
Blackfeet Confederacies. Hockey has been particularly well
received. The world of rodeo has also played a role in improving
the self image of the plains people of native ancestry.

Introduction

The acceptance by the Indian people of Canada's pairies of treaties
6 and 7 marked the end of a social era. Only education might
restore their once noble self-image.
    Indian Treaties and Surrenders, Volume II read as follows with
reference to education.
    And further, Her Majesty agrees to maintain schools for
instruction in such reserves hereby made as to Her Government of
the Dominion of Canada may seem advisable, wherever the Indians of
the reserve shall desire it. (Treaty #6). Vol. II, p. 35, 23-28
August, and 9 September, 1876. By Cree Indians.
    Further, Her Majesty agrees to pay the salary of such teachers
to instruct the children of said Indians as to Her Government of
Canada may seem advisable, when the said Indians are settled on
their reserves and shall desire teachers. (Treaty #7). Vol. II,
p. 58, 22 September, and 4 December, 1877. By Blackfoot, Peigan,
Sarcee and Stony Indians.
    The signing of Treaties 6 and 7 ended the days of freedom for
the proud Indian peoples of Canadian prairies. Promises were made,
and men of God proclaimed that the "Canadian Savage Folk" would
become educated in the ways of the whiteman. The Confederacies of
the Cree and the Blackfeet peoples had capitulated and would now
have their children educated in the residential schools that the

Christian missionaries eagerly errected. Chief Poundmaker, the revered Cree, in 1881 told his people:

> . . . We have a missionary on our Reserve, we have a school, let us profit by them. I have given you an example. Nearly two years since I sent my son to Saint Albert, Big Lake School (sic). My heart was sick when I saw my boy crying at his departure from me, and I find long the time of his absence, but he is at school. Some day he will be able to help himself and to help his fellowmen. He will be able to speak English and French, and he will be able to read and to write, besides know how to work like a white man. Do the same for your children if you want them to prosper and be happy. (Maclean p. 389)

Crowfoot, the famous chief of the Blackfeet, was up to the time of his death in 1890, a peaceful upholder of Treaty #7. He was buried in a service performed by the Oblate priest, Father Lacombe, on April 27, 1890.

Father Lacombe had also been present at the landmark signing of Treaty #7; had heard the bagpipes gaily wail, had seen the Union Jack hoisted and listened to the speeches of Governor Laird and Chief Crowfoot. The most eloquent of the Blackfoot expressed his worry and foreboding that his hard riding braves would find it difficult to become another person. Changes would be slow and he hoped the commissioners and their leaders would be patient with his people as it would take a long, long time for them to be made into another people. The Christian educators did not heed the words of the great Indian leader.

Harold Cardinal, a young Cree intellectual from the land of the mighty Peace River, wrote in 1969 of eighty years of Christian educational failure.

> The unvarnished truth is that the missionaries of all Christian sects regarded the Indians as savages, heathens or something even worse.
> They were interested primarily in a high conversion score. The government was interested in keeping the savages quiet. Their aims dovetailed, and the Indian was the pawn. (Cardinal p. 53)

Cardinal, a rebel of the 1960's, spoke a great number of truths relevant to the education of his people. He clearly and correctly records that during the eighty years following the signing of Treaties 6 and 7, neither government nor church involved the Indian people in the planning for their educational future. The residential school programs that were established and operated into the 1950's operated from the religious and governmental bureaucrats down to the native students.

Were there some aspects of these early subjective educational programs that had a positive effect on the Cree and Blackfoot children? The role of residential schools operated in the south central regions of Saskatchewan and Alberta will be the major sources of data for this paper. Particular emphasis will be

given to the situation of the Cree at Hobbema in Central Alberta
and the Bloods of the Blackfoot Confederacy in Southern Alberta.
These are two of the better economically based Indian populations
in Western Canada. The four reservations visited in Alberta were
the Ermineskin at Hobbema; the Blood north of Cardston; the
Blackfoot located east of Calgary, bordered by the small towns of
Gleichen and Cluny; and the Piegan at Brocket just east of Pincher
Creek. The Cree and Blackfoot Confederacies, which includes the
Piegan, the Blood and the Northern Blackfoot bands, were depicted
by nineteenth century writers and artists to be among the most
athletic of the peoples of native ancestry. Their nomadic nature,
good source of sustenance, horsemanship, and isolation had resulted
in two proud Indian cultures on the Canadian plains. The
establishing of reservations, residential schools, and the
extermination of the buffalo by 1883 created a foreboding
juxtaposition for these once self-sufficient societies.
    The physical nature of the plains Indians and their love of the
horse were two of few positive, quality of life, aspects for the
Cree and Blackfoot.
    The Cree words for running and dancing have a deeper meaning
than their English counterparts. The connotation of running in the
Indian culture was that of an uplifting and an offering of the body
to the Great Spirit. The concept of muscular Christianity that was
espoused by many of the missionaries who established the
residential schools was a good fit with the closely related
physical and spiritual nature of the Indian. Those teachers who
projected this sporting interest were among the more successful in
making a contribution towards and establishing rapport with their
captive charges. The residential aspect, with its required conduct
was however at cross purposes with both the family solidarity and
freedom of movement of the Cree and Blackfeet. All schools
reported truancy from the school's dormitories as one of their
major problems. The confinement of the institution, and the
regimentation of the program was completely alien to the culture of
the Indian people.
    The games of association football, lacrosse, hockey, baseball
were all introduced successfully into the residential school
systems of the then North West Territories before the turn of the
century. Soccer was particularly popular prior to 1890 at the
Industrial School in Battleford. Hockey first came to prominence
when the Dunbow Industrial School team was reported to have
defeated the Dewdney Hockey Club 6 - 1 on February 4, 1898. Hockey
emerged as a strong force in almost all of the large Oblate
operated schools. Following the second world war outstanding
programs emerged among the Cree at Duck Lake and Lebret in
Saskatchewan, and at Hobbema in Alberta. Hockey teams of a high
calibre were also operating for the Blackfeet in Gleichen, Brocket
and Cardston.
    Sir John A. Macdonald, Canada's first Prime Minister, held the
portfolio of Superintendent General of the Department of Indian
Affairs. Reporting on January 1, 1984 to the Governor General, His
Excellency the Marquess of Lansdowne, he noted: "Adverting to the

improvement intellectually, of the Indians of the North West Territories, I am pleased to be able to inform your Excellency that the industrial schools of Battleford, Qu'Appelle and High River, which were referred to in my Report of last year . . . are now in operation."

The industrial schools were to be the flagships of the Indian educational fleet. The muscular Christianity of their principals, particularly the Rev. Clarke (Battleford) and Rev. Fr. Lacombe (High River Dunbow), were an important part in the initial success of these institutions. These schools were well located, comparatively well founded and staffed by certain competent teachers. They were the schools that visiting dignitaries and politicians would visit on their tour through the wilds of the West.

Unfortunately the majority of the smaller schools were poorly funded, unrelated to the Indians' needs and taught by misfits. The results varied from examples of starvation in some school settings in the northwest to an almost total lack of learning in the majority of locations. The Indians were never involved in the planning process and the negative effects of these programs, which lasted until the mid-fifties, is still being experienced on the plains of Western Canada.

Since the mid-fifties the Government of Canada assumed its responsibility for the education of Indian children. Progress for the next two decades was bureaucratic and slow. Recommendations and curriculums continued to come from above and with little consultation with Indian leaders. Social change was occurring on the reserves, urbanization and alcohol related problems were being multiplied, and solutions left wanting. Again because of their superior economic base certain Indian bands emerged with improved educational settings that would hopefully provide a solution. Many of the positive factors and leaders who came forward during the past two decades have a sports related background.

Wilton Littlechild, Ray Ahenakew, Herb Stoneeagle, Hubert Greyeyes, Fred Sasakamoose, David Littlechild, Jim Rattlesnake, Peter Many Guns, June and Jim Gladstone, Fred Gladstone, Rufus Goodstriker and Tom Threepersons, all outstanding athletes from the Cree, Blackfoot and Blood peoples, have provided a proud sporting heritage for young Indians to emulate. Many of the early athletes who learned their hockey and baseball skills in the residential schools are chiefs, counselors and leaders of their bands.

One aspect of sport completely apart from the early school system was rodeo. The Indian Cowboy was a "natural" rider, roper and steer decorator. Since the days of Tom Threepersons winning the steer decorating at the first Calgary Stampede in 1912, to the riding and roping of Jim Gladstone today, scores of Indian cowboys have proudly related to their equestrian roots. Paul Kane noted this quality in 1859. "They were the best mounted, the best looking, the most warlike in appearance, and the best accoutred of any tribe I had ever seen on the continent during my route." (Kane p. 419).

One of the great problems for the person of native ancestry is the lack for many of a positive self-image. The whiteman, his politicians, and educators have too often spoken with a "forked tongue" and have created the stereotype of Canada's native people connoted by the phrase, "not bad for an Indian". Sport within and outside the educational setting has improved their image. Young Indian leaders, who have survived the system, are the hope of their people. Willy Littlechild, a Cree lawyer of the Ermineskin Band, spoke recently of the need for a support system that could follow up the initial gains acquired by young Indians on the rinks, gymnasiums and fields of the prairies. The establishment of such a system must be one of the major objectives of all Canadians of conscience.

References

Interviews:

Duhaime, O.M.I., Rev. A., St. Albert, January, 1986.
Lafonde, Mrs. Leona, Hobbema, March, 1986.
Linder, Mrs. Rosella, Cardston, February, 1986.
Littlechild, Wilton, Hobbema, March, 1986, Edmonton, March, 1986.
Makukis, Ralph, Edmonton, March, 1986.
Sweet Grass Reserve Transcripts, Saskatchewan Department of Culture
      and Youth, Regina, 1975.

Reports:

Dominion of Canada, Annual Report, Department of Indian Affairs,
      for the years 1881-89. (8 Volumes) Maclean Roger & Co.,
      1882-1890.
Indian Treaties and Surrenders, from 1680-1890, in two Volumes.
      Volume I printed by Brown Chamberlin, Printer to the Queen's
      Most Excellent Majesty, Ottawa: 1891.
Minutes, Proceedings and Evidence. Joint Committee of the Senate
      and House of Commons and Indian Affairs. Senator J. Gladstone,
      Chairman. Ottawa: Queen's Printer, 1961.

Newspapers:

Edmonton Bulletin, 1884-1900.
Edmonton Journal. Stuzic, Ed. Choice is Sports or Booze, Say
      Native Young People, March 20, 1986.
Bear Hills Native Voice, Hobbema, Volume 10, Number 8, February 27,
      1986.
The Chronicle, Cardston, Volume 7, Number 2, February 25, 1986.

Books:

Cardinal, Harold. The Unjust Society, The Tragedy of Canada's
    Indians, Hurtig Publishers, Edmonton: 1969.
Catlin, George. Letters and Notes on the Manners, Customs and
    Condition of North American Indians, in Two Volumes. Unabridged
    republication of 1844 work. Dover Publication Inc., New York:
    1973.
James, Edwin. Account of an Expedition from Pittsburgh to the
    Rocky Mountains, in Three Volumes. Longman, Hurst, Rees, Arme
    and Brown, Paternoster-Row, 1823.
Kane, Paul. Wanderings of an Artist Among the Indians of North
    America. Longman, Brown, Green, Longmans, and Roberts.
    London: 1859.
Lowie, Robert H. Indians of the Plains. McGraw Hill Co. Inc., New
    York: 1954.
Maclean, John. Canadian Savage Folk. The Native Tribes of Canada.
    William Briggs, Toronto: 1896.
Morice, Rev. A.G. History of the Catholic Church in Western
    Canada, Musson Book Co. Ltd., Toronto, 1910.
Owen, Roger C., James Deitz and Anthony Fisher. The North American
    Indians. The Macmillan Co., Toronto: 1967.
Renaud, Rev. Andre. Indian Education Today. Athropoligica 6,
    Research Centre for Amerindian Anthropology, Ottawa: 1958.
Robertsen, Heather. Reservations Are for Indians, James, Lewis and
    Samuel, Toronto: 1970.
Zeman, Brenda. Eighty-eight Years of Puck-Chasing in Saskatchewan.
    WDS Associates and The Saskatchewan Sports Hall of Fame, Regina,
    1983.
Zeman, Gary W. Alberta on Ice. Westweb Press, Edmonton, 1985.

AN ATTEMPT TO PERPETUATE A CULTURAL IDENTITY THROUGH TRADITIONAL
GAMES IN THE FACE OF THE INFLUENCE OF WESTERN SPORTS IN PAPUA NEW
GUINEA

A.K. SEWARD
Department of Sport and Recreation, Government of Papua New Guinea

Abstract
Sport mainly in the form of village children's games, existed in
Papua New Guinea in traditional times. These traditional games, many
of which are still played to-day, have the same play characteristics
as modern games although in general, they were games of co-operation
rather than games of high competition. The fragmented nature of
communities within Papua New Guinea society with over seven hundred
different languages and many thousands of autonomous villages, has
nurtured traditional physical skills and hence traditional games.
The introduction therefore of organised sport by successive colonial
governments, the influence of missionaries and the formal education
system, superimposed the elements of competition, structure and a
stricter set of rules upon the country. Western sports have been
introduced with the idea of achieving unity and as an element to help
combat fragmentation of the various tribal and clan groups in the
country. These western sports have mixed and co-existed with
traditional games and an example of a sport, Trobriand cricket,
essentially European but played in traditional fashion is examined in
detail. The promotion of both traditional and modern games is highlighted and the future impact assessed.
Key words: traditional culture, external influences, co-existence.

1. Introduction

A short geographical description of Papua New Guinea sees a major
land mass which forms the eastern part of the largest non-continent
island in the Pacific. It comprises a large mountainous mainland and
some six hundred smaller offshore islands. The country is wholly
within the tropics and the climate is tempered by oceanic and alti-
tudinal influences. Papua New Guinea was colonised in the nineteenth
and early twentieth centuries in turn by Britain, Germany and
Australia and during the Second World War Japan and the United States
exerted considerable influences. It needs to be pointed out here
that there are over 700 languages in Papua New Guinea, 25% of the
total of the world's languages in one country, and because of this
phenomenon there are still many thousands of separate communities.
The basic unit of organisation is the village (approximately 85% of
Papua New Guineans live in villages, and the other 15% in urban

areas). The number of autonomous communities is enormous and these village communities are run in an open, democratic style. A complex system of exchange marks social relationships (mainly revolving around land, pigs or women and in that order!), with warfare determining territorial and many other social arrangements. In some parts of Papua New Guinea to-day, particularly in the highlands, tribal warfare is still a regular occurrence.

The total population of Papua New Guinea in the 1980 census was just over 3 million people and it is worthy of note that the country has a predominantly young population - almost half the population is under 20 years of age. The system of government, since independence in 1975, has pursued a Westminster parliamentary system and reflecting the diverse groupings within the country has many political parties. There are eight operating at present and it is not uncommon for over twenty candidates to stand in an election in one constituency to try and become a member of parliament.

2. Traditional culture

The major point being made here in this short resumé of the country, is the fragmented nature of communities within the society. The mountainous terrain and general ruggedness of Papua New Guinea has seen many pockets of cultural groups evolve where one group's culture could be very different from the rest even if they live fairly close, for example in the next valley. Many Papua New Guineans will tell you of the different languages, dances or customs of friends who may have been brought up geographically very close to them. It is true to say that successive colonial governments before independence have never successfully destroyed the traditional system of government of these various groups. The independent government of Papua New Guinea constantly finds it difficult to satisfy all the demands of the regional groups within the country.

It is against this background that traditional physical skills and hence traditional games have evolved. Physical skill was essential for survival and village Papua New Guineans would not be able to hunt, swim, fish or garden without them. As Kituai (1984) a Papua New Guinean historian, has observed ". . . men ran, heaved stones, cast spears, weaved baskets, chopped trees, built houses in order to prove their skills as hunters, craftsmen, gardeners and builders because survival depended on men's physical prowess". An example of these skills with differences marked by sex was noted by Rosenstiel (1953). ". . . As they (the Motu) grow older, girls learn gardening, pottery making and household skills, from their mothers, and boys learn hunting and fishing skills from their mother's brother." Rosenstiel stressed also that the play activities in traditional Motuan culture evolved around the necessity to develop skills which would be part of adult life. She illustrated this by stating:

> . . . the sea plays a paramount role in Motu life. Motu children learn to swim even before they learn to walk. Children also learn to build and sail small Lakatoi (outrigger canoes) and hold miniature races while the men are away on the hiri (sea trading

expeditions), thus developing assurance in the water and competence in handling the craft which are to be so important to them in
adult life.

Physical skill development largely takes place as Tololo (1975)
saw it through a process of "learning by example, through experience,
by seeing and doing . . ."
The mastery of these physical skills was the test of a man or
woman. In terms of western education no diplomas or certificates
would be awarded but the very mastery of the skills became the badge
of competence. It has been apparent that in each area of Papua New
Guinea children have devised traditional games around the traditional
skills necessary for their parents and themselves to survive indicating the environment they live in. Reflecting the co-operative
nature of the Melanesian group ethic, these traditional children's
games have the same play characteristics as modern games although in
general they are games of co-operation rather than games of high
competition. Orlick (1982) a Canadian researcher into co-operative
games has noted that traditional games in Bougainville, the largest
island of Papua New Guinea, have "no officials, no boundary lines, no
specialization and no exclusion".
Children have traditionally copied the adult group concept and it
has been a natural progression to base games on a "co-operative"
concept.

3. Western sports in Papua New Guinea

The introduction therefore of organised sport by successive colonial
governments and through the influence of missionaries and the formal
education system, has superimposed the elements of competition,
structure and a stricter set of rules upon the country. At this
stage it is important to give a short background to the different
western sports played in the country. Soccer, or "Kik" as it was
popularly called in Pidgin, was introduced into German New Guinea and
although it is now played in every province it is still strongest on
the northern side of the country. Cricket also has a long history in
Papua New Guinea having been introduced into Papua by the early
English missionaries. To-day it is played mainly in the Papuan
region and in some other centres where the players are predominantly
of Papuan background.
Rugby league, rugby union and Australian rules football were
brought to the Papuan region by the Australians. These codes spread
nationally. Rugby union, however, is now played only in the National
Capital, Port Moresby.
Volleyball, basketball and baseball came with the American troops
during the war and were later promoted by American missionaries.
Baseball has now been replaced totally by softball. Athletics was
introduced through schools physical education and sports programmes.
Papua New Guinea's athletics standard is now ranked highly in the
South Pacific region. Boxing, weight lifting and fitness training
have become popular with Papua New Guineans and receive strong
support from defence and police force clubs. Swimming, tennis, golf

and squash are becoming more popular among urban Papua New Guineans.
All sorts of western sports and games have evolved in Papua New
Guinea and it is thought at least a third of the population are
actively engaged in sports participation. Perhaps more than anything
else sport has been accepted in Papua New Guinea very readily. This
is not true of western religion and government where, on first
encounter, early missionaries or government officials were sometimes
killed and eaten! Sport on the other hand, has expanded rapidly to
all provinces in the country and the concept of group participation
and co-operation through sport accepted nation-wide. As it has been
the norm for Papua New Guinean children or adults to traditionally
hunt, fish or swim in groups, they have been ripe for pulling into
organised sport. Many Papua New Guineans take part in localised
teams and "Wantok" (Pidgin for "one talk" or "one language") teams
are commonplace. There have been localised pockets of expansion.
The Tolais of the Gazelle Peninsula, for example, play softball
almost exclusively and the Papuans play cricket.

4. Trobriand cricket

The introduction of organised sport has been a logical step for the
government to foster, to "develop and extend the playing of games
with the ultimate aim of achieving unity through them" (1975). Sport
was seen as an element to help combat the fragmentation of the various tribal and clan groups throughout the country. Since independence and the localising of the teaching force in community primary
schools, traditional games have mixed and co-existed with western
sports and games. This softening of an approach to sport has enabled
the games to have a distinct Papua New Guinean flavour of their own,
for example, Trobriand cricket. To the people of the Trobriand
islands off the southern tip of Papua New Guinea it is a way of life
that has been handed down from one generation to another since the
Europeans first came. According to an expert Kelly Ratu, the game is
played on special occasions, often by invitation of a chief who
invites people from other villages to come and participate. The
biggest occasion for traditional cricket is during the "Kayasa" or
yam festival. During this time the hosting village might invite
three villages to compete in a tournament which is the highlight of
the feasting. There can be upwards of two hundred people on each
side. There is a special code of rules which the players have to
follow: Firstly the batsmen who have to guard the wicket and be able
to hit the ball. Then there are the runners on both sides who have
to make the scores. These runners stand in a clear position in front
of the batsmen.
   The runners change regularly to rest. The game consists of two
rounds. Each team must bat and field twice before a final score is
given. The bats are made of a special wood and can last many years.
The ball also has a special core from hard wood. As the game is
played there is a special chant by the fielders every time a player
is out. There are three different chants. If the batsman is bowled;
if there is a run out, and if a catch is made. These chants are sung
as they dance their famous "Tapioca" dance in order to give the

fielders courage and to belittle the opposition in order to make them nervous. The game is usually played with great singing and dancing which shows the happiness and the spirit of the occasion. The home team has to always win as this shows respect for the side that organised the game. However, the score must not be too great or else the visitors will feel offended.

5. Papua New Guinea sports traditions

This "co-operative competition" is a characteristic of Papua New Guinea traditional games and this is seen regularly in organised sport to-day. For example, in all sports Papua New Guinea teams will run out to the middle of the field as a group, in a line and be introduced both to the other team and to the spectators. This ritual is performed at local village level right through to the inter-national level. All sports teams take great care in obtaining the right sort of sportswear and colours reflecting the dressing up of a "sing-sing" and in fact many Papua New Guineans will wear sportswear as their "normal" dress to work long after the game has finished. After almost every match in any sport, there is a celebration whether winning or losing and feasting similar to that described in the Trobriand cricket occurs regularly. All these things identify sport in Papua New Guinea as very much "Papua New Guinean".

The mixture of traditional and modern has been inevitable and although the imposition of high competition is a worry, traditional games have influenced sport and enabled a distinct Papua New Guinean flavour to emerge. Traditional sporting activities such as canoeing, archery or dance have emerged as more competitive but still retain the co-operative elements of their beginnings. Prizes and feasting are evident and there are no signs these activities are fading.

6. Conclusion

Efforts are now being directed through the policy for sport and recreation and through the Department of Education and National Sports Institute to preserve traditional games alongside the accept-ance of western sports. The policy states categorically:

> Sport, in the form of village games, traditional dance and physical activities such as archery and canoeing, has existed in Papua New Guinea since traditional times. In planning for modern sports development efforts must be made to build on this traditional sports background and on the customs and character-istics of contemporary Papua New Guinean individuals and society.

The development policies are aimed at promoting traditional games and activities to preserve traditional heritage, enriching contempor-ary culture and as a medium for social learning. The Education Department has included traditional games at primary level and a number of games have been included in the syllabus and teaching notes. Schools are encouraged to develop their own traditional games

37

and to celebrate them at occasions such as independence or provincial government days. These traditional activities can contribute to the development of highly desirable personal and social skills such as courage, obedience, determination, justice and co-operation. Increasingly sport world-wide is in an age of competition, aggression and declining social control while traditional games, on the other hand, can engender desirable behaviours such as "co-operative competition". Papua New Guinea which has a rich store of traditional games and activities, can contribute positively towards establishing the right mix of the traditional and the modern for the overall betterment of sport.

References

Kituai, A. (1983) History of sports development in Papua New Guinea (Article) in "Times of Papua New Guinea", Friday 26 August 1983, Word Publishing, Port Moresby.

National Public Expenditure Plan (1985-88) Public expenditure and national development strategy, National Planning Office, Port Moresby.

Orlick, T. (1982) The Second Co-operative Sports and Games Book. Pantheon Books, New York.

Papua New Guinea Government Policy for Sport and Recreation (1985) Report to Department of Home Affairs, Port Moresby.

Physical Education Grades 1-3 Teachers Guide (1983) Curriculum Unit, Department of Education, Papua New Guinea.

Position Statement on Children in Sport with Fair Play Codes (1985) Report by Papua New Guinea Association for Health, Physical Education and Recreation (PNGAHPER), Papua New Guinea Banking Corporation, Port Moresby.

Rosenstiel, A. (1977) "The role of traditional games in the process of socialisation among the Motu of Papua New Guinea", in The Study of Play: Problems and Prospects (ed. D.F. Lancy and B. Allan Tindall), Vol. 1, Anthropological Association for the Study of Play series.

Tololo, A. (1981) "A consideration of some likely trends in education", in Education in Melanesia, 8th Waigani Seminar, Australian National University, pp 4-8.

"Trobriand Cricket" (Article) in "Times of Papua New Guinea", Word Publishing, Port Moresby.

CONCEPTUAL AND METHODOLOGICAL CONFUSION IN ANALYSES OF NINETEENTH CENTURY LEISURE - THE CASE FOR HISTORICAL SOCIOLOGY

J A MAGUIRE
Department of Human Movement Studies, West Sussex Institute of Higher Education

Abstract
This paper has three objectives. Firstly, to highlight that analyses of nineteenth century leisure are flawed in several respects. Secondly, an alternative perspective based on developmental sociology is proposed. Thirdly, illustration of its value will be made with reference to the modernisation of football.

A critical appraisal of the work of Cunningham, Stedman Jones and Eileen and Stephen Yeo is attempted with reference to three issues. Firstly, how historical processes are conceived of. Secondly, the characteristics of popular culture. Thirdly, how change occurs in popular culture. In each of these areas these writers provide insights of some value. However, their weakness lies in their relative failure to analyse the structured nature of social change and to provide a relational and detached view of the 'transformations' which occur in cultural relations in general. Developmental sociology provides a more adequate framework and its value will be highlighted by an analysis of the modernisation of football.

The most recent and influential of writings on nineteenth century leisure centre on the work of Cunningham, Stedman Jones, and Eileen and Stephen Yeo.(1) A critique of their perspectives will be made with references to three main issues. These are, how

(1)
CUNNINGHAM H   (1980)   Leisure in the Industrial Revolution
                          Croom Helm, London
STEDMAN JONES G (1977)   Class Expression versus Social Control? A
                          Critique of Recent Trends in the Social
                          History of Leisure. History Workshop 4
YEO E & YEO S   (1981)   Ways of Seeing: Control and Leisure versus
                          Class and Struggle in Popular Culture and
                          Conflict (ed E Yeo & S Yeo) Harvester,
                          Brighton pp 128-154

historical processes are conceived of, the characteristics of popular culture and how change occurs within popular culture. Let us turn to the first of these issues.

All three writers stress the 'active' making of history. This stems from the rejection of what Stedman Jones calls the 'oft-trodden routes' of analyses of leisure.(2) The 'culmulative picture', he argues is out of focus in that analyses have over-estimated the importance of the 'moral entreprenuers' and 'merchants of leisure'. Class-conflict has been viewed as a one-sided affair in which the powerful manipulate the powerless. In considering the development of nineteenth century leisure, the Yeos similarly reject the view of history in terms of the actions of the elite, refer to the 'noticable incompleteness' of the transition which occurred and advocate that a 'creative social history' should be adopted which focuses on the activities of craftsmen and artisans.(3) Cunningham's rejection of the 'conventional wisdom' regarding the history of football is based on similar premises. Instead of focusing on the activities of the elite and their ability to shape the development of football, Cunningham proposes re-directing the research endeavour to analyse the 'culture- forming processes from below'.(4)

There are a number of advantages to this perspective. Firstly, these writers are correct to point to the element of ideological bias which has pervaded analyses of popular culture and working class leisure. Secondly, by highlighting the purposes of and meanings inherent in the activities of the working classes, they provide a powerful corrective to the 'dismissiveness' of some analyses. However, certain reservations need also to be stated. While it is appropriate to highlight the 'creative culture forming process from below', the sense in which history is the negotiated outcome of all groups, articulating and reflecting structural processes of a relatively autonomous kind, is lost. That is, the relative power potential of particular groups to make history must be viewed in a relational and structured sense, ie with reference to the interdependencies they form together. Secondly, by stressing the role of the working classes in making their own culture, there is a tendency to isolate them from the wider historical process, to see them as some autonomous and undifferentiated entity. Thirdly, while rejecting the stark alternative to this, that the leisure entrepreneurs make history, it is another to lose sight of the issue of power and constraint. Stedman Jones and Cunningham, in considering the characteristics of popular culture are at pains to stress that the view of the

----

(2) STEDMAN JONES G Class Expression versus Social Control?
                      Op Cit
(3) YEO & YEO   Ways of Seeing: Control and Leisure versus
                      Class and Struggle Op Cit
(4) CUNNINGHAM   Leisure in the Industrial Revolution Op Cit

working class as 'cultural dopes' and as passive in response to the culture provided for them by the elite is inadequate. A creative social history which explores the symbolic and meaningful side of popular culture is advocated. Thus, instead of viewing the violent actions of rioters as mindless or as a reflection of a 'deprived', barren culture, the 'moral economy' of their actions is stressed. Not only are the working classes active in the making of their history but their culture, as Cunningham points out, has a creative element which stands in opposition to the dominant values of society. The ideas of resistance and 'rebellion' are the key to unlocking the significance of their actions.

Here again this strand in the writings of Stedman Jones, Cunningham and the Yeos is not without value. It wisely sensitises the researcher to the symbolic nature of the actions of the working classes over time and correctly rejects the view that one is dealing with a passive culture in which its members are dopes who are provided a mass consumer culture by the leisure industries.

These writers also point to the methodological dimension and that 'archival silence' should not infer that a rich and meaningful life was not being led by the 'people'. However, the question arises whether these researchers truly capture popular culture 'as it really was' or is. The danger apparent in their work is to write into popular culture something which is not there - to over-invest the actions of members of popular culture with either too much power or knowledge. It is one thing to point to the 'active' making of history, it is another to interpret all actions in terms of some abstract symbolism imposed onto the evidence.

Equally, a history in terms of heroes or villains needs to be avoided. (5) Neither a view of popular culture as totally encapsulated into a provided culture nor a view of popular culture in terms of total autonomy will do. Equally, while the 'active' making of popular culture allows for the defence of the rights of the free born Englishman, it also allows for the retention of mores which would be seen as problematic by those very writers. The 'rescue' of the artisan cannot be selective!(6)

----

(5)
BURKE, P (1978)   Popular Culture in Early Modern Europe
                     Temple Smith, London
BURKE, P (1981)   People's History of Total History in People's
                     History and socialist Theory (Ed R Samuel)
                     Routledge and KeganPaul pp 4 - 8
(6)
THOMPSON, E. P.   The Making of the English Working Class
                     Penguin, Harmondsworth

This perception of popular culture 'as it really is' links in with the analysis which Stedman Jones, Cunningham and the Yeos offer of change in popular culture. In this sense, their analysis reflects their view of change in history generally. For Cunningham, in examining nineteenth century leisure in general and the development of football in particular, it is necessary to reject the idea that popular culture was 'smashed' by the actions of the elite, that a vacuum was created and that popular culture was thereby filled up by the activities of the leisure entrepreneurs. For Cunningham the activities of the elite have had less influence on the development of football per se but more influence in the historiography of football.

Once more writers such as Cunningham and the Yeos stress the making of history, and popular culture, from below. While it is not appropriate to go into an empirical rejection of the view of the development of football proposed by Cunningham, at a more conceptual level, his analysis is also flawed. His writings can be seen to fall within what Stuart Hall has termed one of the 'unacceptable poles' in analyses of popular culture, that of pure autonomy. While it is right to point to the influence of the working classes in the emergence of football as a mass spectator sport, it is another to over-stress their ability to determine its overall development. Change in popular culture must be viewed in terms of 'transformations' of a kind which stress its structured and negotiated outcome. (7)

How best, therefore, to consider nineteenth century leisure? To do this it is necessary to outline, albeit somewhat briefly, the principles of 'developmental' sociology. (8) Individual human beings both create their social worlds by acting meaningfully within them and are created by them in the sense that the interdependency structures inherited from the past act as limiting constraints on what they can believe and how they can act. The focus of study is thus dependent on recognising that people partake in processes of social development via the meaningful actions they engaged in but that they experience constraints and are not entirely free in this connection and that, out of the interweaving of the meaningful action of innumeraable individuals and groups something emerges which was neither planned nor intended by any of the participants. The analysis of how certain forms of communal life come into being, are preserved and changed must not concentrate solely on the intentions and actions of one or several groups, instead a more adequate approach must understand the structured processes in

(7)
HALL, S (1981)   Notes on Deconstructing the 'Popular' in People's History and Socialist Theory (Ed R Samuel) Routledge and Kegan Paul pp 227-240
(8)
ELIAS, N (1978) What is Sociology? Hutchinson, London

which they live out their lives. It is in this way that the making of history is understood.

Illustration of its value can be made by examining the modernisation of football and the antecedents of spectator disorder in the 1880's and 1890's.(9) In attempting to provide a broad canvas on which to place both the modernisation of the game and subsequent developments regarding the expression and control of violence by spectators in and around football grounds and the related issue of the position of football spectating as part of the clash over popular culture, the present study is at pains to stress the long-term processes involved.

The "decline" of folk football stemmed from changes in the balance of power between groups that occured correlatively with the processes of industrialisation, urbanisation, state formation and a civilising "spurt". During the early part of the nineteenth century the attack on folk football which contributed centrally to its decline was only a part of a more general onslaught on popular recreations and popular culture which stemmed from the middle and ruling classes' desire to colonize working class culture. This desire reflected a perception held by these groups that, in the wake of the changes, then occuring, no commonly affirmed array of values linking different classes existed. For these middle-class groups, there was a need, however dimly perceived, not only to "improve" the public's health but also the public's values and codes of conduct. By so doing, their own grasp on power would be made more secure.

Despite such "moral sanitation", folk football was embedded in mores which formed part of pre-industrial popular culture and expressed the leisure preferences of the lower classes. Not all aspects of these mores declined during the nineteenth century. Those less amenable to control and/or to the "civilising" influences of the middle classes, 'survived", were actively participated in and had significance for sections of the working classes. That is, some sections of the working classes had sufficient power to ensure that the production and reproduction of traditional mores would continue.

Though folk football in its more gregarious forms declined, the public schools, in their adoption of it, provided a haven in which more civilised versions could appear. The status-rivalry between public schools such as Rugby and Eton, combined with the walk-out by the rugby clubs at the inaugural meetings of the Football Association amid the controversy surrounding "hacking"

---

(9)
MAGUIRE, J   The Limits of Decent Partisanship: A Sociological
(1985)   Investigation of the Emergence of Football
                  Spectating as a Social Problem
                  Unpublished PhD Thesis University of Leicester

43

resulted in the birfurcation of football. While the "games cult" assisted in the spread of the modern versions of football in the public schools and in the social circles directly influenced by them, it was the "athletic craze" which led to their spread to a wider social context.

Crucially, though in a more "civilised" form, there was a continued stress in the emerging, more modern forms of football on masculinity. The new game of "soccer" gradually spread to the "masses", a process which signalled the development of football as a spectator sport. The working classes flocked to the ground not because they were sold on the ideas promoted by the rational recreationalists, but because they were still enthusiastic lovers of the mores which underpinned the game. But given the increasing class tension and class awareness of the 1880's and 1890's, this diffusion and democratisation of the game began to be characterised by middle class observers as a "football fever" and a "football mania". (10)

In this way, as a modern game returned to the working class milieu where the traditional mores which had governed folk football persisted, in varying degrees and in more "civilised" forms, spectator disorder was subsumed into the more general debate surrounding working class youth. (11)

The analyses of Stedman Jones, Cunningham and the Yeos have advanced the study of nineteenth century leisure, but, if further progress is to be made, more adequate work must come to grips with the issues referred to. Inadequate conceptions of power and the making of history, the tendency to provide selective and optimistic studies of the characteristics of popular culture and the over-emphasis on the ability of the working classes to make their own culture must be eschewed. Developmental and figurational sociology provides, a more relational, dynamic and relatively detached perspective of the structural processes of continuity and change in popular culture.

---

(10)

ENSOR,E (1898)   The Football Madness Contemporary Review 74.

EDWARDES,C (1982)   The New Football Mania The Nineteenth Century 32.

(11)

MAGUIRE, J   The Emergence of Football Spectating As A Social
(Forthcoming)   Problem 1880-1985 Sociology of Sport Journal

BARRIERS IN FEMALE SPORTS INSIDE A MALE DOMINATED NIF

Gerd von der LIPPE
Telemark Distriktshøgskole, 3800 Bø, Norway

Abstract
Based on the model of analysis, the three issues studied as well
as the three levels which together form the basis of the discussion
dealing with the results, issue no. 3 - physical exercise for
housewives - seems to have been well adjusted to the norms and
values predominant at all three levels: At the central committee
level and also inside the Board and Assembly of the NIF - at least
as far as the objectives and equal rights were concerned. From a
social perspective physical exercise for housewives must have
been considered as an idea which was widely acceptable and safely
placed within the framework of activities adapted to the equal
worth model and the traditional role pattern. Other issues, such
as the handbook for female sports and the idea of a more close-knit
administration of female sports did not, on the other hand, succeed
in passing the barriers 2 and 3. These two issues therefore are
examples of a non-decision process. They have probably challenged
the values and interests of the representatives in the relevant
central boards and committees as well as the decisionmakers of the
NIF.
Key words: The central committee of women: the DSK, barriers, non-
decision process, equal worth, equal rights, handbook of female
sports, a close-knit administration of female sports, physical
exercise for housewives.

1.0 Introduction

The climate for effective cooperation between the sexes seemed
especially favourable in the post-war period in Norway. Respect
for women and an appreciation of their worth seemed to be stronger
in 1945 than in 1939, due mainly to the women's courageous response
to the Nazi tyranny of the war years. Symbolic of an apparently
new relationship between men and women was the presence in 1945
of a woman in the Government for the first time. This new spirit
of reconsiliation and cooperation embraced virtually all spheres
of life and characterised for a time at least, the Norwegian post-
war sports organisations.

In fact, the second World War had brought in its wake a desire for
unity at several levels. In 1946 the Workers Sports Federation
(Arbeidernes Idrettsforbund or AIF) and the National Federation
of Sports (Norges Landsforbund for idraet or NLI) merged to become
the Norwegian Confederation of Sports (Norges Idrettsforbund or NIF).

A Central Committee for Women (det sentrale kvinneutvalget or DSK)
was formed in the same year with consultative status to the newly
formed Board of Sports of the Confederation. The essential purpose
of this Committee was to increase women's involvement in the NIF

which at that time was strongly male dominated. A major task of the Committee was to increase the number of active female participants both as performers and at the level of policy and decision making.

The early years of the DSK were seemingly years of promise. There were committees for women in 6 special associations. In 1947 there were committees for women in 30 out of 35 local associations. Two years later the number had increased to 35 out of 36. Not all of them were operating throughout this period, but up to 1949 most of them were active. Yet by 1953 the number of committees for women had been reduced to 18. The DSK was dissolved at the General Assembly in 1953.

2.0 Approaches and methods

The political system of the western world, its institutions and organisations included, does not always work the way the pluralists thought. Some issues tend to be systematically excluded from serious consideration.

The concept of non-decision making has been defined in several ways. According to Bachrach and Baratz non-decision is:" a decision that results in suppression or thwarting of latent or manifest challenge to the values or interests of the decision-maker. To be more clearly explicit, non decision-making is a means by which demands for challenge in the existing allocation of benefits and privileges in the community can be suffocated before they are even voiced; or kept covert;or killed before they gain acess to the relevant decisionmaking arena; or failing all these things, maimed or destroyed in the decision-implementing stage of the policy process."[1]
It could also be an instant of structural suppression of issues; i.e. suppression where no decisions are made and no agent of this suppression can be identified.

The question to be asked is the following:
What barriers did the DSK have to pass inside the NIF to be able to win the approval of the organisation for their ideas?
The main source of information is written material from Norwegian sources as well as interviews with former leaders of major sports associations.

2.1 Model of analysis

Dahlerup's model for "agenda building" is adapted for analysis of the DSK barriers inside the NIF.[2]

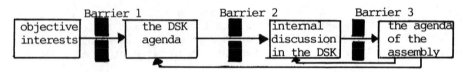

46

Barrier 1 deals with the transition from individual interests to "demands" from a larger group of people, in this case the DSK agenda. Barrier 2 contains the transition from the minutes on the DSK agenda to the corresponding agendas of other boards/committees beside the committee of women, or to the agendas of other boards of special committees. Once barrier 2 is passed, an internal discussion may take place inside the NIF. Barrier 3 deals with the problem of passing from the agenda of the above-mentioned bodies to the agenda of the Board of Sports, the National Assembly or the Assembly. This Assembly is the highest authority of the NIF. During the post-war years the General National Assembly was acting as the highest authority between each session. Both the National Board and the Assembly were bodies competent to issue orders to the Board of Sports.
Barriers 2 and 3 include both administrative bodies and bodies representing elected representatives. We will not go into the size and influence of these two bodies. Their impact on the barriers will not be discussed, and barrier 1 will not be analysed in this respect.

3.0 Special issues

3.1 Introduction

We will start with matters initiated by the DSK and including a formalized cooperation with other bodies and/or elected representatives beside the committees of women inside the NIF. Of the 3 issues selected, one was supposed to be founded on the equal worth model, one on the equal rights model and one was supposed to be neutral in both respects. The two models are more thoroughly described in the report "The central committees of women inside the NIF: 1946-53," TDH 1985.[3])

The following three issues based on the model of analysis in paragraph 2.1 are tentatively analysed:

1. The development of a handbook of female sports (the equal rights model)

2. Suggestions as to a more close-knit administration of the DSK and the committees of women inside "influential" special organisations.

3. The organisation of physical exercise for housewives (the equal worth model).

All three topics are first described in the above-mentioned order and then followed by a brief discussion of any possible explanation why some barriers are passed while others seem impassable.

3.2 The development of a handbook of female sports

The idea of publishing a handbook of female sports was first introduced on the agenda of a meeting held on the 27 November 1947. A sum of NOK 1000 was allocated to this project. The subject matter of this handbook was to be as follows:

- the structure and addresses of the DSK
- Norwegian records as of 1 January 1948
- Norwegian champions of female sports in 1947
- participation in international contests and results obtained in such contests
- rules of competition
- selection of exercises in female sports as well as rules of exercise[4])

The DSK wrote to the committees of women inside the special federations in order to collect material for the planned handbook. At their meeting on 5 March 1948 the committee of women of the NFIF introduced this issue for the first time. Information on the rules of competition and a survey of Norwegian champions were sent to the DSK on 5 May 1948. The committees of women now considered the whole affair settled although they did not forward any of the material they were asked to supply. We know very little of the treatment of this issue as we have very few sources of information. What is certain is that the affair was never discussed in other fora of the NIF as we can see from the minutes available.

The DSK took several initiatives in order to push the affair. The then chairman was asked to contribute. According to the DSK minutes they never received the relevant articles from other persons in influential positions inside the NIF.

The item never reached the agenda of the other central committees and boards as far as we are able to judge. No discussion could be initiated, therefore, and barrier 2 was apparently never passed. The affair was never discussed at any assembly or boardmeeting, consequently barrier 3 was never passed. This is therefore another example of a non-decision process.

3.3 Issue 2: Suggestions of a more close-knit administration of the DSK and the committees of women into special associations.

On 7 February 1947 the DSK wrote a letter to the board of the NIF, explaining why the meeting was being arranged and why the issue was to be discussed. Acurate and precise background information was enclosed. The DSK held the meeting on 27 February 1947 and the leaders of the 6 largest women's sports organisations were present: The Norwegian Gymnastics Federation, The Norwegian Ski Federation, The Norwegian Handball Federation, The Norwegian Amateur Athletic Association, The Orientation Federation and The Natatorial Federation.
The intention behind this meeting was to try and enlarge the DSK to make room for the committees of women inside the special federations.

"The following motion was moved at the joint meeting:
Motion: The committee of the Norwegian Confederatiuon of Sports, working for female sports, is to have the following composition:

A working committee consisting of 5 members to be elected at the Assembly of Sports (CHAIRMAN AND 4 MEMBERS)
The chairman of the committees of women, belonging to the special federations, will join the main committee of women as members."[5]

The meeting was held. The only minutes available from this meeting is the following sentence: "At the end of the meeting everyone agreed to meet again in order to discuss matters of interest both to the individual member as well as to female sports in general."[6]

The minutes from the board meetings of the NIF make no mention whatsoever of this meeting, although there had been some exchange of letters between the organisation and the DSK concerning the arrangement of this meeting. Once again, barriers 2 and 3 remain unpassed. And we have one more example of a non-decision process.

3.4 The organising of physical exercise for housewives

The agenda refers to this meeting for the first time on 13 March 1947. The committee wanted to make physical exercise for housewives more available through the cooperation with the women of the NGTF and other relevant organisations. The committee seems to have been concerned with this idea right from the start.

Representatives from the NGTF and the DSK had a meeting where this issue was treated immediately afterwards. The issue was on the agenda at a meeting in this federation and again in The Board of Sports the year after. A committee was then set up to work out the guidelines for physical exercise for housewives in the keeping with the work already carried out. Its secretary also became the secretary of the DSK. The leader of the organisation. Mr. Fougli, also joined the committee. The issue was discussed at the National Assembly in 1949. The constitutional meeting for physical exercise for housewives was held as early as 26 Januar 1950. From then onwards this type of exercise did no longer belong to the DSK and the NIF, as women's organisations outside the NIF made up the majority of the new working committee. Barrier 2 was passed as the issue was discussed in The Norwegian Gymnastics Federation. The following year barrier 3 was passed when the issue was presented before the Board of Sports.

4.0 A brief discussion of the results
The following three matters will be discussed at three levels:
A.   The competence and authority of the DSK in relation to their partners at the central committee level inside the NIF

B.   The aspect of equal worth and equal rights in places of influence inside the NIF

C.   The aspect of equal worth and equal rights in a social perspectiv

4.1 The professional competence of the DSK in relation to partners

The professional competence of the DSK seems to have been at the highest level in issue no. 3, as several of the members had been working with the physical exercise for housewives affair in various fields before barrier 2 had been passed and the working committee was established. In issue no. 1 - the handbook - the committee seems to have been completely dependent on the professional competence of individuals and on the committees of women inside the special federations. When speaking of the idea of a more close-knit administration of female sports on a central level we find it more complicated to give a general assessment of this issue.[7]

4.2 The authority of the DSK in relation to their partners

The Board of Health and the DSK did not agree on the rules of competition for female sports. Consequently the handbook could not be completed. The authority of the Board of Sports seems to have been considerably higher than that of the DSK in this case as well as in other cases where the physical capacity of women and the various branches in which they might take part were concerned. The DSK did not have much authority in relation to their female partners in any of the three issues. The only exception was the physical exercise for housewives-affair.[10]

4.3 The equal worth and the equal rights model

The equal worth model is based on the traditional role pattern that seems to have been predominant in Norway during the post-war period.[11] Physical exercise for housewives is an activity within this framework, unlike the idea of a special handbook of female sports. Records, national contests and rules of competition were to be presented here. Female competitive sports seems to have been almost non-existent in the yearbooks, reports etc. of the special federations.

Competitive sports and athletics beyond the traditional female sports belong to the equal rights model.[12] The presentation of this kind of sports does, moreover, belong inside the scope of a special handbook.

Neither of the two above-mentioned model seem right one for a presentation of a special administration of female sports. The idea of thus isolating female sports from male sports as a thing apart, and to an even stronger degree, seems to correspond to the equal worth model. A more close-knit cooperation between the DSK and the committees of women on a central level would, on the other hand, probably be considered as a competitive element to the special federations and their own "control" of female sports. Based on this argument issue no. 2 seems to go further than the equal worth model and even to surpass it.

4.4 Equal worth and equal rights

The traditional role pattern seems to have been predominant in
Norway during this period. The equal worth model therefore should
be the more applicable in order to understand and partly explain
the living conditions and life pattern of women. In 1950 95% of all
married women were housewives. Female representation in the Storting
was 5% in 1946-53 and 6% in the municipal boards and committees.[13]
A public debate on equal rights was non-existent, or so it seems at
least, although during the years 1945-52 the women organisations
inside most political parties were working together for the first
time in Norwegian history in order to bring issues like equal
worth and equal rights to the attention of the public.[14]

References

1) Bachrach, P. and Baratz, M., Power and Poverty,New York, 1970
   p. 44
2) Dahlerup, D., Overcoming the Barriers: An approach to the Study
   of How Women's Issues are kept from the political Agenda.
   In Women's Views of the political World of Men, Stiehm, J.H.
   (ed.) Transnat. Pub., New York, 1984
3) Lippe, G. von der; The Central Committee for Women inside the
   Norwegian Confederation of Sports 1946-53, Section for Culture
   and Sports, Telemark Regional College, essay 103, TDH 1985,
   pp. 37-39.
4) Box 310 in the NIF archives: The committee of women 1945-53.
   Minutes dated 27 November 1947.
5) ibid. Letter from the DSK to the Board of the NIF, dated
   7 February 1947.
6) ibid. The DSK minutes, dated 8 May 1947
7) Lippe, G. von der, Lecture notes from Telemark Regional College,
   1984, p. 16.
8) Lippe, G. von der, 1985, opcit., pp. 25-29

9) ibid. pp. 25-31.
10) Lippe, G. von der, 1984, opcit. 24
11) Lippe, G. von der, 1985, opcit p. 32.
12) ibid. p. 15.
13) Lippe, G. von der, 1985, opcit., p 32-33.
14) Løvik, M. The cooperation committee of Norwegian women's
    organisations, 1945.52, The University of Bergen, p. 19, p. 76.

REPRESSED NATIONALISM AND PROFESSIONAL FOOTBALL: SCOTLAND VERSUS ENGLAND

H.F. MOORHOUSE
Department of Sociology, University of Glasgow

Abstract
Most previous studies of professional football and popular culture have ignored problems of football finance and have used class and class relations as the main analytical tools. This approach reveals little about the meanings which Scottish football provokes. Evidence of the financial relation between clubs in the two leagues - Scottish and English - reveal that Scottish football is financially dependent on transfers to England. It is argued that features forced onto the Scottish game by this characteristic relation feed into recurrent (and often contradictory) symbols and images which surround football North of the border, and which, in turn, constantly invigorate a vibrant, but fatalistic, repressed nationalism Scotland.
Key Words: Football, Scotland, Nationalism, Finance

1.   Introduction

"We also must encourage, and I think the most important thing is from the Scottish point of view, it is important we still maintain a solid professional game here, which will generate some form of reference to ourselves overseas. To do that we've got to have a competitive division, which is well paid and which is attractive to maintain revenue. That is the only way we can keep the quality of players up here." Wallace Mercer, Chairman of Hearts FC in The Thursday File on Scottish Football, BBC 1 TV (Scotland), 17 October 1985.

There is a good deal of scholarly analysis of British football, what it 'means', what its exact path and effects are in cultural terms, but most of these analyses relate to English forms and use English evidence. Mostly they analyse football in terms of class relations and class resistance. Now, if we consider: hooliganism, the rebuilding of stadia, or the relation of the game to TV, and all of these have been accorded a prime place in the social analysis of the game's cultural weight, then all have different trajectories North and South of the border. As the above quote might indicate football resonates in Scottish popular culture in different ways than it does in England, and many of these differences arise out of the nature of the Scottish games relation to, the way it has to relate to, the English game. English football conditions, and possible creates, essential elements in Scottish football and these feed themes which turn, not on class and class resistance, but on other kinds of social identities, on a very particular kind of nationalism, on what it means to be Scottish (Nairn 1977, Hunter 1981).

Some random, but far from unusual, examples might suggest what I am alluding to here. The spectator en route to Hampden Park to see Scotland in an international match against, say, Belgium or East Germany, should not be surprised to hear various comments, chants and songs about 'the English', their legal status at birth, and how much they are disliked. Scottish fans invaded the pitch at Wembley in 1977 when Scotland beat England. This was vigorously condemned by the English football authorities and the English media, restrictions were placed on future visits by Scots fans, and the incident is still routinely referred to as 'infamous' and re-shown as an example of hooliganism. It is regarded quite differently North of the border. One Scottish television channel saw nothing wrong in using film of the invasion, including the pulling down of goalposts, as the background for the opening titles of its weekend sports programme for some years. On BBC (Scotland)'s sports review of 1985 an exhange between the presenter and the captain of a Scottish village cricket team which had won a cup competition at Lords ran: "did you bring back any of the hallowed turf?" "No, our turf's better than theirs" [studio laughter] "Ah, I thought we may have given you a few lessons from Wembley!" So what is condemned in one part of Britain is celebrated in another. Again, when, rather rarely, Scottish television chose to show highlights of a crucial English international match (a decision condemned by some Scottish newspapers) the relevant TV guide in Glasgow's Evening Times newspaper (27 April 1983) ran:"Midweek Sports Special: Exclusive Highlights of England's vital match with Hungary ... Come On You Reds!" And when Aberdeen were the only British club to reach the semi-finals of any European competition in 1983 an interview with their manager (now the national team manager) elicited the following thoughts (Daily Record 19 March 1983):

"I'm against Anglos (i.e. Scots who play in England) being in the Scots team. I'd pick a tartan side and they'd give England a run for it - and that's what it's about. Players go south and return with their llama coats and their discipline on and off the park isn't as good as that of the lads at home. I'd worry only about players who stayed at home and shirt-advertising revenue will help. Meantime, encourage them with caps and it would be good for our game. Fewer Anglos are being chosen now than ever but I'd ban them."

2. Scotland Versus England

Professional football in Scotland is, and has been, structured by a number of features which demarcate it from the patterns of the English game and among these are that Scottish football:

(i) has been economically dependent upon transfers of players to the English League which means top clubs face increased competition in the transfer market while, in addition, the post-war period saw increasing activity by English clubs in the initial signing of young Scottish players;

(ii) is involved in a constant and unreciprocated comparison with English football in the mass media. Scottish football receives intensive coverage from media based in Scotland, but Scotland is also served by the national, i.e. English based, media which, despite restrictions on English coverage imposed by the Scottish football authorities, do focus on the English League. This, plus the number of Scots involved in English football, means that Scottish coverage tends to be structured around a comparison with the English game, whereas the national, i.e. English, media tends to ignore the Scottish game and English football certainly does not look to, and is not forced to look to, Scotland for its points of reference.

The financial power of English clubs certainly is an underlying assumption of commentary around Scottish football, relating to a more general view that, economically, Scotland is "at the mercy" of her much larger neighbour. Professionalism was to some extent _forced_ onto the Scots by the English poaching of players. The temptations have continued, and so has the indigenous annoyance revealed in the continual nagging strand in the Scottish media and popular discussion, arguing that international teams should be composed only of Scots playing in Scotland. Nonetheless money counts, and Scottish football gains a large slice of its revenue from selling players to England and buying very few back. The first Chester Report noted that in three years 1963-66 two Scottish divisions (excluding eight clubs who did not provide information) made a profit of £1/2 million from transfers, whereas the English divisions paid out net nearly £1 million. The report noted that there might be a loss in attractiveness in the Scottish game because of this trade but was quite certain that Scottish football depended on such money. In a study for the Chester Report of 1983, the Secretary of the English Football Association considered the accounts for 1978-9 of 80 of the 92 English league clubs, and found a total loss on transfers of around £2 million - most of this going to Scotland.

Most Scottish clubs depend on transfers to balance their books, and this is true even for the most successful. A series of articles (Glasgow Herald March 1982) on "The Crisis in Football" reported that the Vice-Chairman of Aberdeen: ". . . admits that even Aberdeen need a good transfer every three or four years to top up the Pittodrie balance sheet." The article went on to say that it cost £1m a year to run the club and this simply did not come in through the turnstiles. In the years from 1971 to 1979 Aberdeen received a net income of £285,000 from transfers, sold a player to England for £800,000 in 1980, and in 1984 after winning the Scottish League and Cup the club received over £1 million from the movement of two players to England and one to Germany. As their manager put it (Glasgow Herald, 2 September 1984): "That is the sole reason why McGhee and Rougvie left - for money. We have become a big club in terms of recognition, but not in terms of finance so we cannot possibly pay players £2,500 a week." Success in European competitions (and so greater income) can delay the imperative but, basically, almost all Scottish clubs must be sellers in the market for players, especially top class players, a point which must have some effect on the meanings provoked by football in that country.

In contrast, top English clubs are big net spenders in the transfer market and a good deal of this money flows to Scotland. One English club's - Tottenham Hotspur's - squad of players in 1985-6 contained at least seven players who cost between £300,000 to £800,000, and this is not unusual for the English League. In contrast, Scottish outflows are very modest. Rangers have never spent £300,000 on a player (by 1985 only Celtic and Aberdeen ever had, twice each, in Scotland). Certainly Rangers, the richest Scottish club, (Moorhouse 1984) the financial equal of virtually all English clubs, have done little to stop the steady drain of players from Scotland to England (though they have tended to hold onto their own players). Rangers record payment is £210,000 modest even by the standards of quite lowly English First Division clubs. This is not due to a lack of money, a point to which I will return.

This migration is no new thing - eight of the revered Scots team of the "Wembley Wizards" who beat England in 1928 were 'Anglos'. The number of Scots attached to English League clubs was 369 in 1929, 258 in 1965, and 198 in 1975 (of which 82 were in the First Division), but it is doubtful whether the outflow from Scotland of top-class players in their prime or as youths was ever as great as from the 1960s onwards. The new problem for Scottish clubs arose from changes in the law of contract, and the big signing-on fee Scots players could obtain in the South (Crampsey 1978) So here is an aspect of football finance which needs to be considered in assessing its cultural meanings: the constant, and unreciprocated movement of star players out of Scottish football, out of Scotland.

The characteristic relation of the two leagues as seller and buyer, has a variety of effects which feed into Scottish popular culture in complex and, apparently contradictory ways. To begin with, no-one in Scotland, especially the fans, has ever been given the idea that the game has money to burn. Indeed, the profligate ways of some English clubs with regard to transfer fees or wages are occasionally used to highlight Scottish shrewdness and good housekeeping. The deeply imbued notion, that England has more money, serves to supply a convenient vocabulary of motive to explain why players have to be sold (and for players to move) even by clubs - Rangers and Celtic - who, on reflection, might be thought likely to be the financial equals of most, if not all, English clubs. The periodic ringing declaration by Scottish clubs "we will keep our stars" is known to be hollow, and certainly sounds cracked a year or two later. Moreover Scottish clubs often refuse to sell to other Scottish teams. The Chairman of Hearts quoted at the start of this paper was also quoted (Daily Record 25 November 1985) in an article "Hands Off To Rangers": "The only offer we would consider for Levein or any of our other youngsters - would be from a top English club."

Since even the biggest Scottish clubs appear unable to compete it is not perhaps surprising that one thread running through the football culture in Scotland is a distinct sense of loss. The brochure of a recent exhibition about Scottish football contained this as a palpable, but unexamined, element in the Scottish game. Its first action photographs were of two current international players now both in England. Reflecting on the post-war period the author commented: "The besetting curse for Scottish clubs remained the loss of talent to England" but suggested no way the affliction could be lifted (McCarra 1983). Here, then, the structuring of football symbolism in Scotland might well be thought to support fatalism or emigration as responses to the conditions of lower class life. But the reaction to this constant drain of players tends to be much more complex since it is woven in with another strand in Scottish football discussion which asserts that Scotland is a superior producer of high class players. For example, Scotland's popular daily printed an article on teenage players which started (Daily Record, 23 August 1983): "As the cheque book plundering of Scotland's top football talent continued, the fans hunger for fresh faces and exciting new talent grows even stronger. Amazingly this small country can keep on providing enough youngsters with that special magic". While asserting that good young players are constantly emerging to fill any vacuum created by continual sales, the Scottish media plays a double edged role. It deplores the drift of players out of the country, sometimes appeals to them to stay, but conducts a constant discussion about who is likely to be the next to go. While the departure of each star is regretted, the search immediately begins to pin-point "the new...", both to reassure Scots that the indigenous game remains of a quality approximate to the English, but also to indicate the likely next target for English (latterly European) cash. Which English club is prepared to pay how much for who is an off-the-peg story for any harrassed journalist but this English interest is a source of perverse Scottish pride. For English scrutiny and purchases are positive proof of the flow of Scottish talent, and of the similar standard of the two leagues. It should be said that Scotland does seem to possess a remarkable record as a producer of footballers. A recent survey of recruitment to the English League reveals that over the post-war period Scotland more than held its own as an "English region" supplying the English League while, it supplied virtually all the professionals for its own game (Bale 1983). Thus the pride and sense of innate superiority which co-exists with a sense of loss in the Scottish football culture has some objective basis.

Then the diaspora of Scottish players ensures that the Scottish football world has few, if any, super-stars as a cultural type. Many famous Scots footballers never play in their own league, while Scottish professionals who have the footballing ability to serve as the basis of super-star status tend to leave before any cultural identity is established. Once players move, they are much less visible, as are English super-stars (due in part to TV restrictions, the focus of newspaper coverage etc) and while interest is shown in the rather distant echoes of their achievements, this 'absence' and their emigration, do not allow them to serve as appropriate models of lifestyles in the Scottish context.

But this relocation of talent across the Border does mean there is a constant supply of expert testimony about an abiding question in the Scottish football world: how do the two leagues compare?

Expatriates (rarely anyone English) are often called in witness, in
the face of English pretensions, to pronounce on the rather poor
quality of the English League, its reliance on 'foreign' players
(including Scots) to provide 'skill' and 'flair', and the similar
standards of the top clubs. For example, the Scottish League Cup
Final was televised live in Scotland in 1984, at the same time the
equivalent English game was seen in England. Both games ran to extra
time and the Scottish viewer saw hardly any highlights of the
English game (which the English press said was very exciting). In
the studio to provide comments was an ex-Ranger player newly
transferred to Chelsea in England. At the end of the game he was
asked the stock question to Anglos: how do standards compare?
Johnstone was in no doubt. The Scots had seen the better game:
"We've been watching both here (on some video relay presumably) and
ours was much better". He was disappointed by the English League,
Liverpool and Manchester United were out on their own but: "our top
four would do very well down there." And this is fairly
representative of the reassurance that home Scots require and receive
from their distant stars.

In addition, this dispersal of stars allows the myth of the
return to flourish in Scottish popular and media discourse. So, to
take only recent examples, it has been suggested recently that
Macari, Graham, Dalglish, Jordan, Nicholas (Charlie will come
again!), Wallace, and Nevin, - all Scottish international forwards -
might be about to return to the Scottish League. Few emigres ever do
come back, though most are quoted as saying that they want to, but
the belief that talent could flow back persists, with its strange mix
of constant hope and perpetual disappointment. Sometimes, however,
the media laces this myth with a touch of 'economic realism'. In
late 1983 when Ian Wallace was discussing a move from Nottingham
Forest to Rangers, a Glasgow paper explained (Daily Record, 30
November 1983): "Ian Wallace yesterday rejected a move to Rangers
because they would not pay even half his present £1,250-a-week
wages." Or, in early 1984 about rumours that Celtic were to re-sign
Nicholas recently sold to Arsenal, the same paper ran a story
headlined (Daily Record, 3 March 1984): "Why Nicholas won't rejoin
Celtic: £1,000 A WEEK BARRIER" Rarely, if ever, does the media
suggest that any Scottish club could pay rewards equivalent to the
English level. Rangers' wealth is a matter of some interest in
Scotland, but this is not usually developed to suggestions about
transfer fees or wage rates. Now Rangers, at least, should be able
to compete with any English club. They do not but this can hardly be
a matter of money, but must be a matter of policy. Rangers are a
Protestant club who will not sign Catholics (Moorhouse 1984; Murray
1984), but it would seem that they operate other restrictions as
well.

Like all Scottish clubs Rangers do not recruit youngsters from
the rest of Britain (though, of course, English clubs do recruit in
Scotland) and Rangers do not compete, though they certainly could
compete, in a nationwide, now European, market for the very top
stars. Thus while Rangers' policy of not playing Catholics is often
attacked (and, presumably, applauded) in Scotland, to the sociologist

it is just as odd that they have never signed a top-class Englishman.
Up to 1980 the club had had 112 Scottish internationalists among
their players but not one English international. Rangers, then, try
to exist as a top European side while relying almost entirely on a
supply of Scottish (and some Northern Irish) talent increasingly
under competition from England. The football culture in Scotland
sees nothing odd in this, it is scarcely ever discussed. It is
assumed that innate superiority and relative poverty require that the
overwhelming majority of players in Scotland will be Scots. There
can be no doubt that Scottish clubs 'represent the nation' in a way
which is not true of polyglot English clubs - as all Scots know.
Identification is made easier, and cultural nationalism is promoted,
there are the occasional, resonant, victories but, since Scotland's
population is small, and prizes do tend to go to clubs who buy the
best players, Scottish club football's role of national
representation leads, almost always, to ultimate failure. The one
club who could shake this set of assumptions, who could buy players
of all nations to seek success, is unwilling to translate its great
financial power so as to break out of the role of being clearly seen
to represent the nation - of being the more or less unsullied
champion of (protestant) Scotland. Following such a policy might be
supposed to promote fatalism in the force of circumstances as a
characteristic of Scottish popular culture rather than any kind of
resistance.

3. Discussion

Scottish football, then, is bound up in an odd quasi-nationalistic
drama in which its perpetual role is as underdog, if not downright
victim. Often English power (trying not to sell Wembley tickets to
Scots, putting conditions on the release of Scottish players from
English clubs for vital World Cup games etc) are discussed in terms
which are not heard in England, and whose charge might well shock if
they were. So, when the English authorities switched the venue of the
England versus Scotland game from London to Glasgow to "combat
hooliganism", a caller on Radio Clyde's popular soccer phone-in
programme (6 April 1985) asked the resident journalist whether this
made Scots second class citizens, and the exchange went: "I don't see
myself as a second class citizen. I think Londoners are second
class!" "I agree with you but according to the English we have to
prove ourselves all the time. We are not second class citizens here!"
"I don't think we are at all. I think they are. I think they have a
second class football team in a capital that is now third rate!"
     Other football clubs in Europe are also bound quite overtly to
nationalistic projects but the only major European club (and Scots
clubs want to be major) who seem to operate with a similar pure and
exclusive recruitment policy is Athletico Bilboa of Spain who not only
'represent' another submerged 'nation' - the Basques - but will, I
believe, only use Basque players. A more nourishing example for some
Scots clubs might be Barcelona, the acknowledged champions of a third
repressed 'nation' - the Catalans, but they pursue victory not purity.
In pursuit of success they are quite willing to employ Argentinians,

Germans, Hungarians, Scots - even Englishmen, but this does not detract from their symbolic role. Scottish football (and Scotland?) might escape from the dispiriting fug of a doomed, quasi-nationalism, and be confident in its own future if its major clubs:

(i) entered a meaningful British competition in which status and success vis a vis English clubs could be regularly and, eventually, dispationately, measured on the pitch;
(ii) started to recruit via youth teams and transfers, English players, Welsh players and so on so that these major clubs could realistically hope to compete in European terms.

Scottish football might be more successful, more exciting, and more relevant for Scots if it broke free from its pure Scottish identity.

References

Bale J. (1983). From Ashington to Abingdon in A. Tomlinson (ed), Explorations in Football Culture, Brighton, Brighton Polytechnic.
Crampsey B. (1978). The Scottish Footballer, Edinburgh, Blackwood.
Hunter J. et al (1981). Ossian and After: The Politics of Tartanry, The Bulletin of Scottish Politics, No. 2.
McCarra K. (1983). Scottish Football: A History, Glasgow Third Eye Centre.
Moorhouse H.F. (1984). Professional Football and Working Class Culture: English Theories and Scottish Evidence, Sociological Review, Vol. 32 No. 2
Murray B. (1984), The Old Firm, Edinburgh, John Donald.
Nairn T. (1977), The Break-Up of Britain, London, New Left Books.
Shaw D. (1985). The Politics of 'Futbol', Spanish Football Under Franco. History Today, Vol.35, August 1985.

THE PIONEERS OF PHYSICAL EDUCATION IN SCOTLAND

ROY B. SMALL
Scottish School of Physical Education, Jordanhill College of Education

Abstract
This paper will examine the contribution of Robert Owen and David
Stow to the initiation and development of physical education in
Scotland during the 19th century. These men of different nationalities, different beliefs and different social backgrounds were
directly responsible for placing physical education within the
curriculum of their schools. Owen in New Lanark and Stow in Glasgow
had a genuine desire to improve the quality of children's lives.
    At New Lanark Robert Owen introduced physical exercises, dances,
games and military drill into the curriculum in 1817. Apart from
their value as recreative agents, Owen believed them to be amongst
the most powerful inducements to the formation of a good and happy
character.
    In 1835 David Stow, the Scottish Christian philanthropist, found-
ed the Normal Seminary for the training of teachers in Glasgow.
Whilst conscious of bodily health, the cultivation of habits of bodily movement, order, obedience and the value of exercise in a
recreative sense, his overwhelming concern was for moral training.
    It was on the issue of moral training that Stow differed from
Owen. Whilst acknowledging the 'training' at New Lanark as having
physical and intellectual elements he contended that "the system was
not moral training and was nearly destitute of any cultivation of one
most important part of our moral nature viz. the religious affection
and habit".
    New Lanark, originally constructed circa 1785, is today a conserva-
tion village. Robert Owen's school for children, like the mill lade,
spinning mills, store, workshop and dwelling houses, has been refurb-
ished to the original design. It is our intention to visit New Lanark
during the Conference.
Key words: Robert Owen, David Stow, New Lanark, Glasgow, Scotland.

It is my intention to highlight the missionary zeal of two men who,
in their efforts to shape a rational system of education, acknowledged the virtue and necessity of the physical as an integral part of
the total education of the child.
    Since the Reformation of 1560 which was led in Scotland by John
Knox there had been a rcognition of the need for an educated society,
but it was a recognition of education that did not include elements

considered trivial like the physical or the aesthetic. Through the
thought and action of Robert Owen and David Stow who were men of
differing backgrounds, nationalities and beliefs, but of similar
single-mindedness, integrity and compassion, change was initiated
and effected in the lives of working class children in different
parts of Scotland.

Robert Owen

Robert Owen was born in Newtown, Montgomeryshire, North Wales. He
had a brief formal education leaving the local school at the age of
nine. He was however asked to remain as an assistant to the teacher
developing the younger children in arithmetic and English. This
stimulated in him a quest for knowledge and he gained the reputation
of being 'information hungry'. Borrowing books from the intellectuals of the town he involved himself in a process of self-education.
This process encouraged in him rational thinking and from his autobiography we learn that by the age of twelve he had formed the conclusion that religion was the source of many of society's problems.
Despite his Christian upbringing he believed that 'man was responsible for his character, neither God nor his fellows, for he was
despite himself entirely the child of nature and society...nature
gave the qualities and society directed them'. (Owen 1970)

In 1781 he left home to become a draper's assistant in London. In
this context he developed the ability to work with people from all
classes of society. This was an ability which was to be of immense
value to him in the future. John Butt suggests that it was these
early working days and his childhood which were probably fundamental
to his later grasp of the inner truths about society 'It was his
virtually indefinable quality of successful human relationships,often
disregarded, from time to time dismissed as part of 'good luck'
which gives coherence to Owen's success in business and influence in
the social movement'. (Butt 1971)

Following a successful period as a factory manager in Manchester,
during which time he put into practice radical reforms, he moved at
the age of twenty-nine to the village of New Lanark on the banks of
the river Clyde in Scotland.

When Owen arrived at New Lanark he was determined not only to manage the mills but to introduce a code of conduct to the people and
improve their living conditions. (Owen 1970a) He saw in the provision of the right environment the key to the betterment of his
fellow man and in this context education was of primary importance.
In the beginning he concentrated on:

(a) Improving conditions of work;
(b) Improving facilities for education;
(c) Abolishing the recruitment of pauper children as labour;
(d) Attracting new families to New Lanark.

Whilst in Manchester Robert Owen had come under the influence of
friends and colleagues at the Manchester Literary and Philosophical
Society. He had been persuaded 'often at second-hand' by the
philosophers of the Enlightenment and was clearly influenced by the

61

ideas of Rousseau, Helvetius and Bentham.

It is alleged that whilst he was not a great educationist in terms of original philosophy, but in welding together what he considered to be the best of all that had been thought and said, he produced a theory of education the influence of which is still evident today in government reports on Education in Britain. (Butt 1971a) He was concerned with the full development of each man and woman. He believed that people were formed by their environment and circumstances and that through education he could produce the kind of people he sought to populate his new society in New Lanark.

'Children can be trained to acquire any language, belief or any bodily habits and manners not contrary to human nature, even to make them, to a great extent either imbecile or energetic characters'. (Owen 1813)

John Butt asserts that his schemes for education were not the ephemeral daydreams of a philosopher, but a concrete set of principles, aims and values on which he based his educational system at New Lanark. At New Lanark there were two schools - the more famous being the Institution for the Formation of Character which was opened in 1816. The new school was interesting not only because Owen's educational theory was put into practice in an environment planned by him, as his first school had not been, but also because the British infant school movement had their origins here. Children were taken into the school from the age of two thus allowing their mothers to increase their earnings in the mills. There were about 300 children attending the school and the boys and girls were taught together.

In our terms it is important to note the place that Owen gave to physical education. Physical exercise, dancing, games and military drill were all part of the curriculum. Apart from their value as recreative agents Owen believed them to be 'Amongst the best and most powerful surroundings in forming a good and happy character'.

Dancing was taught, to quote his son Dale Owen 'as a pleasant, healthful, natural social exercise calculated to improve the carriage and deportment and to raise the spirits and increase the cheerfulness and hilarity of those engaged in it'. Various types of dances were taught including Scotch reels, country dances and quadrilles as well as dances from different countries. Significantly Owen won much acclaim for according a place in the curriculum to these dances of many nations and the singing of country airs by the children. The fact that he paid his dancing master David Budge at the same rate as masters in charge of more academic subjects is indicative of the importance that he placed upon the activity.

Military drill was taught by a superannuated soldier to give the children the habit of marching regularly from place to place and to improve their carriage and walking. Owen also believed that military drill had a further value 'to prepare them at the best time, in the best manner, when required to defend their country at the least expense and trouble to themselves'.

Physical activity was seen by Owen as a way of recreating the mentally tired and he advocated that neither mental nor physical activity should be pursued if the children showed any signs of lassitude. He believed that mental and physical activities were complementary and if they were applied in this rational manner nothing but good would follow. (Owen 1970c) There is one rather amusing but perhaps indicative reference to dress quoted by Butt. Clothes were an important part of the educational environment at New Lanark. Owen had decreed that school children's clothes should be simply designed in the style of Roman or Highland dress in order to allow the body to move freely. He also believed that such dress would increase sexual delicacy, but not surprisingly his partners, who firmly held the opposite opinion, banned the kilt for boys of six and over.

As one might expect, given the power of the church in Scotland at the particular period, Owen's attitude to religion, together with the nature of his curriculum, was seen as a threat to the established order. There already existed in Scotland a rudimentary form of state education. These schools which were associated with Bell and Lancaster and the monitorial system were assigned to encourage conformity and obedience to both church and state. They were organised in military fashion with children being drilled and forbidden to talk. Any learning was entirely rote learning. Whilst Owen acknowledged the work of Bell and Lancaster he was strongly opposed to their rigidity, their reliance on rote learning and the strong religious bias. He sought real knowledge and rationality rather than rote learning, co-operation rather than competition and freedom for children from the pressures of parents and ministers of the church.

He had a genuine desire to improve the quality of children's lives. He was a deist who rejected the dogma of all revealed religions, a stance which did not endear him to those whose patronage he sought. In 1824 the combined forces of church and business forced Owen to abandon his method of teaching and appoint a Lancastrian teacher. Sadly, with the appointment of the Lancastrian, dancing, music and singing disappeared from the curriculum.

But Owen's success and reputation as an educational reformer flourished and in 1825 he exported his ideas to the United States by setting up another community in New Harmony, Indiana.

David Stow

Whilst David Stow is perhaps best remembered for founding the first Institution for the Training of Elementary School Teachers in Britain there can be little doubt that his overwhelming concern was for the moral welfare and education of children, essentially the children of the poor.

Born in 1793, the son of a Paisley merchant, he was reared in a deeply religious household. It is suggested by William Fraser that although he had been educated at Paisley Grammar School the best preparation for his future work is attributable to the moral guidance of his Christian mother. From his earliest years Stow was familiar with the scriptures and 'had these habits not shed their invigorating influence on his earlier years, there is no warrant to suppose that his career would have subsequently brought with it endless blessings to so many hearts'. (Fraser 1868) He was in

63

essence a Christian philanthropist and, in spite of suffering a succession of personal tragedies, remained so throughout his life.

He came to Glasgow at the age of eighteen. Naturally he joined a Glasgow church and the one he chose was the Tron Church at Glasgow Cross. It was located close to an area of desperate poverty, deprivation and crime. The traditional moral values of the community were in tatters and neither the town council nor the police were able to take any effective action.

Daily as he crossed the river from his home on the south side to his business in the north he passed through Saltmarket, a street unmatched for squalor in a city that knew the full meaning of the word. In an effort to ameliorate the situation he and a number of like-minded citizens tried the charity of money. But as Stow himself records this was both slow and pathetically inadequate. 'For five years prior to 1819 I was one of a number who distributed to poor old men certain funds raised by subscription and which it was expected should be paid to the individuals monthly at their own dwellings. Dispensing sixpence was trivial, ineffective and temporary, providing no long term solutions'. (Stow 1854) Charity could only touch the surface of the problem. Stow believed that the answer to social problems lay in education. 'The real solution lay in training the young so that their moral stamina would enable them to resist the viciousness of their surroundings'. (Cruikshank 1966)

His first efforts involved a Sabbath School, which he opened in 1816, but Sunday Schools could make little impression on children exposed to corruption for the rest of the week. (Stow 1845)

As a consequence he turned to day schools and in 1826 he founded an Infant School Society. This school was similar to Owen's school in New Lanark, but Stow's contention was that Owen's school was wholly secular in its inspiration. Stow differed in that his fundamental aim was the moral regeneration of society based on the scripture maxim 'Train up a child in the way he should go and when he is old he will not depart from it'. (Stow 1845)

In 1828 the Infant School Society started a school in Drygate. The children were admitted between the ages of two and six. His aim was the moulding of character and the development of the whole man He contended that as a young plant was nurtured so must a child be encouraged and directed in habits of mind and conduct. It was important that the school premises were designed to combine physical, intellectual and moral training. Stow's school in Drygate included a gallery of tiered seats to accommodate 100 children. Importantly for physical education the school was set in a large gravel playground.

'Schoolroom routine included marching and singing, clapping hands and exercises, all designed to enable children to 'let off steam' and make them more attentive, orderly and obedient. Indeed they were rarely in their seats for more than fifteen minutes at a time without some form of exercise. However physical exercise was much more than an outlet for superfluous energy. This exercise was an essential part of character training for according to Stow, it was no more possible to develop good habits in children within the restraint of a classroom than it was 'to train a bird to fly in a

cage, or a race horse to run in a stable. The playground was the
'uncovered school' the 'child's little world' where unself-
consciously the child revealed himself' (Cruikshank 1966)
It becomes apparent that physical activity gained its real significance in Stow's school for its contribution to the moral aspects
of the children's education. 'The physical activity of the
uncovered schoolroom in its effect on moral character and in promoting habits of order, obedience and cleanliness, forms three-fourths
of what is peculiar to the infant school, schools or seminaries,
whether for children under six or above that age, without an enclosed
playground are destitute of the best if not the only opportunity
of training children morally and physically'. (Fraser 1868a)
Within the playground Stow laid great emphasis upon the circular
swing. The 'big stab' (as it was called) consisted of a central pole
about sixteen feet high which was firmly embedded in the ground.
Six ropes were attached to a circular iron plate two feet in diameter
on top of the pole which revolved on a strong iron pivot fixed in a
hole. (Stow 1945) The children would run around, then leave the
ground, being propelled outwards by the use of their limbs and centr-
ifugal force. Unlike the normal swing the 'big stab' allowed the
children to control their own movement. It also encouraged dynamic
movement as opposed to the relatively passive movement of the
traditional swing thus preventing the lassitude associated with the
normal type of swing. The action resulted in demanding physical
exercise for children, expanding the chest and lungs and strengthen-
the arms and legs. As the six children were swinging around twenty
or thirty others, who formed a circle round the pole, sang or counted
to thirty or forty when the time was up for those on the ropes to
give place to others. The involvement of the master or mistress
during this activity was to watch for any sign of overstrain or
fatigue. This notion of teacher supervision in the playground was
central to Stow's thinking. 'Without a playground, therefore, there
cannot be an approach to the development of real character and dispositions of the child; also without superintendence by the master
there cannot be moral training, except indeed in a very trifling
degree; and time cannot be afforded for that moral superintendence
without a new and particular arrangement of the method of conducting
the indoor lessons; and also, without the gallery principle, there
cannot be the patient, free and dispassionate review of their playground conduct by the master'. (Stow 1840)
Further, Stow reinforces the responsibility of the masters in the
following quotation: "To no department, however, have young masters
such an innate aversion as physical training. From what cause can we
attribute this feeling but to intellectual pride? What - they say
or feel,am I to condescend to play with children? The exercise of
this pride, however, uniformly 'goes before a fall' or a failure in
training 'the child'" . Stow (1840)
He believed that a playground may either be a moral training
ground or a mischief maker - the latter happens when children are
left alone without an authoritative, superintending eye. 'A monitor
or janitor won't do as a subsitute for the sovereign authority of

the master, which all acknowledge, and whose condescension in taking a game or swing with them, is felt as a kindness and a privilege, and who, in consequence, is enabled to guide them by a moral, rather than by a physical influence' (Stow 1840b)

Within the playground games such as battledore, la grasse, skipping ropes, tig and marbles were all played under supervision. Stow contended that there should not be physical training in one place, the intellectual in another and the moral in a third. Rather the whole learning process should take place each day and under one superintendent.

As a consequence he introduced physical exercises of every description into both infant and juvenile schools. He divided them into four facets: firstly, the bodily health of the children; secondly, the cultivation of correct physical habits or bodily movements; thirdly, the arresting and keeping up of the attention during the ordinary intellectual and religious lessons and fourthly, the cultivation of habits of order and physical obedience which strengthens and assists moral training. (Stow 1840c)

The first division was to be achieved in the playground, whilst at the same time the marching and singing in the school hall tend also to promote bodily health. The second was designed to produce gentleness, gracefulness, proper ways of sitting, walking and running; articulation in speaking, reading and cleanliness.

Under the third heading, as a means of keeping attention there was an unlimited variety of movement. Among these movements were clapping of hands, stretching out of arms, rising up and sitting down of the gallery en masse, movements not being fixed but varying according to the trainer.

Under the fourth and final division of the physical training department was included the element of moral training 'It is evident that as rude, clumsy, boisterous habits are a barrier to moral sensibility and the entrance of Christian truth to the mind, as a principle of moral rectitude, so the cultivation of kind and obliging manners - forbearance and giving each companion his own position at school and play- instant obedience in every physical movement also greatly strengthen and promote the moral training of the child'. (Stow 1840d)

Essentially David Stow accorded physical education a place in Scottish education. It was a place that it had not had previously and in spite of his contribution, over one hundred and fifty years ago, there are still many who hold the belief that physical education - in common with other subjects such as art, music and drama - is peripheral to the main stream of education.

Is our concept of sound learning today still inhibited by traditional views? Is our present overwhelming concern with technology merely mirroring the concern of Stow's contemporaries with industrialisation?

If education is not to exist in a vacuum it must influence as well as reflect the social, economic and intellectual climate of our time.

Stow in the midst of a comparable situation elucidated and practised educational principles which can still be regarded as fundamental today.

He believed that until poverty has been eradicated education cannot be fully effective. Also that education is a matter of the whole being, body, mind and spirit and that moral training must begin with young children. Finally, the most important factor in education is not the physical provision or even the method but the quality of the teacher.

References

Bell, H. (1974) David Stow and Present-Day Problems. Scottish Educational Journal

Butt, J (Ed) (1971) Prince of Cotton Spinners. David and Charles

Cruikshank, M. (1966) David Stow, Scottish Pioneer of Teacher Training in Britain. British Journal of Educational Studies

Fraser, W. (1868) Memoirs of th Life of David Stow. Nisbet

Houseman, R.E. (1938) David Stow, His Life and Work (M.Ed. Thesis) University of Manchester

Owen, R. (1970) Report to the County of Lanark and a New View of (Ed. Gatrell, V.A.C.) Society. Penguin

Owen, R. (1971) The Life of Robert Owen by Himself. Knight

Owen, R. (1813) A New View of Society: Essay First on the Formation of Character. Caddell and Davis

Owen, R. Dale (1969) Robert Owen: An Education Outline of the (Ed. Silver, H.) System at New Lanark. Cambridge University Press

Stow, D. (1840) The Training System. Blackie

HIGHLAND GATHERINGS, HISTORICAL SOCIOLOGY AND SPORT

GRANT JARVIE
Carnegie School, Leeds Polytechnic

Abstract
In making a small contribution to the void of sociological
analysis on Scottish sporting forms this paper considers
the Highland Gatherings as a focus of analysis. In moving
towards an analysis which is both historical and sociological this paper develops three particular themes; (1) a
synthesis and critique of some of the key authors who have
written about this Highland phenomenon; (2) the strengths
and weaknesses of two particular schools of thought which
have contributed significantly to a more historical
sociology of sport; and (3) a brief attempt to situate the
development of the Highland Gatherings within the broader
context of Scottish history and social development.
Key Words: Highland Gatherings, Historical Sociology,
Gruneau, R., Dunning, E., Sheard, K., Webster, D.,
Scottish social development.

1. Introduction

My purpose in this paper is to address three specific
themes which emanate from current research into the
Scottish Highland Gatherings. The first theme is
concerned with the conventional wisdom on this Scottish
phenomenon. More specifically the first part of this
paper considers the work of David Webster (1959 and 1973)
and Sir Iain Colquhoun and Hugh Machell (1927). The
second part of this paper compares and contrasts the
recent work of Rick Gruneau (1983) with the earlier work
of Eric Dunning and Kenneth Sheard (1979). The work of
these authors, although strikingly different in terms of
epistemology, has figured prominently in recent attempts
to develop a historical sociology of sport. Together
parts one and two provide the necessary background and
points of orientation for an analysis of the Highland
Gatherings which is located within the broader context of
Scottish history and social development. Before looking
at these three themes I should like to make two broad

remarks. One concerning a current debate in Scottish
politics and one concerning the need to look at Scottish
sporting phenomenon.

Although the debate is not new there is a current
debate in Scottish politics which urges historians,
educationalists, cultural critics etc to challenge the
dominant cultural power, question its values and
assumptions, enquire into its operations and generate
alternative codes for understanding Scottish culture and
history. The response to this current feeling has been
impressive in some areas. J. Bumpstead's <u>Peoples
Clearances</u> (1982) provides a useful re-interpretation of
<u>Highland</u> emigration to North America. Edward Arnold's <u>New
History of Scotland</u> (1981) and Tony Dickson's <u>Scottish
Capitalism</u> (1980) are noteable landmarks. While in the
absence of any serious challenge Tom Nairn's account and
evaluation of Scottish culture and history in <u>The Break up
of Britain</u> (1981) is fast becoming an authoritative text.

Yet with specific reference to Sociology, although I
suspect the same is true of a number of other areas,
serious analysis of Scottish sporting forms are few and
far between. Whatever the reason the problem still
remains that within the morass of recent sociological
writings on sport work on Scottish sporting forms has been
limited. What is even more disturbing as Bert Moorehouse
(1984) has recently indicated is that many general
theories, in this instance of soccer violence, often fall
short when confronted with Scottish evidence. The
remainder of this paper largely concerns itself with one
Scottish sporting form, namely the Highland Gatherings.

2. The Conventional Wisdom on Highland Gatherings: A
Critique

The subject matter of this initial discussion on the
Highland Gatherings stems directly from what might be
called the conventional wisdom on this subject. To date
the research in this area has been dominated by the work
of David Webster and to a lesser extent the writings of
Sir Iain Colquhoun and Hugh Machell. The term conventional wisdom is not meant to be used here in any
derogatory sense. On the contrary the work of Webster in
particular, up until 1973, provides an invaluable source
of empirical information. Extensive lists are provided of
past champions, records and significant events in the
institutionalization of this Highland event. For instance
in the heavy events legendary names such as Donald Dinnie,
Bill Anderson and Sandy Sutherland are recorded as
noteable champions. It is interesting to note that as
early as 1877 promoters were prepared to pay Donald Dinnie
between £25-£100 for appearing at their versions of the

Scottish Highland Games. Indeed the real strength of the conventional wisdom is that it provides a plethora of descriptive material.

It is also useful to bear in mind that in both cases the authors are careful to note that many of the individual traditions which today contribute to these Highland Gatherings have in many cases a much earlier antecedent form out of which emerged todays modern events. For instance Webster suggests that the origin of Tossing the Caber probably lies with those Scottish woodsmen who developed the sport during their leisure periods, (Webster, 1973, p75). The actual origins of the Gatherings for Webster eminate from an event at Bailemuirn which took place during the Pictish period of control in ancient Caledonia. It is argued that a very definate resemblance to present day ceremonies can be seen but instead of a Chieftain or Queen being guest of honour the Picts relied on the Druids.

One thing that both Gruneau (1976) and Dunning (1971) make perfectly clear is that any definitional attempt which ignores the characteristics which have surrounded sports transformation from an elite or folk recreational activity into a major institutional component of modern life will be seriously flawed. The sociologist may encounter a whole range of historical themes or processes in their efforts to comprehend the nature and meaning of sport. In more modern times these might include the commercialisation, bureaucratisation and nationalisation influences upon sporting development.

Yet despite a certain sensitivity in the conventional wisdom to the early origins of the Highland Gatherings it can be argued that in both cases the entire project is somewhat misleading and in some cases incorrect. The collection of factual data tells us little about the cultural production and reproduction of the Highland Gatherings into different forms. Nor does it adequately explain the relationship between Highland sport and the prevailing social structure of Highland society in particular. For instance anyone who reads Colquhoun and Machell's account of the various Highland Gatherings is left in no doubt about the influence of a particular social figuration in shaping the late eighteenth and early nineteenth century gatherings. A certain flavour of the proceedings can be acquired from the following:

1) It must be remembered that athletes and sportsmen are two different characters. They are frequently combined in one person; indeed it is difficult to find a true athlete who is not a sportsman in the accepted terms of those who have aqcuired the cachet of a public school or the imprimatur of a leading university. p26.

2) Let us return from all of this to the quiet
    seclusion of some Scottish glen, where a
    few days before the great meetings a
    handful of hard-working farm hands are
    practising the caber or shot. Do you think
    the bookmakers are dreamt of in their
    philosophy? Could anything be more
    incongruous with its surroundings than a
    deafening din of 3 to 1 Starkey or evens
    Maitland while these honest Highlanders
    were tossing the caber before royalty in
    the arena at Braemar? p27.
3) Twenty thousand crowd at Braemar now
    annually raises its unanimous voice to
    welcome our good King George V ... Let us
    hope that never, even in another two
    hundred years, will it be necessary for the
    loyal subjects of our sovereign to raise
    the standard. p29.
4) There laird and clansman, crofter and
    shepherd meet for the purpose of keeping
    alive the memories of a great past, and
    furthering either in person, or by their
    attendance, the continuance of those
    contests which will be of the greatest
    value in maintaining the best traditions of
    their race. p9.

On the point of origin it is useful to keep in mind that
one of the major problems that any researcher faces when
trying to pinpoint the exact origin of the Highland
Gatherings is the fragmentary nature of the evidence.
Highland tradition itself helps to explain this occurrence
since so many of the legends, customs and traditions of
the Highland communities tended to be passed on from
generation to generation by word of mouth rather than
being written down. The historian Isobel Grant (1930)
develops this point further when she comments upon one of
the key problems which have pervaded many of the early
accounts of Highland history. On a number of occasions,
remarks Grant, many of the narratives of the Scots
chroniclers from at least the eleventh century onwards
have been misguided by the desire of many writers to
enhance the origins of the countries Highland institutions
and customs in comparison with those of England. In the
case of Pictish and Druidicial cultural practices the
problem is further exacerbated by the fact that the Druids
strictly forbade the use of writing as a means of passing
on folklore and customs from generation to generation.
    In short what is being argued here is that while the
conventional wisdom provides an invaluable source of
empirical data the narrative while being extemely

informative is couched in terms of voluntarism, loyalism and idealistic notions of what sport is like. The problem lies mainly with the descriptive as opposed to the explanatory nature of the problem. The authors rarely question the development of the Highland Gatherings or see it as posing problems which require anything more than superficial explanation.

If the sociology of sport, more specifically the historical sociology of sport is to go beyond purely descriptive atheoreticl expositions then accounts of sporting practice need to be located within the broader context of history and social development and to a certain extent guided by theoretical grounding. It is precisely these factors which are the strengths in the work of Gruneau, Dunning and Sheard.

3. Historical Sociology and Sport

The revival of interest in developing historical sociology, in part marked by the arrival of Philip Abrams text Historical Sociology (1982), has clearly been influenced by theoretical controversies concerning the inadequacy of those sociological accounts that have been insensitive to historical concerns. Renewed attempts to construct historical sociological models of sport have taken a number of different forms. For instance Allen Guttmann's From Ritual to Record (1978) develops a Weberian examination of sports transformation from its traditional to modern forms. It is interesting that Guttmann argues that one of the possible advantages to be gained from the Weberian model is that it does not reduce explanation to the economic determinism which, it is argued, has characterised many Marxist interpretations of sport. Yet an alternative school of thought which has recently influenced a great deal of historical research on sport has been that of political economy and Marxist cultural analysis.

The strategy which Gruneau develops in Class, Sports and Social Development involves relocating the paradoxical features of sport into a broader understanding of human agency, cultural production and their expressions in patterns of social development and social transformation. Having laid out the ground rules the strategy which, in my opinion, is quite brilliantly developed involves locating the analysis of sport within these classical concerns. This involves, (1) articulating the classical concerns of social development; (2) acknowledging the essential unity of critical, interpretive, empirical analysis; and (3) understanding the limits and possibilities governing human choices as they are lived or experienced in different social and cultural settings.

In stark contrast the work of Dunning and Sheard in
Barbarians, Gentlemen and Players lies not so much within
the confines of political economy but within the confines
of Eliasian sociology. As such the concepts of figuration, social bonding and webs of interdependence are of
central importance. For instance the development of rugby
football, it is argued, has been greatly influenced by
various figurations such as the public school, the British
class structure and the conflict and tension in the
amateur and professional responses to the democratisation
of rugby football. The process of development is
continually emphasised through the frequent use of terms
such as urbanization, civilization, modernization and
democratization.

It would be misleading and indeed unfair to both texts
to finish this brief discussion by highlighting the
differences as opposed to the similarities. Both texts
provide serious sociological accounts of sport as opposed
to descriptive, atheoretical types of sociological
analysis. Both texts are sensitive to questions about
social patterns and social arrangements in society. The
problems in both texts are approached from a historical or
developmental position. Yet the historical in both
instances is complemented by a penetating sociological
analysis. Finally both texts attempt to locate the
development of sport within the broader context of history
and social development. For Gruneau this involves
locating the development of Canadian sport within the
development of Canada as a dependent social formation
while for Dunning and Sheard this involves locating the
development of rugby football within an analysis of the
British class structure, to name but one figuration which
influenced the process of development.

4.   Clans, Landlords and Victorian Popularity

In returning to an analysis of the Highland Gatherings it
is useful to mention a point made by Gruneau when he says
that there has been a certain ambivalence of those
individuals working in the field to ask certain classical
research questions. For instance; What is the relationship between the Highland Gatherings and the prevailing
social structure? How have the Gatherings been affected
by the historical epoch in which they move? Why did the
games as an aspect of Highland society Gatherings develop
in the late eighteenth and early nineteenth century? Why
did the Gatherings suddenly become increasingly popular
and respectable after about 1840? In what way are the
Gatherings identifiable with Scottish culture? In what
way do the modern Highland Gatherings differ from the
traditional Highland Gatherings?

I do not intend to provide the answer to all of these questions here, but merely outline some of the possible problems that are posed by placing an analysis of the Highland Gatherings within the wider context by which the Highlands in particular and Scotland in general developed as a social formation. I shall begin by suggesting four possible stages in the development of the Highland Gatherings;

1) A stage which lasted from at least the eleventh century when various elite and folk customs, some sporting, some utilitarian, were gradually transformed and formalised into various Highland Gatherings.

2) A stage which lasted from about 1745 to 1860 when much of the traditional Celtic culture was either banned or destroyed. A number of Highland customs were transported with the emigre to North America. The paradoxical situation developed by the 1780's when in a determined attempt to retain certain aspects of Celtic culture, such as traditional dance and music, many Highland societies actively encouraged the development of a number of Highland Gatherings.

3) A stage which lasted from about 1840 to 1914 when the Games became popularised and respectable sporting events. The patronage bestowed on the games by Queen Victoria attracted a tremendous interest to the Braemar gathering in particular. So much so that by 1866 the event became known as the 'Braemar Royal Highland Gathering'. However, in the wake of this development the Highlands became a playground for the sporting rich.

4) A stage which lasted from about 1900 to the present day which involved the emergence of the modern Highland Gatherings characterised by increased professionalization, standardisation of rules, and the development of this Highland custom into a world sporting spectacle. The Gatherings became increasingly dependent upon a romantic cultural identity.

Implicit in this analysis is the belief that the development of the Highland Gatherings can be traced in order to shed light on various problem areas. Firstly, the significance of sport to the elite members of Highland society. Secondly, the Gatherings provide a useful vehicle for providing further insights into the development of a romantic and somewhat mythical cultural identity revolving around tartanry and the romantic views of the emigre. Finally the notion of the civilizing process provides a further possible problematic concern. The Highland way of life has often been described as the barbarous antithesis of Southern civilization. Yet it is important to ask the question just exactly who amongst the various class or cultural fractions within the British Isles views Highland culture as barbarous or uncivilized.

References

Abrams, P. (1982) Historical Sociology. Open Books
    Publishing Ltd, Somerset.
Bumpstead, J.M. (1982) The People's Clearances, 1770-1815.
    Edinburgh University Press, Edinburgh.
Colquhoun, I. and Machell, H. (1927) Highland Gatherings.
    Heath Cranton Ltd, London.
Dickson, T. (1980) Scottish Capitalism. Lawrence and
    Wishart, London.
Dunning, E. (1971) Sociology of Sport. Frank Cass,
    London.
Dunning, E. and Sheard, K. (1979) Barbarians, Gentlemen
    and   Players. Martin Robertson, Oxford.
Grant, I. (1930) The Social and Economic Development of
    Scotland Before 1603. Oliver and Boyd, Edinburgh.
Gruneau, R.S. and Albinson, J. (1976) Canadian Sport:
    Sociological Perspectives. Addison-Wesley, Ontario.
Gruneau, R.S. (1983) Class, Sports and Social Development.
    University of Massachusetts Press, Amherst.
Guttmann, A. (1978) From Ritual to Record. Columbia
    University, New York.
Moorehouse, B. (1984) Professional football and working
    class culture: English theories and Scottish evidence.
    Sociological Review, 32, 2.
Nairn, T. (1981) The Break up of Britain. Verso, London.
Webster, D. (1959) Scottish Highland Games. Collins,
    Glasgow.
Webster, D. (1973) Scottish Highland Games. Reprographia,
    Edinburgh.

IMPERIAL MANLINESS: E.W.HORNUNG AND 'THE GAME OF LIFE'

MALCOLM TOZER
Uppingham School, Rutland

Abstract
From 1895 to 1915 the last English romantic ideal, that of Imperial
Manliness, flourished at the public schools in this their Golden Age.
The games-player was the exemplar of the ideal, for to represent the
house or school at sport was seen as an apprenticeship for serving
the Empire, with the certain understanding that to fight for one's
country was playing for the ultimate team. Ideals need
propagandists: heroes of the Boer War, politicians of the patriotic
movements, and eminent men of letters toured the schools to spread
the imperialist word. This paper examines the contribution of one
purveyor of patriotic poetry and prose, E.W.Hornung: Old
Uppinghamian, cricketing enthusiast, author of the best-selling
Raffles' tales, brother-in-law of Sir Arthur Conan-Doyle - and ardent
imperialist. Hornung's favourite theme was 'The Game of Life', and
an examination of the message plied by this visiting preacher and
minor poet evokes the spirit of the imperial heyday, when the
sportsman ideal ruled wherever the globe was red.
Key words: Public schools, Imperialism, Manliness, Sermons, Poetry,
Edwardian era, Games.

The year is 1909; the setting is a school chapel. It is a Sunday in
November, and the whole school is assembled for evensong. As the
hymn draws to a close the preacher mounts the steps to the pulpit,
places his prepared address on the lectern, adjusts the shields on
the two flickering candles that illuminate his text, pushes his
spectacles further up his nose, and finally looks out at the
congregation of boys and masters as they seat themselves on the
wooden pews below. But this week there are no yawns of anticipation,
no games of sermon cricket have been prepared, and no thoughts drift
off into day-dreams - for this is a favourite preacher. He is a
famous old boy of the school; not a bishop, nor a politician, nor a
soldier, nor a colonial administrator - but a popular novelist, and
much read by the boys of the school. His annual sermon at his old
school is awaited with interest, for it is always a winner: this year
his theme is 'The Old School List'.

He asks the congregation to imagine the return to the school of an
old boy, one who has not been in contact with the school for many
years. Perhaps he has been buried in the Australian bush, or the
Canadian outback; and perhaps this is his first visit to the old
country for more than a decade. Suppose him to be a typical

76

colonial, 'bearded and burnt to a brick'; sadly out of touch with developments at home, but probably retaining some of his old interest in British sports and games; he may even have had <u>Cricket</u> or <u>The Field</u> sent out to him all these years. He makes his way to the library, pulls out the old School List, and looks up the names of his old chums: he compares the boys as he remembered them with what they had become in after life.

The first names to strike him would be the names of several first-class cricketers - for the school is a famous nursery of the national game. He would say - "Were those the brothers who were captains of the Cambridge Eleven in successive years?": and a little lower down the list - "Was that the man who made a century in his first Test at Lord's?". And if you told him - "Yes, those were the men." - then the man from the bush would say he was proud of them, and of the school that had turned out so many fine cricketers. "But," he might inquire, "they are all young men still; why do none of them play first-class cricket now?" And if you answered - "Because they have something better to do; because they loved cricket as a game, but scorned it as a career in life." - then the old boy from the wilds would feel more than ever at one with a school that turns out the truest and highest type of athlete, but has never yet produced the modern gladiator justly characterised as 'The flannelled fool at the wicket'.

The old boy's thoughts turn naturally to the boys who were best at games, but his eyes will light on other names in the School List. "What happened to Harold Paton; what became of Fergus Murray?" - he asks. "Paton and Murray were the two brilliant footballers of my time. What opposites they were; Paton all dash and verve, Murray one of the steady dogged sort who are never beaten till they drop. What happened to those two?" Then you will bring their old comrade in here, the chapel, and show him the regimental flags, with the tablets underneath in memory of Lieutenant Paton and of Captain Murray. They were both killed in the first few weeks of the South African War, and nothing could be more characteristic of the boys we remember at football than the way each met a soldier's death. Paton, racing ahead of his men, was shot dead whilst making for a ditch: how like him! Murray was shot twice whilst leading a charge, but he continued to cheer his men on until a third bullet struck him down: yes, that was the true Murray!

The old boy is prouder than ever of the school at which they and he were boys together. The preacher reminds his listeners that theirs is only one type of heroism; that hardship, pain and death are enemies that anyone may encounter at any moment without going to the wars. And in conclusion he makes his point: what is School but the threshold of Life, and what are Games unless they teach us to play the Game of Life? To do well here at school and not to go on doing well is to leave something like a blot on the Old School List.

The preacher is E.W.Hornung. Old Uppinghamian, cricketing enthusiast, author of the best-selling Raffles' tales, brother-in-law of Sir Arthur Conan Doyle, and ardent imperialist - Willie Hornung was one of many speakers and preachers who visited the public and preparatory schools at this time to press home the imperial message. All ideals need propagandists, and heroes of the Boer War,

politicians of the patriotic movements, and eminent men of letters
toured the schools to spread the imperial word. The soldiers and
politicians generally spoke as representatives of the National
Service League or the Navy League, and under the guise of lecturing
on military history, inspecting the cadet corps, or opening new
gymnasia, they sought to promote the ideal of national conscription.
Other visitors, like Hornung, were more altruistic, seeking to awaken
the ideal of imperialism in the new generation of public schoolboys.
    Hornung had three interests as a writer - the Empire, public
schools and cricket. After he had left Uppingham, Hornung went to
Australia and spent a couple of years there. The life on the stations
made a deep impression on him, and he turned it to account quite
early in his fiction. It cannot be said that his Australian novels
have lasted well: the first, A Bride from the Bush, turns on the
gaucheness of an Australian girl in English society. Her final
offence is to call "Coo-ee" to a compatriot in Rotten Row, a crime
that apparently had the same electrifying effect as Eliza Doolittle's
famous expletive. In all Hornung wrote nearly thirty books, but only
the Raffles' stories have lasted the test of time. Although it is
fairly common to meet people who have not read about Raffles, it is
comparatively rare to come across someone who has not heard of him,
or to whom the name does not suggest a man about town who was also a
burglar. Two of the four volumes of stories are still on the
publisher's list, and in recent years the hero's adventures have been
dramatised for both television and radio.
    In the tales of this 'Amateur Cracksman' Hornung could combine his
passions for the public schools and cricket, and Australia could add
the occasional imperial flavour. Raffles possesses a healthy,
athletic approach to crime, and the only violence encountered is
reserved for his opponent's stumps. Raffles plays cricket for the
Gentlemen of England, and it is his prowess at the game that is so
indispensable both socially and financially for the hero's
well-being. Cricket and the public schools again happily combine in
Fathers of Men, his story of life at Uppingham in the 1880s. Here
the cricket is well handled, and every ball is lovingly and expertly
described. For a terrible moment the reader fears that Hornung is
going to sink to the luxury of letting his schoolboy hero take all
ten wickets in the Old Boys' match, but he recovers at the last
moment and allows him only nine. Though handicapped by asthma and
short sight, Hornung was an enthusiastic cricketer, and he was
recognised, not least by the M.C.C., as an authority on the game.
    Hornung was a great believer in the English public school system,
and he always protested how much it could make even of unpromising
material. He recognised too that with the privileges of a public
school training went responsibilities - and it was here that the call
of Empire needed to be heard. Throughout the years of his own son
Oscar's schooling, Hornung made it his duty to 'do his bit' at
several public and preparatory schools. The sermon was his preferred
medium, and the Game of Life was a favourite theme. In June 1914,
less than a month before the start of the First World War, Hornung
chose 'The Game of Life' as the title for one of his last school
sermons.

He told his young listeners that it is a very old comparison that likens Life to a Game, so old indeed that there is little that is not expressed in terms of games, and particularly of course in terms of cricket. When you want someone to try hard at something, you tell him to 'play up'; when you find it hard to do the right thing, you tell yourself "I must 'play the game' - because", you may add, "because what I'm tempted to do is 'not cricket'." If it is a case of doing our share in some way to help another, we call that 'keeping our end up'; and if only one good word could be said for us by our friends, and by the world, we would love to be known above all else as 'sportsmen'. Being 'a sport', as we use it among ourselves, has come to signify every virtue which is dearest to our hearts: courage, honesty, unselfishness, chivalry, you cannot have a sportsman without all these; and if you have all these, you must be a good man.

Here Hornung broke off to include some lines from Henry Newbolt's Vitae Lampada, with its refrain 'Play up! play up! and play the game!', together with some lines of verse from Punch:

'He kept a rule, if a thing seemed right -
I hope I may do the same -
To go and do it with all his might,
And hardly a thought of fame.
For it isn't the winning that makes a man,
But it's playing the game on the good old plan,
As hard and straight as a mortal can -
In fact it is playing the game.'

Life, he continued, is the most glorious game of all, right up to the end - in a game we know when we are doing well, but in Life we never do. You cannot keep your own score in the Game of Life, and if you try you will make mistakes. God keeps our score, and He does not tell us what we have made until we are out. It is better not to think what we are making, better just to try to play the game.

Try as we can, we cannot tell the score, for we see so dimly: so dimly that sometimes we can hardly see to play; but never so dimly that we think to appeal against the light, for we must glory in the very difficulties that we have to overcome. Who wants an easy victory? Who wants a life full of pitches to leg? Do you think the Great Scorer is going to give you four runs every time for those? No - for in this splendidly difficult Game of Life these cheap and easy triumphs will be written in water on the score sheet. And the way we played for our side, in the bad light, on the difficult pitch, the way we backed up and ran the other man's runs; our courage and unselfishness, not our skill or our success; our brave failures, our hidden disappointments, the will to bear our friend's infirmities, and the grit to fight our own: surely, surely, it is these things above all other that will count, when the innings is over, in the Pavilion of Heaven.

This then was the message of Hornung's sermons: games were a training ground for life; and service to one's country was the ultimate test of that training. It was a message that was well received at his old school, Uppingham, where Edward Selwyn was the headmaster. The school's reputation at games was high, and a series

79

of very fine cricket elevens had brought national renown. The cadet
corps steadily grew in importance, and in the first months of the new
century Selwyn announced to the school that all boys, whether in the
corps or not, were required to pass a shooting test, and that no boy
would be allowed to take part in any inter-house athletic or sporting
contest, nor could he gain a school prize, until he had passed that
test. In February 1900 C.H.Jones, the commanding officer, left for
active service in the Boer War, and his adventures in South Africa
were reported in the School Magazine in gory detail - 'We hear that
Mr. Jones has killed five Boers single-handed. We congratulate him
heartily on the exploit and hope that he will dispose of many more.'
In the early years of the new century about half the school was in
the corps, and by 1905 over a thousand cadets had passed Uppingham's
'Recruit Drill and Fire Exercise'. To Selwyn the corps was 'one of
the glories of the school'; to the visiting Lord Roberts, who came to
open the school's South African War Memorial - a gymnasium -
Uppingham's lead in military matters was an example to set before all
public schools.
   Though Hornung's literary reputation rested on his work as a
novelist, he was also a competent poet and he wrote much patriotic
and propagandist verse in similar vein to his friends Henry Newbolt
and Rudyard Kipling. In the Forerunners of 1900 he echoes the theme
of 'The Old School List':

   'When I lie dying in my bed,
   A grief to wife, and child, and friend,-
   How shall I grudge you gallant dead
   Your sudden, swift, heroic end!'

But it is in his Lord's Leave of 1915 that the sporting rhetoric is
captured at its most innocent:

   'No Lord's this year: no silken lawn on which
   A dignified and dainty throng meanders,
   The Schools take guard upon a fierier pitch
   Somewhere in Flanders.

   Bigger the cricket here; yet some who tried
   In vain to win a colour while at Eton
   Have found a place upon an England side
   That can't be beaten!

   A demon bowler's bowling with his head -
   His heart's as black as skins in Carolina!
   Either he breaks, or shoots almost dead
   As Anne Regina;

   While the deep-field-gun, trained upon your stumps,
   From concrete grand-stand far beyond the bound'ry,
   Lifts up his ugly mouth and fairly pumps,
   Shells from Krupp's foundry.

But like the time the game is out of joint -
No screen, and too much mud for cricket lover:
Both legs go slip, and there's sufficient point
In extra cover!

Cricket? 'Tis Sanscrit to the super-Hun -
Cheap cross between Caligula and Cassius,
To whom speech, prayer, and warfare are all one -
Equally gaseous!

Playing a game's beyond him and his hordes;
Theirs but to play the snake or wolf or vulture:
Better one sporting lesson learnt at Lord's
Than all their Kultur ...

Sinks a torpedoed Phoebus from our sight,
Over the field of play see darkness stealing;
Only in this one game, against the light
There's no appealing.

Now for their flares ... and now at last the stars ...
Only the stars now, in their heavenly million,
Glisten and blink for pity on our scars
From the Pavilion.'

Innocent this may be, but it was no mere imperial jingoism: rather
this is sincere imperial idealism. It is the culmination of the
late-Victorian and Edwardian ideals of athletic and imperial
manliness, where war was to be fought in a Homeric atmosphere. The
war to end all wars would be won by the public school heroes playing
'The Game of Life'. Hornung's connection with the Eton and Harrow
cricket match at Lord's comes about because his son went to Eton and
not to Uppingham, and that at school he was a well-known games
player. He had left Eton in July 1914 to go up to Cambridge, but on
the outbreak of hostilities he joined the Essex Regiment as a
subaltern. Shortly after the summer of Lord's Leave he was killed at
the front, leading his platoon from the fore - in the manner of Paton
and Murray. The distraught father sought comfort in the compilation
of a privately-printed memorial to Oscar, titled Trusty and
 Well-beloved, and included these verses. The Last Post refers to
the contents of Oscar's last letter home:

'Still merry in a dubious trench
They've taken over from the French
Still making light of duty done;
Still full of Tommy, Fritz, and fun!

Still finding war of games the cream,
And his platoon a priceless team -
Still running it by sportsman rule,
Just as he ran his house at school.

Still wild about the 'bombing stunt'
He makes his hobby at the front.
Still trustful of his wondrous luck -
'Prepared to take on old man Kluck.''

Whilst the war was fought in this Homeric atmosphere so the ideal
of manliness sustained the new heroes - and the propagandists of
patriotic prose and poetry - but the arrival of entrenchment saw the
start of its demise. The enemy became invisble: there was nothing
chivalrous about chlorine gas; there was nothing heroic in dying
under bombardment; and there was nothing idealistic in inhuman
mechanistic warfare. As the mode of warfare moved from the
nineteenth to the twentieth century, so the public school officer met
his limit and the ideal of manliness met its end. The war had moved
away from a level where individual action was vital to one where the
individual was lost in an army of millions: the war that was to be
the awakening of the ideal of imperial manliness instead witnessed
its death in the mud of countless battles.
    In 1916 Hornung went to France with the Y.M.C.A., and helped to
organise a library and a rest hut. He was present at the German
bomdardment of Arras in 1918, experiencing at a mature age warfare
already described in imagination. His contact with schools, and with
Uppingham in particular, remained: <u>The Old Boys</u> dates from 1917 -

    '"Who is the one with the empty sleeve?"
    "Some sport who was in the swim."
    "And the one with the ribbon who's home on leave?"
    "Good Lord! I remember him!
    A hulking fool, low down in the school,
    And no good at games was he -
    All fingers and thumbs - and very few chums.
    (I wish he'd shake hands with me!)"'

Hornung had a great interest in the creation of the 1914-18 War
Memorial at Uppingham. This took two forms - the building of a
memorial assembly hall, and the erection of panels of names in an
alcove in the chapel. The visiting old boy of Hornung's 1909 sermon
on 'The Old School List' found a handful of names on the South
African War Memorial; his successor of 1929, on being shown the Great
War Memorial, would find seven panels of names, with three columns in
each panel - and beneath the panels are inscribed seven texts from
the Bible, Hornung's seven chosen Watchwords.
    Hornung was just beginning to recover from the staggering effects
of the war, and all that he, his family, his friends, and his school
had suffered therein, when suddenly he died in March 1921, at St Jean
de Luz, in his fifty-fifth year. His innings in 'The Game of Life'
was closed - and with it closed an era of British imperial history.

References

Hornung, E.W. (1890) <u>A Bride from the Bush.</u> Smith, Elder, and Co.,
    London.
Hornung, E.W. (1899) <u>The Amateur Cracksman.</u> Smith, Elder, and Co.,
    London.
Hornung, E.W. (1901) <u>The Black Mask.</u> Smith, Elder, and Co., London.
Hornung, E.W. (1912) <u>Fathers of Men.</u> Smith, Elder, and Co., London.
Chichester, S.R. (1941) <u>E.W.Hornung and his Young Guard.</u> Wellington

THE 1911 FESTIVAL OF EMPIRE: A FINAL FLING?

KATHARINE MOORE
Department of Physical Education, The Queen's University of Belfast

Abstract
The coronation of King George V provided the British Empire with an
opportunity to parade its splendour at a time when its status in the
world was definitely changing. The halcyon days of the late nineteenth century had given way to the brewing threat of war, and the
staging of the Festival of Empire came at a time when unity within
the Empire was seen to be of increasing importance in some circles.
Sport had long been identified as one of the most desirable ways of
maintaining links among the constituent countries, and the Festival
included various sporting competitions. Although it went
unacknowledged in 1911, this inclusion of sport in a larger
celebration of the Empire itself had been suggested twenty years
before by John Astley Cooper when he advocated a Pan-Britannic
Festival of culture, industry and athletics.
    The paper seeks to examine the connection between Cooper's
proposals and the Festival of Empire by investigating the purpose of
the Festival, and the role sporting competition played in it,
against the backdrop of Empire social history in the early years of
the twentieth century.
Key words: Empire sport, Pan-Britannic Festival, Inperialism,
J.Astley Cooper.

During the late nineteenth century Britain's great exhibitions came
to be dominated by the imperial theme; "the secret of their success
was that they combined entertainment, education, and trade fair on a
spectacular scale" (MacKenzie, 1984). A celebration of the Empire
had been planned for the summer of 1910, but the death of King Edward
VII in May of that year, and the subsequent period of official
mourning, delayed the start of the festival until the middle of 1911.
The coronation of the new king, George V, provided yet another
ceremonial occasion for the Empire to put herself on display.
Throughout 1910 the Times carried regular reports of Festival plans,
and by August a change in rationale for the event was evident in
the newspaper: "It is now felt that the festival will be of increased
use and value as an 'At Home' to the visitors from the Colonies, who
will be in England for the Coronation of King George" (Times,
August 16, 1910). The scope of the entire event had widened, and for
the first time athletic competition was mentioned as a formal

component of the Festival.

A sports committee, chaired by Lord Desborough, was asked to make arrangements for an Imperial sports meeting. The list of countries invited to take part is particularly revealing. Twenty years before, Cooper had suggested that men from the "White Dominions" alone should be asked to participate in his Pan-Britannic Festival; this attitude was still prevalent in 1911 when Australasia, South Africa, and Canada were invited to compete with the athletes of Great Britain. There is no evidence of any consideration being given to having female competitors in the sporting events, even though the Olympic Games had recently allowed women as participants, nor of including non-whites in the contests.

The Festival of Empire was scheduled to run for several months during 1911, and since the sporting programme was a modest three-day affair, it received only brief mention in the daily newspapers prior to its commencement. The entire festival was to be held at the 200 acre grounds of the Crystal Palace, and in February it was reported that more than 2000 workmen were being kept busy on the site (Times, February 6, 1911). Their two main tasks were the construction of the 'All-Red Route', a mile and a half train ride through the miniaturised colonial Empire, and the erection of a three-quarter size physical reproduction of the parliament buildings of the over-seas Dominions. The houses of parliament were also advertised as featuring tableaux which illustrated the history and life of several dependencies, representing "the development of British civilization in remote and savage regions now converted into prosperous and progressive countries" (Times, February 6, 1911). The era of Imperial propaganda had not yet passed. The overall scale of the Festival was massive, incorporating not only physical displays but also the Pageant of London, involving thousands of performers, in which the history of London, England, and the Empire would be recreated from prehistoric times. It is hardly surprising the capital costs of the Festival were estimated at £500,000 (Times, May 12, 1911).

Although the actual structure and format proposed by J. Astley Cooper for his Pan-Britannic Festival was not reproduced in the Festival of Empire, the powerful sentiment of lavishly celebrating the achievements of the British Empire survived the twenty year gap between suggestions. No evidence of Cooper having been involved in preparations for the Festival of Empire has been discovered, despite the fact that he assisted in the administration of the 1908 Olympic Games in London. What little writing that has been done concerning the Festival of Empire sports programme has stopped short of declaring a direct link between the idealistic suggestions of 1891 and the practical events of 1911, but it is proposed here that the philosophy and sentiment underlying the Pan-Britannic idea, if not the identical content, was reproduced in the Festival. Cooper had called for a celebration of the Empire's industry, culture, and athletics, and although the media promoted the sporting aspect almost to the exclusion of the other two, he felt all these areas had important contributions to make to his plans. When the Festival of Empire did take place in 1911, the cultural and industrial aspects were accompanied by a small but significant sporting programme, and the balance which Cooper had desired was approached.

The athletic portion of the Festival evolved into a three team competition with representatives from Australasia, Canada, and the United Kingdom competing in athletics, swimming, wrestling, and boxing. However, events did not unfold completely smoothly, for there was a certain amount of secrecy connected with the issuing of invitations, and a degree of controversy surrounded the events finally included in the programme. As late as 11 May 1911, it was believed that all four countries - Australasia, South Africa, Canada, and the United Kingdom - had accepted their invitations and would be attending the Inter-Empire Sports. However, the subsequent withdrawal of South Africa meant that the contests became three-sided affairs, which proved awkward in certain individual sports. The programme of events underwent a single but highly significant change in the months preceeding the actual hosting of the sports, and this one issue caused considerable confusion, and some resentment, when the 'winning' country was to be declared. When it issued invitations in February 1911, the organising committee originally decided to include the following sports on the athletic programme: Athletics (100, 220, and 880 yards, 1 mile, and hurdles), Swimming (100 yards and 1 mile), Wrestling (Middle weights), Boxing (Heavy weights), and Lawn Tennis (Singles). It was this last event which commanded a great deal of attention, resulting in the organisers reversing their decisions more than once.

The English governing bodies of the five participating sports were responsible for the sanctioning and organising of the individual events in the Festival. The Lawn Tennis Association, whether due to lack of information or lack of understanding, failed to approve the tennis competition, believing that it would conflict with the hosting of its annual championship. Accordingly, William Henry of the Empire Festival Committee, wrote to the Amateur Athletic Union of Canada in early march to notify the organisation that the tennis fixture had been withdrawn from the Festival programme. Meanwhile, Richard Coombes, the Honourary Manager of the Australasian team, had sailed from Sydney in April without knowledge of the cancellation, and was surprised to learn of the decision when he arrived in London late in May. Coombes sought out the tennis authorities and explained that the competition could be completed in one day, and therefore would not interfere with the English championships. Sanction was soon granted, the Empire Council decided to reintroduce tennis and immediately cabled Canada to that effect on 2 June. But the action came too late, for the Canadian tennis champion had returned to his home on the west coast of the country, and the remainder of the team sailed for London on 10 June, unwilling to support the reintroduction of tennis into the sporting fixtures. Ultimately, no lawn tennis competition was held, but the matter smouldered until the final points tally revealed an extremely close finish between Canada and the United Kingdom.

On 12 May 1911 the King and Queen officially opened the Festival of Empire "amid manifestations of enthusiasm it would be found difficult to equal" (Our Empire, June 1911). A newspaper correspondent captured the familial mood and feelings of the festive crowd with this eyewitness account: "there is only one sentiment that

animates us all, that of personal loyalty and affection quickened by
a common impulse of Imperial solidarity and sympathy" (Times, May 13
1911). The summer months were filled with activities which oozed
imperial sentiment, including The Pageant of London, the Imperial
Exhibition at the Crystal Palace, the coronation of the King and
Queen in June which can be seen as the ceremonial apogee of the year,
the first Inter-Empire sports meeting, and another in the series of
Imperial Conferences. As had been the case in the past, the
Conference was held in conjunction with a major event for the Empire,
and the coronation ceremony guaranteed a full representation of
overseas government officials in London.

Two changes in protocol, indicating the continuing maturation of
the Imperial Conferences, were evident in 1911. It was the first
gathering in the series between His Majesty's Government and the
Dominions to meet at the Foreign Office, not the Colonial Office;
and secondly, it marked the first occasion that the Prime Minister
of the United Kingdom presided over the meetings (Tyler, 1959).
South Africa joined Australia and Canada as the self-governing
Dominions sending delegates to the meeting; representatives from New
Zealand and Newfoundland were also present. The delegates "had to
find a place within the framework of Empire both for local autonomy
and the kind of authority and dignity the Foreign Office and Colonial
Office were determined to retain" (Hancock, 1966). Several meetings
during May and June resulted in no startling political decisions, so
the eventual outcome of the Conference was to endorse the status quo.
But the unsettled nature of life in continental Europe was soon to
provide the Dominions with an opportunity to demonstrate their
allegiance to Britain.

With the apparent exception of Newfoundland, the same Empire
members who attended the Imperial Conference were invited to
participate in the subsequent Inter-Empire Sports Meeting, and just
as the conference was concluding, the initial stage of the Empire's
sporting competition was set to begin. Athletics, the longest
portion of the sports programme, was held on 24 June at the Crystal
Palace. The three competing countries were allowed one representative
in each of the five races. An announcement that Lord Lonsdale had
agreed to present a trophy to the team winning the overall competition
meant that results became more important than simply how the game
was played. The scoring system awarded one point for first place,
two for second, and three for third place, and at the end of the day's
athletic competition Canada had secured three victories for 8 points,
the United Kingdom two victories for 9 points, and Australasia no
victories for 13 points. The two swimming contests were held in the
Crystal Palace Lower Lake on 1 July. All three countries gained
four points, leaving the final two combat sports to sort out the
close race between the United Kingdom and Canada.

It was the boxing and wrestling events which exposed the
difficulty organisers experienced in running three-way contests
fairly; all competitors had to face each other in turn, thereby
necessitating the awarding of a bye in the first round. Middle-
weight wrestling and heavyweight boxing were held at the Crystal
Palace on 5 July. In the wrestling the Australasian was so
exhausted after his long bout with the Canadian he had to default

after the first fall in his match against the United Kingdom.
Fitness was no problem in the boxing competition, when Hardwick of
Australasia scored first round victories over both his opponents.
These results meant that total points scored in the competition for
the Empire Trophy were Canada 16, the United Kingdom 17, and
Australasia 21. The debate about the lawn tennis competition was
stirred again by the close finish, and Richard Coombes claimed he
had reserved the right to demand a match between representatives of
the United Kingdom and Australasia if his country's position in the
Lonsdale Cup points score warranted it; however, "on finding the
position hopeless at the conclusion of the other events" (Coombes,
1911) he withdrew all requests for the playing of tennis.

The record of the exact sequence of events is a bit sketchy, but
it is evident the Lonsdale Trophy was not immediately presented to
Canada after the completion of the sports programme. A series of
letters passed between the team managers and the Festival organising
committee, ending with a letter dated 27 July which confirmed that
the Lonsdale Trophy was officially the property of the Canadians.
Despite the difference of opinion about the tennis competition, the
Inter-Empire Games concluded on a unifying note when Lord Desborough
hosted a dinner on 21 July at which all the competitors and
officials were presented with medals. Several speakers alluded to
the benefits of interaction among Empire members both on and off the
field of competition, and Lord Desborough referred to the series of
meetings between representatives of the competing countries which
could lead to increased co-operation in sport. One result of these
meetings was the suggestion, reputedly put forward by Richard
Coombes of Australasia and James Merrick of Canada, that the Empire
countries should assemble in London a week before departing for the
1912 Olympic Games in Stockholm, train together as an Empire team,
and then travel as a unit to the games. A further suggestion that
a British Empire team, selected from the various member countries,
be entered in the Olympic Games was not as well received, primarily
due to a perceived loss of identity on the part of the dominions.
The growing trend of increasing independence from Britain in
political matters was reflected in the colonial desire for separate
national representation in the Olympics.

Coombes, a well-known Sydney newspaperman, had long been
critical of the lack of interest by Englishmen in sport beyond
England, and even within England itself a casual interest which
resulted in a dearth of British athletic visitors to the colonies.
The modest attendance at the sports meetings during the Festival of
Empire had prompted Coombes to record his displeasure, and he was
particularly critical of England's apparent absence of interest in
the athletic events of 24 June: "All the enthusiasm on Saturday was
shown by the Colonials... The British public did not take the
meeting seriously - and they could scarcely be expected to do so, in
view of the manner in which the authorities dealt with it" (Referee,
August 2, 1911). In contrast to the detailed reports contained in
the minutes of the major sporting organisations in Australasia and
Canada, the General Committee minutes of the Amateur Athletic
Association contain but a single brief reference to athletic fixtures
in the Festival; the annual A.A.A. championships commanded much more

of the association's attention.

At the annual dinner of the A.A.A. on 1 July, held after the conclusion of the association's championships, Coombes took the opportunity when replying to the toast to 'The Visitors' from Canada and Australia to make a few more points about emerging colonial strength. The question of affiliation to the A.A.A. was once again raised, but Coombes said the alliance could now only be on equal terms, and his choice of a political comparison is most revealing: "The Colonies had grown up. In the political world there had been a conference, upon terms of equality, between the Overseas Dominions and the Mother Country; could not something of the same kind be brought about in athletics?" (Referee, August 9, 1911). Real changes within the Empire itself were reflected both in athletic and political matters.

In the fading light of her nineteenth century domination, Britain's attempt to briefly capture the grandeur of her past stature was reflected in the scale and cost of the Festival of Empire. The global balance of power was shifting away from Britain, and even within her own Empire there were significant signs of change. The continuing political maturity of the dominions, marked by achievement of self-government and a desire for more control over their foreign affairs, was a clear indication of the evolving nature of the Empire. The sporting events in the Festival of Empire provided the opportunity not only for long-awaited competition among Empire members but a chance for Australian and Canadian officials to influence the future direction of sport. The narrow Canadian victory, perhaps a bit of a surprise in some circles but graciously acknowledged none the less, coupled with Britain's declining performance in the Olympic Games, presented Australia and Canada with a vehicle to transform increasing political maturity into leadership in the sporting world of the Empire. Coombes and Merrick emerged from the Festival of Empire as respected sportsmen of the two largest dominions, and the success of his athletes in gaining the Lonsdale Trophy added considerable weight to Merrick's views.

The halcyon days of the Pax Britannica had given way to the brewing threat of war, and the Festival of Empire provided an exquisite opportunity to recapture the grandeur of previous days. The reality of Britain's shift from the focal point of nineteenth century world power, and the changing nature of the Empire, were brought home clearly both through political and athletic activity during the extensive celebrations. The self-governing dominions were becoming increasingly bold in their discussions with Great Britain concerning internal autonomy, and while the Imperial Conference resulted in no radical political recommendations, notice was served that the Empire should be moving towards a more equitable partnership. The Inter-Empire sports contributed tangibly to this belief in two ways. First, the success of the Canadians in claiming the Lonsdale Trophy showed that the dominions were perhaps not so undeveloped as had been assumed. Secondly, the emergence of Richard Coombes and James Merrick as leaders in athletics who were fierce nationalists but also saw that value of Empire links in sport demonstrated that initiative could come from outside Britain, and neither man was shy about expressing both praise and criticism

concerning the holding of the sports festival. It was the two
dominions, far more than the home country, who showed enthusiasm for
the continuation of periodic athletic meetings, and the events of
the Festival of Empire unveiled a new-found confidence displayed by
both Canadian and Australian officials. Two decades earlier, Cooper
had anticipated a long term move towards equality among members of
the Empire, but he had identified his Pan-Britannic Festival as a
realistic short term goal, one which would encourage a sounder mind
and a sounder body among the British communities.

In James Morris' evocative words, "the Edwardian age, that mellow
epilogue of Victorianism, died with its eponymous patron in 1910, and
the world became more urgent" (1978). The Festival of Empire
provided Britain with a final chance to recreate her past grandeur,
and the inclusion of the first multi-sport Inter-Empire sports
meeting in the celebrations acknowledged the role and importance of
athletic competition in maintaining Empire unity. J. Astley Cooper
had emphasised the valuable contribution sport made to the Empire
when he promoted his Pan-Britannic Festival in the early 1890's, and
a direct link betweeen his ideas and the actual staging of the
Festival must be acknowledged. The position of Britain as the
dominating force in the world was changing quickly, and the 1911
Festival of Empire provided a final opportunity to celebrate the
past glories of an Empire facing an uncertain future.

References

Coombes, R. "Festival of Empire Games London 1911: report of the
    Tour of the Australasian Team". Mimeograph report issued by the
    Amateur Athletic Union of Australasia. Sydney 1911:1.
"Empire Festival Championships". Referee, August 2 1911: 1.
"The Festival of Empire". Times, August 16 1910: 4.
"The Festival of Empire". Times, May 13 1911: 11.
"Festival of Empire - Crystal Palace Preparations". Times,
    February 6 1911: 6.
"Festival of Empire - To-Day's Opening Ceremony". Times, May 12
    1911: 7.
Hancock, I.R. "The 1911 Imperial Conference". Historical Studies
    Australia and New Zealand Vol. 12, No. 47, October 1966: 364-5.
MacKenzie, J.M. Propaganda and Empire: The manipulation of British
    public opinion 1880-1960. Manchester: Manchester University
    Press, 1984: 129.
Morris, J. Farewell the Trumpets: An Imperial Retreat. Middlesex:
    Penguin Books Ltd., 1978: 146.
"Their Majesties Open the Festival of Empire at the Crystal Palace".
    Our Empire No. 8, Vol. II, June 1911: 202.
Tyler, J.E. "Development of the Imperial Conference, 1887-1914" in
    The Cambridge History of the British Empire Volume III: The Empire-
    Commonwealth 1870-1919. Edited by E.A. Benians, Sir J. Butler,
    and C.E. Carrington. Cambridge: At the University Press, 1959:430.
"Why Is England So Apathetic In Reciprocating In the Matter of Inter-
    Empire Visits?" Referee, August 9 1911: 1.

A UTOPIAN SOCIETY: THE IMPORTANCE OF PHYSICAL EXERCISES AND GYM-
NASTICS IN THE EDUCATIONAL CURRICULUM OF ROBERT OWEN'S AND JOSEPH
NEEF'S NEW HARMONY, INDIANA SCHOOLS.

DIETER JEDAN   College of Humanistic Studies,
                 Department of Foreign Languages,
                 Murray State University (USA)

Abstract
While Neef's method of intellectual education has produced a siza-
ble number of scholarly studies on the topic of schooling, the
question of the place or importance of physical education in his
curriculum has been neglected by scholarship. However, Neef was
one of the first American educators who believed that physical
education and physical activities were important in each child's
schooling and in preparing the pupil for his future vocation.
     Unlike his mentor, Johann Heinrich Pestalozzi, Neef did not
believe that the lessons in physical education should become
formalized, routine or laborious, but rather they should be one
additional means of freeing the pupil's natural energy.
     In his Sketch of a Plan and Method of Education, Founded on an
Analysis of the Human Faculties, and Natural Reason, Suitable for
the Offspring of a Free People and for all Rational Beings (Philadelphia, PA., 1808), Neef expressed his views concerning the
incorporation of all different kinds of sports into the curriculum
and he stressed their general value in the education process.
     This study of early 19th century American educational thought
will follow an interdisciplinary approach, drawing on research from
physical education, educational history, history, foundations of
education, and educational philosophy. The multi-facetedness of
the resultant study is indicative of the multi-faceted studies and
topics to be presented at the VIII. Commonwealth and International
Conference On Sport, Physical Education, Dance, Recreation And
Health, in Glasgow.

1. Introduction
Modern physical education has few practices analogous to Joseph
Neef's schools of the early nineteenth century. Although Neef's
theory and practice with regard to physical education cannot be

established as a major influence on present-day physical education programs, they do have the advantage of being the first singular example of sports being incorporated into an American school prior to Civil War days. According to Billett, "The early date (1809) represents the earliest uncovered evidence of play in Neef's school near Philadelphia." (1)

Indeed, Neef's incorporation of jumping, swimming, skating, climbing, etc., if appearing in the first quarter of the twentieth century, would have been called "pioneer work" to our schools' return to such 'natural' activities as swimming, skating, jogging, jumping, or riding.

2. Analysis of Neef's System of Physical Education

In Francis Joseph Nicholas Neef's system of education the development of the pupil's physical skills played a major role. Indeed, Neef not only recognized the child's desire for physical exercies during the school day, but he considered sports as one of the most important parts of childhood. In 1808, he wrote in his Sketch of a Method that

> "The most superficial observer of children,
> must be forcibly struck with their untameable
> activity; with their great predilection for
> bodily exercises; with their untired fondness
> of running, jumping, climbing, bathing,
> swimming... that they always prefer the fresh
> open air, however cold or hot, to the inclosed
> air of a house." (2)

Alas, the aim of "exercises" in Neef's stystem of education is to bring the schooling of the child into harmony with his inherent nature, which means, to make education more natural. As a result, Neef included physical and military exercises in his program of education which he offered at his schools in Pennsylvania and Deleware. About sports at the school at the 'Falls of the Schuyl-kill', in Philadelphia, Gardette, a former pupil wrote:

> "We were encouraged in all athletic sports, were
> great swimmers and skaters walkers and gymnasts.
> In the pleasant weather we went to bathe twice
> every day in the Schuylkill, with Neef, who was
> an accomplished swimmer, at our head." (3)

Like his mentor, Pestalozzi, Neef believed that sports were important in the development of the pupil, although for different reasons and motives. Pestalozzi stated that the neglect of physical activities, especially by the poor, caused them illness and early aging, thus restricting their capacity to earn their living when they needed it most. Neef's reasons for including sports into the curriculum were different, believing that sports, properly administered, taught the pupil to control his physical powers and to get to know his physical limitations; furthermore, it helped develop such 'moral qualities' as perseverance and courage. Neef wrote:

> "Nature gives every human being physical, in
> tellectual, and moral capacity. The new-born
> infant contains the germines of those faculties,
> as the acorn comprehends the future majestic oak.
> Teach and accustom the young man to make a just
> use of these faculties, and your task as an edu
> cator is done. The unfolding of those powers is
> the real object of education, rather education
> itself." (4)

According to Gerald L. Gutek, Neef's physical education program was not much different from that of his mentor's, arguing that such activities prepared the pupil for his future vocation and in the art of self-defense. He argued that this was really also the goal of Neef's education. (5) The reported experiences of former Neef students such as David Glasgow Farragut, an American Civil War veteran, may, in part, add fire to Gutek's argument. According to Farragut, Neef taught swimming and climbing to his pupils and he praised the school as rendering life-long values. (6) For Gutek, Pestalozzi and Neef must be viewed with regard to their outcomes rather than individual applications. Of course, Monroe, one of the earliest American Pestalozzi and Neef scholars, would have disagreed with such assessments, suggesting that there was little, if any, value in establishing the educational methods of Pestalozzi with regard to sports in the United States because of the different societal needs. (7)

In 1826, when Neef was called by Robert Owen and William MaClure to come to New Harmony, Indiana to assume the principalship of the schools there, he vigorously attacked the neglect of physical education in the schools of his time: "Let not the very learned be alarmed at my project of teaching my pupils to play; education is, as now conducted, a deplorable toil; but by play I mean exercise, and I mean to convert this toil into a pleasure." (Sketch, p. 103) He believed that sports had a definite place in the curriculum of all schools, including those at New Harmony. According to the statutes of 'The New Harmony Community of Equality'

> "All members of the community shall be considered
> as one family and no one shall be held in higher
> or lower estimation on account of occupation.

93

There shall be similar food, clothing, and
education, as near as can be furnished, for
all according to their ages; ... It shall
always remain a primary object of the community to give the best physical, moral,
and intellectual education to all its
members." ⌐Underlining mine⌐(8)

While in New Harmony, Neef was an ardent advocate of planned
physical education and liberally provided for it in his curriculum.
During these years, 1826-28, all students participated in physical
education and sports. Neef believed that sports properly taught,
would not only strengthen the body, but teach discipline, as well
as unite the community. Following a few months of experimentation
with various types of sports and recognizing the pupil's irresistible
disposition to achieve, Neef recognized the possible diversion of
such activities to more useful purposes, i.e., work. In 1826, Neef
began to partially substitute manual labor and trades for gymnastics
and physical education, considering them equally healthful and
strengthening for the young bodies. (9) In this context it must
be remembered that although Robert Owen, William MaClure and Neef
all wanted to liberalize the shcools by making them more in line
with the needs, nature, and interests of the pupils, Neef's contributions can only be properly evaluated within the context of his
benefactors, Owen and MaClure.

Indeed, Neef's educational ideas were parallel to, rather than
derived from Owen's social philosophy. Neef agreed with Owen's
condemnation of private property. Like Owen, he believed that
man is the product of his environment, thus the schools in such
a communitarian society must reflect and transmit communitarian
values. The New Harmony school system consisted of three institutions: infant, higher, and adult schools. In all three institutions physical education played an important role. MaClure
wrote:

"Gymnastics...they acquire by the practice of
all kinds of movements always, preferably, those
that may lead to utility, such as marching, climbing, the manual exercises, etc. They are taught
the greatest part of these branches at the same
time, never fatiguing the mind by giving more
than an hour attention to the same thing, changing
the subject and rendering it play by variety." (9)

Unlike Owen, Neef understood physical education at New Harmony to
mean not only sports, but also vocational and practical training. He
emphasized repeatedly that all physical training is an integral part
of our total education, and that it cannot be viewed as a seperate
subject. He defended this system as not only offering movement but

also variation from the classroom and physical activities routines. Of course a child's physical development had to be exactly in line with his mental and moral development, when it came to selecting work training for various age groups.

Similar to the development of the pupil's intellectual and moral sides, the physical side needed a set curriculum, also. Its best development provides the pupil with health, strength and posture. Physical education, therefore, trains the body in very specialized skills: it may strengthen the legs or the arms with appropriate training, but it will not do the same for that person's soul or heart unless you view the pupil as a whole, a totality. Since Neef did not want to form any singular ability but the whole person, he did not teach jumping, swimming, running, climbing, to make expert jumpers, swimmers, runners, or climbers out of his pupils, but instead, Neef jumped, swam, ran, and climbed with his pupils to develop their hands, feet, arms, toes, fingers,i.e., their bodies, minds, and souls as a whole. Only if we interpret Neef's contributions along these lines, do we comprehend why he wanted to start where 'nature' left off. In Sketch (1808), Neef wrote:

> "That our bodily faculties ought to be unfolded and improved; that, therefore, we ought to have means fitted for unfolding and improving them, is one of the great pivots, on which all my notions of education turn. I shall, consequently, endeavour to contrive proper exercises to effect that purpose; and a very simple and obvious question, will lead me to the discovery of those exercises.
> What motions can we perform with every seperate member of the body, at everyone of its articulations? In what directions, positions, and situations, may those motions take place? How may the motions of several limbs, and several articulations be combined together?" (10)

Neef believed that his vocational training depended foremost on the development of the pupil's physical powers. His curriculum started with elementary gymnastics and ended with the most complicated exercises of movements necessary for work in industry. In this regard we should also point out that Neef differentiated between occupations for women and men: the former consisted of weaving, baking, field work; the latter were blacksmithing, printing, work in various industries such as metalurgy, farming, just to mention a few:

> "The upper part /of the Steeple House/ will serve for upwards of a hundred boys to sleep, the lower part is divided into work-shops for showmakers, tailors, carpenters, tinmen, stocking-

weavers, etc. at which the boys all learn to
work part time as a recreation from more studi-
ous pursuits, besides being occasionally employed in the fields and gardens, all of which
are cultivated on the most improved principles of agriculture adopted in any part of
the world. All these exercises are substi-
tuted for gymnastics of the old school, and
are equally strengthening for the body and
may be made the means of training them to
activity and energy so useful in the common
occupations of life. The boys already can
make their own shoes, clothes, etc., and in
a short time may be able to furnish those articles to the whole community." (11)

According to Neef, the important point of his physical training curriculum was that it was always in line with the child's intellectual
and moral developments. Only when the total person was utilized,
the schools had completed their tasks. Since vocational (i.e.
physical) education, just as intellectual and moral education, were
the property of the community, all children of school age became the
property of the communitarian schools:

"Boys and girls were given the same kind of
education in seperate school-rooms, since the
New Harmony community held to the theory of sex
equality. In addition to the boarding schools
for boys and girls, there was an infant school
.... It was provided that children should
become the property of the community at the age
of two years, when they were first received into
the infant school. This was essentially a play
school; games were taught the children; play-
things were provided, and 'they were taught
nothing that they could not understand.'"
/Underlining mine_/(12)

Because of the fact that these schools were also the home of the
pupils, they were adjoined by playgrounds, complete with balance
beams, swings, and the like. Furthermore, here the playing privileges were exchanged for compliance to teacher expectations, good
conduct, exceptional work, and minding.

3. Conclusion
With regard to Neef's general method of education, neither the
Philadelphia nor the New Harmony schools experiments exerted a wide
influence on American 19th century education. In fact, there was

96

little general adoption of Neef's educational system prior to 1860.
Nevertheless, Neef's system of physical education began to permeate
the schools throughout the country, especially by individual
teachers who incorporated sports and physical education in their
curricula.

The spirit of Neef's methods of teaching sports has also been
felt in the shools of the twentieth century, particularly in the
philosophies of John Dewey, who urged that all learning should
originate in the learner's experience, and in William Heard Kilpa-
trick, who condemned excessive bookish learning, and all that was
purely theoretical and abstract.

References
(1) Ralph E Billett, "Evidence of Play and Exercise in Early Pestal-
    ozzian and Lancastrain Elementary Schools in the United States,
    1809-1845," in Research Quarterly of the American Association
    for Health, Physical Education, and Recreation, edited by Ella
    H. Wright (Washington, D.C.), Vol. 23, p. 127.

(2) Francis Joseph Neef, Sketch of a Plan... (Philadelphia, P.A.,
    1808), p. 103.

(3) C. D. Gradette, "Pestalozzi in America," in The Galaxy (August,
    1867), p. 437.

(4) Neef, Sketch, p. 102.

(5) Gerald L Guteck, Jeseph Neef. The Americanization of Pestaloz-
    zianism (University, Ala., The University of Alabama Press,
    1978), pp. 110-111.

(6) Loyall Farragut, Life of David Glasgow Farragut,)New York, D.
    Appleton and Company, 1879), p. 49.

(7) Will S. Monroe, "Pestalozzi Literature in America," in Kinder-
    garten-Primary Magazine (May, 1894), Vol. 6, pp. 673-6.

(8) "Mr. Owen's School in New Harmony," in American Annals of
    Education and Instruction, I (June, 1826), p. 377.

(9) William MaClure, as quoted in Lockwood, New Harmony, p. 236f.

(10) Neef, Sketch, p. 103-4.

(11) Will S. Monroe, History of the Pestalozzian Movement in the
     United States (Syracuse, N.Y., C.W. Bardeen, 1907), p. 113-4.

(12) Ibid, p. 112.

PHYSICAL ACTIVITY, ACTIVITY FOR LIFE, IN SOVIET CAUCASUS.
A sports- anthropological study in the Soviet Caucasus.

KNUT KARLSRUD
Consultant of P.E. and Sport, Oslo State Prison,
Akebergveien 11, 0135 Oslo 1.

Abstract.
1.   Introduction (a short summary of----).
2.   Methods.
     The question to be asked in this paper is the fol-
     lowing: In what way are the old Caucasian folk
     games flourishing along with modern Olympic sports?
     The methods are interviews with scientific staff of
     the Institute of Physical Culture in Moscow, Lenin-
     grad and Tiblisi. In addition studies of Russian
     literature and national folk sports of the USSR and
     a three months! field work of participant obser-
     vations of the folk games of Caucasus.
3.   Modern sports in Caucasus.

1.   Introduction. A short summary of sports in historical philosophic influence in the period 1917-1980.
   Before 1917 very few people in Russia did active
sports. Sports were influenced by foreigners who were
stationed in Russia, mostly English and French.
   From 1917 - 1921 "warcommunism", (Jensen,Stig 1983).
The government decides the physical training of recruits to the red army to strengthen its position. A
goaldirected function. (Riordan, James 1978).
   From 1921 there were three groups who influenced the
physical culture:
1.   The hygienists who had their basis in health. They
managed to prohibit some hard, very competitive sports
such as football, wrestling, athletics, weightlifting
etc. They promoted open air activities, gymnastics,
swimming, and bicycling. The hygienists had strong
supporters in health personnel and academically educated people. The hygienists connected physical culture with a healthy way of life.
2.   The promoters of proletarian culture were another
group. These had their roots in the extremist revolutionary group. They thought that all former burgeois
sports helped to keep the burgeois culture and should
therefore be replaced by the proletarian physical

culture.

Children played proletarian games on the Lenin heights (formerly Sparrow heights), games like "smuggling proletarian literature across the borders" and "fleeing the fascists". The adults did " production gymnastics",e.g. they aped production movements. Made mass exhibits to strengthen the collective thought in man. The leading philosopher in this field was A. Bogdanor who claimed that social life and consciousness are one. "The social behaviour and the social conscience are identical in the true sense of the word", Bogdanov's theories from 1961 (Jensen, Stig 1983).
This was in opposition to Marx who thought that the social conscience was dependent upon the social behaviour.

The promoters of proletarian culture agreed, but thought this was valid for the prerevolutionary society. They claimed that the working class was the culture-creating factor and combined physical culture with the other cultural areas like science, literature, painting, theatre and music.
3. Lenin created the third alternative, the party's. At first he found the philosophy of proletarian culture positive, but he did not share the ideological viewpoints. Lenin was himself interested in sports and took exercises. But when he said that "religion is opium to the people" and wanted to put something in its stead, he did not think of sports, but imagined the theatre playing this role.

Both the hygienists and the promoters of proletarian culture overlooked the liberating forces of sports.

The youth organisation Konsomol took over sports after order from the party. Sports were now linked to the various activities. We know names like the locomotive Dynamo (security forces) - chka (army). It was the intention that one should identify with the activity at which one was engaged, partly by becoming a member of its sportsteam and also to identify oneself by the starteam, a kind of solidarity. From 1923 pictures of leaders were used on posters that were carried at sportsmeets as they were carried at religious feasts. In this way also sports came to be bearers of symbols. During these years the sign GTO was introduced. GTO - "Prepared for work and defence" - a kind of sportsbanner.

If one looks at a membership card from a Russian club, one will find that the idea of solidarity with the factory and readiness for defence are significant factors in the rules. A conscious aim for the physical education.

In 1930 a Ministry of sports was established. After previous membership of various sports internationals, the international struggle for communism in the world grew feebler as the world revolution did not happen, and Stalin launched the thesis of socialism in a country. Thus one

had to seek out the bourgeois sports in the rest of the
world. The result was a decree which states that "we
shall win gold medals in all the important disciplines in
t he international competitions". Thus the world will discover the excellence of the socialistic state.

One distinguished between Massovost (mass sports) and
Masterstvo (elite sports).

Within the Soviet Union the good sides of the sportsman
are used for propaganda purposes linking this to the production worker.

When Moscow arranged the Olympic Games in 1980 it was
a strong sports nation.

Sports research has been essential throughout. In 1919
Lenin ordered the establishing of institutes for physical
culture. In 1921 the Lesgaf Institute for Physical Culture was opened and the following year the State Central
Institute for sports in Moscow was established. In 1924
the Institute for Physical Culture in Tblisi, Georgia was
opened, and since then all major cities in the Soviet
Union have got their institutes.
Caucasus.
Here are traditionally many old sportsgames - games that
are still practised. This area was in the 1920s a feudal
society and was in 1924 taken up as a member of the Union
of Soviet Republics. In this way they skipped the capitalistic stage. But for this reason they have an unorthodox
transition to socialism (Lenin 1975). It should also be
noted that Stalin was from Grusia and held his hand over
Caucasus.

The area is now fully modernised and industrialised and
consists of the republics of Grusia (Georgia), Armenia
and Azerbajan. The republics do very well in modern international sports, but have to quite an extent kept their
old sports games.

2. Method.
Sports is a part of our natural pattern of movement. The
cells of the body have over millions of years developed
into something most suitable for movement. Movements
which have been of utmost importance for us through centuries. The struggle for daily nourishment among tribes
is a physical exercise often lasting for days on end. The
subsequent seremonies of distributing the food, feasts,
dance and showing of skills, is part of a ritual where we
may have difficulties discovering the element of sport.

It is, however, there. The children's daily imitation
of the parents' pattern of movement, the attempt at throw-
ing a spear, using a bow and arrow, run, throw, jump. The
basic elements in most sports. Here intermingled in the
training to face everyday life, to survive in the environment. But also a test to find out the possibilities of
movement of the body. That gives meaning and content to

the games.

The rituals of dances, wrestling matches are not separate from the hunt, from daily life, it is a question of an entity where the feasts are a tryout of the possible movements of the body.

The bodily skills are not a private matter, but a matter for the whole tribe. The whole tribe bears the responsibility that each individual becomes as skilled as possible because it is the collected skills that count, not the individual.

The French philosopher and social anthropologist Claude Levi-Strauss describes in "The wild thought" ballplay among North American Indians. Here is a footballplay between two teams. If one does not know of their myths and rituals, one does not understand the game. The one team symbolises the living, and the other the dead. And life cannot conquer death, because death always conquers life. They play this game so that the dead may have peace, and so that the dead will know that the living know, in order that the dead will not come and disturb the living unnecessarily. Claude Levi-Strauss thinks that ball games in the capitalistic societies count as a kind of "cheating which is separated from the social unity, not quite tolerated, but in other connections admired, an event which sometimes is an aim, sometimes a means, sometimes apart.

3. Modern sports in the Caucasus.

In all these traditional games there is in the Caucasus a basis for solid engagement around modern sports. The state sports institute in Tblisi was the third to be started in the Soviet Union. The three Caucasian republics have many modern sports fields spread around the country, in the mountains one finds alpine ski centres. As the mountains are the goal of all Soviet mountaineers, tourism is very common - at the Black Sea there are sanatoriums with physical exercises.

But there is a distinct difference between rural and urban environments in this mountain area. At the community farms modern sports facilities are coming up. The various areas have sports schools for the children, and elite sports schools for those with special abilities. Modern sports live side by side with the traditional games.

Sporting games in the Caucasus today.

Ways of life through the ages with different methods for hunting, have influenced the way the population has managed their natural surroundings. To be skilled in hunting, riding etc. are actually a way of doing sports. Their time has not been sharply divided into work/ leisure, but both in work and leisure has one competed in being best in various sports activities. And these activities have been decided by the climatic conditions reigning. The yakutes

102

have been and are skilled reindeerkeepers and do sports
connected with snow. The kirybs and people from Caucasus
are clever horsemen. People from Ukraina and Caucasus
are good wrestlers and weightlifters. The different republics have a cultural tradition to excel in certain
sports, and some republics have sports that do not exist
in other parts of the world. How have these sports survived the revolution and survived in competition with new
sports like football, volleyball, tennis, basketball etc.
with their modern strict set of rules for behaviour, dress
and the weight and shape of their equipment? What social
mechanisms of political, economic and religious kind have
influenced the development of sports?

Caucasus is a wild and fertile mountain area which is
situated between the Black Sea and the Caspian Sea. Three
different republics are here: Grusia, Azerbajdjan and Armenia. The area is known for its good sportsmen: Dinamo
Tiblisi from Grusia which is one of the best football
teams in Soviet, the sisters Irina and Tamara Press who

are the world's leading athletes. Weightlifters
and wrestlers are holding world records, world championships and olympic championships.

Traditionally the many sports are also practised today.
Stonethrowing has always been very popular. The biggest
and strongest are participating here. There are no classes according to weight like in wrestling. And when we
know from physics that height and weight combined with ex-
plosive strength give the longest throws, it is not surprising that most of the stonethrowers weigh more than
a hundred kilos and are taller than average.

In the mountains there is not so much room for ball-
playing, but there are quantities of large stones. And
who has not stood on a mountaintop and thrown big stones
down the slopes?

The children in the north of Caucasus test their relative strength by seeing who can throw the biggest stones
the furthest. Through generations one has developed several disciplines. Today there is a North- Caucasian championship in stonethrowing. (Lukoshin,Y 1980)

A line is drawn on the ground - a stone of about 32 kilos lies on the ground. This is to be thrown with one
hand as far as possible. The best manage between six and
seven metres.

Another variation gives one a choice of three different
stones with various shapes and weighing 8 - 10 kilos. The
stones are thrust from below using both hands. The rules
prohibit the turning of the body. The best manage appr.
16 metres. The name of the record holder is Karacha Kazi
Laipanov who has thrust 16,23 m. It is obvious that a
well-trained body is needed.

A third variety gives the throwers a three- discipline

fight. In the last discipline the stone is round as a ball and weighs appr. ten kilos. The rules allow one a running start of any length, but most participants choose to start standing on one leg and jumping on the other. The best result is about 15 metres.

One might think that this is shotputting with a stone. But closer analysis says that this is not so. It is impossible to hold an uncut stone under one's chin - it has to be held in the hand. During practicing for all three disciplines heavier stones than for competition are used. It seems that the strongest also tend to do well in shotputting. Karacha Kazi Laipanov is also sports champion of shotputting. He could not be given this title in stonethrowing as the title does not exist for this branch. In the Caucasus area athletes are someone to admire in the world of sports. A lot of practising is done, in several places one may see young men practising with weights.

The North Caucasian games have participants from Kabardino, Belkania, Daghestan, Karachaebo-Cherkessia, Chechemo-Ingushetia, Kalmykia, Adykia and North-Ossetia.

Weightlifting is another popular branch in the North-Caucasian games. A handweight of oldfashioned bellshape that weighs 32 kilos. The purpose is to see how many times one can lift the weight. The participants are classed according to their own weight - up to 60, 70, 82 and more than 82 kilos. The weight is lifted by one hand as many times as possible. When one hand is exhausted, one changes hand and continues until exhausted. The lightest of the lifters manage between 35 - 40 lifts, while the heavyweighters do between 60 and 70 puts.

Another variation is to heave from the floor till fully extended posture. The lightweighters do about 50, the heavyweighters the double. The third variety is to lift two handweights simultaneously from the shoulders up. It is regarded as good if one can do more than 25 of these.

The winner of all three disciplines is the one who scores most points. One point is granted for each correct put in the two disciplines with one hand, and three points for each put when using both hands.

Wrestling is very popular, but there are various styles; Tatar Buryat, Yakut, Grusian, Bashkir....

One interesting feature of the wrestling is that it is accompanied by music. The music starts quietly while the wrestlers sum each other up, but explodes as soon as the wrestlers try to overthrow one another. There are eight weightclasses - up to 55 kilos, 60, 70, 75, 80, 90 and above 90 kilos if one wins first or second place in two out of the three competitions which are arranged annually. (Imedashvili, David) One has then earned the right to bear the title "National sports champion".

The highest honour is that the team from your republic wins in wrestling, stonethrowing and weightlifting. The team to win this cup may keep it. The teams from Kabardin Balkar republic and Karachai-Circassian region have both won this cup for keeps.

Another way to test one's strength is to use heavy stones as weights. These are tests with stones weighing no less than 150 kilos. The sport is called "dur isyn". There are also strong men who have even lifted such a weight above their heads. Leather straps are sometimes used for assistance.

In Ossetia there is an expression: "He is a very strong man, he can lift a man with one arm" That means one can lift a man above the head on a straight arm.

Strong men and wrestlers have a long tradition in Caucasus. Travelling strong men have performed on marketplaces and in circus. In the 16th century and onwards travelling musclemen could be seen anywhere. Wrestling with wild bears was a popular way to show one's strength. Human victory was not always a matter of course.

Wrestling had an element of entertainment because those travelling challenged the local strong men and tempted with sums of money if they won over them. One of them was also accompanied by his wife who also wrestled with the men and usually won.

The Caucasians are horsemen. Wrestling on horseback, especially people from Ossetia. Riding is part of the general education. Races were arranged for feasts, even funerals to honour the dead. One year after the day of death it was common to have a race to honour the memory of the dead man. (Keesing, Roger M 1981).The size of the race was determined by the economic ability of the family to present prizes. The most common was to present riding equipment, saddle, dagger or uniform of the dead man as a prize.

If horseraces took place in a flat area, more than ten riders participated. But in the mountains there was room for only four. There were many variations. One long stretch, or back and forth. The mountainride was more than a dozen kilometres, whereas in the flat areas up to 60 kilometres. These were the distances for 12-13 year old boys. The host then slaughtered a cock or a sheep in honour of the riders.

The mountainrides were often dangerous. By overtaking a rider might be pushed over the cliff or the overtaker might fall. Therefore preparations for these rides were careful.

The horses were specially prepared over the last two, three months, special food, riding in cold rivers. The stretches grew longer. All participants have assistants who are in the middle so that they can speed the horses on

when fatigue has started.
Habah, arrowshooting from horseback in gallop.
A long stick is fastened in the ground with a cloth or
a hat on top. Then one is supposed to gallop and shoot at
a certain sign. There are also variations with rifle
shooting, but then the target is exchanged by a coin.
At weddings there is often a challenge of horseracing
with shooting the same way it has been done for centuries.

The old ones.
Caucasus is the area in the world to have the largest
number of old people, and then really old.
The old ones enjoy great respect among the younger
generation. Even today their opinions are heard with respect. When an area has a number of people beyond the age
of 100, living an active life both physically and psychi-
cally and enjoying respect among the young people, these
old people will be a socialising factor for children and
youngsters. Their opinions on attitudes to family life,
nutrition, exercise, self discipline, religion will be important for an understanding of physical culture in the
community.
Everybody wants to remain healthy and active when they
grow old. The old ones claim that cleanliness, regular
eating- and sleepinghabits are important. They are firm
believers in preventive, therapeutic herbs.
Sula Benet finds it remarkable that none of the very
old people She interviewed , independent of their religion, thought their old age was due to "fate". They all
thought the reason was "a good life" i.e. order, physical
work, no excesses and good health. This was valid for all
ethnic groups. (Benet, Sula 1977   )
In the old heroic poems one salutes the old, they are
described as wise people. Today one also shows respect
for the old ones. The oldest is supposed to fire the
first shot during the hunt. The older have first choice
among the best part of the spoil.
But the reverence for the old could easily cease if
these were not so physically strong that they could participate in hunting and war. There are even some awful stories that old men have been thrown into ditches to end
their useless lives. (Benet, Sula 1977   )
Prof. Sula Benet writes in her book: The world's oldest
people, the Caucasians, are very conservative people,
their norms change very slowly. The Caucasians have a
very strong and traditional cultural history where folk
sports have an important place.
There are three republics in the Soviet Union where
there is a sports programme. Where sports politics
are centrally decided. Including the ideological use of
sports. Also financial measures are decided here. By
looking at socialisation I would be able to see the cen

tral political and ideological influ.ence on the local
community and regard changes in the practise of sports.
   By looking at the development of the Sovietrussian
sports after 1917 I shall regard a major influencing factor of sports in its widest sense in the Caucasus.

Conclusion.
   In this tentative study the following may be stated at
this stage:
   The same persons in Caucasus seem to excel in both folk
games and olympian games.
   To some extent the Caucasian republics seem to inspire
the people to be active in both folk games and olympian
games through the introduction of the sports badge GTO.
   It seems that the old Caucasian folk games flourish
along with the modern olympic sports.

References

Levi-Strauss, Claude: The Savage Mind
    London, Weidenfeld and Nicholson 1966
Lukashin, Y: National Folk Sports in the USSR
    Progress publishers Moscow 1980
Keesing, Roger M: Cultural Anthropology. Holt, Rinehart
    and Winston, New York, Chicago 1981
Lenin, V.I.: Imperialismen som kapitalismens høyeste
    stadium. Forlaget Ny Dag 1975
Loy, J.W./Segrave, J.O.: Research Methology in the
    Sociology of Sport, In:Jack H.Wilmore, Exercise and
    Sports Sciences Reviews, Volume 2, New York 1974
Hellevik, Ottar: Forskningsmetode i sociologi og stats-
    videnskap, Universitetsforlaget, Oslo 1977
Thomsen, R.W.: Participant Observation in Sociological
    Analysis of Sport. International review of sport
    sociology,Warzawa 1977, 12 no 4 s. 99-110
Pelto,P and Pelto,G; Anthropological Research, Cambridge
    University Press, Cambridge 1978
Riordan, James: Sport in Soviet Society, Cambridge Uni-
    versity Press, Cambridge 1978
Jensen, Stig: Kontroleret vitalitet, sport i Sovjetsam-
    fundet. Århus 1983
Rasmussen, Svend Gottschalk: Folkeidrætt og elitesport i
    Sovjetunionen.Selskapet for Østeuropastudier,Århus 1980
Imedashvili, David: Sport in Soviet Georgia, From Mass
    Character to Mastery. Novosti Press
Peizel, Mark: "Gyulesh". The wrestling of Bogatyrs.
    Novosti Press
Benet, Sula: Verdens eldste mennesker. Grøndahl, Oslo 1977
Rommetveit: G.H. Meads syn på det sosiale opphavet til
    sjølvet. Sosialpsykologisk ego-psykologi
Kjørmo, Odd: Idrett og sosialisering. Publikasjoner fra
    Norges idrettshøgskole 1980
Karlsrud, Knut: Metodiske problemer og overveielser i for-
    bindelse med en etnografisk tilnærming til idretten som
    fenomen og praksis i et lokalsamfunn. Norges idretts-
    høgskole 1982
Loy,McPherson,Kenyon: Sport and Social Systems. Addison-
    Wesley Publishing Company 1978
Jensen, Stig: Styret vitalitet,-sport i Sovjetsamfundet
    Århus universitet 1983
Karlsrud,Knut: Idrett i Sovjetrussland, filosofisk/ his-
    torisk påvirkning i perioden 1917/1980. Kroppsøving
    vol 2 1986. Oslo
Karlsrud, Knut: Idrettsleker i sovjetisk Caucasus i dag.
    Kroppsøving vol. 2 1986. Oslo

THE DEVELOPMENT OF PROFESSIONALISM IN ENGLISH LEAGUE CRICKET, c. 1900 TO 1940

J. HILL
Department of History, Trent Polytechnic

Abstract

In the late 19th century English cricket developed a structure of authority which reflected the leadership of an aristocratic-upper middle class elite. 'First class' cricket epitomised the elite's influence, and it is this aspect of cricket that historians have concentrated upon, insofar as the evolution of the game has been studied at all. But first class cricket was for a minority of both players and spectators. League cricket, strongly established in the North and Midlands by the turn of the century, acquired rapid popularity, especially among working men and women; but it has been virtually ignored by historians. In some respects its development served to buttress the status quo in cricket; in others - notably in the prominence it gave to professional players - it acted against the natural order and nurtured attitudes that were to be enlarged on during the transformations of the 1960s and 70s in the cricket world.
Key words: Cricket, Leagues, Lancashire, Professionals, Hegemony, Constantine,

Cricket, more than any other popular sport, has symbolised the British class structure. At some point during the third quarter of the nineteenth century the game assumed the characteristics by which it was to be recognised for the next hundred years. Two features predominated. Firstly, social and political leadership (both off and on the field) was vested in an alliance of aristocracy and upper middle class; this group controlled the county clubs and the Marylebone Cricket Club (MCC) - effectively the game's ruling body - thus ensuring some continuity with eighteenth century patterns of control in popular recreations and, at the same time, steering cricket into what might be termed a 'semi-commercial' path. Secondly, it was under the guidance of this hegemonic alliance that cricket assumed its definitive form as a game; although the rules of play had been codified earlier in the century it was only after the formation of the county clubs in the 1860s and 1870s that a specific mode of play - the three day match - came to be seen as the pre-requisite form in which to develop the essential skills of the game. Thus 'county' and, later, 'test' cricket established a political, social and aesthetic primacy encapsulated in its official designation as 'first class' cricket. This particular ideology of what constituted the 'natural order' in cricket was reproduced in a vast literature which developed around the game.

In reality, the modern form of the game was fashioned in the context of a struggle for control over cricket. The ascendancy of the aristocratic-upper middle class alliance was secured by frustrating and eventually suppressing the emergence of a quite different form of cricket - one based upon more thoroughly commercialised 'all-star' touring teams, organised by working class cricketer-entrepreneurs employing paid professional players. The outcome of this contest for influence was, of course, the subordination of the professionals and their incorporation into the county sides under the leadership of gentlemen 'amateurs'. But how complete was the victory? To what extent did the dominant elite guide the way in which cricket was played? By the end of the century cricket was a popular sport, frequently referred to by writers as 'the national game', but most of its practitioners were not part of the 'first class' enterprise. The aim of this paper is to explore the development of cricket outside the first class circuit by focusing upon one aspect of the game - northern league cricket - and to offer some preliminary observations about the relationship between it and the first class game.

League cricket in the industrial regions of the North was established by the 1890s, its rapid proliferation during that decade no doubt stimulated by the success after 1888 of the Football League. In contrast with local cricket in the South, where clubs competed in friendly matches, it was exceptional in the North to find cricket that was not organised into some form of competition on a Saturday afternoon league basis. It was doubtless this feature of highly competitive play, coupled with its close association with the industrial working class, which was responsible for league cricket's image of social and aesthetic inferiority; its image, indeed, as a threat to the natural order, since its mode of play served to deform the essential skills and ethos of the game. The lowly status accorded to northern leagues was reflected in the slight attention paid to them by 'official' opinion. The weekly magazine Cricket, for example, founded by C.W. Alcock in 1882, provided a detailed coverage of first class cricket in England and overseas, as well as match reports and score cards of Home Counties club matches, but until just before the First World War it contained hardly any references to league cricket in the Midlands and North. Its successor journal The Cricketer, edited by the former Middlesex and England captain P.F. Warner, continued this first class, metropolitan bias. The point may be illustrated further by outlining the attitudes expressed in three cricket books from the early 1920s. Jack Hobbs, the Surrey and England professional, typified southern attitudes to northern league cricket in his first autobiography (1924). Hobbs had briefly played in the Bradford League during the War when, owing to the suspension of county cricket, local clubs enjoyed great commercial success by importing star players into the district. But Hobbs clearly found the atmosphere uncongenial:

> League cricket cannot be compared to county cricket. The
> average duration of the game is from 2.30 till 7. The
> standard of play is on the whole not very high; a side may
> have a couple of good bowlers and two or three decent bat-
> smen, but the teams are no better than those fielded by
> good class clubs in London. (p.192)

Similarly, Cecil Parkin (1923), an outstanding league professional whose remarkable bowling skills also brought him success in
county and test cricket, expressed the same sentiments, if in a
rather equivocal sense:

> I am...in a position to answer the question that is often
> asked: "Is league cricket as good as county cricket?" My
> reply is given with all the force and confidence I am cap-
> able of. League cricket is not in the same street as
> county cricket; it is not the same game. From the bowler's
> point of view, it is ten times easier in the league than
> in the county. I don't only mean that in the league a
> bowler has to play only one day a week. I mean that it
> is ten times easier to get wickets in the league than
> against county cricketers. For one thing, the pitches are
> not perfect in the leagues. Then it must be remembered
> that the pace league cricket is played at gives a batsman
> little or no chance of playing himself in...A league bat-
> sman has to get busy with the runs from the moment he
> arrives at the crease. Consequently, he is always giving
> the bowler a chance. He will go after your off balls, and
> even if you keep a perfect length, he must still, in the
> interests of his side, continue to take risks. A league
> club has no use for the batsman who, like the county cric-
> keter, can only score from loose bowling. (p.19)

A.C. Maclaren (1924), though making no direct references to league cricket, nevertheless adopted a similar perspective in suggesting that only at first class level can the subtle arts of
cricket be nurtured. The book is interesting for prefiguring responses to later 'crises' in English cricket. Maclaren was writing in the aftermath of a series of victories over the English
national XI by Australia in 1920 and 1921. His explanation for
the poor English performances rested on the notion of 'incorrect
methods': too many players had been 'innovating', and ignoring
the basic techniques laid down by W.G. Grace in the previous century. Of the innovator Maclaren said: "He is...the Bolshevist of
the cricketing world, and it is about time that he was suppressed".
(p.4) Such views parallel in a number of ways the arguments advanced in the 1970s and 1980s to explain similar problems.
Maclaren's inference was that only by reinforcing the traditional
methods of county cricket could the supremacy of England in test
cricket be assured; by implication, therefore, Maclaren was per-

petuating the image of inferiority of league and club cricket, where 'innovation' (as described by Parkin) was, of course, essential. Latter-day Maclarens (represented, for example, on the working party set up the Test and County Cricket Board in 1984 to report on reasons for the failure of the English test team in the matches of that year against the West Indians) have a more visible target of attack; it is 'limited overs cricket', a mode of play increasingly adopted in the first class game in the 1960s and 1970s and derived directly from the leagues. In attacking this more recent form of innovation, and in assigning to it a major reason for a decline in standards, modern conservatives are continuing to articulate an ideology of the 'natural order' in cricket that goes back to the nineteenth century.

Notwithstanding this sense of the latent threat to standards implicit in league cricket, northern clubs have traditionally reproduced several of the features of first class cricket and, in so doing, consented to its dominance. For example, in contrast to the development of football, the same basic model of club organisation has been shared by both county and league cricket; clubs are democratic associations of members who elect their officials annually, decide policy collectively and derive their working capital from the subscriptions they pay. In financial affairs, league clubs also followed the model of the first class game by pursuing the same 'semi-commercial' approach. Most sought to maximise their spectator appeal and from an early stage were alert to the need to provide adequate seating, refreshments and other services at their grounds. Admission charges were invariably made, 'gate' receipts being the most important item, alongside members' subscriptions, in the Treasurer's annual accounts. But as a game played over a lengthy period of time, and being susceptible to adverse weather conditions, cricket probably possessed too many inherent disadvantages for it to challenge football as a mass spectator sport; and, consequently, neither county nor league clubs found it viable to seek additional capital by converting into limited liability companies, as many football clubs were doing in the years before the 1914-18 War. Exceptionally, however, league cricket did reveal a considerable market potential. An enthusiasm of almost football-like proportions was experienced in the Bradford League during the War, when county cricket lapsed. The same was true of the 1929 Lancashire League season, when a combination of good weather and the appearance of the brilliant L.N. Constantine as professional for Nelson produced a remarkable series of matches. Nelson's fixture with East Lancashire, for example, on July 20th, as well as the return match a month later, attracted a crowd in excess of 10,000 people. In June, at Enfield, Constantine had astonished over 8,000 spectators by scoring 124 out of 175 in just over an hour. Such performances provided a commercial stimulus throughout the League, and the northern correspondent of The Cricketer Annual was able to comment: "...mainly owing to the huge gates and the magnetic influence of Constantine, together with the fine weather, several clubs were lifted out of debt which they have carried for years: a wonderful happening!" (<u>Cricketer Annual</u>, 1929-30, p.66) There was an indication here of a spectator potential in league cricket which placed it, on occasions, closer to association football as a commercial sport than to first class cricket. County cricket, with its antipathy to limited duration play, rarely sought to tap, let alone to develop, the mass market.

There were, on the other hand, several structural features of league cricket which were antagonistic to the assumptions on which the first class game operated. For one thing, league cricket did not embody the very public display of social authority and deference which was a necessary accompaniment to first class cricket. It seems likely that league cricket was much closer to the working class in terms both of its support and its control (though until detailed analysis - following the routes mapped out by T. Mason (1980) for association football - is completed on the sociology of club officials and supporters, this point cannot be made with any force.) What is certain, however, is that a significant difference existed between county and league cricket in their treatment of the professional player, and it is in this respect that the leagues made what was perhaps their most important contribution to the development of English cricket in this period.

W.F. Mandle (1972) shows that, by the end of the nineteenth century, the professional in first class cricket had acquired a respectable though fully subordinated status in cricket's social hierarchy. Except for a very brief period in the 1870s the 'all-professional' team (so common in football by the early 1900s) never existed in county cricket before the 1950s, and the extent to which county committees employed professionals varied a good deal. In some cases (notably the 'Big Six' counties - Lancashire, Yorkshire, Notts, Surrey, Kent and Middlesex) the proportion was usually high; in others it was minimal, with Somerset as late as the 1920s employing only two regular professionals in the team. The deference expected of professionals from amateurs has been well documented and (what has less frequently been considered) the professionals seem generally to have accepted their position. Hobbs, though a truly outstanding player, evinces in his autobiography the kind of deference towards authority that might have been expected from a Cambridge working class tory. Parkin, on the other hand, sounds a more truculent note in his book, demanding the skilled labourer's right to dignified public treatment, though preferring the company of his fellow working men in private: "...I do think that the class distinction that exists between amateur and professional <u>should not be emphasized in public</u> (his italics). Therefore I believe all the players should come on to the field through the same gate. But, frankly, off the field, professionals as a class prefer to be left to themselves." Few players, though, would have dared to offend the social codes as Parkin did; he openly criticized his test match captain in a newspaper article and paid the to-be-expected penalty: he never appeared again in an international side. The vast majority of professionals in first class cricket accepted their lot silently.

113

In the leagues, by comparison, the professional was liberated; he enjoyed a status and esteem undreamed of in the first class game. Although most league clubs employed only one professional in a club of otherwise amateur players there is a very real sense in which league cricket was the cricket of professionals. Well before the First World War it was exceptional to find a club in a major league which did not employ a professional: the North Staffordshire League in 1913 had only one such club (Silverdale). Movement of professionals between clubs was common, as clubs vied with each other to attract 'stars'; thus, Denis Hendren, a leading player in the north-east before the War (and the brother of the more famous E.H. Hendren) played for three different clubs in the Durham Senior League between 1912 and 1914, and generally it was rare for a player to stay with one club for very long. Monetary rewards, expecially for outstanding players, could be handsome. According to a report in the <u>Northern Daily Telegraph</u> (5.7.1920), an unnamed Lancashire League club in 1920 offered terms to Harry Howell, the Warwickshire bowler, which included: £20 a week for the season; a benefit; a bonus of 30 shillings on each occasion he took six wickets (as well as the normal 'collection' for a performance of five wickets or fifty runs); removal expenses; and a 'business' to be found for him by the club; additionally, Howell was to be allowed to honour his football engagements early and late in the season. Exaggerated though this report may have been, it nevertheless helps to explain why players like Parkin retained their attachments to the leagues. Parkin, in fact, played county and league cricket concurrently; following his first appearance for Lancashire in 1914 he did not play a full season of first class cricket until 1922. The extreme example of this practice, however, was S.F. Barnes, generally acknowledged by most observers to have been unsurpassed as a bowler anywhere in the world before 1914. He was a regular England test player in the dozen years prior to the War (27 matches between 1901 and 1914; 189 wickets, average 16.43). During these years he played only two seasons of county cricket (1902 and 1903, for Lancashire). For the rest of the time he was employed as a club professional in the Lancashire and, later, North Staffordshire Leagues, also playing for Staffordshire in the Minor Counties competition. Barnes estimated that league cricket, being less intensive and therefore less physically demanding than county cricket, gave him the opportunity of a longer career and the prospect of long-term financial security. (Duckworth, 1967)

As an international player Barnes was out of keeping with the general pattern of league professionals before the First World War. The vast majority were far less celebrated players whose age, ability or inclinations kept them out of county cricket. An analysis of the professionals in the Durham Senior League in 1912, for example, shows several to have been players with some county experience but none with a national reputation. Probably the most successful was the Sunderland professional Alf Morris, who never played at the first class level. During the inter-war years, however, this pattern began to change radically, especially in Lanca-

shire. The Lancashire League, which in the 1920s still retained
a preference for English professionals, had by the late 1930s
come to regard the acquisition of 'star' overseas players as both
desirable and normal. The Nelson Club had initiated the change
by signing the Australian test player E.A. McDonald for the 1922
season. It was an attempt to revive the club's flagging membership and finances and was carried out with an eye to maximum publicity, McDonald's services being secured midway through the 1921
season, when the player was provoking a mixture of respect and
hostility from the public for the way in which he and his fast
bowling partner J.M. Gregory were despatching English test batsmen in the current series of matches. Such a radical breach of
tradition alarmed several sections of opinion including the
Australian Board of Control, concerned about the possible poaching of its leading players, and even the local Nelson Leader,
which commented that "...the spirit of the game is made none the
healthier by business transactions of this kind." (17.3.1922)
Nelson paid McDonald in the region of £700 during each of the
three seasons he played for them until leaving to join Lancashire
in 1925, and there can be little doubt that his presence in the
League has a generally stimulating effect upon interest: "(his)
departure", observed the Nelson Secretary in his report of 1925,
"is not only a loss to Nelson but to the whole of the Lancashire
League. Every club has benefitted (sic) as a result of our enter-
rprise in signing McDonald, and he brought new interest and enthusiasm into the League when there was a tendency for it to be
weakening."* The precedent was irresistible. By the late 1920s
there was a sizeable cadre of overseas players in the Lancashire
League. By the end of the 1930s the vogue had spread to other
leagues in Lancashire, we well as to the Midlands and the North
East. What more than anything else served to consolidate this
fashion was the success of Learie Constantine at Nelson between
1929 and 1938.

In Constantine league professionalism achieved its apotheosis.
At the peak of his powers in the early 1930s the West Indian cost
Nelson around £1,000 a season in basic wages, making him the highest paid cricketer in England, with earnings in excess, no
doubt, of even the leading professional footballers. In his athletic, social and financial status Constantine symbolised the
immense esteem accorded to professionals by league clubs. In
Nelson he lived a comfortable middle class life, which made his
position exceptional by the standards of league professionals;
but he remained a popular local hero in his adopted community,
and in this respect his role was essentially no different from
that of every professional. They were the cornerstone of the
team, the local champions upon whose exploits the pride and aspirations of the community fed. Their crucial function in the team
was clearly sketched out by Constantine himself (1933). Though
Constantine acknowledged that the professional was not the whole

Nelson Cricket and Bowling Club records (1886-1945), by kind permission of the Hon. Sec.

team, nevertheless league cricket clubs were to a great extent identified by the success of their professionals. Indeed Constantine - 'Connie' - was, for cricket followers at least, the very embodiment of Nelson itself in the 1930s.

Constantine is interesting in another sense. He had no direct links with first class cricket in England. (C.L.R. James described him as "a league cricketer who played Test cricket".) This enabled him to view the established order in English cricket more dispassionately than most. He became, in fact, a stern critic of it. His book Cricket In The Sun (1948), contains a spirited defence of the principles inherent in league cricket, and he seeks to rescue it from the inferior status to which it had been consigned. In so doing he attacks many of the traditional features of the first class game, anticipating in his proposed reforms several of the innovations that were to be introduced in the 1960s and 70s: limited over matches, improved financial rewards for first class players, more emphasis upon fielding and attacking play, knock-out competitions. All of these he had come to know about through his experiences as a league professional. It needed a players' revolt under the patronage of an Australian media millionaire in the 1970s before these ideas could be fully incorporated into first class cricket.

A study of the social relations of cricket offers an excellent illustration from the sphere of popular recreation of Gramsci's concept of hegemony. League cricket, essentially a game controlled by working men, was neither a directly imposed version of first class cricket nor, on the other hand, a direct challenge to the dominant version of the game. Cricket, until the 'Packer Revolution' of the 1970s, produced no equivalent of the breakaway movements that split both association football and rugby football, largely along class lines, at the end of the nineteenth century. League cricket, however, nourished features which represented a latent challenge to the cricket establishment. Eventually the perpetuation of the dominant group's position in cricket came to depend upon the re-fashioning of the mode of play according to features who origins were in the cricket of the northern leagues.

References

Constantine, L.N. (1933) Cricket and I. Philip Allan, London.
Constantine, L.N. (n.d., c. 1948) Cricket in the Sun. Stanley Paul, London.
Duckworth, L. (1967) S.F. Barnes - Master Bowler. The Cricketer/Hutchinson, London.
Hobbs, J.B. (1924) My Cricket Memories. Wm. Heinemann, London.
Mandle, W.F. (1972) The Professional Cricketer in England in the Nineteenth Century. Labour History, 23, 1-16.
Mason, T. (1980) Association Football and English Society, 1863-1915. Harvester Press, Brighton.
McLaren, A.C. (1924) Cricket Old and New: A Straight Talk to Young Players. Longmans, Green & Co., London.

THE CONCEPT OF COMPETITION AND WINNING IN THE DEVELOPMENT OF
HERMANN HESSE'S GLASS BEAD GAME

J. MILTON GRIMES
Department of Foreign Languages, Murray State University

Abstract
To compete and to win form the basis of all games, but the exact
definition of these two concepts within differing game contexts is
an unending source of controversy. In his last major work, The
Glass Bead Game, published in 1943, Hermann Hesse creates an intellectual game which in its actual performance acquires many of the
characteristics of ritual. This article will trace the development
of the game idea as it evolved in Hesse's thought and attempt to
show how Hesse sought to establish historical-social roots for the
game. The concepts of competition and winning will then be analyzed
in order to show how they develop from a feeling of aggressiveness
and domination to the more intellectual concept of contribution to a
whole and then the celebration of its attainment.
Key words: Author Hermann Hesse, Competition, Winning.

In 1943 Hermann Hesse published his last major work, Das
Glasperlenspiel, for which he received the Nobel award in 1946. The
major part of the novel is devoted to the development of the main
character, Josef Knecht, who is chosen master over the intellectual province of Castalia and then leaves it to become a teacher
in the outside world. The central unifying element of the novel to
which Josef Knecht and all other characters of the novel continu-
ously refer and which goes far beyond the importance of a leitmotiv
is the ritual-like activity entitled the Glass Bead Game. Ever
since the publication of the novel, readers and critics have reviewed the game with varying degrees of awe, suspicion, and even
cynicism. More serious readers have sought to understand the game
by drawing parallels to it. Noted critics have compared it to the
Chinese language and to the game of Go; still others have pointed
out general similarities with the system of symbolic logic, the
tarot, and a broad assortment of others. Hesse himself contributes
an impressive list of precursors or parallels to the game idea
(GW 9, p. 13). In all of these analyses of the game, critics have
concentrated on the abstract intellectual symbolism of the game,
an approach that essentially cannot be questioned.

Singular attention to the symbolic character of the game tends, however, to destroy one of its most important elements, namely its historicity, its realness, and therewith its credibility. The establishment of historically verifiable roots for the game, as a game, was a great concern to Hesse, and it was primarily the clarification of this aspect of the game which demanded the greatest time and energy in writing the "Introduction" to the novel. The purpose of the present study is to analyze the Glass Bead Game not primarily as a symbol but as a real game, arguing that such an approach was the intention of the author. In order to establish a more concrete point of reference, I would like to focus on the nature of competition and winning as the essential elements of the activity and how they evolved in Hesse's early plans and then how they developed in the final version of the novel. I do not think that it is necessary to enter here into a philosophical discussion of game theory, including the highly problematic questions which range from definition to function. I think that it is more important to let Hesse's work guide our considerations.

The idea of a game and of a novel which would revolve around a game began to evolve in Hesse's mind in the early 1930's. By early summer of 1932, he had written a preliminary sketch of the history and nature of the game. He subsequently wrote a second and third version. The fourth and final version, completed in 1934, then became the first part or "Introduction" to the novel itself, the second being the life history of Josef Knecht, and the third the writings of Josef Knecht as a young student. It is clear that in each of the four versions Hesse was attempting to establish historical-social roots for the game, whose elements above all would reflect the attitudes of the player.

According to the earlier versions of the "Introduction," the game had its beginnings during those darkest years between 1935 and 1940 when a certain Reinhold Klaiber spent an entire winter working out the details of a pseudo-intellectual game of cards which he based on the game we now call Authors. He did it primarily for his wife who had spent endless hours playing bridge, an overwhelming source of shame for an intellectual man cast in the Germany of the 1930's. I would like to interject a comment by Johan Huizinga which appropriately describes the game which Klaiber's wife played so avidly. "An enormous amount of mental energy is expended in this universal craze for bridge with no more tangible result than the exchange of relatively unimportant sums of money. Society as a whole is neither benefitted nor damaged by this futile activity." In either Klaiber's or his wife's game, the elements of competition and winning are strikingly deemphasized and insignificant mostly because the motive for play was escape from the realities of the day and not a true challenge to stimulate either mind or body toward higher achievement. Hesse calls their activity "childish" clearly wishing to distinguish it from "childlike." However sterile and unimportant this "childish carelessness" of the mind was, as Hesse calls it, it did become a rage of the time, being adopted by nearly every cultural group.

In the second, late 1932 version of the "Introduction," the next
step of the game's development occurred when the various cards were
replaced by glass beads having different colors, sizes, and values.
The game had also acquired considerable social stature, as had also
the essential game elements. In this development there evolved a
more genuine sense of competition and a definite value was attached
to winning. One collected the beads or winnings, traded ones of
lower value for those of higher value and demonstrated the achievement by putting them on strings presumably to be worn. At this
point we approach an activity which Huizinga would begin to consider
a more genuine kind of game. It began to have the seriousness of
childlike play. It was becoming "elevating recreation in the sense
of Aristotle's diagoge" (Huizinga, p. 199). It helped to diffuse
that "limited perfection" which is experienced in play and which
helps to bring order to the confusion of life. This new development
which presumably occurred in the generation following the second
world war was, however, still diluted by its own lack of content.
The beads were merely symbolic of names or works of different
authors, artists, and composers and did not express any of the
qualities of the works involved.

In all of the first three versions, Hesse retains Klaiber's game
as the origin of the ritual glass bead game. In the final fourth
version, however, the plan is scrapped. The entire historic setting
of Klaiber's century is communicated only through the later
historian named Plinius Ziegenhals. Klaiber's game based on Authors
is only alluded to. There are many important reasons for this
significant new approach to the "Introduction," but most are only
tangential to the subject of this study.

More important is the fact that in the final version of the
"Introduction" the game's original form involves both content and
the true spirit of play. In the music academies of Germany and
England the students, as a means of practicing their music, would
play a musical theme as a challenge to another student to either
continue the theme or vary it. The spirit of competition is still,
as in Klaiber's complex card game, a demonstration of prowess and
resourcefulness within the structure of the game. The challenge
which is presented to a responding player is not, however, an
attempt to defeat or trick, rather to call forth affirmation of the
original move by correctly improvising (equivalent to a move in the
game) which in turn creates new challenges and advances the game
toward its successful completion which would in this case be the
performance of a piece of music. Winning in such a game begins to
assume a new dimension. The winner certainly achieves esteem and
honor by successfully contributing a variation or continuation which
out challenges the others. In winning, however, he benefits the
entire group since the accomplishment and significance of winning is
dependent on the contribution of the group. The goal of competition
is no longer essentially to overpower or dominate, rather to excel
in a collective effort. Although not included in the novel, Hesse
outlined in his notes five examples of such exercises in improvi-
sations, the mastery of which is even required for the successful
performance of various musical scores.

Despite these significant developments, Hesse still chooses to call the game "Spielerei" even after Bastian Perrot invented the glass beads to aid in the actual practice of the game. Hesse, or the biographer he creates to relate the history and nature of the game, does not explain the somewhat derogatory description. A brief comparison of the game as practiced in the music academies and following later developments does, however, help to understand the judgment. First, the game practiced by the music students was in fact an essential part of their professional training. Second, the game did not utilize rules independent of those determined by the musical scores themselves. Third, the game had no symbolic language, such as those found on playing cards, in the figures of chess or in abstract formulae, since even the glass beads of Perrot represented nothing more than the notes on the staff. Fourth, the cultural value of the game, although definitely present, was restricted to a closed and essentially non-social group. During each ensuing developmental stage of the game, Hesse methodically addresses himself to these questions thereby lifting the game to its highest level of expression within the intellectual province of Castalia.

Throughout the description of this process which stretches far into the twenty-first century, Hesse is careful to delineate the details of how one actually played the game and what the players' attitudes toward the activity were.

Considerable autonomy was gained when the game was adopted by the field of mathematics (GW 9, p. 31). Its symbols were abstract which freed them from singular applicability; they possessed the capability of sublimating other categories of learning within their abstract quality. Although the symbolic language used by the mathematicians was not used by musicians or the other disciplines which now participated in a glass bead game-like activity, each discipline did develop abbreviated formulae and signs which became independent systems and the characteristics of competition and winning which existed at the earlier music schools were now applied to what can be considered independent games. As the fictional biographer explained: "The game was no longer only complex exercise or recreation, it was concentrated self awareness of the intellectual element in society" (GW 9, p. 32, translated by J.M.G.). In addition, the activity began to play an increasingly significant role in overcoming the trivia and pseudo-intellectualism of the mid-twentieth century, when Klaiber was pained due to his wife's devotion to the tasteless game of bridge and when intellectuals delighted at attending lectures and talks whose significance was more social than educational.

Later developments of the game, which no longer made use of glass beads, brought about significant transitions in the character of and attitude toward competition and winning. The important final changes in the game include the invention of a new language capable of expressing symbolically the content of the various disciplines, and it was this change which prompted the biographer to describe the game as sublime cult, as the expression of the spiritual unity within the universe, and borrowing from Steppenwolf, as magic theater. The practice of contemplation, the counterpart of its new hieroglyphic language, lifted the game out of the realm in which virtuosity and cleverness alone sufficed. The game became a form of religious-like celebration in which not only the player but also the entire human element participated.

In order to view the game more realistically, to define the game elements as practiced, we must go beyond such descriptive titles as Unio Mystica, or Magic Theater, to an actual performance of what Hesse called a public celebration or ritual. At first appearance, the game elements in the public ritual seem to have simply disappeared. Neither in the many lengthy discussions which occur throughout the main body of the novel nor in the one fully described game do we see obvious evidence of competing opponents or of victorious winners. The concepts even seem out of place in a ritual-like activity despite their essential place in the general concept of game. We must first define how ritual is play and second describe what transformations the concepts of competition and winning have undergone in the game-ritual.

Utilizing a standard authority on game theory, I turn again to Johan Huizinga. He states: "The function of play in the higher forms which concern us here can largely be derived from the two basic aspects under which we meet it: as a contest for something or a representation of something. These two functions can unite in such a way that the game 'represents' a contest or else becomes a contest for the best representation of something." The glass bead game ritual is a contest for the best representation of something and that something is the underlying unity inherent in the multiplicity of the disciplines and therewith in nature itself. Huizinga goes into much greater detail in establishing the identity of ritual as play. There is no essential need of repeating it here since the major question concerns two elements within play, competition and winning, and how they are expressed in the ritual presentation of the glass bead game. Let us consider them separately. In the competitive activity there is always a degree of tension present. Beginning with Klaiber's card game and proceeding all the way to the game with glass beads invented in the music academies, this tension is present in a literal sense. It is caused by two players who present competitive or opposing situations, and the game can be considered an alternating process between opposing situations within the order of the defined activity. When more than two players are involved, the alternating process becomes more complex but essentially the same process is at work. In the ritual the tension caused by the juxtaposition of opposing situations is still present but no longer in a literal sense. The tension in the ritual stems from the inherent polar nature of that which the game wishes to represent. The idea of polarity takes the place of or is the symbol of the meaning of the more literal competition found in the earlier forms of the game. According to the biographer, polarity is, in fact, the single most important element in the game. He says close to the beginning of the novel: "It is an old idea that the more sharply and more intensely we formulate a thesis, the more irresistibly it calls forth its antithesis" (GW 9, p. 8). In the game ritual we are no longer dealing with competing contestants but with impartial players who seek to represent the idea of contest or, more appropriately, the idea of polarity. Contest, tension or strife become symbolically represented in the game-ritual.

The concept of winning has undergone similar changes. We have already seen that in the music academies the winner is more than one who is victorious over an opponent as was the case in Klaiber's card game. This gradual transformation continues. Winning becomes more and more associated with the idea of completion or of complete representation of a living whole. Of course, each yearly ritual did have its literal winners--those whose formulae were incorporated into the language of the game or into the archives of Castalia but the winner is not a celebrated victor. He has become an unnamed part of the victory which is the completed symbolic representation.

This does not mean, as is so commonly interpreted, that the game is purely symbolic. The ritual is a symbolic representation, but it has become such only after a developmental process which has clearly demonstrated the empirical reality of that which is being repre-sented. Hesse states that contemplation prevented the symbolic structure from becoming an abstract house of cards ready to collapse at the slightest breeze from "real life." This is true for the Castalian, but for the reader, this symbolic structure of the novel is solid due to its own elaborate historic foundations which required first an evolutionary and then a conscious developmental process lasting over more than a century. Without the historically verifiable foundations for the game, it may conceivably be vulner-able to the criticism that it is an elaborate vessel with no real content. With the historical roots which Hesse builds into the novel and which clearly reveal the nature of the game elements, the vessel is actually determined by the contents, and therewith it becomes a credible core around which the drama of Josef Knecht revolves.

References

Hesse, Hermann, Das Glasperlenspiel, Vol. IX of Gesammelte Werke
  in Zwölf Bänden, (Frankfurt am Main: Suhrkamp, 1970). Cited
  throughout as GW 9.
Hsia, Adrian, "Das esoterische Glasperlenspiel," in Materialien zu
  Hermann Hesses "Das Glasperlenspiel," Vol. II, ed. Volker
  Michels (Frankfurt am Main: Suhrkamp, 1974), pp. 193–203.
Goddgar, Harry, "Hesse's 'Glasperlenspiel' and the game of Go,"
  GL+L, 20 (1966), 1932, pp. 132–37.
Field, G. W., "Zur Genesis das Glasperlenspiel," in Materialien zu
  Hermann Hesses das Glasperlenspiel, Vol. II, ed. Volker Michels
  (Frankfurt am Main: Suhrkamp, 1974), pp. 175–193.
GL. p. Sp. Gesch, p. 3, TS of the 1932 version of the "Intro-
  duction" to das Glasperlenspiel. Located in the Schillerna-
  tionalmuseum, Marbach, Federal Republic of Germany.
Huizinga, J., Homo Ludens: A Study of the Play-Elements in Culture,
  (Boston: Beacon Press, 1950), p. 199.
Hesse, Hermann, "Beispiel für eine Improvisationsübung," in
  Materialien zu Hermann Hesses das Glasperlenspiel, Vol. I, ed.
  Volker Michels, (Frankfurt am Main: Suhrkamp, 1973),
  pp. 316–317.

PEDESTRIANISM TO THE TRUST FUND - ATHLETICS IN IT S HISTORICAL AND
SOCIAL CONTEXTS

ERIC M MACINTYRE
Loughborough Technical College

Abstract
The origins of any modern sport are often hazy and are the product
of many diverse factors. Athletics is a case in point and this
paper highlights one particular aspect of its development - the
'pedestrian' tradition. Emerging in the nineteenth century urban
settings it attracted huge crowds, drawn by the sport and betting
returns. Victorian upper class morality frowned on this sport and
the amateur tradition emerged. However, the sport still survives
today in some small pockets and the amateur branch heads towards an
'open' situation. The social and historical aspects of pedestrianism are investigated, together with any lasting lessons for the
future of the sport.
Key words: Pedestrianism, Amateur, Powderhall, Wager, Highland
Games.

In 1985, one hundred and two years after its formation, the Scottish
Amateur Athletic Association offered an amnesty to those athletes
who had competed for money on the Highland and Border Games circuit.
For a single payment of fifteen pounds, a professional could be
re-instated to take part as an amateur in domestic competitions.
While this news may not have greatly impinged on the world athletics
scene, it tells us a great deal about the development of the sport
from humble beginnings to its present multi-million state on the
verge of being declared a truly 'open' sport. This paper will
address itself to some of these trends and seek to find out if past
experience can shed any light on the possible future which awaits
modern athletics.
    The urge to run, jump or throw better than an opponent is as old
as man himself and the social evolutionary process from hunting and
survival to modern sport has been well chronicled. Alongside these
changes we must place the almost timeless human urges to make money
and to gamble. If we, as the brevity of this paper dictates, combine these human traits into a total picture, then we can begin to
detect the origins of athletics as we know it today.
    The splendid bibliography by Lovesey and McNab (1969) lists
hundreds of items which can tell us a lot about these origins and
their social diversity. At one extreme we find in Shakespeare's
Henry IV, Part I (c1595), Sir John Falstaff challenging Poins that
"I'll see thee damn'd ere I call thee coward, but I would give a
thousand pound I could run as fast as thou canst". At the other end
of the social spectrum men and women could race at village fairs or
wakes, with the prize being no greater than a "hat or a

smock or a handsome satin ribbon". Some of these local events seem
bizarre to our modern refined tastes. Up until 1755 boys used to
run naked in winter across the Derbyshire moors, while the Eccles
Wakes in 1810 included a "race for wooden legg'd women for a purse
of silver". These local festivals, like the present-day Highland
and Border Games, were vital to the social and religious life of
their communities, but they did not advance the development of
athletics very much. First, they were too scattered and locally
based to bring cohesion and organisation. Second, wages were small
and this left little for prize money or gambling. Third, they had
cultural, rather than sporting or monetary significance for the
local community members.

The real developments were to take place in the emerging towns
and cities and with the impetus coming from a more leisured and
monied class. Up until the 18th Century roads and communications
were generally poor and many of the nobility employed 'running
footmen' to carry messages or race ahead to an inn to announce their
arrival. These men must have cut a real dash in their colourful
clothes and carrying a staff with a ball on the end containing a
beaten egg or drop of grog. Some became very gifted runners and
their employers often put them up for wagers against the footman of
a rival. Samuel Pepys comments on seeing such races and Charles II
and the Duke of York went to Banstead Downs to bet on a tyler in a
race against a footman. However, better roads and coach services
made the running footmen redundant and in order to continue in the
sport they began to arrange their own matches and wagers. They now
became known as 'pedestrians'.

The first, and possibly greatest, pedestrian was Captain Barclay,
who in 1809 walked 1,000 miles in 1,000 hours on Newmarket Heath.
He won £16,000 in wagers and Lovesey (1979) estimates it to be among
the biggest prizes ever won in athletics, even rivalling some of the
payments on offer today. Large crowds flocked to see such
promotions which included footraces over distances from 130 yards
upwards to the strength-sapping, sleep-denying six day 'go as you
please' efforts of the 'wobblers'. These latter contests have been
vividly brought to life in Lovesey's (1970) fictional account.

The Industial Revolution and improved transport and communications gave pedestrianism a great boost in the years from 1820 -
1870. The rapid growth of towns and cities brought public houses
and sports grounds and the two amenities were often combined. The
venues - Hyde Park, Sheffield, Hackney Wick, London, Belle Vue,
Manchester, Lillie Bridge, London among them - may have long passed
into obscurity, but it was not unusual for 30,000 of the 'fancy' to
turn up to watch such contests. Challenges would be printed in the
local papers and, on acceptance, the race would be run with vast
wagers. Moreover, there was an international dimension to the sport
with the first 'superstar' being the American Seneca Indian Louis
Bennett, known as 'Deerfoot', who came to Britain in 1861 to
challenge all-comers. Running in moccasins, and sporting his native
head-dress, this curiosity was watched by 150,000 spectators in that
year, among them the future King Edward VII and the Duke of
Wellington. Moreover, he was a wonderful athlete and his distance
of 11 miles 970 yards in one hour was to remain a record for nearly
forty years.

There was no season to pedestrianism and no real organisation. By the 1860's concern was being expressed about the image of the sport, largely on account of its gambling associations. The term 'amateur' began to appear and the Rowing Almanack of 1861 took this to exclude "tradesmen, labourers, artisans or working mechanics". Victorian gentlemen feared that gambling would make the urban working class idle and debauched. They began to wrest control from the pedestrian fraternity and the first Oxford v Cambridge fixture in 1864 was followed by the formation of the Amateur Athletic Club in 1865, the forerunner of the Amateur Athletic Association founded in 1880.

The definition employed by this body was that "an amateur is one who has never competed for a money prize or staked bet, or with or against a professional for any prize, or who has never taught, pursued, or assisted in the practice of athletic exercises as a means of obtaining a livelihood".

These events did not, of course, signal the immediate demise of pedestrianism, but they did move its centres out of the South of England. Amateur and professional meetings alternated at Lillie Bridge in London, but that ended on September 19th 1887. On that day, 15,000 spectators turned up to watch Harry Hatchens race his rival Harry Gent over 120 yards for £200. As the crowd waited, the rival backers fell out and no race took place. Frustrated spectators stormed the enclosures, tearing down the stands and putting them to fire. It was the real death knell for pedestrianism in London.

Though the AAA's now began to exert a strong control over athletics, the pedestrians were not alone in breaking the rules. Betting openly took place at amateur fixtures and was not banned finally until the passage of the 1906 Street Betting Act. Moreover, the top amateur athletes were not averse to accepting appearance money and under-cover payments. In 1896, the AAA's made an example of the great sprinter A R Downer and the distance-runner F E Bacon were banned from amateur competition. Both were welcomed with open arms by the professionals and Downer (1908) wrote a celebrated autoboigraphy exposing the 'shamateurism' of his day.

Sheffield began to exert itself as the centre of pedestrianism and its first major handicap was run in 1857. As a burgeoning industrial city with many public houses and sports grounds it housed events at several venues. Harry Hutchens, mentioned above, became the great star and contemporaries thought him the "fastest thing ever to operate on two feet". Indeed, when he ran in Edinburgh in 1880 a special train load of spectators travelled to support him. The sport enjoyed this 'boom' because football had not yet emerged as the great working-class sporting outlet. A good day's sport, and the chance to augment meagre wages with a betting coup, still ranked high for a steel or railway worker. The Sheffield Pedestrian Handicaps were well conducted but disputes still occurred and in 1883 one local observed "t'handicap's over, t'handicap's past, what a wonder, and what a relief".

The last major Sheffield Handicap was run in 1899, but by then the centre of the sport had moved to Edinburgh and its celebrated New Year Powderhall Handicap Sprint. This event was first staged in 1870 and is still run today. From the outset, the Powderhall organisers stamped on any abuses, even having a man jailed for deception. This probity by the promoters and the special atmosphere of the event are both highlighted in the unique account by Jamieson (1943). The event has always had an international connection with the great Australian, Jack Donaldson, known as the 'Blue Streak', being the back-marker in 1913. Indeed, he was one of the fastest runners ever, as witnessed by his defeat of the 1908 Olympic Champion, Reginald Walker, and the spectacular times which he clocked. In later decades, the famous E J Cumming won the event and in 1983 a Black American, Kipper Bell, triumphed. Of the home-based winners, Willie McFarlane in 1934 stands out as the only runner to win from scratch and many experts rate George McNeill, Centenary Powderhall winner in 1970, as not only one of the greatest professional runners ever, but also of any category. He completed his 'unique double', also the title of his autobiography (1983), when he won the 1981 Centenary Stawell Gift Sprint, the Australian equivalent of Powderhall. This antipodean branch of pedestrianism began when emigrants from Britain introduced the sport into local communities in the 'new country'. The famous Australian film 'Gallipoli' features such a footrace and that country remains, with Scotland, the last bastion of professional running.

Apart from Powderhall and the Scottish Highland and Border Games, the sport died out in the rest of Britain soon after the First World War. The year 1926 was to prove a bitter one in sporting, social and industrial terms. The General Strike left men short of money and many 'peds' gladly competed in small events for small prize money, thereby ruining their self-esteem and their future handicaps. Moreover, the electric hare was introduced into greyhound racing and that sport rapidly took over as the urban working man's main betting attraction. Hyde Park, Sheffield and Powderhall Grounds, Edinburgh both literally went to the dogs and became tracks for the canine, rather than human, fleet of foot. Never again would professional running attract the interest or the money of the local punter as it had done in its great days.

As mentioned above, the Highland and Border Games remain the only other venues, Powderhall and Australia apart, where professional athletics is conducted. Like the wakes or village festivals which predated pedestrianism, these gatherings have been held for centuries and are firmly implanted in the social fabric of their communities. Strength events are probably the major attractions of Highland Gatherings and Webster (1973) catalogues the great feats performed by past and present champions. Highland dancing and bagpipe playing join running and jumping as the other components, but the prime purpose is not sport, rather an annual meeting of friends in a sporting setting. The competitors are deemed 'professionals', but prizes are as nothing compared with those on offer legitimately to the modern 'amateur' athlete. Indeed, no one can make a living from such competitions and, by a strange quirk of fate we can truly say that these 'pariahs', banned until the 1985 amnesty offer, are the last amateurs in athletics, competing mainly for the love of their sport. It will be interesting and probably ultimately sad, to see the long-term effect which the Scottish Amateur Athletic Associations's amnesty offer has on the Highland and Border Games.

The modern sport of athletics is conducted on a lucrative international circuit with the top performers earning vast sums in subventions and from sponsorship which is then invested in trust funds with the help of governing bodies. It is ironic to reflect on the pedestrian tradition, so anathema to the AAA's founding fathers, and to the 'ritual cleansing' which subsequent amateur administrators have found necessary to keep the sport pure. The case of Downer has been noted and after him the legendary Jim Thorpe had his Olympic medals taken away. Paavo Nurmi was banned for monetary infringements on the eve of the 1932 Olympics though he was 'forgiven' and allowed to light the 1952 Olympic flame. The Swedes, Gunder Hagg and Arne Andersson were banned in 1945 when tantalisingly close to the then mythical four-minute mile and Wes Santee and Dan Waern suffered similar fates a decade or so later. In the era of the trust fund such bans are unlikely to be required again.

In conclusion, it is always difficult to draw lessons and parallels from history, especially in a sport constantly evolving in terms of organisation, coaching theories and performances. It has come a long way from the running footmen and the pedestrians, but the basic aim - to win - remains constant. We would perhaps do well to reflect that, compared to Harry Hutchens or Alf Downer taking a few pounds for their splendid efforts, the modern drug taker is guilty of even greater abuse. The stadium may not be burnt down in frustration today like the old Lillie Bridge, but are we sure that the spirit of the modern sport is as pure as when our Victorian forefathers sought to drive out such excesses for ever?

References

Downer, A R (1908). Running Recollections and How to Train. Gale and Polden, London.
Jamieson, D A (1943) Powderhall and Pedestrianism. W A K Johnston, Edinburgh.
Lovesey, P and McNab, T (1969) The Guide to British Track and Field Literature 1275 - 1968. Athletics Arena, London.
Lovesey, P (1970) Wobble to Death. Macmillan, London
Lovesey, P (1979) The Official Centenary History of the Amateur Athletic Association. Guinness Superlatives, Enfield.
Macintyre, E M (1976) The Powderhall: sprinting into the record books. Scottish Field, CXXIII, 9 - 10.
McNeill, G (1983). The Unique Double. Privately published.
Webster, D (1973). Scottish Highland Games. Reprographia, Edinburgh.

THE TROJAN GAMES IN ANCIENT ROME

Dr. Y. SOREQ
Wingate Institute, Israel

Abstract
Bearing the following Caesarean goals in mind (namely, to
incite and stimulate national and patriotic prestige ; to
enhance the unity of Italy ; to regenerate archaic elements
of varied Roman virtues ; to crystalise the noble youth and
keep them in good physical fitness for better implementation
of supreme martial, political and social roles), and
referring to the manifold Greek influences which left their
impression on the Roman civilisation, the Romans were
presented with mythical games, viz the Trojan-Games, marked
with a national and patriotic seal. Such games, restored
as a link between Caesar's family and the legendary Greek
founder of ancient Rome, were excercised by noble youth,
and particularly included chivalric manoeuvres within the
bounds of an interesting sport competition, of a spectacular
nature. These prominent nobles, the loyal trainees of the
Iuvenes (national clubs which provided the noble youths
with physical excercises and horsemanship training) were
destined to openly represent the paradigm of the new-Rome's
virtues.

1. What does Rome have to do with Troy ?

It is interesting to note that Roman mythologists erected
an archaic bridge between the Trojan war and the very beginning of Rome, by underscoring the two famous Trojan
figures (Aeneas and Antenor), the main refugees of the
wrecked Troy who settled in Italy and founded two cities
(bearing the name of the lost and devastated Troy). The
offsprings of Aeneas built, it should be noted, the famous
centre of Rome.
   The link between Rome and Troy was grounded upon a
complex background in which we can include : The Greek
settlements along southern Italy ; the commercial relations
which prevailed between Rome and Greece ; the military
campaigns which Rome waged in Greece and the Hellenistic
east throughout the 2nd century B.C.
   The significant outcome of such phenomena was a gradual
and prolonged process of Greek cultural influence which

129

particularly permeated into the upper crest of the society
whose members endeavored to forge a traditional channel
between their family pedigree and the Greek heroic gallery
Hence the original core of the romantic Greek-Roman essenc

Such a complex background paved an interesting way in
displaying sports competitions of a Greek nature in ancien
Rome, to the extent of a prevailing custom from the mid 1s
century B.C. onwards. This process was well oiled by Roma
rulers and consolidated by persomal, prestige, geneologica
and socio-aristocratic tendencies which the Roman court ha
recurrence to be grounded upon.

Such reasons, it is noteworthy, found themselves groupe
under an educational, ideological and national umbrella,
and were concisely expressed in the way of enhancing the
status of the noble youth (namely the important Roman
reserves). This tendency was certainly nourished by the
Greek romantic influences (where formal and public education was underlined as the main essence of Hellenic society
on one hand, and where athletic contests were strengthened
by national dimensions and pan-Hellenic values on the
other).

Hence, it is no wonder that Roman youth, of the wealthy
strata, were keen on numerous Greek athletics. Such contes
in pursuance of the aforenamed goals, consolidated the pre
requisite atmosphere towards the appearance (and/or)
restoration of the Trojan Games.

2. The Trojan Games throughout Roman historiography

Plutarch, the Roman historian held that the conclusion was
inevitable that Sulla was the Roman ruler who should have
rightly been crowned with the primacy of restoring the
Trojan Games. Plutarch subsequently termed those games as
a sacred competition (in a sense of the archaic Greek
crown-contests which were inextricably interwoven with
national and pan-Hellenic threads), where young noble
horsemen, carefully chosen by the above ruler (which is
evidence enough to underscore the significance this ruller
attributed to such a phenomenon), and led by two captains,
each of whom took care of his company's training.

Sulla, it is worthy of note, was convinced that such
competitions would reinforce the equestrian order,
crystallise solid reserves of military-aristocratic office
cadre and symbolise his prolonged dictatorship (81-79 B.C.

The holding of Trojan-Games gradually became a fixed,
instituted and traditional practice during the sovereignit
of Julius Caesar (59-44 B.C.). It is of a particular inter
that this ruler held the games which were comprived of
young men (Iuvenes) and boys (Pueri), and hence normally
wished to enlarge the above category among the younger age
groups.

All the more so, Julius Caesar endeavoured to mold and

and illustrate, during the above games, the firm link
between Troy, Rome and the Caesar himself as a dispersed
tradition whereas the Trojan Games were celebrated in
memory of Iulus (Aeneas' son), or, put differently, in the
same way that the archaic Trojan refugees were eager to
comemorate their new foothold in Latium and introduced in
such a manner the Trojan Games as a symbol of the beginning
of a new era, the here-discussed ruler, it should be
perceived, found a fertile ground to nourish his ideas upon.

That is to say, not only for the reason that Caesar was
traditionally a pure descendant of archaic Iulus, but also
his main image, as the founder of a new era in Roman history,
would have placed him close enough to the very essence of
the ancient Trojan Games.

Julius Caesar, it is noteworthy, after putting an end
to the civil wars in Rome, and when starting to menage the
state's business and implementing his dictatorship campaign,
introduced the Trojan Games in 46 B.C.

It is by no means certain that such contests were
basically annexed with his main policy and the social
characteristics, to wit : underscoring the youth's
education and its recruitment for the benefit of the state;
the reliance and grounding upon the noble strata of the
Roman society; the balanced promotion of military power,
and in brief, logically consolidating the varied elements
towards the unity and uniformity of the state (as national
factors), bearing the Caesarean mark.

Four years ensuing the assasination of Caesar, the
Trojan Games were celebrated (40 B.C.) by the initiative
efforts of Agrippa the praetor, and introduced once more
in 33 B.C.

So much for the pre-Augustan epoch. During the reign of
Augustus such games reached the peak of popularity and
gradually established by noble, romantic, archaic and
national characteristics. When first displayed (18 August
29 B.C.) the games were intended to vividly celebrate the
dedication of the "Aedes Divi Iuli", and Augustus, the
legal heir of Caesar and the pure descendant of the Iulii
family, endeavoured in such a way to vigorously forge the
mythic-romantic pipe with Aeneas, as if was "bewitched" by
a deep missionary impetus.

Furthermore, the very year when the games were held (29
B.C.) marked the nomination of Augustus as the supreme
figure in Rome, whereat the thrilling dimension of founding
the new era was well noted, and hence colourfully
commemorated by the Trojan Games.

The abovementioned tie between Augustus and Aeneas was
artistically produced by the prominent poet of the Augustan
epoch, Publius Virgil, in his national poetry, Aeneid,
which was influenced by the epos of Homer. Virgil deemed
it his normal duty to basically shape the prototype of the

ideal Roman citizen in keeping with the image of the noble Trojan. Virgil charmingly noted the conspicuous funeral contests introduced by Aeneas when first set foot on the shores of Sicily, and he also vividly elaborated in detail on the Trojan Games. Those contests, as Virgil attested, were consisted of three noble chivalric companies (each of sixteen participants), who, after spectacularly giving an official riding parade, of a martial sort, broke away, then gallopped back, then parted again and carried out various perilous chivalric manoeuvres (including charging, chasing, tackling, barring, evading, waging fronted attacks, flank assaults and the like) in dramatisation of numerous scenes, taken from the archaic battle and siege of ancient Troy.

Those breath-taking excercises were meant, no doubt, to publicly demonstrate the riding proficiency and the indispensible chivalric skills of belligerent-competitive nature, to instill national and romantic elements among the cheering public. It should be noted that Augustus instituted, or more probably restored the games in which the equestrian order came prominently before the eyes of the public.

The whole exuberant demonstration was poetically portrayed by Virgil in a historical excerpt, pertaining to "the ancient practice of horse-riding competition", as he put it, the very same that Iulus (Aeneas' son) first held when he erected the walls of Alba, and the latter (Alba) bequeathed the discussed scene to Rome as a legatus ad aeternum.

3. The original sources of Trojan Games

Two significant archaeological finds may cast an interesting light upon the Trojan "mystery". The first, a 6th century B.C. Etruscan vase upon which two horsemen are drawn next to a labyrinth scheme bearing the inscription, termed Truia. We may endorse with little hesitation the view that this term refers to the phyrric dance (a Greek-Spartan dance of military dimensions) which was practised by the Saliic priests of Rome (who, it should be noted, choreographically dramatised interesting military scenes). Such a theory, together with the above discernible inscribed "Truia", which the Romans mistook for Troy, both reasonably point to the Trojan Games.

The second find, an interesting inscription which was excavated in Pompei, consisted of four verses in praise of the Iuvenes of Pompei and recorded a strange term, to wit, "the serpent ride".

Both the above labyrinth and the "serpent ride" were found, it is worthy of note, in Virgil's verses of Aeneid, while referring to the Trojan Games. The equestrian manoeuvres of the skillful riders metaphorically represented in Virgil's composition the legendary labyrinth in the mythic palace of Minos, the Cretan king, and the noble horsemen who weaved circles within circles in mimic warfare, symbolised in such a manner the serpent's tracks.

Besides the significant allusion to one of the Games' displays (to wit, the daring riding courses/lanes of circles within circles, as a labyrinth and the serpent's twisting), the above geographical radius of the finds, obviously refers to the main southern centres of the Etruscan empire in Italy (prior to the Roman rule).

The Etruscan civilisation was heavily influenced, for many reasons, by the Aegean and Asia-Minor culture (including the area of ancient Troy), and as a result emphasised horse-riding competitions and spectacular funeral games, as attested to in Virgil's verses. The Greek-Asian influences on Etruscan civilisation are quite conspicuous in the archaic Greek settlements throughout southern Italy.

The data above presented give us a reasonable assurance to allege that the Trojan Games was but an interesting complex of Greek mythology (Trojan legends); legendary traditions which bound up together the Trojan remnant (Aeneas) and the birth of Rome; Greek contests and Etruscan culture whose impressions were deeply left in Roman civilisation and maintained a long time after the Etruscan decline in Italy (end of the 6th century B.C.).

4. The place and roles of Trojan Games in Roman policy

The importance and prominence (not to mention the unbroken continuity) of the Trojan Games are well attested to by the fact that such games were an important instrument of the Caesarean Roman policy, and its potential applications.

Throughout the Augustan epoch the educational institution of sports-military characteristics, named Iuventus (note both its resemblance to the Greek ephebeion and its interesting annexation to the "young men" (neoi), that is the Greek gymnasium trainees) flourished significantly.

Boys of upper classes, even before they assumed the Toga virilis, became members of clubs which provided them with physical exercises and training in horsemanship, the outcome of which was their habit of displaying in the spectacular "Lusus Troiae" (i.e., the Trojan Game) on the 19th of March every year in front of masses of citizens, including their parents.

They remained at this stage until they were seventeen when they passed into the Iuventus proper, and their activities took a more definitely martial form.

These clubs, scattered throughout Italy provided appren-
ticeships for high-ranking military service, opportunities
for social and political advancement and centres for the
propagation of correct sentiments about the government.

Note that such a picture was very closely interwoven
with the aforenamed trends as the foothold and mainstay of
the Trojan Games (namely, symbolising the Caesarean rule;
the inaugeration of a new era; the attention that was paid
to the youth reserve) consolidated during the Augustan era
and were enriched with other dimensions, following the
particular characteristics of Augustus' policy, namely :
the national unity of Italy by ideological education of
the youth which included various values (such as chivalry,
loyalty, bravery, discipline and the like, within the
mythic symbol of the Homeric knights). Therefore, no
wonder that the games were defined as the "patriotic
contests", as an integral part of Augustus' national
program, and were dispersed throughout Italy in his epoch.

If so, it would be plainly erroneous to assume
otherwise than the following : the pragmatic outcomes of
Augustus' policy and trends would have logically been
doomed if he had grounded his mission only upon slogans
and national spirit. The consortium of both values and
military-political benefits was an apt key for the
implementation of romantic and national policy during his
interesting era.

Moreover, I would say, parenthetically, that those
national threads were inextricably interwoven as a linkage
between the Iuvenes clubs and the Trojan Games, and might
have been examined from another angle. Augustus, it is
true, achieved and initiated the total imperial peace
(known by the term Pax Romana). However in order to
preempt possible future dimensions of indifference among
the military orders, he was wise enough to keep the noble
belligerent forces in good physical shape and sharpen
their martial skillfulness. Hence he founded the Iuvenes
clubs as honourable and suitable means of achieving his
goals.

The Iuvenes, as mentioned above, were also intended to
be propagative centres for the recruitment of the trainees
in favour of the central regime and a device for
demonstrating its policy among the spectators who watched
the Games. Of their importance we may draw analogies from
the mere fact that from Augustus' period onwards such
contests were highly supervised and patronised by the
emperors, and to such an extent that Augustus himself
deemed it essential to personally nominate the clubs'
leaders (princeps iuventutis), as a title of honour for
his grandsons, Gaius and Lucius.

Furthermore, it should be noted that the solid

continuity of the Trojan Games was ensured by sacred and ritual characteristics, initiated by Augustus. Or put otherwise, due to the fact that religion was the moral mainstay of Rome's power, the emperor was determined to bind up the Trojan Games with the temple of Mars Ultor, known as the sacred centre of the Roman army, and was identified with the tradition and ritual of the emperor's house.

In doing so, Augustus used the Games to strenghthen his personal image, as the peak of Roman nationalism (it is worthy of note that the tradition created a significant identification between Augustus and Virgil's Aeneas. Hence, two years following the colourful inaugeration of the temple of Julius Caesar (29 B.C.), who was the true descendant of Aeneas' son, Augustus vividly and stunningly held the Trojan Games.

5. The decay of the Games

The solid evidence which verifies the far-wide and deep flourishing of the Trojan Games during Augustus' epoch, their particular characteristics (that is national, romantic and the like) and martial-political dimensions, is paradoxically also explains the reasons for their decline.

Augustus' heirs found themselves beset by courtyard intrigues and personal turmoil. The Augustan ideals, instilled by the Iuvenes among the noble youths and the citizens, disintegrated in no time and became impotent cliches. It is true indeed, that the ensuing descendants were ardent supporters of performing the Trojan Games. However, lack of patriotic and national education; the absence of mythic-religious dimensions which were annexed to the Games, and a marred gallery of emperors who were slaves to personal prestige, paved the way towards the decay of the glorious Trojan Games. The romantic and national Games became a thing of the past.

References

Bendorf, (1890) Ueber des Alter des Trojaspiels, Sitzungsberichte den kaiserlische Akademie der Wissenschaften, 123, pp. 47 ff.
Cicero, M.T. Ad Atticum, 5 ; Id., De Respublica, I.
Cook S.A. (et alia), The Cambridge Ancient History,(1952), p. 462.
Cassius Dio, Roman history, XLIII, 23, 6 ; Id., XLVIII, 20, 2 ; XLIX, 43, 3 ; LI, 22, 4.
Harris, H.A. (1964) Greek Athletes and Athletics, Hutchinson of London, pp. 44 ff.

Livius, L. Ab Urbe Condita, I, 1.
Mommsen Th. (et alia), (1863) Corpus Inscriptionum
    Latinarum, IV, 1595 ; 2437 ; IV, pl. XXXVIII, I.
Ovidius, Metamorphoses, X, 560 ff.
Sallustius, C. Bellum Catilinarium, 1.
Seneca, Troades, 777.
Suetonius, G.T. Divi Iulii, 39 ; Id. Divi Augusti, 38 ; 43.
Syme, R. (1968) The Roman revolution, Oxford university
    press, pp. 445-447 ; 482.
Tacitus, P.C. Annals, XIV ; XV ; Id., Agricola, 4, 4.
Taylor, L.R.S. (1924) Seviri Equitum Romanorum and
    municipal seviri, A study in pre-military training
    among the Romans, Journal of Roman Studies, XIV, p. 160.
Vergilius, M.P. Aeneidos, V, 286-288 ; 303 ; 340 ; 368 ;
    545-605.
Willis, H.W. (1941) Athletic contests in the epic, T.A.P.A.
    LXXII, pp. 392-417.

CANADIAN INTERNATIONAL SPORT POLICY AND THE GLENEAGLES AGREEMENT

G.A. Olafson, Ph.D.
Faculty of Human Kinetics, University of Windsor

Abstract
The parallel developments of Canadian sport and foreign policies
between 1959 and 1978 as they pertain to the question of apartheid
in South Africa are traced. Canada's role as a middle power
led to a major foreign policy review which culminated in the
1970 White Paper entitled Foreign Policy for Canadians.
Sub-section four, "Reconciling Canadian Objectives in Southern
Africa," emphasizes the theme of social justice which became
an important cornerstone of Canada's international policy. The
evolution of the Canadian position as evident in the House of
Commons, in the Commonwealth, and in the United Nations, from
that of a compromiser viewing South Africa's internal affairs
as her own business to that of a leader for change in her racial
process, is documented. The reflection of the themes guiding
foreign policy in the establishment of a sport policy under which
the Olympic Games and the Commonwealth Games would be hosted
in Canada in 1976 and 1978, respectively, is illustrated. The
concurrence of this Canadian sport policy with that of the
Commonwealth and world opinion as expressed in the Gleneagles
Agreement, 1977, is also noted. Thus the policy of denying funding
"to any Canadian athlete or group of athletes who intend to travel
to South Africa to participate in an athletic competition, and
of not providing moral or financial support to any event in Canada
to which South African athletes have been invited," as a result
of their policy of apartheid is established both in theory and
practice by 1976.
Key words: Canada, Foreign policy, Sport, Apartheid, South Africa,
United Nations, Commonwealth, Olympics.

In 1970 the Canadian government undertook a major foreign
policy review as a result of its emerging role as a middle power
in world affairs. New policy initiatives resulting from this
review were related to the dovetailing of existing national
policies and the maintenance of our diplomatic relations within
the international community. The major aim of Canada's foreign
policy was to achieve those conditions "in which Canadian interests

137

and values can thrive and Canadian objectives be achieved."[1]
The shaping of this policy was based upon: fostering economic
growth, safeguarding sovereignty and independence, working for
peace and security, promoting social justice, enhancing the quality
of life and ensuring a harmonious environment.[2] Together these
objectives provided the conceptual framework for our foreign
policy. The factors associated with social justice, quality
of life, and economic growth will become closely linked with
Canada's development of a consistent attitude toward racial
discrimination and international sport.[3]

A major section of the White Paper entitled Foreign Policy
for Canadians which resulted from the above process is dedicated
to Canada's role in the United Nations (U.N.) and indirectly
in the Commonwealth of Nations. Sub-section four, "Reconciling
Canadian Objectives in Southern Africa," discusses the economic
implications for Canada of a stand against apartheid as well
as the moral aspects of support for African aspirations for racial
equity.[4] The government stressed its intention of emphasizing
the theme of social justice in its international policy.[5]

The question of apartheid had been addressed in the U.N. on
numerous occasions and the Canadian delegations had "indicated
our disapproval of any form of racial discrimination."[6] In 1959,
however, a resolution before the U.N. contained specific reference
to South Africa. The Canadian view was that "such criticism
was unlikely to contribute to the solution of the problem,"[7]
and thus "we abstained on the vote on the whole resolution."[8]
Canada's role in international affairs up to this time had been
as a mediator/arbitrator in terms of attempting to derive the
best policies for the Commonwealth as a whole. The Hon. Paul
Martin, Secretary of State for External Affairs, summarized this
function as it related to South Africa as follows: ". . .any
effort to exclude one Commonwealth country from the Commonwealth
is a course that is not to be encouraged or supported."[9]

---

1. Foreign Policy for Canadians (1970). Ottawa, Information
   Canada, p. 19.
2. Ibid, p. 16.
3. Refer to Olafson, G.A. and Brown-John, L. (1986). Canadian
   International Sport Policy: A Public Policy Analysis, in
   Sport and Politics, Human Kinetics Publishers, - for an elaboration of the public policy process.
4. United Nations, Foreign Policy for Canadians, p. 20.
5. Ibid, p. 20.
6. Report of the Department of External Affairs (1959). Ottawa,
   Information Canada, p. 3.
7. Ibid, p.3
8. Canada, House of Commons Debates, Third Session,
   February 10, 1960, p. 940.
9. Ibid, p. 941.

Article II, sub-section 7 of the U.N. Charter, which stated that "the United Nations is not in any way permitted to interfere in the domestic affairs of the country,"[10] provided Canada with only one option at this time, however - to abstain from vote of censure. The interpretation of the implications of "to interfere," became the central focus of a long debate in the Canadian Parliament on the implications of the U.N. apartheid resolution. Prior to the upcoming Commonwealth Conference, members of the House discussed the direction Canada should take on the issue of apartheid and South Africa's pending withdrawal from the Commonwealth.[11] Discussion suggested that alternatives such as "throw them out of the Commonwealth, impose an economic boycott, and use of formal protests through diplomatic channels," should be considered. The Prime Minister, however, closed the discussion by noting: " . . . a commonwealth drawing its strength not from sameness but from diversity . . . That is my idea of the commonwealth."[12] Thus the debate closed on a note of optimism that a compromise with South Africa could be reached.

Upon his return from the 1960 London Conference, however, the Prime Minister concluded that "the proceedings of the meetings did not result in any perceptable change in the attitude of the South African Government. It was not be be expected. . ."[13] The policy of non-interference in the internal affairs of another country continued to be the major directive in guiding Canadian foreign policy decisions on apartheid. Employing informal diplomacy, the Prime Minister met with Mr. Louw, the official representative of South Africa, who had recently been appointed a vice-president of the U.N., to explain Canada's position. "I left Mr. Louw in no doubt that in Canada there is no sympathy for policies of racial discrimination, on whatever grounds they may be explained, and that such policies are basically incompatible with the multiracial nature of the commonwealth association."[14]

During the London Conference, the continuation of membership of South Africa as a Republic was debated and the consensus of the meeting was that "membership in the commonwealth was not a formality . . . the consent of the other commonwealth governments will be required . . ."[15] With this statement, Canadian foreign policy "hardened" and the implications of this changing attitude would impact on sport policy in the years to come.

During the early 1960's, the moral problem of racial discrimination in U.N. member nations, the question of South Africa's commonwealth membership, and the practical consideration of trade

10. Canada, House of Commons Debates, Third Session,
    February 10, 1960, p. 966.
11. Canada, House of Commons Debates, Third Session,
    April 17, 1960, pp. 3319-3341.
12. Ibid, p. 3340.
13. Canada, House of Commons Debates, Third session,
    May 16, 1960, p. 3898.
14. Ibid, p. 3899
15. Ibid, p. 3901.

relationships, challenged Ottawa's bureaucrats to direct and interpret Canada's middle power course. The adoption of an Act for the Recognition and Protection of Human Rights and Fundamental Freedoms by the House of Commons reinforced the Canadian policy of social justice and quality of life.[16] In the following year, 1961, Canada continued its strong support of the U.N. position. The question of South Africa's status as a new republic was to be resolved at the Commonwealth Ministers Conference. The Parliament of Canada debated the importance of a "proposed declaration of basic accepted principles with regard to human dignity."[17] The Prime Minister summarized the Canadian position by stating: "it would be a desirable objective if it could be attained that the Commonwealth stand for a certain body of principles."[18] Thus the passage of the above noted Act (1960) protecting human rights and freedoms, combined with these sentiments, represent the first signs of Canada's policy congealing on the question of apartheid. At the 1961 meeting of Commonwealth prime ministers in London, Diefenbaker from Canada, in an attempt to avoid a split in the Commonwealth on racial lines, proposed a compromise which instead of expelling South Africa, would declare racial equality to be a Commonwealth principle. As South Africa could obviously not accept this in light of its own policies, it "withdrew its application to remain in the Commonwealth after becoming a republic"[19] on May 31, 1961.

Over the next five years, members of the House repeatedly questioned Canada's continued economic involvement with South Africa, and our continued abstention on U.N. resolutions condemning South Africa's racial policies. Finally a U.N. resolution calling for an arms embargo was supported and implemented as part of our foreign policy position. Thus, another cornerstone was added to Canadian foreign policy with the imposition of sanctions on South Africa.[20]

The necessity to provide a coherent sport policy for Canada was recognized with the creation of a Task Force on Sport for Canadians (1969) and the formulation of a Proposed Sport Policy for Canadians (1970). The sections of the aforementioned white paper entitled Foreign Policy for Canadians dealing with apartheid and South Africa will have great significance in formulating Canada's international sport policy as it relates to South Africa's participation in the 1976 Olympic and 1978 Commonwealth Games which Canada was to host.

16. Report of the Department of External Affairs, (1960). Ottawa, Information Canada, p. 25.
17. Canada, House of Commons Debates, Fourth Session, March 3, 1961, p. 2544.
18. Ibid, p. 2544.
19. Canada, House of Commons Debates, Fourth Session, March 15, 1961, p. 3011.
20. Canada, House of Commons Debates, First Session, February 3, 1966, p. 697.

On January 20, 1971, the first direct question of the effect of apartheid on Canadian sport policy was addressed by Mr. Skoberg (Edmonton-Strathcona) to the Minister of National Health and Welfare responsible for Canada's sport programs:

. . . considering the firm decision of the International Olympic Committee to adhere rigidly to the principle that there shall not be racial discrimination in sports, can the Minister give some indication to the House of the position to be taken by the government on that principle so far as the 1976 Olympic Games are concerned?[21]

With the granting of the Olympic Games to Montreal, Canadian politicians expressed concern about our stated policy and its impact on international sporting events. The official policy of not tolerating any form of racial discrimination was repeatedly addressed in the House. In reply, the Secretary of State for External Affairs referred to the stated policies of social justice and quality of life as the basis for government policy.[22] The interpretation and implementation of a policy decision "involves hard choices which require that a careful balance be struck in assessing the various interests, advantages, and other policy factors in play."[23] This delicate balance between and among the intervening variables operative through this period will be frequently discussed by Canadian politicians as the time for the Olympic and the Commonwealth Games approaches.

In the meantime, the Secretary of State for External Affairs visited Ivory Coast, Nigeria, Democratic Republic of the Congo, Tanzania and Zambia. Upon his return, he advised the House that the "governments are preoccupied with the intractable problems of South Africa . . ."[24] Canada's position on South African issues was well understood and accepted." Commonwealth ministers had recently issued a Declaration of Commonwealth Principles (1971), which addressed in detail equal rights and racial prejudice - both central issues in the emerging policy on sport.

The position of the Canadian government on apartheid had now hardened to the point where "The sooner apartheid ends in South Africa the better the world will be."[25] Canada's foreign policy was now being put to the test.

21. Canada, House of Commons Debates, Third Session, January 20, 1971, p. 2589.
22. The reader is directed to Foreign Policy for Canadians (1970) for an explanation of these themes, pp. 15-17.
23. Foreign Policy for Canadians, p. 17.
24. Canada, House of Commons Debates, Third Session, March 22, 1971, p. 4454.
25. Canada, House of Commons Debates, Third Session, November 25, 1971, p. 9912.

As the External Affairs Department developed our foreign policy on racial discrimination, the international sporting community continued its own campaign against apartheid in South Africa.[26] Continued concern was expressed in the House on Canada's trade relations with South Africa, on the Canadian Crown Corporations Polymer operating in South Africa, and on Commonwealth preferential tariff agreements. Not withstanding these factors, the co-sponsorship by Canada of a U.N. resolution which was placed before the Special Political Commission "censuring the restrictive practices by South Africa in the selection of its athletes who take part in international competitions,"[27] is of major significance to the development of our international sport policy and ultimately to the support of the Gleneagles Agreement. The melding of our foreign policy themes of social justice and quality of life and our international sport policy appears to be taking place.

With the Olympic Games less than a year away a member of the House asked the Prime Minister if South Africa were to change its selection process, would Canada be bound by the resolution forwarded to the Politicial Commission? Mr. Trudeau replied: "the athletes . . . are the guests of the I.O.C. and . . . this committee has excluded the South African Republic from these games . . ."[28] Canada moved another step away from the position of compromise. The Minister for National Health and Welfare stated in the House in reply to questions concerning the government's South African policy, "the government's position has been to withhold its financial aid to sporting events involving South Africa because of its apartheid policy."[29] As a further clarification of the government's position, the Minister for National Health and Welfare indicated that "The Canadian government policy denies funding to any Canadian athlete or groups of athletes who intend to travel to South Africa to participate in an athletic competition."[30] A further statement of the government's position on sport is offered by the Minister in his closing remarks: "I wish to confirm the position taken by the government . . . of not providing either moral or financial support to any event in Canada to which South African athletes have been invited.

---

26. The reader is directed to Lapchick, R.E. (1975). The Politics of Race and International Sport - The Case for South Africa, London, England, Greenwood Press, for a detailed account of reprisals by sport governing bodies.
27. Canada, House of Commons Debates, First Session, November 6, 1975. p. 8907.
28. Ibid, p. 8907.
29. Canada, House of Commons Debates, First Session, April 12, 1976. p. 12711.
30. Canada, House of Commons Debates, First Session, May 11, 1976. p. 13428.

This policy is being implemented in concert with many nations."[31]
The Secretary of State for External Affairs concurred with this
statement of policy. For the first time the two ministers
responsible for sport and external affairs, respectively, publicly
supported a foreign policy decision related to sport.

Diplomatic channels were being employed, meanwhile, to secure
a unified position within the Commonwealth on the question of
apartheid and sport. A major factor in this scenario was the
statement issued by the Organization for African Unity which
called upon its members to refrain from participating in sports
events in which New Zealand planned to take part because of its
sporting contacts in South Africa.[32] During this period, Mr.
Ramphal, Secretary General of the Commonwealth, had visited Canada
and "the matter was discussed at great length. Various proposals
were canvassed at that time and various actions will now be taken
as a result."[33] As these discussions were occurring in the international arena, the External Affairs Department, rather than
the Minister of State (Fitness and Amateur Sport) now assumed
a major role. Canadian concerns were conveyed to the Prime
Minister of New Zealand. On the last day of May, 1977, Prime
Minister Trudeau summarized the involvement of Canada as follows:
"On many occasions we have tried to solve this question. If
it is not solved before the London Conference next week then
we must find some way of solving it there."[34]

One week later, the Parliamentary Secretary informed the House:

What we envisage is a statement by all heads of government
reaffirming their opposition to the practice of apartheid
in sport and to contacts with South Africa by Commonwealth
sports bodies and individuals.[35]

The Gleneagles Agreement on Sporting Contacts with South Africa
was issued by the Commonwealth First Ministers in June, 1977.
The following year, the Canadian government withdrew its trade
commissioners, closed its consulate in Johannesburg, and issued
a code of conduct to companies operating in South Africa. In
July, 1978, the government announced that "South African sportsmen
and sports officials would "henceforth be denied Canadian visas."[36]

31. Canada, House of Commons Debates, First Session
    May 11, 1976. p. 13428.
32. Canada, House of Commons Debates, Second Session,
    April 4, 1977. p. 4595.
33. Ibid, p. 4596.
34. Canada, House of Commons Debates, Second Session,
    May 31, 1977. p. 6110.
35. Canada, House of Commons Debates, Second Session,
    June 6, 1977. p. 6349.
36. External Affairs Annual Review (1978), Ottawa, Information
    Canada, p. 8.

This paper has traced the evolution of the Canadian government's policy on sport and apartheid. Canada's role as a compromiser within the U.N. and the Commonwealth had matured and she had become a leader for change. The problems associated with hosting the 1976 Olympic and 1978 Commonwealth Games were a factor in motivating the Department of External Affairs and the Fitness and Amateur Sport Directorate to cooperate in formulating a Canadian policy concerning racial discrimination and international sport which is presently in effect.

References

Canada (1970) Foreign Policy for Canadians, Ottawa, Information Canada.

Canada, House of Commons Debates, 1959-1985.

Canada, Annual Report, Department of External Affairs, 1959-1984.

Brown-John, L. (1981) Canadian Regulatory Agencies. Toronto: Butterworths and Co.

Kanin, D.B. (1981) A Political History of the Olympic Games. Boulder, Colorado: Western Press.

Kidd, B. (1983) Boycotts That Worked: The Campaign Against Apartheid in the Commonwealth. J. Can. Assoc. Health, Phys. Ed. and Recreation, Vol. 49, No. 6 (July-August 1983), pp. 8-11.

Lapchick, R.E. (1975) The Politics of Race and International Sport: The Case of South Africa. London: Greenwood Press.

Leeds, C.A. (1969) The Racial Factor in Commonwealth Relations with Special Relevance to Africa, in The Impact of African Issues on the Commonwealth, Commonwealth Studies, University of London, pp. 48-70.

Newman, P.C. (1963) Renegade in Power: The Diefenbaker Years. Toronto: McClelland and Stewart.

Nossal, K.R. (1985) The Politics of Canadian Foreign Policy. Toronto: Prentice-Hall Canada, Inc.

Olafson, G.A. and Brown John, L. (1986) Canadian International Sport Policy: A Public Policy Analysis, in Sport and Politics, (Ed. G. Redmond), Champaign, Illinois: Human Kinetics Publishers, Inc. pp. 69-75.

Olafson, G.A. (1984) Structural Variation and Sport Policy: A Comparison of Canadian and British Sport Systems in Sport and International Understanding, (Ed. M. Ilmarinen), Berlin: Springer-Verlag. pp. 352-357.

Tomlin, B. (1978) Canada's Foreign Policy: Analysis and Trends, Toronto: Methuen.

THE INFLUENCE OF THE STATE SPORT OF FASCIST ITALY ON NAZI GERMANY. 1928 - 1936

ARND KRÜGER
Institut für Sportwissenschaften, Georg-August-Universität,
Göttingen, Fed. Rep. of Germany

Abstract
Italy has been generally considered in Weimar Germany as unorgan-
ised, unreliable and somewhat chaotic. One of the few exceptions has
been its sport system in which the fascist government succeeded to
achieve great international acclaim, particularly in bicycling,
motor-racing, and boxing. Italy's athletes were labeled diplomats in
track suits - just like those of the GDR 40 years later. Italy
placed a surprising second in the 1932 Los Angeles Olympics,
improving from 5th, while Germany fell back from 2nd to 7th from the
previous Amsterdam Games. The Italian fascist sports model from the
Carta dello sport (1928) to 1936 is presented. It served as a model
for the sports of the Yugoslav military dictatorship in 1929. Its
influences on Nazi sports from 1933 to 1936 are discussed. It is
shown which German sports related agencies were newly constructed
according to the Italian model and which were changed according to
the model, and which maintained its stength in its own right. It is
concluded that the Italian fascist influence has generally been
underestimated, and that even a number of present day features of
state organised sports were first invented in fascist Italy and not
in Nazi Germany as has been previously suggested.
Key words: Fascism, National Socialism, Italy, Germany, International
Olympic Committee, Propaganda, Nationalism.

1. Introduction

The Olympic Games of 1936 have been considered as the most powerful
demonstration of what a strong monolytic state can create in a short
time to demonstrate its national strength. Three years after taking
over power from a weak and divided democratic government, a strong
nation emerged which demonstrated its virility by classic monumental
athletic architecture, by the superb organisation of the largest
amount of international competitors assembled until then, by perfect
crowd management of more international spectators than ever before,
by a perfect sports complex which provided more medals for the Vater-
land than any other team could reach, and telling the success story
to a world wide audience using the most modern and sophisticated
propaganda machinery known by that time.

When the Nazis came to power in early 1933, nothing in any of their previous speeches or writings had suggested this formidable rise from an international seventh place at the 1932 Los Angeles Games to an unprecedented first. Nothing had suggested the enormous investment of the state into elite sports. In fact, all the evidence pointed to the contrary: The Völkische Beobachter, the party news-paper, had used little space to deal with sports at all.

Table 1. Average sports pages per week in the Völkische Beobachter.

1921	1,89	1930	0,23
1923	1,55	1931	0,69
1924	0,74	1932	0,86
1925	1,47	1933	10,32
1926	1,53	1934	16,43
1927	0,69	1935	11,92
1928	0,41	1936	22,89
1929	0,48		

The statements therein concerning top level sports were nega-tive and only occasionally neutral. This was due to the fact that there was no official party policy towards competitive sports, and that it used the news service of the völkisch and antisemitic Deutscher Turnerbund whenever it made an ideological statement relating to sports. This organisation which had seperated itself from the mainstream Turner organisation in 1889 because it prohi-bited jews from becoming members, drew its followers from the same Austrian and southern German tradition as many of the Nazis of the first hour (Becker 1980). Like many of the larger Deutsche Turnerschaft their members resented athletic specialisation, the prerequisite for successful international competition. They also resented international comparison with athletes from non-Germanic countries or at least with athletes from countries which had been on the winners' side in treaty of Versailles. Their student Turner movement dug up the running track of the famous Berlin Reichshochschule für Leibesübungen, the German National Institute for Sports, and planted oak trees in the spring of 1933 symboli-sing the end of athletic specialisation. They expected a return to Turnen in the sense of the Turnvater Jahn as preparation for able soldiers, strong and well versed in many athletic skills and not just in one. Coubertin had acknowledged this tradition of German Turnen. When he described the various roots of the natio-nal athletic movements he linked the German one only to warfare (Coubertin 1894; Krüger 1986a).

Commentating on the 1932 Olympic Games in Los Angeles, the Völkische Beobachter demanded the exclusion of jews and negroes from the Berlin Games (VB Aug.19, 1932). This worried the members of the International Olympic Committee (IOC) to such an extent that they asked their German member Karl Ritter von Halt who was a Nazi himself(Omgus 1985, 57ff.) to ask Hitler's position on the Olympics before he even took power (Nov. 6, 1932). Hitler gave a lukewarm statement confirming that he would not hinder the Olympic Games from taking place(Krüger 1972, 31).

The German Olympic movement was also worried how the Nazis
would handle elite sports. To maintain their formal independence
they set up a seperate non-profit organisation as organising
committee for the Games a week before the swearing in of Hitler
as Reichskanzler. After the Hitler take over the organising
committee presented to the secretary of the interior, responsible
for elite sports, the budget of the 1936 Games. The budget was
balanced at 5.5 millions RM. This was as late as July 1, 1933. It
expected the Reich to prefinance the organisation, the fixing of
some of the already existing stadia, and wanted to pay for all of
this by the ticket sales of the Games themselves. This meagre
balanced budget did not presuppose any monumental buildings, nor
a large organisation, but had a spartan approach to money. It did
not even attempt to ask for extra favours of the Reich but had
planned to receive almost 80 p.c. of the prefinancing from the
city of Berlin, which had been ably represented on the organising
committee by its mayor.

Inspite of the previous inner party opposition, inspite of the
scepticism by the German sports leaders, inspite of the utter un-
athletic appearance of Hitler, Goebbels, Göring, and the inner Nazi
circles, the Nazi movement absorbed elite sports and its greatest
international symbol, the Olympic Games. The Olympic movement was so
enthrilled by this complete state support that it honoured Leni
Riefenstahl's movies of the Berlin Games (Fest der Völker and Fest
der Schönheit) with the highest Olympic distinction, the Diplôme
Olympique du Mérite in 1938 thus stressing that it saw the Games just
like the German artistic director for whom this was a grandious show
of manliness, strength, and vigor, symbols of the rise of the new
Germany (Mandell 1971).

The following paper will try to explain how this change came about
in such a short time. It will be suggested that inspite of the
lengthy German tradition of highly organised sports which received
its first financial support from central government sources as early
as 1913 (Krüger 1982), it was not the German tradition but the
Italian fascist model which brought about this rapid shift. For this
it will be necessary to look at the situation in Italy prior to 1933
and in Germany to show that only the existence of an established,
powerful model can explain the speed and the proficiency with which
the situation in Germany was changed, generally accepted, and successful - more successful even than the Nazi sports leaders expected
themselves. They had prepared for a big propaganda machine, for the
splendid organisation - but were surprised themselves to win the
medal score - having hoped to place second to the US.

2. The situation in German sports. 1920 - 1932

After World War I the first democracy in Germany was characterised by
a multitude of subdivisions, polarisations, and atomisations in every
field of life. Parliament consisted of members from eleven parties
(and sometimes more), agitation ran high from left and right, street
fights took place between activists of all sides, political parties
maintained semi-military organisations to defend their political

rallies, elections took place with a high frequency as multi-party coalitions broke up on a fairly regular basis. Just like the political scene, sports was organised by many rivaling bodies. Most of them cooperated under the roof of the Deutsche Reichsausschuß für Leibesübungen (DRA) and in Olympic years the Deutsche Olympische Ausschuß (Krüger 1975a). The Deutsche Turnerschaft maintained, however, that it should actually be an umbrella organisation itself. In the Reinliche Scheidung it left the DRA to speak up for itself, maintaining an extremely conservative position and avoiding international competition (Becker 1984). The catholic sports organisation Deutsche Jugendkraft, the protestant Deutsche Eichenkreuz and the Jewish Makkabi Bund did have their own German championships in all sports, but generally cooperated under the DRA-roof. The socialist Deutsche Arbeiter-Turn- und Sportverband and the communist workers' sports organisation did neither cooperate with each other nor with the "bourgeois" sports organisations (Krüger and Riordan 1985). Physical activities of most of the para-military groups often called themselves sports as well(Bach 1981).

For the purpose of Olympic Games most sports organisations cooperated. The communist athletes even joined the teams, while the socialists had their own Games. Table 2 shows the relative strength of the various organisations for 1932.

Table 2. Membership of sports organisations in 1932

Deutsche Turnerschaft	1.574.000	members
Deutscher Turnerbund	112.000	"
Deutsche Jugendkraft	253.000	"
Eichenkreuz	265.000	"
Arbeiter-Turn-und Sportbund	515.000	"
Betriebssport	170.000	"
Kampfgemeinschaft für Rote Sport Einheit	200.000	"
Deutscher Fußballbund	935.000	"
Deutscher Schwimmverband	185.000	"
Deutsche Sportbehörde für Athletik	450.000	"
All DRA organisations	6.400.000	"
All workers' sports organis.	1.200.000	"

Under the leadership of Theodor Lewald(Krüger 1975b), former secretary of state for the ministery of interior, and with the professional help of the first full time sport administrator Carl Diem, the DRA developed into an umbrella organisation which worked for the interest of its members but leaving each one maximal autonomy. The joint efforts resulted in the creation of a physical education and sports academy, into the bill to put the space available for sports onto a unified basis (the law failed, but the guidelines were very useful), an increase of physical education classes in all schools, a national sports badge, creation of local and area sports coordinating bodies to speak with a unified voice with the authorities.

Ever since the parliamentary debate about the purpose of elite

sports and the financial support of the central government for the
organisation of the 1916 Olympic Games in Berlin, it was established
practice that elite sports received a subsidy for the purpose of
national representation (Krüger 1982). Prior to World War I this left
out the workers' sports organisations. After the war with a social
democratic government the workers' sports organisations participated
in the funding. In 1928, when the most money was spent for sports,
its organisations received 25.1 million RM, of which 1,5 million came
from the central government, 3,2 million from the states, 0,8 million
from the Prussian provinces, 2,1 million from the counties, and 17,5
million from the cities and communities. Of the 1,5 million from the
central government 100.000 RM were for workers's sports organisations
and 1,4 million for "bourgeois" organisations(Krüger 1975a, 46). In
addition to these subsidies for sport organisations and their projects, the authorities spent vast sums on the building of sport facilities. Thus the sporting infra-structure of Germany was comparatively good. This resulted in considerable athletic success.
When Germany was permitted to participate in the Olympic Games
for the first time after the World War I in Amsterdam in 1928, Germany placed second in the medal score behind the US, ahead of Finland, Sweden, and Italy. The depression hit Germany hard, resulting
in more interior upheaval, divisions, and political unrest than most
other countries. Politically, this prepared the path for the Nazis,
in sports this brought a lengthy discussion, whether under the circumstances it was feasible to participate in the Olympic Games of
Los Angeles at all - finally finishing 7th with a small team there.
During the Weimar Republic Germany was becoming more and more
involved in international sports organisations. Lewald and Ruperti
became members of the IOC in 1925, the isolation after the world war
was broken in most sports even before this date. In workers' sports
it never existed(Krüger and Riordan 1985). The first Workers Olympics
took place in Frankfurt. In 1931 the Olympic Games for 1936 were
given to Berlin and Garmisch-Partenkirchen.
Although the German sport organisations relied upon the state for
subsidies, voiced the desires of the state to gain even greater
subsidies (health, national prestige, Ersatz for the compulsory
national service which the treaty of Versailles had prohibited), and
tried to unify the efforts of the divided sports to speak with a
common voice, the different political, religious, and philosophical
groups all used the field of physical activity for yet another area
of debate and often bitter fighting.

3. Sport in Fascist Italy

After World War I the political and economic situation in Italy was
extremely chaotic. Benito Mussolini who had moved from the political
left to the leadership of the fascist right was asked by the Italian
King to form the new government after the fascist March on Rome. The
fascist government reduced the rights of parliament in 1922, reduced
the rights of the press, the trade unions, and abolished most civil
liberties. By 1926 the government could pass laws without asking the
consent of parliament. As Mussolini always had the support of the

Italian King his taking of power seemed to stay within the bounds of
legality. By a treaty with the Pope and the Catholic church the power
in catholic Italy was consolidated.

Mussolini himself was a very athletic man. He played actively a
number of sports, had himself frequently photographed as fencer,
rider, swimmer, skier. His image of the new Italian man was that of
an active patriot. "Magnanimity, courage, enthusiasm, vigour, readiness, and the nobility of purpose" were supposed to be aims of
fascist sport to bring the state back to Roman greatness within less
than one generation (Longostrevi and Mantovani 1931,xx).

The various counteracting sport organisations which showed a similar degree of inner rivalry as in Germany, cooperated for the Olympic
Games but did only slightly improve over their pre-war situation
until the fascist took over the organisation of sports by the state
itself. The position of Italy at Olympic Games is shown in table 3.

Table 3. Italy's place at Olympic Games

Year	Position
1900	7
1904	–
1908	9
1912	7
1920	7
1924	5
1928	5
1932	2
1936	3
1948	5
1952	5
1956	5

The drastic improvement was the direct result of the Carta dello
sport (Dec. 30, 1928) in which the sport organisations were "coordinated" in Rome. There were five agencies left which governed
sports:
- Comitato Olimpico Nazionale Italiano (CONI), responsible for all
elite sports. It was the roof for all sports federations, each responsible for one sport. The head of each federation was appointed by
the head of CONI, who himself was appointed by Mussolini as head of
state on proposition by the secretary general of the fascist party.
- Opera Nazionale Dopolavoro (OND), responsible for all low level
sport mainly organised on factory or pub level. It organised all
other sports of workers' leisure activities, including cultural
events and tourism.
- Opera Nazionale Balilla (ONB), responsible for all youth activities including sports up to the age of 18. Balilla was the nick-
name of the boy Gian Battista Perasso who was said to have started spontaneously the uprising in Genova against Austrian rule in
1746. Every child and youth who wanted to take part in any competitive sport had to be a member of the ONB.

- Gruppi Universitari Fascisti (GUF), responsible for all university students activities including sports. The GUF had already participated in the March on Rome and maintained their position as fascist elite organisation. They governed all student activities of which sports were only a minor part.
- Milizia Volontaria di Sicurezza Nazionale, responsible for paramilitary activities including sportlike exercises.

Only for CONI and its federations was sport the only activity, while for the other four sport ranged among their activities. This at first gave the greater leverage to the others as they had a powerbase within the party of a somewhat longer tradition. The CONI did catch up, however, as the fascist realized very soon that athletic success made the regime popular. For the "culture of consent"(De Grazia 1981) sport did play a major role.

The Carta dello Sport described precisely the competence of the various organisations, thus reducing the amount of rivalry and forcing each one to look at inner consolidation rather than expansion into areas which were already dominated by others. § 9 of the Carta ordered all sports federation to take office in Rome, to make sure that they could be better coordinated. 25 of 33 federations had their seat in various northern cities and moved into new quarters which were provided by the fascist party.

The differenciation between elite sport and low level sport did create further difficulties: Football was and still is Italy's sport number one. The football federation succeeded in maintaining control of all football, which meant that teams of the lowest leagues had to affiliate with a CONI club rather than with their dopolavoro group which often had recruited them. The OND therefore pushed volata, a selfcreated nine-a-side football-rugby mixture, which had received the name of classical Roman football. Although nobody knows which rules Roman football had, volata was supposedly the classical game. Achille Starace (1933, 48), head of Fascist Party propaganda, and from 1933 on head of CONI, characterised the game as "not identified with English degeneracy", with more "logical technique", more in accordance with "Italian temperament". On the other hand, the game could be played where football was not really possible, on poor pitches where the ball would bounce in any direction and in villages so small that one could not muster eleven a side. As the OND was solely responsible for this sport, it created the first Italian championships in 1930 with 44 teams, 1931 already 809 participated, 1932 - 513, 1933 - 444, then the championships were abolished again. With Starace as head of CONI and the Football World Cup in Italy the very year, it was not in the national interest to continue this sport with national exposure. As Italy won the World Cup, football became so strong nationally that volata was never established on championship level again.

All sports clubs continued under fascist rule with their normal program. The Carta dello sport did bring major shifs about in youth sports in that it required that all Italian youth had to be an active member ONB if they wanted to affiliate with a sport club. The balilla was formed at first as the youth organisation of the party but later transformed in the state youth. It was wearing uniforms and much of

151

its structure resembled the boy scouts. It did prepare for military service, however, and enstilled a strong patriotism using national symbols, medals, and much military discipline.

The balilla were subdivided into age groups each sporting a name which contained already the program: 6 through 8 years: Figli della Lupa (sons of the wolf, symbol for the new beginning in classical Roman tradition), 8-12 Balilla excursionisti (excursions in the same sense as in the boy scout movement), 12-14 years Balilla Moschettieri (musketeers), 14-18 years Avanguardisti (vanguard). With this program the physical and moral education was placed outside the responsibilities of the schools and the minister of education into the hands of an opera. Opera are foundations based on long tradition (some of the opere del duomo are of mediaeval origin). On this legal basis former organisations like the boy scouts could be coordinated under the same roof, without having to disband first.

The Opera Nazionale Dopolavoro (dopo lavoro = after working) was founded on May 1, 1925 as substitution for the dissolved workers' sports clubs which had been members in the Socialist Workers Sports International (Krüger/Riordan 1985). Although the dopolavoristi were supposed to be prepared as able soldiers for war (Ferretti 1928, 118ff.), most of them played boccia - hardly a war game. Under the roof of this opera many of the case del popolo could continue to exist. Any organisation could become a member of an opera without much of a legal problem. This way only functionaries on a provincial or national level had to be changed. Of course, the leaders of the socialist and communist parties, and trade union leaders, who had been active on grass root level were also excluded. But much of the structure was maintained which led to difficulties between the fascist party and the fascist trade unions once the actions which required a unified strength (1926-7 new apparatus to generate support, and economic battle, assistance effort under the slogan "reach out to the people", 1931-1934 connected with a membership drive, national defence against the sanctions 1935-1936) were no longer necessary. When the Italian Communists startes to follow the "popular front" policy of the Comintern in 1935, it was only logical to use the dopolavoro groups to try the "frontist" tacties.

Italy has had an Olympic Committee since 1906. It was represented by Count Palli (1894-1907) and the Duke of Andria Carafa (1894-1898) on the founding committee of the IOC. Afterwards it continued to send a fair amount of members, including General. C. Montu (1913-1939), Count Guglielmi (1920-1930), Count Bonacossa (1925-1953), Augusto Turati (1930-1931), Count Ravel (1932-1964), Giorgio Vaccaro (1939-1949). From this it can be seen that internationally nobody objected that fascists were sent, that they were fully integrated into the IOC, and that they stayed on, when the fascist regime was overthrown in 1943. Even the secretary general of the fascist party, Augusto Turati, who was also head of CONI from 1928-1930, could manage to become a member of the world's most exclusive club without any protest.

An interesting personality in this group is Count Bonacossa, who was the owner of the Gazetta dello sport, Italy's leading sports daily. He had opened his paper early for pro-fascist propaganda, his editor Lando Ferretti (1925-1928) became head of CONI. A sporting man himself, he was close to the line of Mussolini, who used the athletes as "ambassadors in track suits" (Bonacossa 1932).

The centralisation of sports, national investment into sports, the use of money from the football pools for basic sports like athletics, the taking over of a number of international events by Italy to make them a public affair in the country itself, helped to bring about success and enthusiasmm for top level sport. Bicycle racing has a long tradition in Italy. Radio transmissions of long distance races into the Italian provinces brought national fanatism into the most remote areas which were difficult to reach otherwise. In the professional bicycle world championship 1927 Alfredo Binda won, and three more Italians on the places 2 through 4 made the triumph complete. Binda also won in 1930 and Learco Guerra in 1931. This was the era of Italian success in bicycling, which led to many great names, up to the "Campionissimo", the legendary Fausto Coppi. The <u>Giro d'Italia</u> although started for the first time in 1909, received tremendous popularity through radio coverage and Italian success. Every year the Giro took a different route to bring complete ecstasy to the remotest parts of the country. For the same propaganda effect the fascists started the <u>Mille Miglia</u>, the world's longest motor-car race, performed on ordinary roads, all through Italy following the structure of the <u>Giro</u>. It demonstrated the Italian military ability to mobilise with the existing infra-structure. Italian triumphs on the roads made this race even more impressive. Between 1927 and 1939 only once (1931) a foreign car (<u>Mercedez</u>) could win, while the rest of the time <u>Alfa Romeo</u>, <u>Maserati</u>, <u>Fiat</u>, and <u>Ferrari</u> dominated. Only the French Bugatti team could occasionally keep up. When Germany wanted to get even after 1933, <u>Mercedez</u> hired an Italian team manager (Fagioli) to get the world's best.

The greatest international success was achieved in the 1932 Olympics at Los Angeles, when the so called "Mussolini Boys" won 12 gold, 12 silver, 11 bronce medals, 12 4th places, 6 5th, and 2 6th places, beating everybody but the favoured American team. Mussolini had visited the athletes himself in their training camp, he congratulated every winner by a personal cable. Inspite of the economic crisis the Italian team was large, well prepared, and well equiped. It was the most numerous European team (101 male, no female participants). More than every second athlete on the team placed, more than every third (2.7) won a medal; this was per head far better than the Americans (3.3 athletes per medal) and was only surpassed by Finland (1.7). The sending of the team was paid for by a special national lottery. This way, everybody was involved in sending the team. It helped to bring the country closer together. The identification of the Duce, people, and Italy could nowhere be sensed easier than in the national representation by the athletes.

The national fervor was increased even, when Primo Carnera won over Jack Sharkey the heavy weight crown of the world in professional boxing. From a national Italian point of view, the soccer world cup 1934 and 1938 were, however, the highlights of the fascist era. Italy had not participated in the first world cup in Uruguay in 1930, but it organised the world cup of 1934. During the competition there was a high degree of violence on and off the field, as clashes were also taken as very nationalistic encounters. Perhaps the worst game was played between Italy and Spain which ended in a 1 : 1 draw. When it had to be replayed under tournament rules, Spain had to replace 7 and Italy 4 injured players. In the final Italy beat Czechoslovakia in Rome. The 1938 World Cup tournament was held in France. Brazil played a violent game against Czechoslovakia in which 3 players were sent off the field and 3 others were hospitalised. Italy beat the Brazilians in the semi-final and then went on to retain the world title by defeating Hungary. In between, Italy retained its supremacy by winning the Olympic soccer tournament in Germany 1936, defeating Austria in the finals.

The success of the Italian athletes, amateurs and professionals, strengthened the position of the CONI in their rivalry against the other sports related organisations. The identification of the dopo-lavoro with the less strenuous activities, bocce, and the wine circles, improved the athletes role, as they could demonstrate Italian superiority on a world basis. Already 1924 Gazetta dello sport had written that "all nations have understood today, that Olympic Games are the true international expostions of the efficiency of the various races and of the degree of their civilisation" (Will Power 1924).

In true Roman fashion most of the Italians did, however, prefer to watch the circenses rather than to participate. This improved the position of the CONI as here at least the athletic ideal of the Duce was followed and the scandals were less obvious. In 1936 large scale frauds were discovered in the dopolavoro management, causing a major shift in the organisational structure. The membership of the organisations reached so far out, that there were more people actively involved in fascist mass leisure groups than in any other sector: 3.1 million members in dopolavoro (1936), 5.5 million in the balilla. This was an impressive apparatus in which the fascist party and the state overlapped, the groups competed for membership and national favours, thus insuring that eventually nobody who was interested in leisuretime activities at all, could avoid getting involved and being controlled by the fascists.

Only after 1936 the fascist propagandists repeatedly used the word "totalitarian" to characterise the fascist state, using as examples the centralisation under the immediate authority of the Duce of the Italian mass organisations and the rapid increase in its membership. This may have been already the case under German influence.

4. Sport in Nazi Germany

When the Nazis came to power in early 1933, they did not have any clear cut idea how to manage the leisure time activities of the population. As a fighting organisation they had spent so much time and effort into getting to power, that many of their aims in "minor" fields such as leisure and sport were not clearly defined. While for some organisations it was obvious who would continue to head them after 1933, for others it was not. Obviously Baldur von Schirach the NSDAP youth leader since 1930 would continue in the same position with increased possibilities as the party was now in power. Obviously the paramilitary SA would improve their role and position now that the party was in power, and claim all paramilitary exercise. Bruno

Malitz, a former sprinter and representative of the SA, was permitted
to write in the official Nationalsozialistische Bibliothek and later
in a book on the occasion of the Olympic Games:

Nationalsocialism can only be experienced in the SA. Man
by man, student and apprentice, preacher and bricklayer,
clerk and manager, all are in the brown shirt side by side. One
is helping the other. One man is supporting the other.
This is nationalsocialism. Only those who have passed through
this school, are permitted to be leaders. German sports can only
and shall only be led by SA-men as the true carriers of the
nationalsocialist spirit. Everything else can only be a passing
through stage (Malitz 1936, 260).

But the storm troopers of the SA did not have any organisational
grip on any of the sports fields. In 1932 the Nazi party decided
against a party sport organisation. The Reichsorganisationsleiter
Gregor Strasser was being asked whether the party should start to form
their own sports clubs and a regional or national sports organisation - yet another in the already atomised sports field. He said that
this was not feasible as it would take too long to have one which
would have better performances then the others already existing. If
the party came to power

we will have a sport Kommissar for all of Germany according to
the fascist model, who will give out the new guidelines
in the name of the Reichsleadership. He will dissolve all
clubs, associations, and federations which do not fulfill the
prerequisites and the physical, moral, and spiritual
conditions (May 25, 1932 BA Slg. Schumacher 275).

Yet for such an organisation there was no immediate choice as
leader. Just like Italy Germany had some factory sport in the Weimar republic sponsored by the employers for their employees. This
was mainly done to improve the health of the workers and thus their
efficiency. By 1933 this organisation had 175.000 members. It
became the basis for the German copy of the dopolavoro movement,
which at first was also called "Nach der Arbeit" (after work) before it received the name which included the program:"Kraft durch
Freude" (Strength through Joy). In the discussion about the reorgani-
sation of German sports in spring 1933 this could not have played a
major role, as it was too small. However, when the decision was taken
to follow the Italian model, the counterpart to dopolavoro was founded within the Deutsche Arbeitsfront, the work organisation, on
Nov. 27, 1933.
    In September 1932 a Reichskuratorium für Jugendertüchtigung had
been founded, in which the efforts of the Reichswehr, and all right
wing paramilitary organisations were combined to have the material
basis for regular paramilitary training in Wehrturnen. As the German
forces were permitted to have only 100.000 men, regular fitness and
military skill courses for male youth were in the interest of the army.
It had therefore supported the construction and maintance of 13
"people's sports schools" (Volkssportschulen) as early as 1924, to give

155

military basic training to those who wanted it. Now this was put on a broader less clandestine basis. General von Stülpnagel who was put in charge of the _Reichskuratorium_ died, however, shortly after the formation of the organisation. His successor was Franz Seldte, head of the _Stahlhelm_, the paramilitary organisation of the former participants in the world war, who became Minister for Public Works (_Reichsarbeitsminister_) in the first Hitler coalition government. The _Stahlhelm_ was, however, soon integrated into the larger SA, so that the _Stahlhelm_ stopped to be a powerful entity in itself. Its leader therefore could not attract the new responsibility for sports. In contrast to Switzerland where the minister of defense is responsible until our days for sports in the national interest, i.e. elite sport and paramilitary training the Reichswehr in Germany did never have this role. In Germany ever since the parliamentary debate of 1913 this was in the responsibility of the minister of the interior.

When Dr. Frick, who had run a NSDAP dominated government in the state of Thüringen for three years, became minister of the interior in 1933, it was obvious that he was strong enough not give up responsibilities which his newly acquired house had always had. Another minister became interested in top level sport, however. When three days after the swearing in of the new government Lewald had a short interview with Hitler concerning the realisation of the Olympic Games, Goebbels was present. Lewald, a former secretary of state for the minister of the interior, used the situation, assumed that the new minister was there, as the Olympic Games were considered a propaganda affair, and started to correspond right after the interview with Goebbels. In his note to the chancellery he summarised his wishes in five points:
- Hitler should take over the patronage of the National Olympic Committee,
- Hitler should publicly call upon the German youth to prepare for the Olympic Games in the national interest,
- the Reich should take over the guarantee of the 6 million RM to be paid back from the ticket sales,
- Goebbels should give the full support of the propaganda ministery,
- the chancellery should make an appointment for him with Frick, as responsible minister for sport (BA 43 II/729).

This interview took place soon after, so that when on April 1st, 1933 the Nazi press started to call for a change in leadership in the sport organisation (Lewald's father had been jewish, he was strongly associated with the Weimar Republic), he could complain to the chancellery that the press attacks were contrary to the favorable agreements between him, the chanceller, and the ministers of interior and of propaganda.

This fell in the time of the complete shake-up of the sports organisation when all interested parties started to get into the position to take over the responsibilities for sport. Who then were the intersted parties and what did they offer:
Dr. Frick wanted to keep the responsibility for sport, just like he did not like to give up any other responsibilities. In fact he rather wanted to strengthen his position. And sport was good public relation. On ministerial level nobody else had the apparatus and the

definite interst to get the responsibility. Although Franz Seldte's ministery was supposed to be enlarged as "work and youth training" he received the leadership over the Reichsarbeitsdienst (labour service). This included the responsibilities for the material of the Reichskuratorium. Neither minister had the personal interest to become head of sports, but both liked to keep or take this major responsibility into his office. The SA and the Hitler-Youth likewise wanted to increase their share of physical education.

On the other hand the struggle between the sports federations broke out again. Particularly the Turner movement used the possibilitiy to get even with the sports movement. It claimed that it has always been working in the best national interest for para-military youth education. Their president resigned immediately making room for his Nazi vice-president Edmund Neuendorff who attempted to "make the Deutsche Turnerschaft a third column of support side by side with Stahlhelm and SA" (Ueberhorst 1970, 70). Lewald resigned as head of the DRA but stayed on as head of the Olympic Committee and organising committee for the Berlin Games. The DRA did not have the will nor the strength to present a candidate of their own. Carl Diem, their secretary general, attempted to make himself Kommissar for sports, but he offered his services to the wrong ministery. With the help of his old club mate General von Reichenau (later on field marshal and a member of the IOC) he was accepted for the expansion of the Seldte ministery which never took place (Diem 1976, 137). Von Reichenau and the Reichswehr also offered Dr. Carl Krümmel, director of the sports school of the army in Wünstorf, who had participated in the Hitler coup of 1923. Krümmel, a former German 10.000 m champion, and editor of the best German language book on coaching for three decades (Krümmel 1930), was also proposed for the wrong ministery. Krümmel was considered later on and became head of all school physical education and physical educa-tion teacher training in the ministry of education (Ueberhorst 1976). As everybody was looking out of a Kommissar and not for another mini-ster of state, the NSDAP and the SA were trying hard to put their own men into the proper positions. Members of parliament, the party and the SA hierarchy wanted to get well paid jobs, and according to the political spoils system, the party bosses had to be recompensed.

Between April 1st and April 25th 1933 there were considerable acts of terror to "coordinate" people into the new order. In this revolutionary act the SA in Prussia received power as police deputies. Hans von Tschammer und Osten, the former head of the SA groups "Central" (i.e. Berlin und west of the city) from March 1st, 1932 trough April 1st 1933, by this became Kommissar for his police deputies in his area. He was in charge of somewhere between 40.000 and 50.000 storm troopers who are said to have killed over one hundred people. He was feared by the communist workers' sports movement as his storm troopers broke into the gymnasium of one of their clubs in Eisleben and killed four athletes, including a boy of thirteen, and injured many others. He justified this act of terror, by pointing out that the communist athletes were preparing a coup and that his storm troopers were acting in self defense (Pätzold and Weissbecker 1982, 210). When the terror wave was over and the Prussian police had been "coordinated" to follow Nazi orders, it was mandatory to reestablish the authority of the state, now the Nazi state, and thus to get rid of the appointed and a number of self-appointed _Kommissare._ Von Tschammer, who was also a member of parliament, was high on the list of those to recompense with a decent position. His experience in the SA, but also the way he had handled the communist workers' paramilitary sporting groups made him a number one choice for the new position of a _Reichssportkommissar_. This he could become within the ministery of the interior, which had to give him the proper compensation anyway, as it was also in charge of police activities. The Nazis could not be certain, that the communists and possibly some of the social democrats would not hit back. In such a case the communists workers' sports groups were considered the most dangerous. As it was planned to dissolve them, infiltration of the sports movement by former workers' sportmen had to be kept in mind. Somebody with blood on his hands, who could be considered a personified threat was therefore very useful at the top of the sports movement at the particular time.

Against such a candidate nobody else had a chance. People from within the sports movement who tried to put themselves into a position of availability, may have had the expertness and the name like world record holder Otto Peltzer (1955, 270) or the skill and the Nazi background like the former head of the swimming federation Hans Geisow (John 1986, 165), or the skill and the reputation (like the new leader of the Turners Edmund Neuendorff) (Ueberhorst 1970), but nobody had to trade something so valuable in the political deal. Von Tschammer also had another definite advantage: He did not have a plan. Although the SA had been permitted to use his land to build a rifle range, he did not have much of a sporting background. A world war officer who could no longer move his right hand due to a war injury, he knew little about sports. As he was to receive a position in the ministery of the interior responsible traditionally for sports in the national interest, it was usefull that he had his exams as interpreter for English and French.

He was appointed three days before the Nazis were to dissolve violently the trade unions. At this time it was feared that the unions might make a last stand. Von Tschammer immediately dissolved the workers' sports organisations - but he did not prohibit their athletes from doing sports. As about 20 per cent of those who were members of sports clubs belonged to the workers' sports organisa-tions, he did permit that they would become members of the general sports clubs on an individual basis. To avoid that the clubs would not be swallowed by the workers, none was permitted to take up more than 20 p.c. new members of these workers' sportsmen. Each of them had to have two affidavids affirming that they had not been "Marxists".That way the organisation of the workers' sportsmen was in fact dissolved. There were very few groups which could maintain their integrety as workers clubs throughout the 12 years of the Nazi era.

Although Hitler and Goebbels wanted to keep sports in the international field and thus use the Italian model of sports, there was still trouble ahead. Already on April 18 the New York Times carried the headline over the whole first sports page "1936 Olympic Games may be chancelled due to Germany's Campaign Against Jews". American sporting officials were quoted as feely "uneasy" and were quite certain that many teams would not go to Germany if Jews were not permitted to participate. The decision would be in the hands of the IOC having its regular annual meeting in Vienna in June. The New York Times did not leave it at that but asked the German Olympic officials. Carl Diem answered for the German Olympic Committee expressing "a mixture of shock and incredulity". He was also qouted saying that the German committee "stands squarely on the ground of the Olympic idea" he could, however, pledge only that "all athletes coming to Germany... (would be) greeted with open arms...irrespective of nationality or race." (NYT April 19, 1933, 21:6). This seemed to be widely expected, the problem appeared to be rather, whether Germany would permit its own jews to represent Germany in sports. Immediately after von Tschammer (whom the NY Times at first labeled "sport dictator") went into office he was asked to give his official position in the matter:"Chancellor Hitler has given full approval of holding the Olympic Games at Berlin. For us this means we are continuing our preparation of the Games and nothing untoward need be feared organizing them. What changes, especially in personal matters may happen later, cannot yet be stated, but in any case, foreign guests will be cordially welcome" (NYT May 1, 1933, 12:2). The continued opposition to the Games in Germany particularly in the American press kept the question open whether the Olympic Games were really to be held in Germany. This worried the German leadership. While the "coordinated" German press mentioned the IOC meeting in Vienna for the last time a month earlier on May 5, the issue made 9 times news in between for the New York Times, including twice front page (June 5 and 6). From this it may be concluded, that while it was not certain that the Olympic Games would really take place with a large international participation, the national _Turner_ way to organise physical activity was still considered as a possible alternative in case the Games would be taken away.

There was under the headline "Reich now says status of German Jews in next Olympics has not been settled" von Tschammer had learned his lesson. He had learned that the IOC considered its members as its ambassadors to Germany and would not permit that they lose influence. He therefore guaranteed that the organising committee would stay untouched. For the German team he came up with a new formula, claiming that the admission to the German Olympic team would not be based only on the candidates performances but also on their "general and moral fitness to represent Germany" (N.Y. Times May 29, 1933, 11:6).

This formula was mutually acceptable. The Olympic Charter did not permit discrimination on the basis of creed, colour, or religion. But the criteria for the selection of the actual team had always been in the hands of the national organisation. General criteria had always played a role. It is traditionally the way to establish the authority of the federations over their athletes.

There was a growing movement in the IOC to take the 1936 Olympic Games away from Berlin and to give them to Rome (N.Y. Times June 4, III, 1:4). From this proposal it can be seen, that the fascist way to run sports, was perfectly accepted by the IOC, it was the question of legal racial inequality which caused the trouble for Germany.

American IOC-member General Charles Hancock Sherrill, the inventor of the crouch start, and a former Ivy-League sprint champion, brought the situation to the point in Vienna and two years later again in a personal 90 minute interview with Hitler. In Vienna he explained that the way Germany put up her team was not an internal matter as "Olympic rules" were involved (N.Y. Times June 5, 1933, 1:3). Therefore the negotiating went on, until with the help of the German ambassy the German IOC-members could produce a cable by the interior ministery "that on principle German jews would not be excluded from the German team" (Mayer 1960, 138). This helped to calm down the international opposition. Now again the German press mentioned the Vienna meeting with its results favorable to the new regime.

Von Tschammer had learned that the fascist model was acceptable. He continued to build the German sport according to the model. It has to be kept in mind through, that as late as 1935 the alternative was still in everbody's mind - and the Turners were there to keep reminding that there was not only the international way but also the national.

When in fall 1935 there was a large international boycott movement towards the Olympic Games, it was again General Sherrill who tried to come up with a solution. He went straight to Hitler. He had a 90 minute interview for which there are lengthy minutes by the interpreter Paul Schmidt (PA 36 Bd. 1) and by the secretary of state in the chancellery Meissner (BA R43 II/729). Sherrill who had drawn up the Vienna agreement learned that Hitler knew nothing about it and discussed under the assumption that, of course, German jews were not permitted on the German team. When pressured by Sherrill, he exclaimed that he could not change his position, and that when a movement coming from the United States would boycott the Olympic Games, Germany herself would no longer participate in international sports. If the Olympic Committee would give the Games to another country, this would also not change his position. In that case pure German Olympic Games would be held in Berlin (PA 36 Bd 1, August 24, 1935). It can be safely assumed that this was the old position of the Reich in 1933, going the international way, but keeping the national alternative open.

While the other sports federations were soon dissolved and converted into sections of new umbrella organisation, the Deutsche Turnerschaft was kept in July 1933. Von Tschammer got himself appointed as their leader (Bernett 1983, 21) and kept the organisation alife to have also the national option. Only after the Olympic Winter Games of 1936 did the Turnerschaft dissolve itself for September 30, 1936. With this long range planning von Tschammer had smartly kept his second option open. With the Olympic Games in Berlin the last stage of following the carta dello sport was introduced. There was then no longer the need nor the possibility for any other alternatives.

5. German state sport

While the <u>carta dello sport</u> was one treaty which settled the
interrelation between the various bodies responsible for sport in
fascist Italy, von Tschammer set up a number of seperate agreements,
which in their entirety was its equivalent. The <u>Reichssport-Führer-
ring</u>, later the <u>Deutsche Reichsbund für Leibesübungen</u> (DRL) had the
same built-up and the same purpose as the CONI. It was responsible
for international sports, for elite sports within the country. It
assured that all sports leaders of seperate sports had their offices
in Berlin and followed orders. On November 27, 1933 the German <u>dopo-
lavoro</u> was founded. Von Tschammer became head of its sports section
(Bernett 1979). This form of personal union had taken place in Italy
as well at certain periods, e.g. the <u>carta dello sport</u> had been
passed when Augusto Turati had been leader of the CONI and of <u>dopo-
lavoro.</u> But while the division between elite, competitive sport and
non-competitive sport in Italy was relatively clear cut, the DRA had
such organisations like the <u>Turners</u> who had always had many members
with a non-competitive tradition. As <u>Kraft durch Freude</u> went into
this tradition, it attracted many disenchanted <u>Turners,</u> including
people like Neuendorff after he had resigned from the <u>Turner</u> leadership (Ueberhorst 1985).
  The <u>Hitler Jugend</u> was the party's youth organisation until 1935
when it became the state youth. At the same time the religious groups
were dissolved which meant that they were also no longer permitted to
practice sports. The agreement between the DRL and the HJ had several
stages, the most important one was passed at the opening day of the
Berlin Olympic Games. In this the sports clubs gave up all children
sports up to the age of 14. The club coaches had to become HJ-leaders
to continue to coach the youth now as part of the HJ-program. Only
for those who were members of the HJ, sport was possible. All 15 and
16 year old HJ-members were encouraged to participate in competitions. Von Tschammer was given an honorary HJ-rank and the responsibility for the HJ-sport. This way, the Italian model was followed with
slight differences in the age groups.
  As von Tschammer had come from the SA, it was only logical that
he would receive the responsibility for sports in this paramilitary
organisation. There was a close cooperation between the <u>Turnerschaft</u>
and the SA. On November 1, 1934 von Tschammer was promoted in the SA
and put in charge of all paramilitary sports. As the SA had lost
some of its importance in the Röhm coup, it put considerable emphasis
on sports to keep a major public role. 1936 Hitler gave the Nationalsozialistischen Kampfspiele, a Spartakiade - like national sports
festival, to the SA and made it responsible for the new Nürnberg
stadium with a capacity of 300.000. In a last treaty between DRL and
SA on January 21, 1938 the same seperation of paramilitary sport in
the SA plus the <u>Kampfspiele</u>, physical education and competitive sport
on the other side in the DRL - both under the leadership of the
<u>Reichssportführer</u>, as in Italy with the <u>milizia volontaria</u> and the
CONI took place.
  The NS-student organisation (NSDS) was responsible for the
physical training of all students. Compulsory sports was intro-

ty of von Tschammer. When a Reichsministery of education was
founded all school and university sports as well as physical
education teachers' training was coordinated in the office Carl
Krümmel was appointed for. The reopened Reichacademy for physical education was now a foundation of the ministers of the interior and of education with von Tschammer as president and Krümmel
as director (Bernett 1979b). The role of the NSDS was somewhat
different from the GUF, which remained an elite organisation
(Ostenc 1980, 320).

As can be seen the Nazi sport consisted like the Italian of
many conflicting organisations. They were coordinated in the
office of the Reichssportführer. The state took over more and
more charges which previously had been private. It was required
to do active service for the state in any of its organisations.
In 1934 von Tschammer explained:"Sports today are a matter of the
State" (v. Tschammer 1934, 387). When therefore the DRL was
converted in 1938 into the NSRL, a subsidiary of the Nazi-party,
a long process had come to an end. In this process there was
considerable competition between the variuos organisations to
reach many athletes, to prepare sports coaches and leaders, as
sports had become immensely popular. This competition was most
obvious after 1938 when SA, SS, Army, Airforce but also traditional sports clubs in the NSRL recruited potential athletes for the
1940 Olympics to show that their organisation had the highest
quality of men (Krüger 1975, 80).

The Italian model of state sports had been followed already by the
Yugoslav military government as early as 1929 (Radan 1984). It was
slightly changed, adopted to German needs, but served as a guideline
for the rapid falling into line of the German sports system from 1933
onward. In this model all had their place, no part was considerd
superior, with coordination agreements similar to the spirit of the
carta dello sport Nazi sport became so successful that still today it
is often considered the inventor of state sport, but it was only able
to bring to it the element of Prussian order. Particularly the
leaders of the DRA like von Halt were active in promoting the Italian
model, as for them it seemed to be the most rational way to achieve
the highest success (Krüger 1986). While the Turners wanted to avoid
international comparisons, the representatives of the athletic
federations wanted to win. So the monthly of the track and field
federation, later the track and field section of the DRL, praised the
Italian model in February 1933 and still in June (Start und Ziel,
1933, p.36; p.171).

As the Italians were the first to form a fascist government,
and as a number of constituent elements of the fascist movements
in Europa are very similar, one need not be surprised that sport
as a major vehicle for nationalism and prestige for the state and
the race was taken up by other fascist movements and developed
along the same lines (Nolte 1966, 66ff). They still serve as
guidelines for state sports today.

References

Bach, H. (1981) Volks- und Wehrsport in der Weimarer Republik, in Sportwissenschaft 11, 273-294.
Becker, H. (1980) Antisemitismus in der Deutschen Turnerschaft. Verlag H. Richarz, St. Augustin.
Becker, H. (1984) Die reinliche Scheidung. Versuch einer Trennung von Turnen und Sport in den Jahren 1921 - 1924, in Die Entwicklung der Turn- und Sportvereine (ed. A. Krüger), Forum für Sportgeschichte, Berlin, pp.118-130.
Beckmanns Sportlexikon (1933) Verlagsanstalt Otto Beckmann, Leipzig/ Wien.
Bernett, H. (1979a) Nationalsozialistischer Volkssport bei "Kraft durch Freude", in Stadion, 5, 89-146.
Bernett, H. (1979b) Wissenschaft und Weltanschauung - Sportlehrerausbildung im Dritten Reich, in Ursachen der Schulsportmisere in Deutschland (eds. A. Krüger and D. Niedlich), Arena Publications, London, pp. 32-44.
Bernett, H. (1983) Der Weg des Sports in die nationalsozialistische Diktatur. Verlag Hofmann, Schorndorf.
Bianda, R., Leone, G., Rossi, G. and Urso, A. (1983) Atleti in camicia nera. Lo sport nell' Italia di Mussolini. G. Volpe Editore, Roma.
Bonacossa, C. (1932) L'idea olimiopica e le vittorie degli ambasciatori a Los Angeles, in La Gazzetta dello Sport, October 5.
Buss, W. (1975) Die Entwicklung des deutschen Hochschulsports vom Beginn der Weimarer Republik bis zum Ende des NS-Staates. PhD.Diss. Göttingen.
Coubertin, P. de (1984) Le rétablissement des Jeux Olympiques. Revue de Paris, 1, 170-184.
Diem, C. (1976) Ein Leben für den Sport. Erinnerungen aus dem Nachlaß. A. Henn Verlag, Ratingen.
Fabrizio, F. (1976) Sport e fascismo. La politica sportiva del regime. 1924-1936. Guaraldi editore, Rimini-Firenze.
Ferretti, L. (1928) Il libro dello sport. Libreria del Littoro, Roma.
Grazia, V. de (1981) The culture of consent. Mass organization of leisure in fascist Italy. Cambridge University Press, Cambridge.
Hoffmann, P.G. and Breitmeyer, A. (eds., 1937) Sport und Staat. 2 vols., Verlag des Reichssportblattes, Berlin.
Joch, W. (1986) Zur Sportberichterstattung im Jahre 1933 am Beispiel von Wassersport und Der Leichtathlet, in Sport zwischen Eigenständigkeit und Fremdbestimmung (ed. G. Spitzer and D. Schmidt), P. Wegener Verlag, Bonn, pp. 171-192.
John, H.-G. (1986) Die Affäre Geisow und der Deutsche Schwimmverband - auf dem Wege ins Dritte Reich, in Sport zwischen Eigenständigkeit und Fremdbestimmung (eds. G. Spitzer and D. Schmidt), P. Wegener Verlag, Bonn, pp. 154-170.
Krüger, A. (1972) Die Olympischen Spiele 1936 und die Weltmeinung. Bartels & Wernitz, Berlin.
Krüger, A. (1975a) Sport und Politik. Vom Turnvater Jahn zum Staatsamateur. Fackelträger Verlag, Hannover.
Krüger, A. (1975b) Dr. Theodor Lewald. Sportführer ins Dritte Reich. Bartels & Wernitz, Berlin.

Bartels & Wernitz, Berlin.
Krüger, A. (1982a) Sport, State, and the Olympic Games. The origin of the notion of sport as a medium of political representation, in Proceedings 5th Canadian Symposium on the History of sport and physical education (ed. B. Kidd), University of Toronto, pp. 369-379.
Krüger, A. (1982b) Deutschland und die Olympische Bewegung. 1918-1945, in Geschichte der Leibesübungen (ed. H. Ueberhorst) vol. 3/2, pp. 1026-1047.
Krüger, A. (1985) Heute gehört uns Deutschland und morgen...? Das Ringen um den Sinn der Gleichschaltung im Sport in der ersten Jahreshälfte 1933, in Sportgeschichte: Traditionspflege und Wertewandel (eds. W. Buss and A. Krüger), Mecke Druck, Duderstadt, pp. 175-196.
Krüger, A. (1986a) De Coubertin and the Olympic Games as symbols of peace, in Sport and Politics (ed. G. Redmond), Human Kinetics Publisher, Champaign, Ill., pp. 193-200.
Krüger, A. (1986b) Sport im faschistischen Italien (1922-1933), in Sport zwischen Eigenständigkeit und Fremdbestimmung (ed. G. Spitzer and D. Schmidt), P. Wegener Verlag, Bonn, pp. 213-226.
Krüger, A. and Riordan, J. (1985) Der internationale Arbeitersport. Der Schlüssel zum Arbeitersport in 10 Ländern. Pahl-Rugenstein Verlag, Köln.
Krümmel, C. (1930) Athletik. Ein Handbuch der lebenswichtigen Leibesübungen. Lehmanns Verlag, München.
Longstrevi, P. and Montovani, G. (1931) Cultura Fisica d'ogni giorno. Salute-Forza-Linea-Sports. Ulrico Hoepli Editore, Milano.
Malitz, B. (1933) Die Leibesübungen in der nationalsozialistischen Idee (=NS-Bibliothek vol. 46). Eher, München.
Malitz, B. (1935) Die Leibesübungen in der nationalsozialistischen Weltanschauung, in Olympia 1936 und die Leibesübungen im nationalsozialistischen Staate (ed. F. Mildner).
Mandell, R.D. (1971) The Nazi Olympics. Macmillan Company, New York.
Mayer, O. (1960) A travers les anneaux olympiques. Pierre Cailler, Geneva.
Nolte, E. (1966) Die faschistischen Bewegungen. Deutscher Taschenbuch Verlag, München.
Office of Military Government for Germany (OMGUS) (1985) Ermittlungen gegen die Deutsche Bank 1946/1947. Greno Verlagsgesellschaft, Nördlingen.
Ostenc, M. (1980) L'éducation en Italie pendant le fascisme. Publications de la Sorbonne, Paris.
Pätzold, K. and Weissbecker, K. (1982) Hakenkreuz und Totenkopf. Die Partei des Verbrechens. Deutscher Verlag der Wissenschaften, Berlin.
Peltzer, O. (1955) Umkämpftes Leben. Sportjahre zwischen Nurmi und Zatopek. Verlag der Nation, Berlin.
Radan, Z. (1984) Sport und Politik in Jugoslavien, 1918 - 1941, in ICOSH Seminar, Sport und Politik, Sömarka, Norway.
Starace, A. (1933) L'opera nazionale dopolavoro. Panorami di vita fascista, collana edita sotto gli auspici del PNF, PNF, Roma.
Steinhöfer, D. (1973) Hans von Tschammer und Osten. Reichssportführer im Dritten Reich. Bartels & Wernitz, Berlin.

"Neuordnung" des deutschen Sports im Jahre 1933, in Sport zwischen Eigenständigkeit und Fremdbestimmung (ed. G. Spitzer and D. Schmidt), P. Wegener Verlag, Bonn, pp. 227-247.

Tschammer und Osten, H. von (1934) Sport eine Sache der Nation, in Nationalsozialistische Monatshefte 5, -.

Ueberhorst, H. (1970) Edmund Neuendorff. Turnführer ins Dritte Reich. Bartels & Wernitz, Berlin.

Ueberhorst, H. (1976) Carl Krümmel und die nationalsozialistische Leibeserziehung. Bartels & Wernitz, Berlin.

Ueberhorst, H. (1985) Ferdinand Goetz und Edmund Neuendorff - Wirkungsgeschichte zweier Sportführer, in Sportgeschichte: Traditionspflege und Wertewandel (eds. W. Buss and A. Krüger), Mecke, Duderstadt, pp. 147-160.

(1924) "Will Power", Problemi olimionici, in La Gazzetta dello Sport, August 15.

Archives

Bundesarchiv (Federal Archives), Koblenz (=BA).
Politisches Archiv des Auswärtigen Amtes (Political Archives of the Foreign Office), Bonn (=PA).

PHYSICAL CULTURE, NATIONALISM AND TECHNOLOGICAL IMPERATIVES

E.A. WRIGHT

Supply Teacher – Manchester LEA, Formerly: Department of Vocational
Education, The Polytechnic, Huddersfield.

Abstract
Education is conceived as political socialisation, within the modern
state which depends upon nationalistic sentiments and military-
economic expertise to maintain itself. Thus nationalism, and its
attendant, military/technological imperatives are products of modern
systems of education. Within this process of political socialisation,
"physical culture" is seen as the most effective aid. This area
includes physical activities which permeate particular societies, via
school systems, youth movements, industry and the armed forces.
These activities, moreover, range from relatively unstructured
physical situations – to highly organised sport, paramilitary
training and productive labour. The hierarchical affective and
anti-rational qualities of physical culture demand and impose the
enthusiasms, skills and disciplines demanded by militant, nationalistic ideologies. An historical outline of the conjunction of
physical culture and nationalism will conclude that the related
concepts of militarism/nationalism have come to subsume the concept
of economic warfare. This is a product of the technology which
gives motive power to nation states – obviating distinctions
between worker/soldier/athlete. Fascist Italy and Nazi Germany will
be used to explicate the rationale. Finally, present day societies
will be compared and contrasted, and consistent trends in the
development of nationalism, technological systems, and systems of
physical culture outlined.
Key words: Physical culture, Sport, Nationalism, Militarism,
Ideology, Technology, Collectivisation.

Introduction
Hence... rooting the national future in the national past – this is
what people ask its schools to do. The schools should tell the story
of its great men, victors as well as martyrs, who have formed the
state politically as well as culturally, of the great ideas of the
nation has contributed to civilisation, of the battles it has fought
for its survival and aggrandizement... (Ulich 1965).

For the purpose of this paper, education is convceived of as a
process of political socialisation, a far from modern construct, as
exemplified by Aristotle (1967a). This argument may be extended to
suggest that the state depends upon feelings of nationalism and
enough military–economic expertise to defend and extend itself. In
more recent times, the conjoining of nationalistic outlooks and
systems of education has become more overt. When Peschell (1967)
said: "The victory of the Prussians over Austrians was a victory of
the Prussian over the Austrian schoolmaster," and Von Moltke
(1967) averred: "The Prussian schoolmaster won the battle of Sadowa,"

they were merely emphasising that modern nationalism and its attendant military imperatives are the products of modern systems of
education.

Physical Culture
Within any particular system of education, certain curricular areas
are variously weighted in relation to their effectiveness as political
socialisers. Obvously, the study of the national language, and its
manifestations   as literature and histroy is a prime agent in this
process. My thesis is, however, that the part of the curriculum
which is most effective in calculating responses of an overtly nation-
alistic/militaristic nature, is that which goes under the titles of
sport and physical education, although interpreted on a far wider
spectrum than in contemporary British society, and for which I prefer
to use the term "physical culture." This term is widely used in
Eastern Europe. It includes physical activities in the school
system, youth movements, industry, the armed forces - indeed, society
as a whole. It encompasses a far wider range of activities than
those contained within the aegis of physical education/sport, as
understood in the United Kingdom today. This all-but global concept
ranges from relatively simple physical activities; taking in events,
displays and demonstrations of a physical-cultural nature; leading
into the spheres of highly structured sport and physical training;
reaching as far as para-military education, and even extending to
productive labour.
    I believe that the nationalistic/militaristic function of physical
culture is so immediate because of the instrinsic nature of physical
activities, which both demand and impose affective responses on the
sportsman, which are those traditionally expected of the soldier - the
so-called military virtues. At the same time, such activities generate "militant enthusiasm," which is all the more a potent force,
because of its unquestioning and basically anti-rational nature.
...militant enthusiasm is a specialised form of communal aggression...
All obstacles in its path become unimportant, the instinctive inhibit-
ions against hurting or killing one's fellows lose, unfortunately,
much of their power. Rational considerations, criticism, and all
reasonable arguments against the behaviour dictated by militant
enthusiasm are silenced by an amazing reversal of all values....
Men enjoy the feeling of absolute righteousness even when they
commit atrocities. Conceptual thought and moral responsibility are
at their lowest ebb. (Lorenz 1967)
    I would strongly maintain that the collective, anti-rational
aspects are central to most physical activities, and that such
activities can engender all the qualities considered desirable by
militant ideologies, and their nationalistic/militaristic aims.
Interrelated to these aimes are the concepts of elitism and hierarchy illustrated by Aristotle (1967b), when in questioning Plato's
blueprint for society, he speculated whether the ancient Cretan
custom of denying the right to carry arms, or to participate in
physical culture to the lower social classes, might be an effective
ploy in social control.

Historical Outline

Harris (1964) maintains that at one time all athletic competition was
a part of training for war. Moreover, he stated that

> "There are a few recorded instances of long–distance races run
> outside the stadium. The most famous of these was the Eleutheria
> at Plataea, a race in armour founded to commemorate the great
> victory over the Persians in 479 BC. The starting point was the
> trophy set up on the battlefield."

This orientation can be traced to the modern pentathalon, itself an
event specialised in by soldiers competing in the para–military
disciplines of riding, shooting, fencing, swimming and running.
Again, in the modern winter Olympics, the Biathlon alternates
vigorous bouts of cross–country skiing with rifle, target shooting,
the weapon being carried throughout the event.

Military values and physical culture have always been emphasised
in the training of elites. Plato (1960) expected his Guardians and
Auxiliaries to be prepared for their military tasks via physical
activities – "I mean a suitably simple physical training, concentrat-
ing particularly on training for war." This theme can be traced on
a historical continuum via Castiglione (1967), Machiavelli (1925),
Elyot (1966), and Milton (1963). Time and again, the importance of
riding is stressed, and indeed, Bronowski (1973) suggests that "warfare was created by the horse," and that: "The strategy of the mobile
herd depends upon manoeuvre,on rapid communication, and on practised
moves... The remnants of that remain in the war games that are still
played... War strategy is always regarded by those who win as a kind
of game."

The conjunction of physical culture and nationalism appears to have
reached its modern apogee in England. (Hiuzinga, 1970). McIntosh
(1963) traces what he calls "a specific function," in the production
of a managerial elite – trained on the sports field, with the battle-
field in mind. However, at the present, sport, physical training –
subsumed as physical culture, have moved on from a general preparation for war, through a specific function of elite–preparation and
beyond the process of achieving fitness from mass–mobilisation and
national, industrial development.

The relationship between physical culture and nationalism/
militarism is still real and cogent, but now the emphasis is more
upon the political and economic advantages which can accrue to one
particular nation or ideology. Indeed modern sport could well be
categorised as war in trackshoes. In prefiguring these views, Kipling
(1966) could describe war as "The Great Game," whilst General Von
Reichenau (1963), Hitler's representative on the committee of the
Olympic Games, stated that sport was a substitute for national
service, and Carl Diem could claim that "War is the noblest sport of
all."

Fascist Italy

Gentile (1929) who became Minister of Education after the Fascists assumed power, was totally immersed in the philosophy of Hegel and, therefore, saw the schools of Italy as seminaries of nationalism. "We affirm our belief that the State is not a system of hindrance and external juridicial controls... but an athical being... and capable of expanding ¸as a collective and yet individual will. The nation is that will...

The idealists who supported Gentile's reforms were, however, out-numbered by a majority who preferred the Futurist concept of educat-ion. This aimed to concentrate on the practical, at the cost of theory. Sport and the skills of industry were to be extolled, and education should be made to serve the ends of industry and militarism according to Lyttelton (1973). Eventually this orientation won the day, and when Bottai became head of the Ministry of National Educat-ion, he produced a blueprint for the future of Fascism – The School's Charter, which had three Key-stones – study, physical fitness and manual labour (Tannenbaum 1973).

The claims of the militant nation were bound to conflict with the interests of the Catholic church and, not surprisingly, these claims were explicitly stated by a nationalist senator.

"What would happen if in Italy alone the education of the young were directed exlusively to the conquest of the Kingdom of Heaven, during which time all other nations are equipping them-selves both mentally and militarily for physical conquest, for the acquisition of the material things of this earth?" (Jemolo 1960).

In pursuit of national goals, the Minister of Education announced that "every difference between the life of the citizen and the life of the soldier will be eliminated," and that "Our fine youth move-ments, our glorious army and the school will be joined intimately." (Tannenbaum 1973a). In a further strengthening of the equation between citizen and soldier, the Fascist Party planned to give each student a "Personal Book for the Evaluation of Physical Fitness" so that he could eventually be classified as either soldier or worker. Moreover, it was postulated that:

"Health and strength and discipline were more necessary than anything else to those who were to become soldiers and conquerers. Physical education was organised accordingly to a plan meant to give a regular scientific development of the body."

This plan entailed four distinct grades of training, for both sexes, from eight to eighteen, progressing on a continuum from relatively pure recreational type –movement activities, through games and competitions, into differing types of specialised calisthenics and athletics, with a continuing bias on collective physical culture. (Minio–Paluello (1946).

Certainly in the earlier stages of the regime, there were serious philosophical disagreements, as Tannenbaum (1973b) has outlined, about the place of sport, especially in the youth movements.

Ricci, supported by Mussolin frowned on purely competitive athletic events, which he disparagingly termed Campionismo. So much so that he even had swimming pools constructed which were ten centimetres short of Olympic standards, so that they could not be used for contests. Scorza agreed with this view and agreed to emphasise collective activities and team sports in the Young Fascists, justifying such a bias by asserting that "the regime has more need of fine tireless hikers, agile mountain climbers, and courageous sailors than perfect athletes".

Finer (1935) describes a vast march past of 15,000 athletes, watched by Mussolini. In a ceremony binding the young to the ideals of physical and national conquest, twenty-six olympic champions handed over rifles, each with the name of a former champion, killed in the war or revolution, inscribed upon it, to twenty-six of the junior youth movement. At this ceremony the Duce said:

> "You athletes of Italy have particular duties. You must be tenacious, chivalrous, daring. Remember that when you fight beyond our frontiers, to your muscles, and above all your spirits, is confided at that moment the honour and sporting prestige of the Nation. You must, therefore, put all your energy, all your will, to attaining the first place in all tests of the earth, the sea and the sky."

It is obvious that despite the dislike for Campionismo, the Fascists soon realised, as other idealogues did after them, the value of sporting triumphs on the international scene. Preti (1966) in his novel about a group of university fascists gives us a graphic description of how they felt having witnessed Nuvolari triumph at the Nurburgring in 1935.

> "The young men returned home with hearts swollen with national pride, more so than they had ever felt. Never before had they witnessed such a sporting spectacle. They were also warmed by the happiness of the Duce, who sent a congratulatory telegram to Nuvolari. Obviously, the regime regarded sporting contests as patriotic battles which must ever affirm the courage of Italy, revived under the symbols of the Littorio."

It can, therefore be seen that the regime understood the value of physical culture to the militant nation, and when the absorption of the Italian National Olympic Committee by the Fascist Party caused surpise in Italy and shock abroad, the secretary of the Party stated: "Since everything which is Italian is placed under the nation's flag, it was only logical that the sporting world should likewise be ranged under its shadow." (Salvemini 1936).

The range of activities offered in the After Work movement truly represented a manifestation of physical culture. Many of the options offered did not fit into traditional definitions of "Sport", but this in no way appeared to weaken the effect of the programme. The emphasis on collectivisation led to the organisational measures one might have expected from the Corporate state, and to some obvious bad taste. For instance, Italian tennis players had to wear the black shirt and give the Fascist salute at international matches – football was claimed as a native Italian invention, and administered via a tightly structured bureaucracy, including a chief referee in Rome with a gold whistle. Party Secretary Starace went even further and invented a game called Volata, said to epitomise the Fascist "style", and therefore, that of the nation. (Smith 1959)

Nazi Germany
To the Fascist worship of the nation state, the Nazis added the concept of race. Thus, to them, all culture was based on racial values, and nationality, or rather race, was contained in the blood. Kandel (1970) maintains that Nazi educational theories were securely based in German Romanticism, which found its home in extreme nationalism. The interests of the individual were to be subsumed in the corporate national whole, based securely on historical traditions, and given motive power by the disillusionment and sense of injustice generated after Versailles. Within this system, physical culture was given prime place, with Minister of Education, Rust, allotting five periods a week to the theory of the subject, with every afternoon, often up to six o' clock devoted to organised sport. (Ziemer 1941).

This emphasis had always as its prime motive that of nationalistic militarism. Indeed, as fas as Hitler was concerned, sport had a purely preparative function for war, and a propaganda one for politics as an extension of war by other means. Several incidents can be cited to illustrate the purely utilitarian concept of physical culture which he held. Speer (1970) describes how he approached Hitler in 1937 with the news that the projected stadium for the 1945 party rally did not meet Olympic standards. Hitler brushed this objection aside with the comment:

"No matter. In 1940 the Olympic Games will take place in Tokyo. But thereafter they will take place in Germany for all time to come, in this stadium. And then we will determine the measurements of the athletic field."

Again, at the 1936 Olympic Games, he at one time threatened to cancel them quite arbitrarily, until his box was made to match his own architectural standards. In 1942, in the drive for the oil-fields of the Caucasus, a group of mountain troops climbed Mount Elbrus and placed a swastika flag on the summit. Far from meeting Hitler's approval, this so enraged him that Speer remarked: "For hours he raged as if his entire plan of campaign had been ruined by this bit of sport."

Notwithstanding the motivation, the primacy of physical culture was institutionalised by law, as the following decree from Rust, the Minister of Education illustrates:

"To avoid confusion I decree that students who were hampered in attending lectures and exercises during the current term on account of the stronger claimes of athletics, Storm Trooper Sports, Labour Service, and national political training may not be rated as worse than other students, especially in the distribution of grades." (Wiener 1942).

Moreover, the ideal type to be produced by this programme was delineated by Hitler before the massed ranks of the Hitler Youth: "... In our eyes the German youth of the future must be slim and slender, swift as the greyhound, tough as leather, and hard as krupp Steel." (Noakes & Pridham 1974).

The main agent in the realisation of this ideal was the Hitler Youth, rather than the educational system per se. Kneller (1942) quotes the Reich Sport's Leader, Hans von Tschammer und Osten, who stated categorically: "Physical training is the highest service of the German to his native land... It is a means of the preservation and advancement of our race."

Therefore, in aggrandising the German state, to which all racial Germans had to belong, physical culture became completely militarised reaching its logical conclusion in the mock-battle - Gelandesport - described by Mann (1939) as "tactical exercises without arms." Again, at all times, this yen to warfare had an economic bias, as Beumelberg (1933), posited:

> "And now the Reich youth leadership and Labour Front call German working youth to a fresh and joyful battle. This will be no boring school hour, no scrambling for high marks, but a struggle as if fought on the battlefield - except that here it will be in the vocational sphere."

The factors of compulsion and collectivisation were, of course, central to the Nazi world view, where economic achievement was an adjunct to military conquest, whilst physical culture was a preparation and training ground for both sets of activities. The young had already been entrapped in the schools and youth movements, but it was still necessary to gather in the economically active adults and adolescents, so that through a collective appeal to patriotism and common purpose they would provide the economic foundation for military conquest. This, in fact, was achieved in the Strength through Joy organisation.

Conclusion

Betts (1953) sees a straightforward relationship between technological development and economic contributions to sport. However, there are other factors to consider, such as the birth of modern ideologies, the growth of consumerism, and a general move towards a destabilised mode of social organisation, as distinct from a homeostatic one. Modern ideologies such as Fascism, National Socialism, communism and capitalism are made possible to implement by modern technology, and so are, to that extent, the products of technological development. The essence of such creeds, if they are to be effective, is the production of mass-attitudes, skills, beliefs and values - above all the production of mass-man. Technology makes these aims possible, yet also needs their product to ensure its continuance, through its particular ideology.

The values of the consumer society were prefigured in the beliefs of the Futurists. Marinetti (1973) was obsessed with the worship of machinery and technical skills, engines of speed, death and warfare, together with the cult of the body and techniques of sport.

It is a world view wedded to the production and consumption – to making, using–up – perhaps even wasting, all in the service of yet more experimentation and production, and it demands a society which is never in stasis, but always in flux. Within such societies, physical culture is used as a form of social control, of social-isation and training of entire populations, for the needs of the technologically based, nation state, in production and consumption, in work as in warfare.

The concept of physical culture which rules in the communist, and much of the Third World is a product of technology. It is about achieving, refining, experimenting and, above all, winning. It does not exist of itself, but as part of a society, that it must serve, ideologically, educationally, economically and militarily. I would maintain that the thesis holds with regard to our own and other western societies.

Obviously, there is not the centralised control, evident in communist societies, within our own. However, the sponsorship, without which modern sporting forms with their mass–participation and lavish facilities and services, would fail to operate, originate from financial interest groups, most of which have an international nature. One might speculate that in our society, physical culture is being used by those who would propogate their own ideologies – in default of the existence of a militant national ideology. Without rigid central control, technology proliferates and sporting forms become more complex, using more of the machinery of technology, whilst science and experimentation become prime agents in this process.

Reference

Aristotle (1967a) The Politics, Harmondsworth, Penguin Books Ltd., pp 299–300.

Aristotle (1967b) op.cit., p66

Betts, J.R. (1953) The Technological Revolution and the Rise of Sport, 1850–1900. Mississip Valley Historical Review , XL, pp 231–256.

Beumelberg, W. (1933)Arbeit ist Zukunft : Ziele des deutschen Arbeitdienstes, Oldberg I.D. Gerhard Stalling, p66.

Bronowski, J. (1973) The Ascent of Man, Book Club Associates, pp 79–82

Castiglione, B. (1967) The Book of the Courtier, Harmondsworth, Penguin Books Ltd., pp 62–63.

Diem, C. (1963b) in Natan, A., Sport and Politics, in Sport, Culture and Society, (ed. J.W. Loy & G.S. Kenyon), London Collier–Macmillan Limited, p209.

Elyot, Sir Thomas, (1966) The Book Named the Govenor, London, Dent, p64.

Finer, H. (1935) Mussolini's Italy, London, Victor Gollanz Ltd., pp 403–404.

Gentile, G. (1929) in Schneider, H.W. & Clough, S.B., Making Fascists, Chicago: Illinois, University of Chicago Press, p85

Harris, H.A. (1964) Greek Athletes and Athletics, London, Hutchinson, pp 74–75

Huizinga, J. (1970)Homo Ludens, London Palladin, p223
Jemolo, A.C. (1960) Church and State in Italy: 1850-1950, Oxford,
  Basil Blackwood, pp 243-244
Kandel, I.L. (1970) The Making of Nazis, Westport, Connecticut,
  Greenwood Press, Publishers, pp 35-38.
Kipling R (1966) Kim, London, Macmillan, p209
Kneller, F.C. (1941) The Educational Philosophy of National
  Socialism, New Haven, Yale University Press, pp 154-155
Lorenz, K. (1967) On Aggression, London Methuen & Co. Ltd.pp231-232
Lyttelton, A. (1973) The Seizure of Power: Fascism in Italy,
  1919-1929, London Weidenfeld & Nicholson p406
Machiavelli, N. (1925) The Prince, London, Dent, p116
Mann, E. (1939) School for Barbarians, London, Lindsay Drummond p106
Marinetti, F.T. (1973) The Futurist Manifesto, in Italian Fascisms:
  From Pareto to Gentile, (ed. A Lyttelton) London
Jonathan Cape, pp 209-215
McIntosh, P.C. (1963) Sport in Society, London, G.A. Watts & Co.Ltd.
  p190
Milton, J. (1963) Areopagitica and of Education, London, Macmillan,
  pp107-109
Minio-Paluello, L. (1946) Education in Fascist Italy, London, Oxford
  University Press, pp129, 142, 179.
Noakes, J & Pridham, G. (1974) (eds) Documents on Nazism 1919-1945,
  London, Jonathan Cape, p.354
Peschell, (1967) Ausland, No.19, 17 July, 1866, in The Home Book of
  Quotations, ed. B Stevenson, New York, Dodd, Mead & Co, 10th
  Edition, pl 970.
Plato, (1960) The Republic, Harmondsworth, Penguin Books Ltd. p.146
Preti, L. (1966) Giovinezza, Giovinezza..., Arnaldo Mondadori,
  Editore, VIII Edizione, pp18-19.
Salvemini, G. (1936) Under the Axe of Fascism, London,
  Victor Gollancz Ltd., p364.
Scheibe, W. (1938) Aufgabe und Aufbau des Reicharbeitsdienstes,
  Leipzig, pp 19-21, 25.
Smith, D.M. (1959) Italy: A Modern History, Ann Arbor, University
  of Michigan Press, p 426. See also Finer, op. cit. p 488,
  Littleton, op. cit. p 402.
Tannenbaum, E.R. (1973a) Fascism in Italy: Society and Culture:
  1922-1945 London, Allen Lane, p 189
Tannenbaum (1973b), op. cit., p 185.
Ulrich, R. (1965) Education in Western Culture, New York, Harcourt
Brace & World, Inc., p8.
Von Moltke, (1967) Speech to the Reichstag, 16 Feb. 1874, in
  The Home Book of Quotations, ed. B. Stevenson, New York, Dodd,
  Mead & Company, 10th Edition, pl 970.
Von Reichenau, (1963a) in Natan, A., Sport and Politics, in Sport,
  Culture and Society, (ed. J.W. Loy & G.S. Kenyon) London, Collier
  Macmillan Limited, p 209.
Wiener, P.E. (1942) German with Tears, London, The Cresset Press,p.50
Ziemer, G. (1941) Education for Death. The Making of the Nazi,
  London, New York, Toronto, Oxford University Press, p 87.

Section II

Sociological Themes

RECREATION MANAGEMENT EDUCATION: SOCIAL CULTURAL AND RESEARCH
PERSPECTIVES

W.J. MURPHY: Department of Sport and Recreation Studies,
                   Liverpool Polytechnic.
J.J. SHUTTLEWORTH: Department of Physical Education and Recreation,
                   Brisbane Institute of Higher Education.

Abstract
The preparation of Recreation Management generalists has become a
major concern within the occupation, within certain academic
institutions and within certain government departments. Also, the
recent attempt to integrate recreation managers in the local
government sector has reinforced the need to examine and debate the
occupation of recreation manager and many other wider issues
associated with the occupation.
    The paper indicates the potential socio cultural impact of the
occupation by discussing selected salient aspects of the topic.
First, it considers recreation management as an academic field of
study. Secondly, the educative potential of recreation activities
is debated as a significant factor in emphasising the importance of
professional preparation. Finally, the paper identifies the role
of social research in investigating the occupation of recreation
manager.

Introduction

Examination of the growth and development of leisure time provision
in local government recreation delivery systems in the United
Kingdom, reveals sporadic, unstandardised and often unilateral
development (Murphy, 1982). Consequently the development of
general recreation management personnel within the system has also
experienced uneven progress.
    Client crisis reduction demands upon recreation managers varies
considerably because of the diffuse nature of the occupation and
the clientele. Chief among such demands are probably positive
health requirements and the expressive objective of self fulfilment
through recreative activity. While the presence of recreation
managers facilitates in many ways achievements related to such
values, their absence would not prevent those and similar
objectives from being attained. It is possible to rationalise the
existance of recreation managers however utilising three major
perspectives. First there is a conceptual rationale which derives
from the perceived values which society associates with play and
recreative activity together with the belief that contemporary

society provides leisure time for most of its members. Secondly there is an empirical rationale based on the statistical evidence of demand for organised recreation opportunity demonstrated by the large numbers of actual and potential participants. The third rationale relates to social values. It is concerned with the contribution that recreation management can make to the improvement of the quality of life for some individuals, particularly those in areas of social deprivation. However a lack of formally qualified general recreation managers has been evident and has attracted the attention of central government (Yates, 1978, 1984). Hopefully courses of preparation devised to ameliorate the situation will benefit from the combined efforts of practitioners and academics. Collaboration will facilitate the development of philosophies indicating practical and theoretical approaches to the broader social and cultural issues related to leisure and recreation and demonstrating educative qualities which can be recognised by educators, providers and consumers alike.

The subsequent sections of the paper consider firstly recreation management as a field of academic study; secondly, the more specific claim of physical reaction as an educative force and finally the role of social research in investigating the occupation of recreation manager.

Recreation Management Education

The study of recreation management within a specific structured and essentially vocational orientation has emerged very recently, and in company with other recently emerged fields of study is experiencing problems in adequately delineating its area of operation and in formulating a coherent rationale. A search for systematisation in recreation may be readily identified within the socio-cultural domain. Indigenous and exogenous influences upon the occupation may initiate a process of collective introspection in an attempt to define a rationale for its role within society. Concern for values may tend to persuade researchers within the sociocultural domain to support attempts at introspective professional analysis. Also, it is likely that recreation managers themselves, consciously or otherwise will indulge to some extent in the process of personal professional self analysis. It is appropriate, therefore, to investigate the search by recreation managers for systematisation since it is crucial to the basic assumption from which this discussion eminates.

Management education in institutions of further and higher education has traditionally adopted a generalised approach within the confines of a clearly highly defined framework of the discipline.

Recreation management, until little more than a decade ago, relied for educational courses upon two significantly different types of organisations. On the one hand it utilised the general management schools of further and higher education, and on the other hand the highly technical in service provision offered by the specialist Institutes. More appropriate courses have emerged in recent years however, but recreation management, although essentially vocational continues to draw upon a largely interdisciplinary body of knowledge, a fact which may contribute to conflict and dissonance which has been identified within the occupation group (Torkildsen, 1983; Murphy, 1982). It is not surprising therefore that one of the strongest recommendations of the Yates Committee (1984) is the amalgamation of the various factions within the occupation. The Committee also suggest that amalgamation will facilitate the implementation of an efficient educational policy.

The acquisition of academic knowledge at a theoretical and scholarly level should not be accepted as the sole or adequate objective for recreation managers. Responsibilities must be accepted as agents of change and as community 'catalysts'. In fact they should demonstrate the vocational utilitarian aspect advocated by entwistle (1970) and Rapaport (1975), Hitchin (1977), Atha (1979), Bevan (1979). Also, academic knowledge offered to complement practically acquired management expertise should utilise relevant aspects of contributory disciplines to examine the provision and administration of opportunity for leisure time activity and man's interaction with his environment in the pursuit of recreation while recognising possible significant social and cultural influences.

Thus, the study of leisure and recreation is essentially cross-disciplinary and ecumenical. It identifies with Bernstein's cocept of open education "not so much a subject as an idea - say topic centred interdisciplinary inquiry" (Bernstein, 1971, 167). It investigates the use of leisure time and the interactions of human behaviour, together with the leisure time opportunity which is available and its management. Study of recreation management therefore, reveals a potentially powerful agent of socialisation and education. Whether or not the specific field of physical recreation qualifies for similar status needs to be debated.

Educative properties of physical recreation

If recreation and its management are accepted as potential agents of change then an equally strong case may be put for including recreation as an educative force. Few people would deny the educative qualities associated with libraries and museums, drama groups and art and craft groups. Physical recreation, however, might not demand such spontaneous support. The Director General of UNESCO presented a persuasive case for recreation and sport as educative leisure time pursuits.

"Sport, which in its different forms accounts for so much of leisure time, can play a vital part in making it a factor for the full development of the human personality. But to do this, sport must not be viewed and practised merely as a means of whiling away time but as a definitely educational occupation. The term 'educational' here, which I use in its fullest and deepest sense should not cause surprise, and sport should play in adults leisure time the same formative and educational part as it does in the education of youth." (Maheu, 1964, p.4).

Maheu's statement fails to recognise variations in attitude or motive and does not consider alternative points of view. Nevertheless, it echoes well a concept of recreation which this paper attempts to postulate. The provision and management of recreation may make a positive contribution to the social and cultural enhancement of communities. Physical recreation as a choice of leisure time activity may encourage the development of personality outside of professional role function. Recognition of the attributes of physical recreation may engender direct conflict with and encourage a determined stand against passive commercial leisure, which may reduce man to the state of a simple leisure consumer.

"This is why the profession of the active leisure time leader must be recognised as a social necessity" (Lengrand, 1970).

The fundamental theory of the integrated development of the whole person is difficult to discount, even though sport and recreation have often been victims of narrow unremitting views which are sometimes hard to change. The situation appears to be improving since more people are in a position to take advantage of the benefits which accrue from physical recreation (Sports Council 1982). These benefits have also been recognised in the educational sense.

"To fight against the various forms of physical illiteracy is in fact one of the major objectives in life long learning" (Lengrand, 1970, 67). Groombridge, (1969) reinforces this point of view but develops the argument, maintaining that the field of physical recreation provides socially harmless, personally expressive actual experience as opposed to the arts where the experience, although valuable, is vacarious.

Recreation management in its broadest aspect employs cross disciplinary systems to structure a body of knowledge. This does not weaken the subject, its strength as a field of higher study is based upon the fact that it is an ecumenical and teleological discipline. It does, however, introduce the debate centred around the relative merits of pure and applied research related to the subject.

Recreation Management and Social Research

Pure and applied research are not mutually exclusive. However, applied research is sometimes accused of being inhibitive within the confines of the problem's frame of reference. Clarke & Clarke

(1970) indicate some of the dangers of applied research particularly in terms of the demand for immediate success in the solving of a problem and the evaluation of the worth of the research in light of a suitable solution being found. Although not intending to convey the impression that all research should be conducted in the confines of a formal laboratory, Clarke and Clarke contend that when the basic problems are solved the practical applications will follow naturally. Nevertheless, Goode and Hatte (1952, 39) indicate that provided the researcher designs his work within the scientific as well as the social problem framework, practical applied research permits the application of knowledge to concrete social problems.

The study of recreation management employing sociological methods within a socio cultural perspective relies upon an interpretive and directive function. The objective is to identify the social significance of an integral component of the leisure service delivery system in terms of personal identity and occupational role and status. Mindless empiricism and purely descriptive analysis of quantitative recreation activity data which dominated recreation research so noticeably for some years, generated marked scepticism in many observers, and indicates the potential dangers of certain methodologies. However, quantitative data describing recreation managers are currently so rare that justification may be found for establishing a data base from which to progress towards a more qualitative interpretation. A research rationale may thus recognise a structural-functional utilitarian perspective as well as the need for a qualitative, interpretive and formative perspective of a case study approach. That is, the utilitarian descriptive analysis of quantitative data in conjunction with the qualitative interpretation of recreation management within the wider social matrix.

"a quantitative study can provide a beginning that leads to progressual research in some depth....social explanation in this Weberian rather than structural mode consists of more than concommitant variation of statistical aggregates" (Kelly, 1980, 310).

Molyneux (1970) was not surprised to find an emphasis on the use of facilities in early recreation studies. Most of these studies have concentrated on catchment areas, modes of travel and socio-economic characteristics of the users themselves. Some have probed the capacity of the facility under varying forms of management (1970, 58). Little effort has been made however to investigate the managers and elicit their personal characteristics and attitudes. Preoccupation has been with the derivation of demographic and socio-economic characteristics of participants in particular activities. National, regional and local surveys have all demonstrated a close correlation between participants and certain key variables such as sex, age, marital status, income, education, occupation, car ownership, parenthood and family size, thus identifying specific groups of participants with pronounced activity relationships.

The result has been the proliferation of socio-demographic data related to participation and repeated matrices of activity preferences. It has produced what Roberts referred to as "a data mountain" (1980, 1). The validity of the data is not in doubt but some authors have questioned the pre-suppositions of surveys and voiced concern about interpretation of the data (Roberts, 1980, Bacon, 1980, Kelly, 1980). Roberts is critical of the lack of sociological input applied to the interpretation of the evidence gathered and the failure to build upon past achievement. He maintains that the data mountain or 'sociographic tradition' has been built substantially by non-sociologists since only recently (in the 1970's) have specifically sociological leisure studies emerged in Britain. With the general growth of sociology, however, there has been a tendency for certain sociologists to include the study of leisure with the more traditionally accepted parameters of social investigation.

The study of occupations is one of those traditional parameters. Thus, the study of recreation management provides the opportunity of compromise between two perspectives. It facilitates the investigation of an occupation which is inevitably influenced by recreation and leisure theories and concepts both intrinsically and in the context of the wider social structure dictated by the communities to be served.

Conclusion

Thus, the management of recreation opportunity should not be viewed narrowly as the manipulation of temporal and spacial demands by some consumers. Managers should be encouraged to accept the potentially broader contribution which they can make to the social and cultural environment. Their roles as agents of change, community catalysts or animateurs will be affected by the degree of systematisation, consensus and integration within the occupation. Common policies related to education, integration and research should form a basis for improved concensus within the inter-disciplinary subject area. As a prerequisite however, pure and applied researchers, academics and practitioners, teachers and coaches, generalist and specialist recreation managers all need to be reconciled within this emerging occupation.

References

Atha, B. (1979) "Recreation Management Training: If not B.E.C. or T.E.C., then what?" Parks and Recreation December.

Bacon, A.W. (1980) Social Planning; Research and the provision of leisure services. Centre for Leisure Studies, University of Salford.

Bernstein, B. (1971) "Open School Open Society" in Cosin et al (Eds). The School and Society. Oxford University/Routledge and Kegan Paul.

Bevan, R. (1979) "The Management of an Integrated Leisure Service Department". Proceeding of Seminar: Leisure into 80's. A.R.M.

Clarke, D.H. and Clarke, H.H. (1970) Research Processes in Physicsal Education, Recreation and Health. N.J. Prentice Hall Inc.

Entwistle, H. (1970) Education, Work and Leisure. Routledge and Kegan Paul.

Goode, W.J. and Hatte (1952) Methods in Social Research. N.Y. Mcgraw-Hill.

Groombridge, B. (1969) "Sport" Convergence Vol. 11. No.4.

Hitchen, H.T. (1977) "Recreation Management Training" Baths Service May/June.

Kelly, J.R. (1980) "Leisure and Quality: Beyond the qualitative barrier in research." in Goodale, T.L. and Witt, P.A. (Eds). Recreation and Leisure: Issues in an era of change. State College Pennsylvannia. Venture Publishing.

Lengrand, P. (1970) An Introduction to lifelong learning. UNESCO.

Maheu R. (1964) "Message by Mr. Rene Maheu" in I.C.S.P.E. Declaratin of Sport. Paris, UNESCO.

Molyneux, D.D. (1970) "A Framework for Recreation Research" in Burton, T.L. Recreation Research and Planning. George Allen and Unwin.

Murphy, W.J. (1982) Recreation Managers: The Study of an Emerging Occupation. Unpublished PhD Thesis, University of Salford.

Rapoport, R., Rapoport, R. and Strelitz, Z. (1975) Leisure and the Family Life Cycle. Routledge and Kegan Paul.

Roberts, K. (1980) Sociology and Leisure Research. Centre for Leisure Studies, University of Salford.

Shuttleworth, J.J. (1975) Community Education and Recreation in England and Wales: The Derivation of a General Approach. Unpublished PhD Thesis, University of Alberta.

Torkildsen, G. (1983) Leisure and Recreation Management. E. and F.N. Spon.

Yates, A. Chairman (1978) Recreation Management Training Committee: Interim Report. Crown copyright, July.

Yates, A. Chairman (1984) Recreation Management Committee: Final Report. Crown copyright.

RECREATION DEVELOPMENT IN GLASGOW
AN OVERVIEW

W.B. ATKINSON
City of Glasgow, Parks and Recreation

Abstract
The City of Glasgow reflects many of the difficulties and
aspirations of a proud community having come through the
development of an Internationally acknowledged growth from rural
development built upon the River Clyde to the use of that great
resource as the springboard for its industralisation.   The
subsequent de-industrialisation;   an awakening of community pride,
a political, commercial and professional commitment to ensure that
not only will Glasgow survive, but will, through its many
activities, not least of which will be its sport and recreation
developments, demonstrate that it can be an International leader in
creating a diverse range of opportunities for its citizens.   Such
opportunities have their roots in a healthier, caring society and
it is the purpose of this paper to demonstrate through the
historical perspectives, and the planned programmes for the future,
how Glasgow is indeed Miles Better!

Key Words Community,   Industrialisation,   Recreation Development,
Planned Programming.

1 **Introduction**
Glasgow has a population of 744,000 distributed over an area of
approximately 90 square miles.   However, it is projected that the
population will reduce to 709,000 by 1991, and the significant
changes that will take place are as follows:

Population Structure

This change in population will play a major role in determining the
type of facilities to be provided over the next 5/10 years as there
are very significant changes in the traditionally recognised
performance groups
10 year - 24 years of age - 28% reduction represented by an actual
population sector drop of 41,000

25 year - 39 years of age - 15% increase represented by an actual
population sector increase of 23,000

In addition to the resident population the City has a fast developing visitor and tourist business, and therefore it is towards its residents and visitors alike that the sport and recreation provision is aimed, based on three particular programmes through its Recreation Plan:

      (a) Facility Development
      (b) Sport and Recreation Programmes
      (c) Major Event Promotions

It is these three matters that are to be developed in this paper

2 Facility Development

2.1 The History
It can be said that the history of Glasgow is encapsulated within the history of Glasgow Green, its most famous parkland near to the heart of the City and it certainly reflects the real heart of Glasgow and its people.

From its early days 800 years ago when it was used for common grazing to the present day when Glasgow's most recent sports development, the Sports Medicine Centre, was opened in early 1986, the "Green" has been the inspiration for inovative sport and recreation development.

2.2 The Review
In 1980 the City amalgamated its Parks and Baths Departments to create the new Department of Parks and Recreation with a very clear brief to re-align its policy objectives in accordance with the Council's Corporate Plan. Its new role was to develop and promote the active and passive recreational and amenity opportunities for residents and visitors to the City using all of its indoor and outdoor resources.

2.3 Existing and Potential Resources
The City recognises that whilst it took a major step forward almost 100 years ago in providing a substantial swimming pool provision and again in the 1960's with the introduction of Community sports halls and new swimming pools, the next two decades represented a standstill position. This, at a time when the demand for leisure facilities was expanding has created a major pressure on the Council to undertake upgrading work and the addition of exciting, modern facilities, able to meet the aspirations of todays leisure orientated communities.

2.3/Existing and Potential Resources

To briefly summarise the Councils provision, the following sports and recreation facilities are operated:

Swimming Pools	11
Mixed Wet and Dry Sports Centres	2
Major outdoor Sports Centres	2
Dry Sports Centres	4
Childrens Recreation Centres	14
Bowling greens	61
9 Hole Golf Courses	4
18 Hole Golf Courses	3
Tennis Courts	82
Boating Ponds	10
Putting Greens	17
Football Pitches	168

2.4 The Cost

To support this structure, of provision requires an increasing commitment from the Councils Capital and Revenue resources, and through the Recreation Plan the level of allocation is currently being assessed.

In terms of Capital investment, to simply refurbish the existing indoor wet and dry facilities requires an expenditure of approximately £5 million.

This must be set in the context of the present level of use and current level of annual subsidy that is incurred to support such services.

In Glasgow, the level of subsidy is much the same as the annual level ie. 80%. In other words for every 100p spent providing a service, only 20p income is received.

2.5 The Demand

The above level of subsidy, related directly to a level of underutilisation clearly indicates that our potential users are indeed "voting with their feet" and choosing other forms of leisure time activity.

At first glance this is not an unusual situation considering that many facilities require major improvements. However, recent studies in the City indicate that whilst there may be a level of under-use, there is a theoretical requirement, based on the population structure, for an additional:

90 Sports Halls
4 Swimming Pools

2.5/The Demand
The answer is coming through very clearly from our users that they
are not prepared to accept a low quality of provision even if it
means that we have to concentrate our resources at fewer locations
but those to be of a higher quality of service, meeting the
aspirations of our users which is fueled by the opportunities they
see being provided in other cities.

2.6 **The Opportunities**
Glasgow faces the unenviable task, not dissimilar to many major
industrial cities of managing many outdated facilities, with a
decreasing user demand and yet having to satisfy political
requirements to maintain a level of service that the public has
come to expect, almost at whatever cost and quality of service.

However, the solutions are never simple and must not be seen as a
typical compromise, but rather an extremely pragmatic approach to a
deep seated problem requiring extensive financial and management
resources.

Whilst the theoretical requirements have been identified, the needs
have been used as a guide and no more. The realities of limited
finance from the public and private sector for inner city provision
has determined an integrated approach utilising all possible
resources.

> a. **Existing Facilities**
> A detailed physical assessment has been made of all
> buildings currently in use together with a review
> of the service being provided, but more
> importantly, their potential for development to
> meet future needs. During 1986/87 £1.53 million
> has been directed to:
>
> Major repairs to 4 swimming pools
> Conversion of 2 swimming pools to leisure pools
>
> b. **Joint-Use with Education Authority.**
> Following extensive discussions with the Regional
> Education Authority three very significant joint
> ventures will be implemented during 1986/87 to
> ensure that facilities operated by both Authorities
> are fully available for educational and public use
> with virtually no restrictions on public access
> during non-school times.

b./Joint-Use with Education Authority.
This represents a very significant step forward whereby the City recreation authority will manage these facilities for educational and public use with costs being shared in relation to the proportion of time given to each authority. This has ensured full use of public resources with almost no additional capital resources required, but still adding to the range of provision available to the public.

c. **Conversion of Buildings**
Under this simple heading rests the Council's most ambitious recreation project. The Internationally known Kelvin Hall is being transformed into a Sports Complex and Museum of Transport. The sports areas will include a 200m indoor running track and two major sports halls equivalent to a 5 court sports hall provision, together with all of the supportive activities expected of an International Sports Centre. The project cost is £5.5 million and it has been estimated that the sports area alone as a new build facility would cost in the order of £12 million. Again, a very high value for money project using all resources available to the Council, including major financial support from the Scottish Sports Council, and equally importantly a joint venture with Glasgow University in terms of capital investment and a 25 year commitment to joint revenue funding - a unique example of co-operation between all leisure agencies.

d. **Community Management**
The Council has taken a decisive step forward in devolving its decision-making process to more accurately reflect community aspirations, and this is very much apparent in the management of facilities by community groups. The recreation service is actively transferring facilities to responsible groups, be it tennis courts, bowling greens, or community recreation centres.

It is of course quite clear that after many years of management by the authorities, it is wholly unreasonable to expect such groups to operate unsupported, at least at the outset.

d./Community Management

The Council provides a range of support relative to each community's needs, such as recreational/administrative/technical advice; financial grant aid; physical repairs to buildings, until such time as the group can be self supportive. This timescale can range from a matter of months to a long term agreement on limited financial support and ranges from a sports centre in the special initiative area of Drumchapel to the City of Glasgow Swimming Club.

e. **New Build Projects**

However well one attempts to make better use of people or buildings, the time inevitably comes when new build is the only realistic solution. This decision has clearly been taken in Glasgow and during 1985 and 1986 three very important additions are being made:

Alexandra Sports Hall   –   £270,000
A simple but vitally important local sports hall directed at community use.

Crownpoint Sports Park   –   £2,200,000
The most significant Scottish outdoor recreation development including a polymeric running track and similarly surfaced pitches for a variety of team sports to operate in conjunction with a joint-use venture with the education authority.

Pollok Leisure Pool   –   £3,400,000
The first leisure pool for the city, including flume; wave machine; catering and bar facilities. In conjunction with competitive swimming facilities it is predicted that this will be an admirable complement to reflect the demand for fun orientated water sports provision and will be an indicator for future demand by the public.

f. **Joint Ventures**

The opportunities for shared developments with the private sector are now beginning to emerge as a real possibility to overcome the local authority's difficulties in raising capital funding. In Glasgow this has been successful in respect of the new Scottish Exhibition Centre opened in 1985. Additionally the City is discussing the possibility of jointly funding a sports development with a long term management agreement. The City plays host to the 1988 National Garden Festival with substantial financial co-operation from trade, commerce and industry. The lead has now been taken and it is for recreation developers and managers to capitalise on the opportunities now available to us. It is now in our hands to grasp the initiative.

g. **Private Sector Investment**

Whilst joint ventures are being developed, the private sector is also indentifying those activities with a potential good return on capital and in Glasgow this is certainly happening. As local authority managers we can learn much from this market targeting and segmentation. We can learn from more positive attitudes to the needs of the customer. If we fail to respond to this challenge and indeed the opportunities for co-operation, we shall find the more profitable areas of our service being drawn away from us, and being left with the most expensive, underused activities, on a downward spiral of use and acceptability. The private developments in Glasgow include a new ice rink opened in 1985, inumerable health and fitness centres and a projected water theme indoor centre.

These opportunities briefly summarise some of the routes along which the recreation service is progressing. These have to be flexible, and as managers we must however be aware of the capital cost of development and the need to respond to changing aspirations and expectations of the customers.

3 Sport and Recreation Development Programmes

3.1 The Development Opportunities

Within the context of the Recreation Plan it is clearly recognised that the development of the built facilities is but one facet of the service provision. In some ways, the capital funding is seen as the "easiest" part of the programme with the long term development and promotional activities the most difficult to sustain over many years.

Whilst this programme of sport and recreation development can be the most difficult, it is undoubtedly the most satisfying in seeing the full spectrum of age and ability performing and achieving their own goals and targets. It is this which is the essence of leisure development in its broadest sense - personal satisfaction and achievement.

This element of the paper will describe the activities currently being pursued in Glasgow to create the opportunity for increased participation.

3.2 The Community Response

Glasgow has long had a tradition of self help and this is well demonstrated through the multitude of Sports Clubs operating in the City, ranging from street league football groups to Internationally recognised clubs encompassing athletics; hockey; swimming and many more besides. The community club resource is there, but how to harness this untapped source of skill and talent and ensure that it is applied to the expansion of sport in the City?

a. Glasgow Sports Promotion Council

Twelve years ago the city recognised that as part of the structure of sport participation and spectator needs, it was necessary to create an environment in Glasgow, together with financial support, to encourage the promotion of International events. The Council consists of lay members of the community who have a special contribution to make to this activity, together with elected members of the District Council and is supported by full time staff to seek out and promote major events in the city.

b. **Sports Council for Glasgow**
   This more recent development acknowledges the collaboration necessary between all local sports clubs in the city to provide a forum for the development and promotion of a sports lobby and co-operation between all sports agencies operating in Glasgow. It is a democratically elected body, and whilst having limited funds, has an increasing degree of influence on the development of sport. The most encouraging development is seen in the cross-fertilisation of initiatives between totally different sports in respect of:

   Sports Injuries
   Club Administration
   Coaching Programmes
   Equipment Hire

Having positively encouraged the development of international and local sports initiatives, side by side with facility development, it is clearly necessary to ensure that the individual sport programmes run parallel with such actions.

3.3 **The Development Programme**
To support the District Council facilities as well as encouraging community groups and clubs, three significant programmes of action are being pursued by facility management staff throughout the city, together with a unique recreation development team of 15 staff. The staff involved have clear objectives in satisfying customer requirements and where this is not immediately possible, develop opportunities for improved satisfaction using all resources available, be this on an in-house basis or by co-operation with other agencies.

   a. **Increased use of Council Facilities**
      As indicated previously, the Council operates a very significant range of facilities and the initial objective is to ensure more extensive use of these sports areas by as wide a cross section of the community as possible. It is recognised however, that manpower and financial resources are not unlimited and to make significant advances, segmentation will be necessary with the identification of:

      Target sports
      Target groups
      Target geographical areas

192

Target sports have been almost "self identified" as a result of significant co-operation with, and demand by, local sports groups, specifically:- gymnastics; basketball; table tennis and football. However, a more considered, structured approach is now being promoted, particularly in co-operation with the Scottish Sports Councils re-launched Actionsport Programme as part of an extensively funded Manpower Services Commission project. Target Groups are related closely to National Campaigns to ensure maximum publicity and integration. Over recent years this has included Women in Sport; 50+ Campaign; Disabled in Sport and more recently the Ever Thought of Sport promotion specifically aimed towards the transitional period between the school environment and the work, or sadly in many cases, the enforced leisure environment. In each case, these are progressed as on-going programmes.

Target Geographical Areas relates directly to the Council's Priority Areas of which there are six in Glasgow, although two, namely Easterhouse and Drumchapel have special initiative area status.

It is the objective, wherever possible, to have the Target groupings running parallel with each other to maximise the effort by all agencies working within the City.

b. Increased co-operation between agencies. Whilst at first glance the resources for development are limited, a closer examination shows that by co-operation between the Council's recreation service and the two wings of education, namely mainstream education and the community education service, a major improvement in service delivery can be achieved. I am glad to report that this is now in a very active state, through the development of shared use of facilities, allowing more extensive public access, but also the integrated development of coaching programmes and the "Bridging the Gap" scheme after school.

c. Increased support to local sports organisations. The encouragement of self-help schemes is perhaps the area of greatest advancement over the last 3 years, with a major expansion of support to local clubs. This has taken the form of an increase of the activities of the Sports Council for Glasgow by giving technical and administrative support to their endeavours, and a fundamental involvement by that Council in the financial grant aid scheme. The scheme has expanded from offering £4,000 per annum 3 years ago to a position where £150,000 is available annually, covering Capital grants; Talented Sports Performers Awards; Awards for Coaching; Disabled groups and Specialised equipment purchase.

4 Major Event Promotions

4.1 The City Promotions

The District Council and the Glasgow Sports Promotion Council have developed exciting attitudes to the promotion of sporting events in the City. Such promotions are seen to have two contributions to make to the development of Glasgow.

The first is in support of its drive to build on the reputation of the City whilst at the same time recognising that the industrial base of Scotland, and Glasgow in particular, has undergone a radical transformation. The development of the City as a tourist attraction in itself, as well as being a sound base for other tourist opportunities in Scotland, has seen the financial support for events increase rapidly, in direct relationship with the recognition of the high level of publicity this brings to the City.

This is clearly demonstrated in events such as:

Glasgow Marathon - with well over 11,000 participants in the 1985 event, this is now clearly in the top three of its kind in the world, and has brought a level of prestige to Glasgow that would have been impossible through standard marketing activities.

Kellogs Inter-City Cycling - part of a National circuit of road racing around City centres, this achieves prime time, live television coverage.

World Silver Broom - this most prestigious ice curling event was hosted by Glasgow in 1985 with International television coverage as well as bringing more than 2,500 relatively long stay visitors to the City, so complementing the hotel trade expansion.

Kodak 10 Kilometre Championship – first hosted in March 1986 as part of a national circuit of events, this included the Scottish 10K championships with almost 2,500 participants from the fun runners to the peak performance athletes.

World Netball Tournament – this will be hosted by Glasgow in 1987 at its new Crownpoint Sportspark and will include entries from 20 nations involving 400 participants and 2-4,000 specators on each of the twelve days of the tournament.

With the development of the Kelvin Hall, the opportunities to use the 5,000 seat athletic arena from 1988 onwards are almost endless and advances are now being promoted to secure events not previously seen in the United Kingdom.

The second element of importance in the promotion of such events is their relationship with the sports development programmes. This will ensure clear opportunities for performers to develop from the bottom rung of achievement through to the pinacle of success, all within Glasgow.

5 Summary

It is difficult to summarise what has had to be a brief excursion through the development of sport and recreation in Glasgow, and it would not do justice to the effort and committment given by Councillors, officials, sporting groups, community organisations, and perhaps above all, the individual who simply sets his or her own goals.

It is perhaps best summed up in Glasgow's promotional initiative entitled "Glasgow's Miles Better". Glasgow is indisputably better than it has been, for residents and visitors alike, and I leave it to your own judgement, ladies and gentlemen, as to whether it has created better opportunities than other Cities, but in any event I commend it to you as a better place to live and work.

SOCIAL AREA INFLUENCES ON SPORTS CENTRE USE: AN INVESTIGATION OF THE
ACORN METHOD OF SOCIAL AREA CLASSIFICATION

A.M. NEVILL and C. JENKINS
Department of Physical Education and Sports Science, University of
Birmingham

Abstract
The ACORN method of social area classification was used to investigate the influence of the socio-economic and demographic characteristics of residential neighbourhoods and site location on sports
centre take-up. Seven dual-use sports centres in Wolverhampton and
one large, centrally located multi-sports Centre in Rugby were sur-
veyed for one week, producing 7697 questionnaires from respondents
whose home could be pinpointed by enumeration district.

Census data for 700 enumeration districts were cluster analysed to
identify and describe the ACORN areas for which mean rates of sports
centre attendance were calculated. Adjustment for the effects of
distance on take-up was made by means of analysis of covariance and
the relative influence of distance and socio-economic characteristics
on take-up in Rugby was investigated by means of stepwise multiple
regression.

Dissimilar social areas showed significant differences in mean
attendance rates, with higher take-up from the more advantaged areas.

It is concluded that ACORN is an important discriminator with
respect to sports centre use. Given the relative ease with which
census data can be accessed, aggregated with survey data and manip-
ulated statistically, ACORN has great potential in monitoring, investigating the effects of site location and more generally in sports
planning and research.
Key words: Sports centre take-up, social area analysis, ACORN method.

Introduction

The major aim of this paper is to explore the potential of the ACORN
classification of residential neighbourhoods to investigate the
social factors at neighbourhood level which influence sports centre
use.

The sports centre attendance data were collected by means of site
surveys of one week's duration in March 1979 at Rugby and at Wolverhampton in March 1981.

The ACORN social area classification and its application in
leisure and sports research is explained fully in Sport and Leisure
Participation and Lifestyles in Different Residential Neighbourhoods

which was commissioned and published by the Sports Council/SSCR Joint Panel on Leisure and Recreation Research (M. Shaw, 1984).

Briefly, the ACORN method uses 40 variables derived from census data to classify social areas and neighbourhoods according to their social environment into eleven different types. Collectively, the ACORN variables describe the age structure; household and ethnic composition; housing conditions; employment characteristics; socio-economic status and travel-to-work patterns of each area. This wide range of social, economic and demographic characteristics is claimed to provide a multi-dimensional view of people's social environment which is believed to exercise a profound influence over patterns of participation in sport and leisure activities. Specifically, with respect to sport, Shaw argued that ACORN had been proved to be a powerful discriminator, which can differentiate between the lifestyle patterns of different types of area, though not, he warns, between different types of person.

Shaw went on to suggest that ACORN offers potential for sport research and planning by providing a means of examining the relation-ship between lifestyles and sports participation in a spatial con-text. Furthermore, he argued that ACORN "provides an invaluable method of estimating the likely demand for different types of sports facilities in different areas by combining data on the social compos-ition of each area by ACORN group and data on the propensity to play a particular sport by ACORN group." This, he suggests, can be useful in determining what types of facilities should be provided and where they should be located.

There is no space here to discuss the ecological fallacy or to examine the problems inherent in using past propensity to play a certain sport to determine the type and location of future facility provision. The ACORN approach is used, as Shaw recommends, merely as a framework for analysis which attempts to relate to people who live in particular types of area "not to types of people per se".

The major working hypothesis of this study is, following Shaw, that areas which are shown by census data to have dissimilar socio-economic and demographic characteristics will tend to exhibit differ-ent patterns of sports centre use, even after controlling for the effects of distance.

Methods of conducting the study

1. The Sports Centres
The Rugby Sports Centre is situated almost exactly in the centre of the town, the population of which live within three miles of the sports centre. Facilities include swimming pool, sports hall, small hall, catering facilities, bar, squash courts, conditioning room and extensive car park. There was no other sports complex offering this range of facilities within ten miles. The seven Wolverhampton sports centres are distributed around the town following the recommendations of the Structure Plan.

197

The sports centre visitors' survey
In the context of this paper the major purpose of the surveys was to pin-point each visitor's home so that attendance from different EDs and social areas could be compared with base populations.

Each visitor completed a questionnaire designed to elicit general information on user characteristics, and showed where he or she lived on a large scale map on which had been superimposed ED boundaries. The OPCS code and the bee-line distance were recorded.

2. Rates of attendance
Census information for each ED was obtained by means of computer access to 1981 data held at the University of Manchester. The programme SASPAC (version 2.5) was used to create files containing the census data required to calculate the ACORN variables which were transferred to SPSS files at Birmingham University and merged with the raw sports centre data. Rates of attendance per 100 population for each ED were calculated by dividing the number of visitors from each ED by its base population.

3. The ACORN social area classification
The 40 ACORN classifying variables were subjected to hierarchical cluster analysis to classify the EDs into the ACORN groups used to describe the different types of residential neighbourhoods found in the two towns. Mean attendance rates were calculated for each ACORN group.

4. The distance factor
Analysis of covariance was used to calculate adjusted mean rates of attendance for the ACORN groups after controlling for the effects of distance. In order to further investigate the effects of distance and socio-economic factors, the 40 ACORN variables and distance, for the Rugby data, were subjected to stepwise multiple regression with attendance rate as the dependent variable.

Results and discussion

1. The ACORN groups
For Rugby, seven clusters adequately classified the different social areas, whilst for Wolverhampton, although nine clusters emerged as the 'best' solution, only eight of these matched the original ACORN groups.

    Group A. Areas of modern family houses for manual workers. Not
found in Wolverhampton.
    Group B. Areas of modern family housing for white collar workers.
    Group C. Areas of better terraces and mixed housing.
    Group D. Poorer quality older terraced houses.
    Group F. Areas of urban local authority housing.
    Group G. Severely deprived tenement areas and council estates.
Not found in Rugby.

Group H. Low status multi-occupied and immigrant areas. Not found in Rugby.
Group I. High status non-family areas.
Group J. High status suburbs.

2. Rates of attendance per 100 population aged 5-49 years by ACORN groups.

Wolverhampton
Figure Ia shows the mean rates of attendance for the aggregated data before and after adjusting for the effects of distance. Groups I, J, B and C, which are the more advantaged areas, have much higher rates of attendance than the less advantaged, with the differences greatest at the extremes. Groups I and J, for example, have a rate of attendance approximately ten times greater than Group G. Groups B and C occupy an intermediate position. The difference of means before, and after, adjusting for distance are highly significant (p<0.001).

Fig. I Rates of attendance per 100 population aged 5-49 by ACORN group before and after adjusting for distance: aggregated data for Wolverhampton and Rugby

(a) Wolverhampton (N = 2,583)   (b) Rugby (N = 5,114)

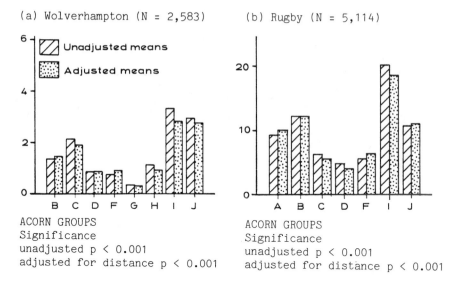

ACORN GROUPS
Significance
unadjusted p < 0.001
adjusted for distance p < 0.001

ACORN GROUPS
Significance
unadjusted p < 0.001
adjusted for distance p < 0.001

Note the differences in the scales of the dependent axes.

Rugby
Rugby (Fig. Ib) shows a similar pattern to that found in Wolverhampton.
The relatively large number of respondents in relation to the town population made it possible to disaggregate the attendance data and Figures IIa to j show rates of attendance for different categories of visitor. Again the pattern persists with differences in mean attend-

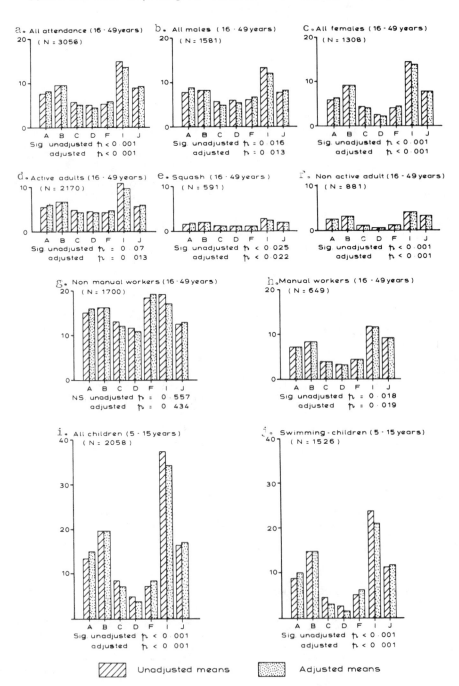

Fig.II Rate of attendance per 100 population by ACORN Group
before and after adjusting for distance : disaggregated Rugby data

a. All attendance (16 · 49 years) (N = 3056)
Sig. unadjusted ℏ < 0·001
    adjusted ℏ < 0·001

b. All males (16 · 49 years) (N = 1581)
Sig. unadjusted ℏ = 0·016
    adjusted ℏ = 0·013

c. All females (16 · 49 years) (N = 1308)
Sig. unadjusted ℏ < 0·001
    adjusted ℏ < 0·001

d. Active adults (16 · 49 years) (N = 2170)
Sig unadjusted ℏ = 0·07
    adjusted ℏ = 0·013

e. Squash (16 · 49 years) (N = 591)
Sig. unadjusted ℏ < 0·025
    adjusted ℏ < 0·022

f. Non active adult (16 · 49 years) (N = 881)
Sig. unadjusted ℏ < 0·001
    adjusted ℏ < 0·001

g. Non manual workers (16 · 49 years) (N = 1700)
NS. unadjusted ℏ = 0·557
    adjusted ℏ = 0·434

h. Manual workers (16 · 49 years) (N = 649)
Sig. unadjusted ℏ = 0·018
    adjusted ℏ = 0·019

i. All children (5 · 15 years) (N = 2058)
Sig. unadjusted ℏ < 0·001
    adjusted ℏ < 0·001

j. Swimming · children (5 · 15 years) (N = 1526)
Sig. unadjusted ℏ < 0·001
    adjusted ℏ < 0·001

▨ Unadjusted means   ▨ Adjusted means

200

ance rates significant, except for active adult participants and non manual workers.

Inspection of the disaggregated attendance rates reveals some interesting differences. For example, differences between the more advantaged and less advantaged ACORN groups are greater in the case of females than males (Figs. II b and c). The differences by ACORN group recorded for non active adult attenders are much greater than for all active visitors and squash players. These differences can be explained in part by the fact that male actives outnumbered female actives in the ratio 2:1 (4:1 in the case of squash), whereas the majority of the non-active females were middle class mothers accompanying young children (compare Figs. IIf and IIi and j).

Figures IIg and IIh, which show class differences in attendance, require careful interpretation, but it is clear from the data that take-up generally is much higher by non manual workers and that in the case of manual workers there are greater differences between the more advantaged and less advantaged ACORN groups than amongst non manual workers. In the case of children's attendance (Fig. IIi and j), which is influenced strongly by class differences in parental support, differences between the more advantaged and less advantaged ACORN groups are at their greatest. This suggests that children's attendance from the less advantaged areas is strongly influenced by proximity to the centre whereas attendance from the more advantaged areas relies heavily on parental involvement. Adjustment for distance has the general effect of lowering the attendance rates of ACORN groups C, D and I and increasing that of groups A, F and J. On aggregate, EDs in groups C and D which are less advantaged are situated in quite close proximity to the Sports Centre. Group F is doubly disadvantaged by its social composition and by the distance of the EDs from the Sports Centre.

With respect to both Rugby and Wolverhampton the major hypothesis, that areas with dissimilar socio-economic characteristics, even after adjusting for the effects of distance, will have significant differences in mean rates of sports centre attendance, is accepted.

3. The multiple-regression analysis
Tables Ia to Ik present in summary form the results of the multiple regression analysis. The ordering of the independent variables and the Beta coefficients indicate their relative importance.

Indicators of relative advantage such as number of rooms per person (the first selected variable in five cases), cars per household, and % of population in non manual occupations have a positive influence on attendance rates, whilst indicators of disadvantage, for example, concentration of New Commonwealth born, overcrowding, % who walk to work and household size have a negative influence. In every instance the selection of variables and the Beta weights confirm the impression gained from the close analysis of the original questionnaire data. For example, in the case of non-active adult attenders, these were predominantly middle class females in their thirties and early forties who brought children by car, whilst children were again mainly middle class who were brought by car. The variables selected in both cases reflect the social composition of the two groups and

TABLE I

Relative Influence of distance and the ACORN variables on Sports Centre attendance

[a] All attenders aged 5-49
1. Rooms per person   0.55
2. % households with 1 car   0.54
3. Households with 1 or 2
    rooms   0.22
Multiple r=0.68
Standard error of prediction 4.3

[b] All adults aged 16-49
1. % with professional
    qualifications*   0.45
2. % overcrowded (1-1.5
    persons/room)   -0.30
Multiple r=0.52 S.E.P.=3.81

[c] Males [16-49]
1. Rooms per person   0.30
2. % aged 15-24   0.49
3. % New C'wealth born   -0.48
4. % in Social Class II   0.27
Multiple r=0.61   S.E.P.=3.7

[d] Females [16-49]
1. Overcrowding (1-1.5)   -0.35
2. % aged 15-24   0.64
3. % unemployed   -0.38
4. % New C'wealth born   -0.38
Multiple r=0.73   S.E.P.=3.7

[e] Swimming [5-15]
1. Rooms per person   0.36
2. % who walk to work   -0.32
3. % New C'wealth born   -0.46
4. % population aged 5-24   0.46
5. Distance   -0.28
Multiple r=0.78 S.E.P.=5.92

[f] Squash [adults 16-49]
1. Furnished rented accom.   0.79
2. % in Social Class II   0.37
3. % New C'wealth born   -0.29
4. Distance   -0.21
5. Marriage rate   -0.35
Multiple r=0.68   S.E.P.=0.94

[g] Non-Active Adults [16-49]
1. Cars per household   1.32
2. Household size   -0.30
3. Households with 2+ cars   -0.70
4. % aged 25-44   0.24
Multiple r=0.69   S.E.P.=1.33

[h] Active Adults [16-49]
1. Rooms per person   0.39
2. % in Social Class II   0.25
Multiple r=0.47 S.E.P.=2.81

[i] Manual workers [16-49]
1. % in Social Class II   0.42
2. Dwelling size   0.30
Multiple r=0.59 S.E.P.=4.3

[j] Non-manual workers [16-49]
1. % households no bath   -0.23
Multiple r=-0.23 S.E.P.=8.3

[k] Children [5-15]
1. Rooms per person   0.56
2. % who walk to work   -0.47
3. % in Social Class IIIN   0.24
4. % Bus/train to work   -0.22
5. % aged 15-24   0.23
6. % Households w/o bath   -0.23
Multiple r=0.8   S.E.P.=7.9

the type of social area in which they tend to live as characterised
by the selected ACORN variables. Size of household, dwelling size
and car ownership (or % who walk to work) appear to exercise a pervasive influence on take-up. Although none of the multiple correlations confer predictive value, the stepwise multiple regression
analysis has selected the ACORN variables which were expected, both
on the basis of the attendance rates of the ACORN groups, and the
detailed analysis of the social characteristics of the visitors.
Further close comparison of the attendance rates of the ACORN groups
for the different categories of user and the related multiple regression results confirm these general impressions.

Despite the loss of fine detail, the ACORN method does discriminate sharply between different neighbourhoods in terms of sports
centre take-up and it is possible to identify social areas at ED
level which have, for example, very low take-up.

Although regression models derived from the analysis are of
limited predictive value, the selected ACORN variables could provide
the basis for a shortened form of ACORN designed to monitor use of
sports facilities and access to them by social area at ED level.

Conclusions

Although it is not possible to generalise from this modest study, it
does provide a promising crucial test of the potential of the ACORN
method in monitoring take-up of these sports facilities. Used in
combination with measures of distance from existing facilities, ACORN
provides an important means of investigating the effects of site
location on take-up from different neighbourhoods at ED level. By
implication, ACORN has potential, as Shaw claims, in informing
planning decisions on the location of new facilities.

The relative ease with which census data can be accessed, merged
with social survey data and processed statistically suggests that
ACORN has considerable potential in research and planning in sport
and leisure.

Acknowledgements

The authors wish to acknowledge the contribution to the original
Rugby study of their colleagues Keith Bonser and Barbara Knapp, other
colleagues and former students who helped with the survey and data
preparation, and the Sports Council for funding; David Seddon, who
collected the Wolverhampton data, and Debbie Wheeler and Shirley
Chambers who carried out the 'ACORN' analysis.

TARGETTING THE UNEMPLOYED: A REVIEW OF PUBLIC SECTOR SPORTS POLICIES
AND PROVISIONS IN THE U.K.

C.M. PACK, T.A. KAY and S.A. GLYPTIS
Department of Physical Education and Sports Science
Loughborough University of Technology

Abstract
Public sector sports providers increasingly recognize the need to cater
for the unemployed. The extent of current local authority provision
throughout the U.K. is examined, based on research undertaken in 1985-6
comprising a census of authorities by postal survey.
    Five types of provision were identified: off peak price concessions
for all users, price concessions for the unemployed, concession cards,
organized sessions and sports leadership schemes. Provision has become
both more widespread and more complex since a similar survey in 1982.
The response of the unemployed to this provision is considered, particularly the results of detailed monitoring of three experimental leadership schemes. The problems and successes perceived by providers are
also considered. In conclusion the benefits and shortcomings of the
different types of scheme are presented, and guidelines for future
provision given. Providers are urged to be realistic in their expectations of schemes for the unemployed.
Key Words: Unemployed, Sports schemes, Local authority.

1. Introduction

In January 1986 registered unemployment in the U.K. reached a record
level of 3.4 millions, representing 14.1% of the workforce. (The Times,
Jan 31 1986). Even the overall unemployment rate conceals the fact
that certain sectors of the population are hit still harder. Firstly,
there are variations by age, with the oldest and youngest sections of
the workforce being most vulnerable. Secondly, although male unemployment is higher, female unemployment is rising more sharply and much is
unnoticed as many women fail to register. Thirdly, the unskilled and
unqualified (and hence the least well off) are more vulnerable to re-
dundancy and long term unemployment; the more highly skilled can "down-
grade". Finally, certain localities experience far greater than average unemployment eg Strabane (in Northern Ireland) 37% (Dept. of Employment, Jan 1986). Whatever the effects of "new technology" on working patterns in the long term, high unemployment seems set to persist
in the immediate future.
    Central government policies for the unemployed have been mainly
geared towards provision of work experience, job opportunities and giving enterprise grants. Some 495,000 people are involved in special

204

employment and training measures (The Times, Jan 31 1986) - notably the Youth Training Scheme and Community Programme. Public sector leisure providers too feel they have a role to play in helping the unemployed while they are out of work. Few would argue that leisure can substitute for work, given the deeply rooted work ethic in society. But leisure can provide some of the satisfactions traditionally associated with work, such as a sense of achievement, social contact, and a routine. The unemployed, however, - and other disadvantaged groups - are constrained in their participation - by financial, social and psychological factors; they comprise precisely those sectors of the working-age population which have a low participation rate in sport.

At the national level the Sports Council has been the leader in working with target groups, and specifically the unemployed. However, it is local authorities who are the main providers of leisure opportunities in the community. Glyptis and Riddington reviewed the extent of local authority provision for the unemployed in England and Wales in 1982. This paper updates their review, extending it to cover the whole of the U.K. It is based on research undertaken in 1985-6 comprising three stages: a census by means of postal questionnaires of all local authorities in the U.K; interviews with selected authorities to discuss schemes in more depth; and detailed fieldwork in a small number of case studies. The paper also draws upon the results of monitoring three Sports Council experimental schemes.

2.   The extent of local authority provision for the unemployed

The questionnaire survey achieved a 90% response rate (454 replies). Of the authorities responding, 323 (71%) were making some sort of provision directly or indirectly benefitting the unemployed. This compares with only 60% in 1982, and excludes a further 20 authorities who were planning to introduce a scheme or had run one in the past. Provision for the unemployed has therefore become more widespread.

Table 1   National and Regional variations in provision for the unemployed

Country	Authorities making Provisions (%)	Sports Council Regions (England)	Authorities making Provision (%)
Scotland	81	Greater London	86
Wales	77	North West	83
N. Ireland	59	South	77
England	70	North	77
		Yorks/Humberside	70
		West Midlands	67
		East Midlands	65
		East	65
		South East	64
		South West	55

As Table 1 shows, however, there remain significant national and regional variations.

Authorities making provision were asked about their aims in introducing the scheme. Most replied that it was to encourage the unemployed to participate in sport and recreation, in particular by removing the financial barrier to participation by reducing entry charges. Several authorities hoped that their schemes would provide other benefits too; for example "To help relieve the psychological and social stresses of unemployment; to encourage the unemployed through individual and group activity to develop sporting and social skills which may help in gaining confidence and self-esteem".

The second most stated reason for introducing a scheme, and for some the sole motivation, was to increase usage of facilities at slack times. Thirdly, many authorities introduced schemes for broadly political reasons, such as to make a token gesture to the unemployed or "to be seen doing something", especially when neighbouring authorities were making provision. These reasons were not so apparent in the 1982 review.

Authorities not making provision were asked if there were particular reasons for this. Over half gave no such reason, suggesting that the issue had not been seriously considered. Amongst the others the most common reason was a real or perceived lack of demand - ie low unemployment rates. Other reasons included lack of available facilities, lack of finance and staff, and an unwillingness to single out the unemployed for special attention.

3. The nature of provision for the unemployed

From the results of the questionnaire survey five basic types of provision, according to the nature and scale, were identified.
1. Off peak price concessions for all users (7% of all authorities)
This was the only type of provision in these authorities and often benefitted the unemployed indirectly rather than targetting them specifically. Off peak usage was offered free or at a reduced price and no proof of unemployment was required. Authorities introduced these concessions to avoid singling out the unemployed, and to include all disadvantaged groups. Many authorities also introduced the concession to increase off peak usage.
2. Price concessions for the unemployed (33% of authorities)
This was the most common type of provision and often extended to other specified disadvantaged groups. Proof of unemployment, usually the UB40, was shown to obtain the concession, which in 60% of cases applied only at off peak times. Authorities introduced these concessions to remove the barrier of cost for the unemployed, whilst maintaining some control over the number of concessions given.
3. Organized sessions (5% of authorities)
This was the least common type of provision and the hardest to define, but in general consisted of organized sessions for the unemployed on a low key and small scale basis in terms of staff involvement, frequency of session and sports offered. The aims of the sessions were partly to provide low cost recreation but also to perform a social function for the unemployed.

4. <u>Concession cards</u> (14% of authorities)

Price concessions, free usage or benefits of centre membership were offered to users holding a concession card or "passport to leisure". Most authorities made the card available only to the registered unemployed or to other disadvantaged groups though in some cases <u>all</u> borough residents could benefit. Precise details of pricing, validity and card design varied greatly. Authorities introduced concession cards to avoid the stigma and abuse of schemes where the UB40 is shown; they were often introduced after trying such schemes. Other aims were to allow families of the unemployed concessionary use, and to create a feeling of "membership" among users.

5. <u>Leadership schemes</u> (9% of authorities)

Again these varied greatly in detail and were often run alongside other types of provision. The distinguishing feature is that they all employed sports leaders or motivators working solely with the target group organizing sessions, leagues, trips and often doing "outreach" work in the community. Many schemes targetted all those "with time on their hands". Sessions were generally free or at a nominal charge, and staff were usually employed via the Manpower Services Commission (MSC) or Urban Aid funding. The rationale behind leadership schemes was that reduced charges alone were insufficient to attract the unemployed and that staff were needed specifically to motivate them and overcome their fear and rejection of sport.

A further 3% of authorities had schemes which do not fit into any of the above categories - e.g. the Regional Councils in Scotland.

Apart from the Type 3 provision (organized sessions) the others were all identified by Glyptis and Riddington in their 1982 survey. Table 2 compares provision in the two years. Provision for the unemployed has not only become more widespread but has also changed in nature, with a shift in emphasis to more 'complex' schemes, with a significant increase in concession card and leadership schemes.

Table 2   Nature of local authority provision: 1982 and 1985

Type of Provision	Authorities making provision (%)	
	1982	1985
No provision	40	29
1. off peak concession for all	7	7
2. Price concession for unemployed	42	33
3. Organized sessions	-	5
4. Concession cards	5	14
5. Leadership	5	9
Other	1	3
	100	100

----

4. The response of the unemployed

At the time of writing only preliminary results from the national review are available on scheme usage; more will be available in July 1986. Provisional findings include the following.

1. Numbers: many authorities reported lower numbers of users than anticipated, problems of expanding beyond a small nucleus of users and apathy amongst the unemployed.
2. Characteristics: the unemployed were often regarded as the hardest target group to reach. Most users were aged 18-25 and male, although many schemes achieved high usage among older females. Younger women and older men were more elusive.
3. Frequency of attendance: many authorities commented on a lack of commitment from users; large fluctuations in usage occurred for no apparent reason.
4. Feedback from users: in most cases this was positive, suggesting that the schemes can play an important role for the unemployed, especially where they fulfil an informal, social function. Negative comments related to price (free use was sometimes viewed as desirable b users who had to pay, and as a 'handout' by those who did not), havin to show proof of unemployment, restriction of concessionary usage to off peak times, and exclusion of families from the concession.

The most detailed statistical information currently available abou the response of the unemployed to sports schemes comes from the monitor ing of three experimental sports leadership schemes in Leicester, Birmingham and Derwentside, established as national pilot projects in 1981 by the Sports Council, in conjunction with other agencies. Usag of these schemes may be summarised as follows.
1. Numbers: All 3 schemes generated impressive levels of participatio - the Leicester 'STARS' scheme for example achieved 30,000 attendance from 6422 users over a 3 year period. Two thirds of users participate in sport only at the STARS Scheme, and 40% had never previously taken part in the activities they did at STARS.
2. Characteristics: The schemes successfully reached the target grou - the unemployed accounted for 98% of attendances at STARS, many by th long term unemployed. This was despite no proof of unemployment bein required. In terms of age/sex characteristics the users mirrored national differentials in participation - 75% of STARS users were unde 25; 73% were male. As the national review further corroborates, olde men and younger women were hard to attract.
3. Frequency of attendance: Retaining users was much harder than attacting them in the first place - a problem again echoed by the nat ional review. In Leicester 70% of users attended five times or less and one third attended just once. Except for a few individuals the unemployed did not become frequent users.
4. Feedback from users: This was almost entirely positive, and emphasized the social contacts provided through the scheme, the feeling o "having something to do", and increased confidence and self-esteem. The few negative comments centred on levels of coaching, lack of publicity and the stigma of being part of a special scheme for the unemployed.

The three experimental schemes provide valuable data on usage of leadership schemes, but very little comparative work has been carried out on other types of provision for the unemployed. Data from the cas study monitoring will be an important input into this area.

5. The response of the providers

Many local authorities stated that they lacked the necessary yardsticks against which to measure and define their success, and that it was much easier to identify the problems. The national review however revealed that certain successful aspects of provision and certain problems were common to many authorities and these are summarised below.

5.1 Successes
1. Increased usage. Many authorities felt that they had been successful in their aim to increase facility usage, and that there was also a "spin-off" effect of usage of sports and associated facilities (catering, amusement machines) outside the scheme itself.
2. Activities. Certain activities were repeatedly mentioned as being successful in attracting the unemployed - notably swimming, netball, weights, aerobics and bowls. Outdoor pursuits and residential trips proved popular, and many authorities reported that unemployed leagues and competitions generated the greatest participation and enthusiasm from users. In some cases leagues were now being run by the unemployed.
3. Staff. Sociable leaders who were liked by participants were crucial in achieving and sustaining high rates of usage, and in creating a feeling of group identity.
4. Employment prospects. Many authorities cited cases where volunteer helpers or users had obtained qualifications via the scheme and had then been employed in council facilities, and most authorities felt the experience helped MSC staff to get jobs or college places. In some cases scheme staff helped users with job applications and references.
Many other individual successes were reported.

5.2 Problems
1. Defining and identifying the target group. Many authorities had problems deciding which groups to include in concessions, and in particular whether to include families. Where schemes were restricted to borough residents this often led to criticisms from those living outside. Identifying those unemployed without a UB40 was a common problem, and misunderstandings at reception were often caused by unclear rules regarding times and pricing.
2. Publicity. The unemployed are a difficult target group to locate. Many authorities thought awareness of their schemes was low. Promotion was often sporadic and was specifically blamed for low take-up in several cases. Job Centres and DHSS were often accused of being uncooperative in displaying publicity material.
3. Facilities. Access to facilities was a problem for many of the leadership schemes, generally because of poor cooperation with community or county agencies. In some cases authorities felt this was due to a reluctance to allow access to unemployed groups. A few authorities commented on the need for informal facilities: leisure centres could be intimidating for those not used to sport.

4. <u>Staff</u>. Providers using MSC staff identified several associated problems - in particular the lack of continuity and low staff motivation which one year MSC contracts imposed. MSC bureaucracy was seen as time consuming and average wage level regulations limited recruitment of enough full time staff. The nature of sports leadership work also placed great demands on MSC staff - themselves long term unemployed
5. <u>Abuse of schemes</u>. Authorities operating price concession and concession card schemes frequently perceived a substantial level of abuse through UB40 swapping etc. A few also mentioned rowdy behaviour and minor incidences of vandalism - in some cases sufficient to deter the paying public.

Other problems identified by providers included the transport of users and equipment, lack of finance, lack of time to monitor provision effectively, and excess demand from the unemployed clashing with that from existing users.

6. Conclusions

6.1 Evaluation of current provision
It is difficult to summarise the extent to which these schemes for the unemployed are successful in reaching their target group, not least because few are being monitored in terms of usage and user characteristics One lesson that can be drawn from monitoring of the three experimenta schemes is that even with large budgets and the support of several agencies there were problems reaching certain sectors of the unemployed and achieving regular and sustained participation. However, particularly in areas of high unemployment, many authorities <u>are</u> successful in terms of numbers (albeit less so than anticipated) and the evidence is that they provide a valuable service for the individuals who use them. The benefits and shortcomings of the various types of scheme are summarised as follows.
<u>Off peak concessions for all users</u> are simple to operate, they avoid the problem of stigma, they include the whole community and they increase off peak usage. The problems are a potential income loss, and that the concession presupposes self motivation on the part of the user. This criticism also applies to <u>price concessions for the unemployed</u>; other criticisms of these schemes are stigma, abuse and exclusion of families. However, they are easy to administer, at little cost and enable particular groups to be targetted. The advantages of <u>concession cards</u> are that they largely overcome the problem of stigma; families and other disadvantaged groups are easily included; and cards can be marketed as an attractive package and create a 'feeling of belonging'. The disadvantages are that the system can still be abused and that the administration may be time consuming. The major advantage of <u>Leadershi Schemes</u> is having staff, free from other responsibilities who through outreach work can attract the unmotivated and fulfil a social role as well as providing leadership and coaching. Employing MSC staff brings additional finance to schemes and more diverse activities can often be provided, tailored to the needs of users. The disadvantages are the problems associated with MSC staff (outlined in 5.2), the input needed by the local authority and the lack of continuity or certainty about the future.

6.2 Guidelines for the future

The main guidelines to emerge to date are as follows:

Firstly the <u>aims</u> of the scheme should be clearly stated - whether to increase usage or cater for the unemployed. The <u>target group</u> needs defining - many authorities had not decided who constituted "the unemployed" for the purposes of their schemes. <u>Simplicity</u>, for user and provider, is essential in concession schemes, with clear details of proof of identity needed, times and prices, to avoid problems at reception. Families should be eligible if possible.

<u>Publicity and promotion</u> should be attractive and appropriate to the target group; 'high profile' publicity such as stunts and shopping centre displays tend to be more successful than traditional methods. Providers invariably identified <u>word of mouth</u> as the best method of all and time should be spent on personal contact with the unemployed. <u>Contact with other agencies</u> is vital in gaining access to facilities and space for publicity, and for maintaining good will.

<u>Activities</u> should be geared to what the users want; programmes should be flexible. Outdoor pursuits, residential trips and unemployed leagues tend to be popular, especially if <u>transport</u> is provided.

<u>Session leaders</u> should realize that formal instruction is not always appropriate and that the social function of sessions is important. The personality of the leader largely determines the success of organized sessions; many authorities found that the best sportsmen do not always make the best leaders.

<u>Forward planning</u> is vital - details such as a base for the scheme, staggering staff contracts and arrangements for administrative support need to be clearly thought out.

<u>Statistical monitoring</u> of schemes is useful but only if the time is made to examine results and to act accordingly. Records of usage should be standardized across facilities.

Finally, one lesson which has emerged clearly is that local authorities should not expect too much. Schemes take time to gain momentum, and providers should be prepared to admit mistakes and adapt. Perceived failure may only be due to unrealistic expectations - as one officer said "everybody thinks the unemployed should just jump up and use the facilities whenever you ask". The unemployed will not all turn into dedicated sportsmen just because they are unemployed: providers should perhaps be less concerned with numbers and more ready to view success in terms of the obvious financial, social and psychological benefits obtained by those who do take part.

Acknowledgement

The research projects on which this paper is based were funded by the Sports Council whose support is gratefully acknowledged.

References

Department of Employment (1986) <u>Employment Gazette</u> 94,1
Glyptis, S.A. and Riddington, A.C. (1983) Sport for the Unemployed: a review of local authority projects Sports Council Research Working Paper 21. London.

YOUTH UNEMPLOYMENT, SPORT AND LEISURE

K. ROBERTS
Department of Sport and Recreation Studies, Liverpool Polytechnic

Methods

During 1985 854 17-18 year olds were interviewed in an investigation into the changing structure of youth labour markets.[1] The young people were random samples of the age-group who had completed full-time education and entered the local labour markets in Chelmsford, Liverpool and Walsall - areas with contrasting economic histories, current business mixes and levels of unemployment. In Chelmsford eight percent were unemployed when interviewed, 28 percent in Walsall and 41 percent in Liverpool. The remainder were in employment or still on the Youth Training Scheme (YTS), except for a handful who had withdrawn from the labour market to become housewives or to return to full-time education. The interviews were deliberately timed so that 16 year old school-leavers would have spent 18-24 months in the labour market, by when those who entered would mostly have passed through the then one-year YTS and into the next stage of their careers. Most of the unemployed were products of this training scheme. Those in employment held a variety of occupations. Some were training for professional and management careers. Others were in routine sales and unskilled jobs with no prospects of career progression. Gross earnings of those in employment ranged from under £30 to over £140 per week.

The interviews dealt primarily with the individuals' careers since leaving school in jobs, youth training and periods of unemployment, but detailed information was also collected about family and educational backgrounds, gross and net incomes from all sources, plus out-of-home leisure activities. The following discussion focuses, eventually, on the implications of unemployment for sport participation, but understanding these implications becomes easier when sport is set in the context of total uses of leisure, and when differences between employed and unemployed 17-18 year olds' leisure can be compared with the sometimes equally impressive differences between males and females, in similar and in different occupations, and with various levels of income.

Gender

Boys had 'been out' slightly more frequently than girls during the previous week. However, the main gender difference in out-of-home recreation was not that the males had or did more, but that the boys and

---

1. This research was funded by the Department of Employment, but all conclusions drawn are solely the authors'. For a full report on the research methods and findings see Roberts et al (forthcoming).

girls tended to 'go out' to do rather different things . They were equally involved in social gatherings in pubs, clubs, cafes, restaurants, discos and similar places, but the girls were slightly more likely to have been to places of entertainment such as cinemas, theatres and concerts, while more boys had watched and played outdoor and indoor sport. The other main sex difference was that the women were the more likely to report steady relationships with the opposite sex. The different proportions of boys and girls claiming such relationships does not necessarily indicate under- or over-reporting by either side. Girls tend to 'go out' with, and eventually marry older partners.

On average boys were earning more than girls in similar occupations and there were even wider differences in the sexes' future career and income expectations. Boys were the more likely to be receiving extended training and time-off for further education, and their current jobs led to the better career and income prospects. We asked about gross and net earned income, and also, when respondents lived with their parents, how much they retained for personal spending after paying 'board'. Girls were not being treated more generously by parents to compensate for their generally lower earnings. Males and females who were unemployed and on the YTS were retaining similar sums, whereas employed males tended to have more to spend than females.

The possessions to which many teenagers aspire, and which many acquire as soon as their incomes permit, include cars and motor-cycles. Twenty-three percent of employed males who were earning less than £40 per week had personal motor transport, rising to 64 percent of those earning over £80. Girls were less likely to have motor cars or bikes than boys with similar earnings. Only 9 - 23 percent of girls in the different income-bands had such possessions. Young men and women spend similar incomes in different masculine and feminine ways, but it is also the case that the girls are less able to afford motors because, in general, they earn less and, therefore, have less to spend. Out-of-school males and females who use their leisure in masculine and feminine ways are not just enacting previously internalised norms and responding to social pressure to conform with gender stereotypes. Teenage girls are encouraged to become socially attached to, and economically dependent on older men because in general, such males have the greatest economic power.

Occupations and incomes

Employed respondents' rates and patterns of leisure activity did not vary by occupation so much as by income. The more they earned, the more likely were males and females to go out in the evenings, to possess motor transport, and steady opposite-sexed partners. Income was making a difference to levels of activity, and also to the types of leisure interests that respondents were pursuing. However, in the latter case the effects of income differed for males and females.

The lowest paid males were the most active in indoor and outdoor sport, though income was unrelated to watching live sport. Among the teenage boys in employment, low income was proving no barrier to sports participation. Rather, high earnings and spending power, and the acquisition of motor transport, appeared to be accelerating males' social development to the stage where their leisure evolved around cars, girls and social gatherings, while 'juvenile' sporting interests were dropped. Among employed girls, variations in income had entirely different leisure associations. The highest earners were the least frequent visitors to places of entertainment, but the most involved in participant indoor sport, and the most likely to have watched live sport. High income appeared to be allowing 17-18 year old males to spend their leisure in milieux and relationships where they could act in masculine ways towards women, while relatively low incomes played a complementary role in confining girls' out-of-home leisure to places and activities where they were socially and economically dependent on men. Relatively high earnings appeared to be releasing girls from some constraints to which other females were subject, and permitting the development, retention and enjoyment of independent leisure interests, including sport. This is not to suggest that the high-income girls were feminist and separatist. They were the most likely to have boy friends. Nevertheless, such young women seemed the best-placed to develop relatively equal, symmetrical relationships with their partners, to bring their own interests to these partnerships and, if they wished, to sustain independent interests and pastimes.

Unemployment

Our sample included enough unemployed individuals to separate those who had been out-of-work for over and less than six months, and this division proves useful. It shows that the effects of unemployment on young people's leisure depend not only upon who the young people are, but also for how long the predicament lasts. In general, compared with those in employment, the short-term unemployed were simply doing less of most things. They had been out on fewer evenings, had attended fewer social occasions, and had played less sport than employed respondents. Unemployed boys' rates of sport participation resembled the highest paid's, but the former were not compensating with high levels of other, more expensive activities. The sole leisure activity that the unemployed were preserving, and then only the males, was watching live sport. Our Merseyside sample included some dedicated Liverpool and Everton fans who, it seemed, were prepared to sacrifice virtually all else to remain loyal supporters.

In some respects the long-term unemployed were doing least of all. Social gatherings and visits to places of entertainment dropped to even lower levels that among the shorter-term unemployed. Approximately a quarter of long-term unemployed males and females appeared to have dropped virtually all normal teenage leisure. During the previous four weeks they had been to no parties, pubs, clubs, cafes, or discos - outings that were almost universal among those with jobs.

Jobless girls were as likely as those in employment to have steady boy-friends. Unemployed boys seemed to be holding onto their sports teams, and the girls to their men. However, over 60 percent of the unemployed girls had been out on less than three evenings during the previous week compared with 41 percent of the lowest paid, and only 18 percent of those earning over £80 per week. Among unemployed girls, with and without steady boy-friends, leisure was primarily home-based. In so far as the longer-term unemployed girls were adjusting to joblessness, this was by becoming domesticated (see also Willis, 1985).

In contrast, there were signs of longer-term unemployed males reviving certain forms of out-of-home leisure. Short-term unemployed males had been out on fewer evenings during the previous week than even the lowest paid, whereas the longer-term unemployed had been out as frequently as all but the highest paid. Short-term unemployed boys were less likely to have steady girl-friends than all employed groups, whereas the longer-term cases appeared to be enjoying as much heterosexual success as all but the highest paid. However, the longer-term unemployed males were not going out, whether alone, with male companions or girl-friends, to play sport, to commercial night-spots or any other places of entertainment. Previous research (Banks et al, 1984; Cashmore, 1984) has found evidence of the long-term young unemployed gravitating into separate social networks and developing distinctive life-styles, and our evidence confirms that adapting to unemployment means becoming more separated from rather than maintaining normal leisure activities.

Lack of income must be a major reason why the young unemployed's leisure is relatively impoverished. Previous investigators have stressed the difficulty of disentangling the effects of poverty and joblessness (Kelvin et al, 1984). This certainly applies among young people. There was little overlap between the incomes and spending power of those in and out-of-employment. It is difficult to quantify teenagers' real standards of living. Neither total income nor personal spending are always accurate guides when young people live with their parents. Some receive gifts of clothing and holidays, and have the use of family cars to supplement their own money. Whether unemployed teenagers are impoverished can depend as much on their households' living standards as their personal incomes. The young unemployed do not all suffer grinding hardship any more than all school and college students. Nevertheless, all the cases of acute poverty that we encountered involved unemployed respondents. Some were extremely poor. One male had no income at the time of the survey because his benefit had been stopped. The young people at greatest risk of unemployment are in high unemployment areas, from poor families, often with unemployed parents. Making the family responsible for supporting these teenagers intensifies family poverty.

Policy issues for further enquiry

There is an obvious sense in which the findings just reported are disappointing. All three research areas, like most parts of Britain, had benefited from recently-opened sports facilities, some deliberately sited in disadvantaged, high unemployment districts. All the local authorities had some special provisions to encourage unemployed teenagers to participate in sport. Despite this, the young unemployed were not even maintaining normal levels, let alone compensating through sport and other leisure activities. It is tempting to conclude that the young unemployed's primary need is for jobs, and that improving their quality of leisure must await solutions to their employment problems. In our view this tempting conclusion must be resisted. This implies no hostility to measures that would drive closer to the roots of women's and the young unemployed's limited opportunities. Awaiting such progress simply seems a poor excuse for 'doing nothing' as a leisure policy. Our evidence may not indicate that the unemployed's leisure disadvantages are yet disappearing, but it offers grounds for optimism. The findings do not imply that low income, gender or lack of employment erect barriers that neither the individuals on the wrong side nor leisure providers can penetrate without exceptional sacrifice. Whether young males or females, relatively affluent or impoverished, in or out-of-work take part in sport must depend, to some extent, on the types of sport offered and the socio-economic contexts - the pricing policies, the marketing strategies, the types of buildings and, maybe above all else, the surrounding images and identities.

Our on-going research is pursuing hints derived from the investigation just reported on how the benefits of sports participation might be broadcast more widely. The enquiries in progress[2] are assessing the extent and ways in which different types of indoor sport provisions are used by, then impact on the quality of life among different sections of the public. The fieldwork is being conducted in six urban areas in different parts of the United Kingdom, and will distinguish types of sports, buildings, management and marketing strategies that prove more and less successful in reaching various target groups, including young adults, males and females, in and out-of-work. The research is also studying panels of participants - males and females, in different age-bands and socio-economic groups, plus controls, in order to measure the costs and benefits, and different groups' reasons for taking part and not participating in various types of sport.

2. These investigations are supported by a research grant from the Health Promotion Research Trust.

We suspect that, with appropriate provisions, it will be possible to achieve a further general rise in sports participation among young adults and, in the process, to close the gaps between young people who continue in full-time education beyond 16, those with jobs, and the unemployed. One ground for optimism is the young unemployed's willingness to 'do something' to improve their own situations, given suitable opportunities. Very few unemployed respondents had become demoralised, resigned and apathetic. The majority were determined to remain 'normal', to obtain jobs eventually, then participate in normal leisure. Unemployment seems rather less demoralising for young people than adults. School-leavers have no established occupational identities to shatter, and they can realistically expect time to improve their prospects. Moreover, the fact that youth unemployment has become so widespread helps to dissolve any stigma (Roberts, 1983). Most unemployed informants complained of boredom and desperately wanted things to do apart from job-hunting. This is why we are optimistic that many will respond to the right opportunities to participate in sport and other leisure activities.

Secondly, there are no class-cultural barriers to break. The appeal of sport among young people transcends class boundaries. Young people with different social class origins and destinies may play different types of games, in different buildings, under the aegis of different organisations and mainly in the company of their social peers. The fact remains that they can all be attracted to indoor and outdoor sports facilities. There is no evidence of potential working class participants being repelled by smart and expensive buildings. Commercial bingo and discos have nailed this myth. The obstacles to delivering sport to the young unemployed do not include their membership of social classes that are generally unattracted by the facilities already on offer.

Thirdly, income is currently a major restraint on the young unemployed's leisure, but there is evidence that it need not inhibit sports activities. Entrance charges are not the sole financial obstacle. There are the additional costs of transport, plus any special clothing and equipment that participation involves. Equally important, just playing the game may not be the sole purpose when young people use sport facilities. The socialising that precedes or follows may be a normal part of the occasion, and an inability to take part, especially when others have the cash to do so, can be a reason for not attending. Many young people are reluctant to go out anywhere without the cash and, sometimes, the clothing to make the right impression. Young people with limited spending money must ration their trips out. Some opt for just one or two weekly leisure excursions that involve significant outlays -watching sport or clubnights, depending on their preferences. Playing sport is then dropped if not a main interest.

Public authorities can reduce some costs of sports participation by cheap admissions, hire of equipment and concessionary travel. The other financial impediments are less easy to tackle, but we can be confident that they are not insuperable. Limited spending power does not inhibit sports participation among some groups of young people. Male employees with the lowest earnings are the most active. Students are even more involved. A stream of Britain's international competitors are now using the dole in lieu of sports scholarships.

A Final ground for optimism is that present patterns of sports participation among young men and women are hopeful bases from which to build. The highest-earning female employees are the most active. Among teenage girls, participant sport seems a distinctly upmarket, high status activity which is a promising springboard for stratified diffusion. Among male teenage employees there is a substantial decline in participation as incomes rise and the opposite sex becomes a central life interest. However, participant sport has a widespread appeal among students, and also among young professionals and managers in their twenties - the Yuppies, as Americans describe them. It should be possible to construct bridges between the sports cultures of young male adolescents and the sport scenes preferred by older, more affluent players. Any future spread of sport participation among females will be an added inducement for males to retain the habit.

Our current enquiries will lead to practical conclusions on how best to widen sports opportunities for all young people, but especially those who are most disadvantaged by family and educational backgrounds, and in the labour market. One hypothesis, consistent with the evidence already assembled, but requiring confirmation, is that the most successful local provisions will not pin all hopes on any single formula. 'Young people' and 'youth' are adult society's terms. Those labelled are more discriminating. There is no single youth market. Sport seems to play very different roles in the lives of different groups. Young males whose out-of-home leisure evolves around mono-sexual peer groups may be attracted by low-cost facilities, and may not only be tolerant of, but sometimes prefer spartan surroundings. However, retaining these players is likely to require bridges to different sports, played in different social and physical settings where young adults can distance themselves from 'juvenile' teenagers. In general girls are more interested in music and entertainment than sport. At the moment young sportswomen tend to be drawn from the better-educated and more prosperous members of their age-group. Like most out-of-school females, they are involved in relationships with men, usually slightly older men, and will probably be most keen to practise sport in surroundings with an ambiance to match their social identities and aspirations.

A second hypothesis derived from completed stages, but awaiting corroboration or refutation in the on-going enquiry, is that explicitly targeting provisions at the young unemployed is inept. Unemployment is not a status that many individuals wish to parade. Out-of-work teenagers often define themselves as 'between jobs' or 'looking for work'. Unemployment is a predicament from which most are trying to escape, not a condition in which they want to settle. Moreover, most youth unemployment is short duration. Young workers, youth trainees and the young unemployed can be the same individuals at different points in time. Only a minority of young people may be on the dole at any moment, but in many areas, nowadays, the majority of school-leavers can anticipate unemployment at some early stage in their working lives.

REFERENCES

M Banks, P Ullah and P Warr (1984), 'Unemployment and less qualified urban young people', Employment Gazette, August, 343-346.

E E Cashmore (1984), No Future: Youth and Society, Heinemann, London.

K Roberts (1983), Youth and Leisure, Allen and Unwin, London.

K Roberts, S Dench and D Richardson (forthcoming), The Changing Structure of Youth Labour Markets, Department of Employment Research Paper, London.

P Willis (1985), The Social Condition of Young People in Wolverhampton in 1984, Wolverhampton Borough Council.

PHYSICAL EDUCATION, SPORT AND RECREATION AND THE QUALITY OF LIFE

R.H. Chappell
Department of Physical Education, West London Institute of Higher
Education

Abstract
Several researchers would manintain that involvement in physical
education, sport and recreation improves the quality of life,
although there has hardly been any consensus on the significance of
the term 'quality of life'. Others would argue forcibly in favour
of sport as a means of enhancing moral values among young people.
    Following the Wolfenden Report, several other reports were
published. These reports were issued by various bodies and
examined the role of physical education in schools and the use of
leisure and recreation programmes in the community as a means of
improving the quality of life.
    The aim of this paper is to investigate several of these
reports to see if that is the case. In particular, the paper will
focus upon the role of physical education, sport and recreation as a
means of increasing participation amongst young people, thereby
attempting to improve moral awareness in them, as for example,
helping in the fight against criminal habits.

The debate has continued for some time whether participation in
physical education, sport and recreation improves the quality of
life. For example, Unolle (1984) and Allhardt (1984), in relation
to the role of sport in Scandinavia; Moustard (1983), in relation
to French sport; and Illmarinen (1984) in relation to sport and
international understanding all maintain that this is the case.
    There has hardly been any consensus on the significance of the
term 'quality of life', which according to Allardt (1984) denotes
'something which is valued and which is nor has been missing'.
Therefore people with different life-styles will lay stress on
different things, societies will emphasise different qualities, and
different need-satisfaction will result in different things being
held as crucial to the quality of life.
    Many of those involved with physical education, sport and
recreation maintain that a participation in sport improves the
quality of life, while others would argue forcibly, in favour of
sport as a means of enhancing moral values among young people.
    During the period between 1950 and 1980 in particular, various
reports such as the Newsom Report, Crowther Report, Wolfenden Report
and Albermarle Report, were issued by local and national bodies

which examined physical education in schools and also had far-reaching effects on sport in the community; hence, they directly influenced the quality of life for a great majority of the population.

These reports and papers became integrated into a debate relating to the role of physical education and sport. Much of the information contained in the reports and papers indicated that physical education and sport were used as a means of improving the quality of life. An investigation into these reports shows that this is the case.

The Birmingham University Report 'Sport in Britain' (1957) stimulated the C.C.P.R to act and, consequently, the C.C.P.R established the Wolfenden Committee in the same year, who reported in 1960 with terms of reference to:

'examine the factors affecting the development of games, sports and outdoor activities in the United Kingdom and make recommend-ations to the C.C.P.R as to the practical means which should be taken by voluntary or statutory bodies in order that these activities may play their full part in promoting the general welfare of the community'.

The implications for physical education and sport concentrated on the area devoted to improving the quality of life and this is revealed in the following statement included in the final Report itself:

'a considerable proportion of delinquency among young people springs from the lack of opportunity or desire for practical activity...it is a reasonable assumption that if more young people had opportunities for playing games fewer of them would develop criminal habits'.

Therefore, it would appear that there was to be a strong plea for a commitment towards more active participation for all sections of the community, especially those who previously had not been given the opportunity to participate in physical educaton, sport and recreation programmes. It was advocated that there should be equality of opportunity in terms of participation.

In this respect, active participation is linked to improvement in moral awareness, such as helping in the fight against the development of criminal habits. Consequently, in an attempt to develop participation and to increase the influence of organised recreation programmes a massive programme of facility development began; dual-use of existing facilities was advocated; coaching schemes were developed under the direction of the various sporting bodies; and it was suggested that there should be more direct links between schools, clubs and coaching organisations.

All such schemes had far-reaching implications for the development of sport and recreation programmes in an attempt to improve the quality of life for all sectors of the community.

Similar suggestions were made by the Crowther Report in 1959. The Crowther Report recommended amongst other things, more structured use

of leisure pursuits in an attempt to alleviate social problems such as
juvenile delinquency. Again, it was felt that physical education
and sport were important in the improvement in the quality of life.

The Albermarle Report of 1960 on the Youth Service supported the
findings of the Wolfenden and Crowther Reports. Concern was
expressed in relation to the social and moral development of young
people and this had been prompted by the increasing rise in the
levels of juvenile delinquency. This indicated an interest by local
and national bodies intent on improving the quality of life, more
specifically, the social and moral development of young people by
organised physical education and sports programmes.

It is interesting to note that the Newsom, Crowther, Wolfenden
and Albermarle Reports were established by the Conservative
Government, but their recommendations were developed by the Labour
Party after 1964.

The recommendations of the Newsom Report of 1963 had an immediate
effect on physical education in the schools. The Report contended
that:

'the essential needs of physical education for older pupils
could perhaps be summed up in the words of variety, choice,
better facilities and links with adult organisations'.

Consequently, the philosphical framework for physical education
shifted towards variety and choice especially for those children in
the 5th and 6th forms in schools. A wide range of options became
available in an attempt to involve all children in a sporting
activity, and in order to facilitate this change in the nature of
physical education. Furthermore, as children became involved with
a wider range of activities, additional facilities, such as local
sports centres and swimming baths, were utilized and these necessit-
ated links with adult organisations. Such links were made in an
attempt to ensure that children could remain interested in a sports
programme on leaving school, thus ensuring that the quality of post
school life was enhanced. Education for leisure became a central
issue.

The 1972 White Paper 'Framework for Expansion' emphasised the
need for the 'development of practical and human skills'. It was
implied that there should be a slight change in the role of the
teacher of Physical Education towards involvement with health and
fitness. This is emphasised in the work of such authors as Kane
(1974) and Whitehead and Hendry (1976).

Of great significance was the 1973 'Quality of Life' experiment
which was established by the Department of Education and Science and
the Department of the Environment, and took place in three English
cities. The scheme resulted in local action being taken to improve
leisure time activities, mainly through the utilisation of existing
facilities. The scheme which lasted two years, proved to be a great
success in raising the quality of life of those people involved and
made the point that the quality of life can be improved in every
neighbourbood.

The 1975 White Paper 'Sport and Recreation' returned to the role

of the physical education teacher in the improving of the quality of
life, especially in the provision of opportunities for young people.
The paper maintained that:

'By reducing boredom and urban frustration, participation in
recreation contributes to a reduction of hooliganism and
delinquency amongst young people. Teachers of physical
education play a valuable part in this programme; they have a
dual role to encourage young people to take part in physical
recreation and to develop standards of excellence amongst the
gifted.'

It would appear, therefore, that the document returns to the
central issue advocated by previous reports of physical education,
sport and recreation being extremely important as a means of
improving the quality of life.

With a view ot the talents of gifted sportsmen and women, a
Ministerial Working Party was set up in 1975 to investigate the
possibility of establishing Centres of Excellence. The purpose of
the Centres of Excellence was to provide facilities, coaching and
medical back-up for the development of top-class performers in
numerous sports. For example, at the West London Institute, the
facilities are used as a Centre of Excellence for rowers and volleyball players, while further developments have included the formation
of a sports fitness unit, basketball and summer camps. All such
schemes are an attempt to make available the facilities to members
of the community as a means of improving the quality of their lives
and raising the standards of potential international sportsmen and
women.

The Sports Council 'Sport for All' campaigns, initiated by Roger
Bannister in 1972 had had many successes and failures as indicated
by McIntosh and Charlton (1985). According to Coghlan (1986):

'a measurable indication of success is seen in the number
of new public facilities created by the schemes...The growth
of popularity of sports such as basketball and volleyball, owes
much to the proliferation of sports centres and adequate space,
surfaces and lighting'.

A major success of these campaigns according to Coghlan (1986)
is the development of 'pay at the door' which has allowed the vast
majority of the population to become involved in physical education,
sport and recreation programmes, thus fulfilling a useful function
in the maintenance of good health and the constructive utilisation
of leisure time.

The most recent Sports Council campaign 'Ever Thought of Sport?'
for example, is an attempt to encourage more participation for the
13-24 year old age group. The publicity campaign costing £500,000
orientated thoughts towards active participation in an attempt to
create:

'a dialogue between those teenagers who want to play sport
and the adults who can provide it'

In this context, sport offered youngsters the opportunity to take
part in something exciting and fulfilling, when, in many cases, there
will be no other glimmer of excitement or fulfilment in their lives
other than what they see on the TV screen or in advertisements.
As the 'Ever Thought of Sport' manual maintains:

'The latent energy, particularly of our young people between
the ages of 13 and 24, can lead to unsocial behaviour. Vandalism
and disruptive behaviour, has sometimes become their way to
express their frustration and to combat their new-found boredom.
We all have a duty to help our young people, and assist in
directing their energy into areas which would help them to cope
with this very different and changing society'.

In 1976 the British Government, in accepting the principles of
the Council of Europe's 'Sport for All' Policy implicitly committed
itself to the use of physical education and sport as a means of
improving the quality of life. Article I of the Charter stated that,
'every individual shall have the right to participate in sport', and
further articles explained how opportunities to exploit this right
were to be created
In 1978, the General Conference of UNESCO accepted the International Charter of Physical Education and Sport. Article I of this
Charter laid down that:

'Every human being has a fundamental right of access to physical
education and sport, which are essential for the full development of his personality. The freedom to develop physical,
intellectual and moral powers through physical education and
sport and must be guaranteed both within the educational system
and in other aspects of social life.
Everyone must have full opportunities, in accordance with his
national tradition of sport, for practising physical education
and sport, developing his physical fitness and attaining a level
of achievement in sport which corresponds to his gifts'.

This is a clear indication that the British Government is
committed to the development of social and physical qualities through
organised sport and recreation programmes.
The paper has attempted to investigate the role of national and
local government in improving the quality of life for the nation by
the provision of leisure programmes. There are many other schemes
which have not been mentioned in detail. They include the 'Football
and the Community Scheme'; 'Sport for the Disabled'; '50+ All to
Play For'; the 'Urban Aid Programmes', all of which have been
concerned with improving the quality of life for the participants.
Sport for all is not about elitism, it is not only about young
people, it is about the whole of society. If you believe that
physical eduication and sport contribute to the quality of life then

you must believe that society must do all it can to bring the same opportunities to the widest possible market.

References

Albermarle Report. (1960) The Youth Service. H.M.S.O
Allardt, E. (1984) 'The Ever Changing Nature of the Quality of Life and in the Sources of Dissatisfaction: Scandinavian Experience' in Olin, K. Contribution of Sociology to the Study of Sport. Jyvaskyla. Univeristy of Jyvaskyla.
Central Advisory Council for Education. (1960) The Crowther Report. H.M.S.O
Central Advisory Council for Education. (1963) The Newsom Report. H.M.S.O
Central Council for Physical Recreation.(1960) Sport and the Community. The Wolfenden Report.
Coglan,J. (1980) Sport and People. The British Journal of Physical Education. Vol.17. No.2:59-60.
Department of Education and Science. (1972) Education: a Framework for Expansion.
Department of Education and Science. (1978) 'The Development of Sporting Talent'. Circular 16/78.
Department of the Environment. (1975) Sport and Recreation.
Illmarinen, M. (1984) Sport and International Understanding. New York Springer-Uerlong.
Kane, J.E. (1974) Physical Education in Secondary Schools. MacMillan.
Laitinen, A. (1984) 'Women's Sports - Overview of Finnish Women's Physical Culture and Physical Activness'. in Olin, K. Contribution of Sociology to the Study of Sport. Jyvaskyla University of Jyvaskyla
McIntosh, P.C. and Charlton, V. (1985) The Impact of Sports for All Policy 1966-84. Sports Council.
Mouetard, R. (1983) The Sport Populaire, Paris. Meseidor Editions Sociales.
Sports Council. (1976) Council of Europe. European Sport for All Charter.
Sports Council. (1985) Ever Thought of Sport.
U.N.E.S.C.O (1978) Internastional Charter of PLhysical Education and Sport.
Whitehead, N.J. and Hendry, L.B. (1976) Teaching P.E in England. Lepus.

THE USE OF LEISURE TIME

H.A. McINNES and S.A. GLYPTIS
Department of Physical Education and Sports Science,
Loughborough University of Technology

Abstract
The aim of this paper is to examine time use and leisure activities,
with particular reference to the role of sports and active recreation.
    This paper is based on an empirical study comprising time-budget
diaries for a random sample of 460 individuals in Nottingham. This
gives prominence to the role of particular activities within the whole
lifestyle of the individual, a form of analysis which is not possible
in conventional leisure participation surveys.
    Activity patterns revealed remarkable consistency in terms of the
most commonly pursued activities, yet considerable diversity with regard to minority pastimes and those activities that constituted an individual's leisure time.
    Leisure occupied a considerable proportion of the individual's
daily routine. The nature of leisure was both complex and varied.
Leisure lifestyles appear to be increasingly home centred, with three
quarters of all leisure events based in the home. It was found that
sport and active recreation received very little prominence in everyday lifestyles.
    The nature of leisure lifestyles is of significance both to leisure
providers and our understanding of leisure behaviour.
Key Words: Leisure lifestyles, Activity patterns, Time-budgets,
Sports, Home.

1. Introduction

Research enquiry into the use of leisure time has centred primarily on
recreation or the active use of leisure, focusing particularly on the
scale of activity and the concomitant pressures on facilities and resources. Participation surveys (BTA/University of Keele, 1967, 1969;
Patmore and Rodgers, 1972) have provided an important data base from
which much descriptive material about the popularity of activities has
been gleaned. Whilst such surveys describe leisure behaviour, they do
not explain it.
    The bulk of leisure research has focused on activities and facil-
ities rather than people, and on social aggregates rather than individuals. This approach is not without justification, given the concern for facilities and resources in planning and management issues.
Nevertheless, such omissions render our understanding of leisure

226

behaviour substantially imcomplete. Very little is known of the total
'package' of activities and experiences which make up an individual's
routine. In any attempt to explain the behaviour of an individual,
rather than merely describe it, such contextual 'life-style' considerations must be taken into account.

The notion of lifestyle may be defined as "the aggregate pattern of
day-to-day activities which make up an individual's way of life"
(Glyptis, 1981). As such it includes all of an individual's activities and experiences, and enables leisure behaviour in particular to be
placed into broader context.

This paper adopts the concept of leisure lifestyles as a means of
investigating time use and leisure activities, with particular reference to the role of sport and active recreation within these lifestyles.

2. Research procedures

2.1 Time-use studies

Time-use studies and activity accounting have assumed increasing importance in social science research. This has been primarily through
the application of time-budgets, systematic records of an individual's
use of time over a given period. The time-budget diary (or time-space
diary, if activity locations are included) provides a complete account
of time use, including the timing of activities, their duration and
sequence. The main advantage of time-space diaries is their comprehen-
siveness: they include all the informal activities that are not easily
reached by conventional interview and recall techniques. As well as
providing a complete picture of an individual's actions, they impose a
temporal exactness rarely attained by other types of survey. Duration
itself may be a reflection of the importance of different activities
(Young and Wilmott, 1973), although the quantitative measure of time
may ignore the subjective significance of the activity (de Grazia,
1962). Further, by providing an on-going account of time use, there is
less dependence on respondents' memories; accuracy and detail often
lost in other types of survey approach may thus be preserved. There
are problems too, mainly concerned with design and implementation, and
these are referred to, as appropriate in connection with the Nottingham
fieldwork on which this paper is based.

Overall, the use of time-space diaries is well suited to the lifestyle approach outlined previously, as they accommodate the investigation of activities or behaviour in the context of the total lifestyle
of the individual.

2.2 The Nottingham time-use survey

The issues addressed in this paper have been drawn from an exploratory
investigation of Leisure and the Home (Glyptis and McInnes, 1985) commissioned by the joint ESRC/Sports Council Panel on Recreation and Leisure
Research. The project comprised an empirical study of the significance
of the home as a venue for leisure, as well as examining time and space
usage in the home and elsewhere. By applying the concept of lifestyles
to the findings of this work, it is possible to examine the role of
active recreation within the overall use of leisure time.

227

Time-space diaries were employed in conjunction with a questionnaire survey to provide information on individuals' total lifestyles, time use, and activities both in home and out. The diaries provide a complete record of time and space use over a three day period, including a weekend. They thus afford a base for assessing the role of leisure in total, and of particular activities, within everyday lifestyles. The diaries also record the location, social context, and respondents' own perceptions of their activities as work, leisure, duty or whatever. All events lasting 15 minutes or more were to be included, regardless of their character; relaxation or dozing equal to playing football or walking the dog. The stipulation of a minimum time period inevitably meant that some time and events were lost. However, a full account of the main activities was most important as an indicator of daily routine.

A random sample of 460 individuals from North West Nottingham completed the time-space diaries. Fieldwork was carried out in 1984 and early 1985. Of 822 households contacted, 523 (64%) completed a questionnaire. This apparently low response was mainly due to the nature of the survey which was a cumbersome package to administer and demanded considerable time and effort from respondents. Extensive information was sought on the characteristics of the house and household and generally the interview took from 45 minutes to an hour, though up to 2 hours in some of the largest houses. From those households, 502 individuals agreed to fill in a diary; of those 460 (92%) actually completed diaries. Considering the complexity of the survey and the fact that no incentives were offered, both the rate and quality of response were high. (Table 1 shows the profile characteristics of respondents).

Table 1. Profile of characteristics of respondents

Total (%) (base=460)	Sex		Age							
	Male	Female	12-15	16-19	20-24	25-29	30-44	45-50	51-59	60+
100	42	58	4	7	19	15	29	5	7	14

3. Results

3.1 Time use

The 460 completed time-space diaries provide a remarkably penetrating insight into individuals' lifestyles. Although spanning only a three day period, the diaries nonetheless reveal the nature and range of activities undertaken, as well as the timing, location, and social context of each event.

Diary records for the whole sample contained 21,948 "events", an average of 48 per person, and 16 per day per person. These events comprised 119 different activities. Whilst this represents a wide variety of events, it must be noted that individual diaries revealed much less variety, containing on average only 15 different activities.

The activity patterns of women were more fragmented than those of men (51 events per diary for women compared with 43 for men). Further, the activities undertaken by women were generally of shorter

228

duration and more home centred than those of men. Age differences also existed, with older groups exhibiting more fragmented patterns of activity. Such social group differences are investigated further below.

3.2 Leisure and work
As outlined earlier, the lifestyle of an individual incorporates both work and leisure. Most leisure research has tended to pre-define leisure, and hence impose upon respondents the researchers' ideas of what constitutes leisure. The diaries used in the present survey allowed respondents to give their own perceptions of leisure.

"Leisure" accounted for 33% of all events recorded, compared with only 5% defined as "work". One explanation of this low representation of work, is the diary period which only included one 'weekday'. In addition, the majority of work events are single incidents of lengthy duration. Over half of all events lasted less than 30 minutes, yet the average time spent on work events was 123 minutes, and that on leisure events, 82 minutes.

Whilst there were fewer incidents of work activity, they lasted for considerably longer than leisure events. However, the average amount of leisure time per diarist per day was four times that of work. Leisure, therefore, occupies a considerable proportion of the individual's daily routine.

3.3 Activity patterns
Despite the significance of work and leisure, they only accounted for about ⅓ of the total lifestyle. "Personal care" activities, including eating, sleeping and washing, used up 40% of time, and the remainder was filled primarily with "duties" or "chores", and other miscellaneous activities. Although individual diarists had rather specialised lifestyles in terms of the range of activities they undertook, the nature and duration of these events varied widely.

Participation rates in most activities were similar to those of national surveys such as the General Household Survey (1980), although direct comparisons can be misleading. The Nottingham survey has a brief reference period of just 3 days, compared with a month in the G.H.S. Further, the G.H.S. smooths out seasonal variations through year-round fieldwork. In addition, national participation habits may be mirrored exactly in any particular survey area.

The most commonly pursued activities out-of-home were shopping, going to work, visiting friends and relatives, and going to the pub. Within the home, the necessities of life such as sleeping, eating, and washing featured prominently. Among the less essential activities, television achieved its usual prominence and reading involved over a third of respondents.

Walking and walking the dog were the most popular active pursuits outdoors, whilst sports participation and countryside visits were conspicuously lower than usual. This may be due, in part, to the restrictions of the three day record which would underrepresent those activities pursued relatively infrequently.

Overall, the daily activity patterns of individuals displayed remarkable consistency and similarity in terms of the most commonly

229

pursued activities. Sleeping, personal hygiene, eating, watching television, and shopping had by far the highest participation rates; all but shopping being home based pursuits. These 5 activities also accounted for half the total number of events. This reiterates the consistency of activity patterns, and stresses the considerable influence of the home in peoples' lives. The diversity in individual lifestyles was revealed by the less frequently pursued activities and minority pastimes; these activities that constitute an individual's leisure time.

3.4 Leisure lifestyles
It has already been indicated that leisure plays a prominent part in daily routines. The nature of leisure is complex and varied. For the purposes of this paper, active pursuits include all active out-of-home leisure activities, ranging from sport through countryside visits, to drives and informal outings; and excludes passive entertainment such as watching sport or going to the cinema.

Leisure accounted for ⅓ of time use. Three-quarters of leisure was based in the home. In other words only 8% of all events can be classed as out-of-home leisure. However, leisure events in the home were generally frequent and of brief duration, in contrast to those out-of-home which were far more sporadic but for longer duration. General home based pursuits seen as leisure included having drinks, listening to records, watching television, knitting and many others. The nature of these activities is such that they are generally informal and of short duration. The briefest out-of-home activities were walks, walking the dog, or stops at cafes; the longest were visits to the countryside and places of interest, going for drives, and parties at friends' houses. It must be stressed that few forms of out-of-home leisure can be undertaken for short periods, and this is particularly so for active recreation and sport. Active leisure accounted for some 544 events for the whole sample, or expressed as part of the total lifestyle, an average of only 2.5%. Active leisure assumed little prominence in individuals' lifestyles. In the context of the leisure lifestyle it fared little better, occupying only 11% of all leisure events. This does however disguise the actual amount of time devoted to active pursuits. Whilst there were very few of them, active recreation pursuits lasted considerably longer than most other forms of leisure. If sport alone is considered then it effectively only accounted for 0.5% of the total lifestyle, and just 2% of leisure events. The question of duration of events takes on greater significance with sport, as some 80% of events lasted more than 90 minutes.

Leisure lifestyles appear to be diverse and complex, made up of a large number of activities, frequently undertaken but for short periods of time. The home is the single most important venue for leisure and affords individuals a resource that is put to extensive and varied use. For those who participate in sport and active recreation, such events last a considerable time, yet nontheless sport and active recreation constitute only a very small proportion of leisure lifestyles.

3.5 Social group differences

3.5.1 Gender
For the sample as a whole,the average number of events was 48; for women it was 51 and men 43. In addition to the activity patterns of women being more fragmented, they were also much more home-centred. A roughly equal proportion of events were classed as work, yet 38% of male events were seen as leisure compared with only 27% for women. On the other hand, twice as many female events were described as duties or chores (31% compared with 15%). This would support claims that men lead a more leisured lifestyle than women, particularly given the propensity for leisure events to be of greater duration.

Apart from the necessities of living, women were generally over-represented in activities concerned with servicing the home and family. Active recreation comprised 9% of leisure for men and 7% for women, but male leisure time devoted to sport was four times that of women.

3.5.2 Age
Activity patterns were highly consistent across all the age-groups. Whilst leisure preferences may vary through the life cycle, the activities making up everyday lifestyles were remarkably consistent. Young people were generally less home-centred, and more orientated towards social and sporting activities out of the home; the 12-15 years age group being by far the most overrepresented group in sport and active recreation. Much of the sports participation may be explained as part of the school curriculum, but nevertheless the 12-15 age group and to a lesser extent all those under 25 years revealed lifestyles which included above average participation in active recreation.

3.5.3 Occupational status
For the majority, except for the unemployed and full-time housewives, work or school were the dominant out-of-home activities. Home-based activities were most prevelant for almost all groups, particularly clerical and professional workers. The pub featured prominently for semi and unskilled manual workers, whilst social and entertainment activities were overrepresented amongst those groups still in full-time education. Apart from the personal care and necessity activities common to all groups, the unemployed and housewives were by far the most home centred.

Unskilled manual workers, the unemployed, and school children were overrepresented in team sports; likewise skilled manual workers, clerical and professional non-manual workers in racquet and individual sports. Active recreation and sport fulfilled a lesser role in the lifestyles of the unemployed and full-time housewives; those groups that have the greatest amounts of time in which to fit leisure.

3.5.4 The social context
As many as 50% of all events were undertaken alone, yet for leisure only ⅓ fell into this category. Leisure was quite markedly a more social experience than work, duties or personal care. Leisure activities were far more likely to be undertaken with spouse or family (41%), than work and duties. Some 12% of all leisure took place in the company of friends, more than twice that of any other type of activity.

A greater proportion of active recreation events took place alone than with the family, and particularly so for sport. However, the company of friends was by far the most important social context for sports. The family was a strong factor in leisure lifestyles generally though less so for active and sporting recreation.

3.6 'Typical' lifestyles
To illustrate the points outlined above, it is useful to look briefly at two 'typical' diarists, an adult couple from an owner-occupied semi-detached house in West Nottingham. Both are employed, the man as a skilled manual worker, and the woman a non-manual clerical worker; both are aged between 25 and 29, and they have no dependents.

In overall terms, the number of activities and events undertaken were broadly similar, though the duration and nature of these activities differed markedly. For example, the man spent ⅓ of his time in leisure pursuits, taking part in 10 separate activities. The wife, on the other hand, spent just ⅕ of her time on leisure and on only 5 different activities. The woman occupied a greater amount of her time with personal care and duty activities; the proportion spent on work being roughly equal.

The man pursued more sport and active pursuits than his wife. He spent ⅓ of all his leisure time engaged in sport, and on 4 different sports, while the woman only took part in one sporting activity, a 2 hour game of squash with her husband. In this case, the lengthy duration of sporting activity perhaps overstresses the prominence of sport.

There were marked differences between the sexes, both in overall lifestyles and leisure lifestyles in particular. Attention must be drawn not only to the units to which individuals belong, such as the family, but to each individual person.

4. Conclusions

This paper set out to examine time use and leisure activities, with particular reference to the role of sport and active recreation. An approach hitherto rarely applied, namely that of lifestyles, has been developed to assess the prominence of various types of leisure in everyday lives.

The activity patterns of the whole sample were very varied, yet the lifestyles of individuals were much more specialised. Leisure constituted a third share of people's time, and in support of previous participation surveys, those pursuits that involve physical activity and going places attracted a far smaller proportion of people.

In the context of everyday routines, the most remarkable finding was the consistency of activity patterns across different social groups, the same few activities predominated in the lives of most people. However, outside the common 'necessity' activities there was far greater diversity of pursuits. This diversity was most apparent in the wide range of minority activities that make up people's leisure lifestyles. In the main, it was leisure lifestyles that distinguished between different groups. For women, leisure time tended to be more home-centred than for men. Likewise, the elderly and retired were less likely to undertake out-of-home leisure pursuits than teenagers and young adults.

Active recreation and sport played little part in the leisure life-styles of the majority of people. For some individuals, most commonly young, single males sport was far more prominent, yet in the context of all their available leisure time it was still fundamentally a minority pastime. That sport is a minority pursuit is nothing new, yet to reveal that even to those for whom sport is important, it still nonetheless forms only a small proportion of their lesiure time is significant.

The implications of this scale of activity are important for academics and leisure providers alike. Leisure lifestyles are increasingly home-centred. Only 8% of all events were out-of-home leisure pursuits and three quarters of all leisure was based in the home. This is of some importance with regard to facility management. Demands on purpose built facilities appear to be low, and the demand for sports facilities is most certainly a minor one. Leisure-time demands focus most strongly on the 'informal' facility of the home. The apportionment of time by individuals, and the activities undertaken in that time must be closely examined to ensure the best possible use of resources.

Leisure plays a prominent part in daily routines, but the nature of leisure is complex and varied. Active recreation and sport however, receive little prominence in the leisure lifestyles of the majority of people.

Acknowledgement
The research project on which this paper was based was funded by the joint ESRC/Sports Council Panel on Recreation and Leisure Research, whose support is gratefully acknowledged.

References

British Travel Association/University of Keele (1967, 1969) Pilot National Recreation Survey, Report Nos. 1 and 2
De Grazia, S (1962) Of Time, Work and Leisure, Twentieth Century Fund
Glyptis, S.A. (1981) Leisure Life-styles Regional Studies, Vol.15 No.5
Glyptis, S.A. and McInnes, H.A. (1985) Leisure and the Home Draft Report to the Joint Sports Council/Economic and Social Research Council Panel on Recreation and Leisure Research.
Office of Population Censuses and Surveys (unpublished) Leisure statistics from General Household Survey, 1980
Patmore, J.A. and Rodgers, H.B. (1972) Leisure in the North West North West Sports Council
Young, M. and Wilmott, P. (1973) The Symmetrical Family Routledge and Kegan, Paul. London.

HEGEMONY - ANOTHER BLIND ALLEY FOR THE STUDY OF SPORT?

LES HAYWOOD
Department of Applied & Community Studies, Bradford and Ilkley
Community College

Abstract

The paper examines critically recent attempts to establish "hegemony
theory" as the key perspective for the study of sport within a
sociological and historical framework. This critique focusses initially on themes discussed inter alia, by John Hargreaves in his
writings on "Sport and hegemony" by questioning the following assumptions:

    (i)   that the multi-faceted nature of sport may be adequately
explained by a single, comprehensive theoretical framework
    (ii)   that prior to the work on hegemony no real sociology of
sport had emerged.

Subsequently the paper argues that such approaches fail to address
the special, even unique, characteristics of sports and contends that
sports are radically different from other aspects of popular culture,
and thus may be seriously misunderstood if they are treated as simply
another cultural form, susceptible to identical methods of study and
analysis.

The paper concludes in an attempt to outline a model for the sociological study of sport forms, which takes account of their diversity
and variety, and which is not locked into any circumscribed ideo-
logical/theoretical stance.

<u>Key words</u>: Hegemony, Nature and structure of sport, Social theory.

Introduction

In the early publicity material for this Conference, 'Sport and
hegemony' was identified as one of the areas in sociological and
historical studies for which papers were invited. In a sense this
illustrates that the topic has already attained a certain status in
Sports Studies, and may even be in process of a sort of academic
colonization of the mainstream of sociological approaches to the
subject. The aim of this paper is to question both the approach and
the substance of the 'hegemonists' and to suggest that hegemony
theory may well be a blind alley which will not lead us far in the

quest for better understanding the nature and significance of sports practice and involvement. My argument will consist of three strands: first, a critique of the work of John Hargreaves (1982a, 1982b), the major published writer in the field; second, some thoughts on the nature of sport as an aspect of culture; third, proposals for alternative perspectives offering more productive insights for sports study and understanding.

Critique of hegemony theorists

It appears to be fashionable among neo-Marxist writers* to preface the construction of their definitive theory with the systematic assassinations of rivals and predecessors. Thus Hargreaves condemns to the scrap heap of atheory and idealism not merely functionalist and figurational sociologists such as Loy and Kenyon (1969) and Dunning (1979), but dispatches as equally naive structural Marxists such as Brohm (1978) and Hoch (1972). This ground-clearing proceeds with a minimum of discussion, leaving the way clear for hegemony theory which is then staked out with equal haste ... determinism and idealism must be eschewed, a dialectic between agency and structure will allow both the repressive and liberalising strands in Marxian theories to co-exist. Capitalism and modern sport (the twin evils for neo-Marxist sport sociologists) remain stubbornly attractive and resiliant in the Western democracies - send for a theory which keeps faith with Marx, but doesn't treat people as dupes. Gramsci's theory of hegemony looks promising for it allows for a degree of cultural autonomy while at the same time locating ideological control with dominant groups in such a way as to carry moral and not merely coercive force... This is something of a caricature of Hargreaves' position but is certainly no more cavalier than his wholesale rejection of the majority of alternative sociological writings on sport.

Having established the pre-eminence of hegemony theory, Hargreaves (1982b) develops his analysis drawing on empirical evidence from British sports practice, in an effort to identify the extent to which particular sports, and sporting occurences, exhibit tendencies towards autonomy or compliance. However it is here that problems inherent in the theory become most apparent, for while the possibility of freedom, change and opposition is constantly evoked as a promise, Hargreaves denies them much space in the exemplars on which he draws. For example in considering the ritual element in sports as inherently political, and thus inevitably servicing the hegemonic class interests, he seems almost to ignore his own condemnation of determinism. Ritual is described as "traditional and cognitive" yet still serves the ruling hegemony.

A further element of sporting practice discussed is that of media presentation. Again the analysis is virtually completely one-sided,

---

* See also for example R. Hollands (1984) The role of cultural studies and social criticism in the sociological study of sport. Quest, 36.

the media acting as a hegemonic filter through which sport becomes
ineluctably oppressive ... "In modern capitalist societies ... the
media re-dramatise and represent what are already potent dramatic
spectacles within a framework of interpretation, which facilitates
the passing of encoded messages, that is preferred ways of seeing
sport and society"(1982 p.127).   Little room for autonomy here, and
little room either for the editorial independence of T.V. presenters
for example, or any discussion of the aesthetic qualities of sport
which seem remarkably and enduringly potent across cultures, whatever
their particular political/ideological stance. Does, in fact, T.V.
presentation of sport's nature per se, shift from culture to culture
once one dips beneath any unsubtle nationalistic/chauvinistic veneer?

A further exemplification of the paradoxical nature of the theory is
its adoption of what might be called the "double metaphor" principle.
Here some of the positive elements of sport are identified - the
equality unavailable elsewhere as Caillois (1961) put it; evenhanded
rules; chance and luck held in balance - and to subordinate classes
these qualities are held to demonstrate how life should be, while at
the same time to elites sports may "serve as exemplifications of the
bourgeois ideal of the individualistic competitive, meritocratic
society" (1982, p.129). Surely there is an inherent contradiction
here: certainly sport values and practices were   re-shaped in the
image of industrial capitalism in the middle to late 19th century and
its modern structure of rules and canons and patterns of action
reflects that image to some degree, but the underlying test of human
skills is of much older origin and enduring appeal, drawing a response
that cut across lines of dominance and subordination as much in the
past as it does in the present. This is not to say that the class
analysis of sport is not relevant or important, but it is to question
whether it is the most important issue in considering the shaping of
people's perceptions of sport.
    In sum, the examples which Hargreaves has chosen to illustrate the
explanatory power of hegemony theory do not do particular justice to
the claim that dimensions of both autonomy and compliance may be
embraced within a coherent framework. Equally there is no strong
evidence that the theory is especially potent in the study of sport in
all its ramifications, as I shall go on to argue in the next section.

The nature of sports

Sports at root are tests of gratuitous difficulty, artificial human
constructions devised and moulded to maximise opportunities for the
exercise of certain human qualities. While they share this common
rootage, sports are nonetheless incredibly diverse in their forms and
structures, the challenges and responses they proffer, and equally
diverse in the levels and types of organisation in which they are
situated. It would be possible to arrange sports on a series of
matrices (see for example Haywood and Kew 1984) using such features as
type of challenge/mode of interaction/categories of skill/levels of
organisation, etc., for their classification. Such an exercise, if it

achieved nothing else, would attest to the plurality of the concept
sport and alert us to the danger of proposing all-embracing theories
for its explanation.

A second point concerning the nature of sports,not unrelated to
the above, is that there are particular problems in applying neo-
Marxist perspectives to such a social phenomenon because of its fun-
damently 'artificial' non-work nature, and its consequent unsuscep-
tibility to analyses which are predicated on the centrality of the
labour process. This is the issue raised by Morgan (1983) in his
consideration of the application of the ideas of the Frankfurt School
of sociology to sport, and hinges on the issue of the essentially un-
productive, inefficient nature of the way in which sports' goals are
achieved. The process, according to Morgan, being a complete
reversal of the normal rationalisation of work processes, the aim
being always to maintain the gratuitous difficulty of the exercise in
spite of the efforts of players and coaches to streamline the activity in production terms. A look at the efforts of modern sports
administrators to counter this tendency to rationalise their game or
sport demonstrates the centrality of the concept of sports as
'occasions of pure waste' (to borrow again from Caillois) - a concept
which again renders hegemonic interpretations as problematic.

A further feature of modern sports, and one which is particularly
pertinent at this Conference with its link with the Commonwealth
Games, is that sports in many ways are a unique (or at least very
unusual) cultural form. Their idiom is international in form and
practice, and their very structures remain remarkably similar under
a great variety of political and social systems, and this is certainly
not the case for most other cultural forms. It is one thing to say
that the rationalisation, commercialisation, chauvinism, etc., of
sports must be viewed contextually across societies as Hargreaves
argues, but equally we are unlikely to progress our understanding of
the nature of sports if we fail to account for the remarkable dura-
bility and universality of the actual structures (rules, skills, etc)
of particular sports across time and across cultures. What is it
about this largely British 19th century cultural form whcih renders
it so universally appealing to players and spectators alike, and so
apparently malleable to the needs of very different political
systems? Of course we can account for its spread to the former
colonies and elsewhere along with British trade imperialism, but that
is not to explain its particular power to take root and flourish once
introduced. Again my argument is that hegemony theory may divert us
from a proper analysis of the international idiom of sports in its
preoccupation with its extrinsic rather than intrinsic properties.

Alternative perspectives

If the preceding paragraphs seem to be hard on hegemony theory it is
not because of a belief that this approach has no relevance for the
study of sport for, as I shall argue below, it can provide useful
insights into some aspects of sports practice. Rather my concern is
with the apparent attempt to establish the pre-eminence of such a

perspective and the consequent distortions of social reality required in order to fit such multi-faceted phenomena as modern sports into an ideological/theoretical straitjacket, which in any event was originally devised with a quite different patient in mind.

My initial value assumption in approaching sociological studies of sport is that the enterprise is at heart about understanding the involvement, direct and indirect, of people in sports. Sports are at the same time amazingly diverse in their forms and structures, but also display striking similarities and universality along other dimensions. They exist on a multiplicity of levels, are capable of offering enormous intrinsic satisfactions, but are equally subject to pervasive extrinsic exploitations. Sports may be located on continua from playform - workform; freedom - constraint; recreation - athletics; autonomous - incorporated; process - product. Equally sports have diverse histories (careers) and origins; some remain culturally specific, others cross frontiers with ease; most are in a constant state of flux. Given the foregoing it is perhaps not surprizing that my contention is that to understand such a complex multiplicity of dimensions of sports, we need to employ a plurality of theoretical perspectives and consequent methods of analysis which are not locked into a pre-set ideological cage.

The starting point may be any exemplification of sport involvement set in its particular historical period and cultural context, and the focus may be micro or macro, game structure or game organisation, etc.Specificity is important. Dependent then on the nature of the specific problem or issue, we bring to bear those perspectives which will illuminate our understanding. For example if a sport form was highly incorporated into a social system (as in education) at a particular time, then both Marxist and functional perspectives may prove useful in probing the particular circumstances then current, and in tracing the ongoing institutional relationship between sport and education. In fact I have argued elsewhere that cultural reproduction theories (Haywood 1982) may be very effective in analysing the modernisation of certain sport forms in 19th century Britain, and certainly hegemony theory would add to our understanding of that process in that specific context. On the other hand if our concern is with how players make sense of the rules of a game, or what the key elements are which render a game viable or non-viable, then micro-sociological approaches drawing on symbolic-interactionist or ethno-methodological perspectives may be the most appropriate way into understanding the fleeting, processional interactions which actually constitute the game. Equally if our interest lies in examining the particular tensions and balances that exist within a sport at particular levels, and in probing the source of developments in play (e.g. variation in importance of attack/defence; individuals/group) than Elias & Dunning's figurational sociology may be productive.

Other examples could be given, but the foregoing should suffice to indicate the lines on which I am proposing that we should proceed. Sports sociology is clearly still in its infancy and if it is to be of benefit to sporting practice, rather than becoming a blind alley, and consequently ignored by most sports practitioners and fans, it should employ all the tools that are available - not uncritically, but by the same token not prejudically. The next step may be to construct a classificatory meta-theoretical model in order to map out the dimensions and interrelationships of insights gained via divergent theoretical approaches - a task in which the recent work of Giddens (1979) may be a fruitful starting point.

References

Brohm, J.M. (1978) Sport - a prison of measured time. Ink Links, London.

Caillois, R. (1961) Man, Play and Games. Free Press, Glencoe.

Dunning, E. and Sheard, K. (1979) Barbarians, Gentlemen and Players. Martin Robertson, Oxford.

Giddens, A. (1979) Central problems in social theory, Macmillan, London

Hargreaves, John (1982a) in Hargreaves, J. (ed) Sport, culture and ideology. Routledge & Kegan Paul, London.

Hargreaves, John (1982b) Sport and Hegemony in Cantelon, H. and Gruneau, R. Sport, culture and the modern state. University of Toronto Press.

Haywood, L. & Kew, F. (1984) New directions in leisure studies. Papers in Community Studies No. 2. Bradford & Ilkley Community College.

Haywood, L.J. (1982) Sport and cultural reproduction, in Sport and the Community, June Newsletter supplement, leisure Studies Association.

Hoch, P. (1972) Rip off - the big game. Doubleday, New York

Loy, J. & Kenyon, G.S. (1969) Sport, culture and society. Macmillan, London

Morgan, W. (1983) Toward a critical theory of sport. Journal of sport and social issues. Vol. 7.

CRITICAL REMARKS REGARDING SPORTS AID
FOR DEVELOPING COUNTRIES

by PROF. HARALD DUBBERKE (rtd.)
President, International Sports Academy, West-Germany

Abstract
Sports and physical education are not independent activities. Administrators,
coaches and competitors as well as teacher in physical education and their
participants train in a field of definite philosophical and political conditions.
It has to be seen that there exist innumerable cultural differences in all
the various societies.
One half of the world - the industrialized world is determined by commerce,
profit-making and subjective high performance. That is a relative
philosophical change which has grown in the last two centuries and is
influencing all aspects of life and culture. It has nothing to do with
happiness or peace or self-reliance and so on. It may be contrary. Who
feels competent to answer this question adequately ?
Sports and physical education mirrow the philosophy of a high-performance-
society, although sports and physical education **is not** a basic need in poor
countries.
Key words: sports aid, cultural cooperation, self-reliance, humanity,
high-performance-society, healthy youth, mass-sports.

Sports and physical education are part of education. As such we have to
see the point that the help of one country given to another will never be
free of criticism - it can not be!!
For example, the education in any European country has a special contents
which has grown from the past and has adapted itself to the needs of
industrialized and economic requirements. If we transfer these ideas to
non-industrialized countries it will not function properly. It has also to be
considered that in many countries of the ' Third World ' education is not
spread all over. The result can be that only a minority will benefit of a
given help in the field of education. With other words - if we understand
sports and physical education as a part of education only an elite has the
chance to be taught in physical education !
   Georg Bernhard SHAW (the former Irish poet) once said that if
somebody wants to teach someone, he will never learn it. He is right in
as far as we understand education as an active process. Education has to
be **wanted** by the interested person. Taking this in mind we have to state

that support in physical education and sports should be granted only if it is requested for by a country ! You may reply that sports aid is not possible against an independent country, correct !

But I have in mind many attempts where in the field of educational aid and assistance others tried to convince someone that only a particular sport is the right one for a specific country. At this point I would like to mention that true partnership has to be the basis for a cooperation in sports and physical education. The selection of the type of sports is therefore a decision that has to be made by the receiving country itself.

Sports and physical education are not independent activities. Coaches, administrators and competitors as well as teacher in physical education and their pupils train in a field of definite philosophical and political conditions. It has to be seen that there exist innumerable cultural differences in all the various societies.

Based on the above statement and the experiences I got as a sports expert in Nigeria where I lived for five years to establish a NATIONAL INSTITUTE FOR SPORTS in Lagos I would like to make some critical remarks regarding sports aid being offered to developing countries. I have to say that I speak for myself and I don't pretend to be right ! My intention is to open a discussion and I would be glad if I could contribute to a small extent in finding a passable solution for the future.

If we put the question ' How can sports and physical education be organized in developing countries ? ' we first have to define what a developing country concerning sports and physical education is ! It may surprise you if I say that we don't have any developing country in this respect. Each society or country has its own original sports or physical education activities related to its culture. It is not right to state that an economically poor country is automatically a developing country in sports !

What matters is the modern contents of sports which has been set up in the European or Western World exclusively. The main competitions nowadays are the Olympic Games and World Championships and if we have a close look at the types of sports practise there, there is none of the original sports from the so called ' developing countries '. At least the rules are new, see for example wrestling. Therefore I believe that the programme of the Olympic Games are not quite fair to countries which have started later going in for modern sports. I am certainly not the first who ask the question, why cannot the programme of international competitions be changed ? Somehow it should be possible to bring in original sports from the different countries in the **right balance** - that is important. If this idea would be accepted European countries may become developing countries in the area of sports or do you think I am dreaming ?

Coming back to the present reality it is a fact that countries of the ' Third World ' are trying to find their identity through sports in the very same way as developed countries do. This attempt is very hard and therefore they ask for assistance from more developed countries - but do they meet the interest of their people ? As I said before, we are living in a world of differences. One half of the world - the industrialized world is determined by commerce, profit-making and subjective high performances. That is a relative philosophical change which has grown in the last two centuries and is influencing all aspects of life and culture. It has nothing to do with happiness or peace or self-reliance and so on. It may be contrary. Who feels competent to answer this question adequately ?

Most countries have decided to accept the idea of modern sports above to promote their people and to improve life. Sports and physical education mirrow the philosophy of a high-performance-society. Through sports there is an influence on various aspects of culture. That is what we have to realize and to pronounce. The question which comes next to me is whether this is the only one to be considered. Is there no way to find individual and collective satisfaction and a valuable life apart from the above thesis ? May be there is no alternative but then it is nevertheless a question of whether we have to practise the idea of high performance to the extent it is presently done or not. Of course, all cultures had a stage in the past where their people had to fight and to compete with nature or with each other to survive. But is this reason an argument to continue to regard sports as the exclusive field of the highest efficiency ? I don't know - but to give a personal answer I would like to see the pressure created through the idea of high performance reduced for the individual human being !

I have always attempted to differenciate between sports and physical education. That was by intention. I see physical education as most important and consider it as a right for everybody because I believe in the image of a pyramid. The bigger the foundation of a pyramid is, the higher can we build the pyramid of physical education. The top of the pyramid can be the high performance sports, why not. Somewhere in the middle of the pyramid I would place the interest of sports. To remain within the picture I guess it is very dangerous to turn the pyramid on its top. It will shake and fall down at any time. Even if we support the idea of high performance sports there is no doubt that more attention should be given to mass-sports, including schoolsports. 2ooo years ago DIOGENES said in Greece that the foundation of each state or nation is the education of **youth**. A healthy youth will be the best guarantee for the welfare and progress of a country !

Now, if we check what has been done most then it was to send coaches to non-industrialized countries to improve high performance sports and to enable these countries to compete on international level with developed countries. Is that the only way to present sports aid ?

There is another point we have to consider or remember which is that sports or physical education **is not** a basic need in poor countries. People who are hungry are more interested to get food. The World Bank has found out that about 1.3 billion human beings are living with a minimum of food and only 2 - 3 % of the total population in these countries are active in sports. These are facts !

Most of us believe that sports and physical education are values in themselves and think that even poor people have a right to practise sports, to play and to prove their abilities in the area of sports and physical education for their own satisfaction and self-reliance. An answer or compromise to this contradiction should be : only if the main attention

242

is given to school- or mass-sports it is justifiable to promote high performance sports. Many countries have problems to find their national identity. For this reason it seems understandable if priority is first of all given to high performance sports or elite sports and I am convinced that success in national or international sports championships then will influence the mass-sports positively. Therefore I see nothing being wrong as long as mass-sports (sports for all) and schoolsports is recognized as the foundation of the pyramid.

Up to here I spoke more or less about the people who practise sports and physical education. The majority, unfortunately as we know by reports of the World Bank is passive. For many of them sports is only an amusement on the weekend. Do they enjoy sports when they go to the stadium to watch a football match, for example ? I very often saw that at the end of the match spectators started to fight or showed other forms of aggressive behaviour in case their own team lost. This happens even in Europe and I guess we cannot use the argument of amusement without limiting this function if we try to defend sports.

You can see there are many problems in the field of sports aid which have to considered. What about the countries which are willing to assist in the development of sports in the ' Third World '? Do they offer their help only for reasons of humanity ? Sometimes a country starts with the offer of sports aid to establish a certain form of cultural cooperation which then serves as a first step for economic relationships. I am not against these contacts. For me this is legal. In many cases sports is the entrance for general political partnership. But the receiving country has to realize this intention. By all means I share the opinion of Leopold SENGHOR from Senegal who said that the cultural cooperation can be imperialistic and dangerous and another type of colonialism. And sports is a part of any cultural transfer as I said already.

Before a country asks for sports aid it should be examined in which field of sports good sportsmen can be more easily sponsored and which one is most healthy for the people. As we know - each human being has his own individuality, constitution and talents. I reckon this applies also to tribes and nations. If we look into the list of records it will be verified. Sure, with a good coach and optimal conditions under the right circumstances, everything is possible, no question. But in most of the non-industrialized countries there is a lack of means. Considering this big disadvantage man has to be modest.

From the practical point of view we have to take into account that modern sports needs special equipment and facilities, but especially a lot of good administration. However, effective administration depends on general and specific education. In most of the affected countries the educational system has not fully expanded yet. It appears to me that already sports aid has to start at this stage, which means assisting in setting up effective and functional bodies in sports administration and to educate sports organizers. The second step, not in time, should be the training of coaches and teachers in physical education to enable them to help themselves as soon as possible and to train their own competitors. In the maintime it would be favourable if foreign coaches could train the athletes. This would be in line with many countries which are interested in fast progress. When I first mentioned the necessity and advisability of a support in the sense of personal staff I did so because I believe that human thinking is the basic requirement at all. Even if we spend a lot of money on sports it will not help if there is a lack of qualified staff. On the other hand sports aid cannot be successful without financial means to provide adequate facilities and equipment. A very simple example is pole vault. You cannot compete with a bamboo stick against your opponent who is using a synthetic pole ! Schools without any space around cannot practise football or athletics - how can we introduce physical education in this case ?

Let me come back to those who really initiate and promote the idea of sports: ORGANIZERS, COACHES and COMPETITORS. Sports is often appreciated as something good for health but not to the extend of support or choise to become a member of the big family of sports, unfortunately ! What can be done ?

An easy and useful undertaken is to guarantee regular lessons in physical education at schools. This is a serious challenge to the respective government. But even if the government has approved regular lessons in physical education it takes a long time to realize it. I know it very well.

Those who are professionally active ' workers ' in sports have to get adequate recognation and suitable payment and promotion. Otherwise good staff will go away to business or students of teaching will choose other subjects and so on. Nobody can make a livelihood on honour alone. The 'job' has to be attractive. For competitors we have to create a particular ' scale ' of awareness and social security, too. If we want them to train hard and to keep away from some other exiting attractions we have to think of compensation, somehow. But promotion and other gratitude should be bound to qualification and progress and not to tribalism or political coherence. Unfairness in this respect will spoil all efforts in the long run.

I would have liked to talk more about schoolsports to emphasize the importance of it or about the topic ' women in sports ' but the time is much too short to discuss this points extensively. I rather would prefer to answer questions on the end of my speech.

As I mentioned there is no doubt that through the promotion of school sports high performance sports can be achieved. I would be glad if I was able to transfer my belief to you. The other, and to me more important side of the coin is that the health of thousands of people can be improved through schoolsports or mass-sports to help people to fulfil their duties in society but moreover, they can enjoy life more than a medically weak person.

Coming to the end of my topic - it should be stressed that the countries of the so called ' First World ' or industrialized area are still developing especially if we consider the speedy technical progress and we don't know where and when it will end, probably never. Sports is not excluded. New techniques in sports or better equipment will be researched. For this reason we all belong to a developing community. Only the stages differ in the countries. The term ' development ' is therefore relative and development is not the sense of all. Other dimensions like happiness, freedom, cultural tradition etc. are equally, or decisively more important.

So far - so good ! Countries with a lower standard in sports should think twice about the chances and danger involved when other countries offer them sports aid. It has to be found out what a country finally wants to be advised, what are the needs, what is necessary, what is in line with the tradition and what can be realized. Sports aid for the so called ' developing countries ' should always be newly and properly discussed. It seems to me as if some ideological positions have to be changed or at least modified if the idea of health and other needs should be given ' green lights '.

To make it clear - I was a gymnast on national level for more than 1o years. I am not against high performance sports. Undoubtely it is better to compete on the track instead of quarrelling with weapons. Sports and physical education without high performance sports are like a child without arms and legs. My criticism mainly aims at one-sided and unreflected promotion of high performance sports and sports aid. How can we ever argue for sports aid if many people die because of lack of food and if at the same time by means of sports aid we only advance a small elite.

Sports and physical education should get more attention everywhere and sports aid as a part of international aid programmes should be considered in good time and at early stage.

A STUDY OF FAMILY'S ROLE AS A SOCIAL SYSTEM IN SOCIALIZATION OF SPORTSMEN INTO SPORTS IN NIGERIA

AMARJIT SINGH SOHI   Department of Physical and Health Education,
                      University of Ibadan
                      Nigeria.

KANWALJIT SINGH   Ondo State Sports Council,
                      Akure, Nigeria.

Abstract
The purpose of the study was to see the role of family as a social
system in socializing sportsmen into sports. A sample of 200
sportsmen of different sports and who have particiapted at higher
levels, were randomly selected. A pretested questionnaire, pertinent in nature was used to collect the data. The analysis of the
data showed that significantly more number of sportsmen's parents,
siblings and relatives participated in sports. The sportsmen
were encouraged to participate in sports by the members of the
family - parents, siblings, relatives. Parents and siblings also
exposed the sportsmen equally to the values of sports participation and competition, whereas the relatives did so but to a lower
tune. The overall analysis showed that family as a whole played a
significant role in socializing the sportsmen into sports.
Key words: Socialization, Family, Sports, Values.

1. Introduction

Among the social systems, the family has been seen as playing a
pivotal role in socializing the children into various roles which
they assume and enact as functional members of the society.
McPherson (1968) observed that first interest in sport among
children was aroused by and within the family. Greendorfer (1979)
observed that family was seen as an influential social system in
getting the youth involved in sports. However, both these studies
indicated that family's influence decreased as children grew up
which was contrary to what was concluded by Sohi (1985). Synder
and Spretzer (1973) and Orlick (1972) claimed that parents of
the athletes themselves participated in sports and hence presented
a social milieu conducive to the inculcation of interest of their
children in sports. It would not look a far fetched idea to stress
the fact as suggested by other studies that parent's participation
and family's sports environment as a whole were found related to
the process of socialization of the children into sports (Hackman,
1978; Maluphy 1970). Apart from the parents, the siblings being
close to each other in age and immediate in interaction
over long time, have been seen as having sociali-

zing influences on their brothers and sisters developing a meaningful propensity towards sports participation (Landers 1970; Portz 1972). While using social-role social-system approach of Kenyon and McPherson (1971), the study intended to test the following hypotheses about the family's influence in socializing sportsmen into sports role.

(i) Significantly more number of members of the family of sportsmen participated in sports.
(ii) Members of the family motivated the sportsmen to participate in sports.
(iii) The family taught the values of participation in sports to the sportsmen.
(iv) The family exposed the sportsmen to the values of sports competitions.

2. Method

A total of 200 athletes of various sports who have participated at national and international levels were selected randomly from a state in Nigeria. A pretested and relevant questionnaire was used for data collection. Family's role as social system in socializing the athletes into sports was considered as influence of parents, siblings and other relatives. The socializing efforts of the family were seen as members participation in sports, the encouragement given to the sportsmen and its emphasis on values of sport participation and competition. To see an association between the variables or significance in difference chi-square statistics have been used.

3. Results

To ascertain whether the family provided a favourable social milieu, the participation of its members was considered as shown in Table 1. The parents, siblings and other relatives participated in some sports. In each case the number of participating members was significantly high. The number of parents and siblings participants was found to be similar but their number was significantly high compared to other relatives. The analysis supported the hypothesis one.

Table 1. Sportsmen by their family's participation in sports.

Family	Participated				
	Always	Sometimes	Never	Total	x^2
Parents	126	36	38	200	79.318*
	63.0%	18.0%	19.0%	100%	
Siblings	131	25	44	200	95.926*
	65.5%	12.5%	22.0%	100%	
Other relatives	101	51	48	200	26.779*
	50.5%	25.5%	24.0%	100%	

* Significant $P < .05$

The data in Table 2 indicated a degree of latent and active motivational momentum given by the family to sportsmen during their later childhood and adolescence to continue participating in sports. During these years significantly more number of sportsmen were encouraged to participate in sports to various extent by their parents, siblings and other relatives. The encouragement by parents and siblings was of similar extent whereas the other relatives did not match them in this endeavour. The motivational support of the family to the sportsmen during their later childhood and adolescence remained same in magnitutde. The analysis supported hypothesis two.

Table 2. Sportsmen by the encouragement given to them during their later childhood and adolescence by the family.

Age	Family members	Encouraged				
		Always	Sometimes	Never	Total	x^2
Later childhood	Parents	120	60	20	200	75.006*
		60.0%	30.0%	10.0%	100%	
	Siblings	140	40	20	200	124.001*
		70.0%	20.0%	10.0%	100	
	Other relatives	98	66	36	200	28.865*
		49.0%	33.0%	18.0%	100%	
Adolescence	Parents	97	73	30	200	34.572*
		48.5%	36.5%	15.0%	100%	
	Siblings	127	50	23	200	87.377*
		63.5%	25.0%	11.5%	100%	
	Other relatives	95	69	36	200	26.231*
		47.5%	34.5%	18.0%	100%	

* Significant, $P < .05$

The socialization into a role being gradual, socializing agent has to keep on emphasizing the importance of the outcomes of the role enactment in the present case participation in sport. In order to make the sportsmen to descriminate and cope up with negative reactions due to frustration emerging from sports participation, the family as a system emphasized on the values of enactment of such a role. The data are shown in Table 3. A significant more number of parents taught the values of sports participation to the incumbents during their later childhood and adolescence periods. However, more parents did not lay much emphasis on two values, i.e., "to be physically fit" and "to get a better job." The parental emphasis on teaching these values of sports participation remained the same during later childhood and adolescence periods of life of the sportsmen. The siblings contributions in socializing the sportsmen in this regard were identical in nature to that of parents. The other relatives did teach these values but their number was significantly less. On the other hand, they kept on teaching these values to sportsmen with almost same zeal during later childhood and adolescence periods of life the sportsmen.

The comparisons were carried out to know who in the family emphasized more on the values of sport participation. The parental and siblings emphasis in this regard was of equal magnitude, but they were found to be more influential than the other relatives. More parents as compared to siblings made sportsmen to realize the value of participation in terms of physical fitness and job opportunities during later life. The other relatives tried to inculcate the values of participation among sportsmen with similar zeal during later childhood and adolescence of the sportsmen. The hypothesis three with its ramifications by and large has been supported with help of the analysis.

The data about family's emphasis on values as outcomes of sports competition are given in Table 4. The parents, significantly more in number, made the sportsmen to recognize and internalize the values of competition. They, however, did not do so in the case of two values, i.e., "to be aggressive" and "to win at all cost." The parental teaching of these values remained at the same tune during sportsmen's later childhood and adolescence. However, the parental emphasis increased in the case of two values during the adolescence period. The siblings socializing influence was observed to be similar to that of parents both in extent and nature. The other relatives did teach these values but to a lower extent. The hypothesis four on the basis of the analysis was found to be tenable to greater extent.

It was of special interest to note that family as a system was both module and model in socializing the sportsmen into sport. The social closeness and intimate but enduring interaction between the sportsmen and their family members were of special significance in the process of sports-role socialization.

Table 3. The extent of values of sport participation taught to the sportsmen during their later childhood and adolescence by the family.

Family members	Extent of values Taught	Values									
		To be physically fit		To be popular		To defeat opponents		To get better job		To bring laurel to the country	
		6-12 years	13-20 years	6-12 years	13-20 years	6-12 years	13-20 years	6-12 years	13-20 years	6-12 years	13-20 years
Parents	Always	77 38.5%	67 33.5%	103 51.5%	97 48.5%	88 44.0%	109 54.5%	70 35.0%	82 41.0%	93 46.5%	105 52.5%
	Sometimes	49 24.5%	62 31.0%	14 7.0%	24 12.0%	15 7.5%	15 7.5%	14 7.0%	9 4.5%	16 8.0%	15 7.5%
	Never	74 37.0%	71 35.5%	83 41.5%	79 39.5%	97 48.5%	76 38.0%	116 58.0%	109 54.5%	91 45.5%	80 40.0%
Siblings	Always	67 33.5%	79 39.5%	119 59.5%	102 51.0%	102 51.1%	119 59.5%	71 35.5%	74 37.0%	82 41.0%	112 56.0%
	Sometimes	78 39.0%	60 30.0%	14 7.0%	25 12.5%	14 7.0%	12 6.0%	8 4.0%	15 7.5%	22 11.0%	6 3.0%
	Never	55 27.5	61 30.5%	67 33.5%	73 36.5%	84 42.0%	69 34.5%	131 60.5%	111 55.5%	96 48.0%	82 41.0%
Other relatives	Always	46 23.0%	51 25.5%	46 23.0%	44 22.0%	51 25.5%	52 26.0%	36 18.0%	43 21.5%	52 26.0%	57 28.5%
	Sometimes	19 9.5%	23 11.5%	20 10.0%	44 22.0%	11 5.5%	22 11.0%	15 7.5%	21 10.5%	16 8.0%	20 10.0%
	Never	135 67.5%	126 63.0%	134 67.0%	112 56.0%	138 69.0%	126 63.0%	149 74.5%	136 68.0%	132 66.0%	123 61.5%

Table 4. The extent of values of sport competition taught to the sportsmen during their later child-hood and adolescence by the family.

Family members	Extent of Values taught	Values									
		To win at all cost		To play fairly		To play to the best of ability		To be aggressive		To obey the rules of the game	
		6-12 years	13-20 years	6-12 years	13-20 years	6-12 years	13-20 years	6-12 years	13-20 years	6-12 years	13-20 years
Parents	Always	50 25.0%	73 36.5%	109 54.5%	110 56.0%	117 58.5%	130 65.0%	46 23.0%	55 27.5%	102 51.0%	118 59.0%
	Sometimes	25 12.5%	29 14.5%	9 4.5%	16 8.0%	5 2.5%	16 8.0%	14 7.0%	19 9.5%	11 5.5%	10 5.0%
	Never	125 62.5%	98 49.0%	82 41.0%	74 37.0%	78 39.0%	54 27.0%	140 70.0%	126 63.5%	87 43.5%	72 36.0%
Siblings	Always	67 33.5%	69 34.5%	105 52.5%	113 56.5%	129 64.5%	134 67.0%	61 30.5%	64 32.0%	121 60.5%	132 66.0%
	Sometimes	21 10.5%	29 14.5%	7 3.5%	25 12.5%	9 4.5%	19 9.5%	15 7.5%	25 12.5%	5 2.5%	9
	Never	112 5.6%	102 51.0%	88 44.0%	62 31.0%	62 31.0%	47 23.5%	124 62.0%	111 55.5%	74 37.0%	59 29.5%
Other relatives	Always	26 13.0%	23 11.5%	46 23.0%	52 26.0%	56 28.0%	60 30.0%	21 10.5%	30 15.0%	62 31.0%	120 60.0%
	Sometimes	27 13.5%	32 16.0%	22 11.0%	27 13.5%	22 11.0%	27 13.5%	16 8.0%	21 10.5%	11 5.5%	17 8.5%
	Never	147 73.5%	145 72.5%	132 66.0%	121 55.5%	122 61.0%	113 56.5%	163 81.5%	149 74.5%	127 63.5%	63 31.5%

References

Greendorfer, S. L. (1979) Childhood sport socialization
    influence of male and female track athletes, in Women Sport:
    From Myth to Reality (ed. C. A. Oglesby), Lea & Febiger,
    Philadephia, pp. 115-140.
Hackman, C. (1978) Factors in the development of sport for
    women, Physical Educ. Review, 1, pp. 41 - 55.
Kenyon, G. S., B. D. McPherson (1971) An approach to the study
    of socialization - A paper presented at the Int. Congress of
    Physical Activity Science, Quebec, July 11 - 16.
Landers, D. (1970) Sibling-sex-status and ordinal position effects
    on females sport participation and interests. Journal of
    Social Psychology, 80, pp. 247 - 258.
Maluphy, T. M. (1970) The College women athlete questions and
    tentative answers. Quest, 14.
McPherson, B. D. (1968) Psycho-social factors accounting for
    learning the role of tennis and hockey players, unpublished
    study, University of Wisconsin.
Orlick, T. D. (1972) Family sport environment and early sports
    participation, in Proceedings of the Canada Psycho-motor
    Learning and Sport Psychology Symposium (ed. I.D. Williams
    & L. M. Wankel), pp. 503 - 513.
Portz E. (1972) Influence of birth order and sibling sex on
    sport participation. H.P.E.R. Series, 2.
Sohi, A. S. (1985) Socialization of elite sportsmen into
    competitive sports - A·social system approach, unpublished
    paper.
Synder, E. E. and E. A. Spretzer (1973) Family influence and
    involvement in sports. Research Quarterly, 44, pp. 249 -
    255.

PLAY, GAMES, AND SPORT PREFERENCES OF TSWANA CHILDREN

J.T. CORLETT: Faculty of Human Kinetics, University of Windsor

M.M. MOKGWATHI: Faculty of Education, University of Botswana

Abstract

The existence of certain types of play behaviours in a given
society is understood to depend on various biological, psychological, and cultural antecedents. Very little is known, however,
about how these factors are related to participation in free time
activities by people in southern Africa. Since planning and implementation of physical education curricula in developing countries
must be responsive to local conditions, this study was undertaken
to investigate the play, games, and sport preferences of school
children in Botswana where P.E. programme development is now
underway. School children throughout Botswana were asked to respond
to a questionnaire by which their choice of leisure activities
and preferences for various games and sports were examined. Responses for leisure time activities were categorized according to
their physical or sedentary nature and their playful or non-playful (e.g. work) characteristics. Responses for preferences for
specific games and sports were tabulated and a rank order established. Differences between urban and rural children were found
with regard to choice of free time activities. Urban children
stated a clear preference for spending free time in a sedentary
and non-playful way (e.g. reading, sleeping, listening to music)
while rural children indicated a preference for active and sedentary work in such circumstances. This might reflect a lack of
distinction between work and play in rural areas. Few children,
urban or rural, chose play, games, or sports as favourite ways
of spending free time. Differences between preferences for various
games and sports were found between urban and rural areas. Although
football was the boys' first choice in both areas, rural boys also
stated high preferences for running and jumping activities and
for games of make believe and low organization. Urban boys preferred
more organized activities requiring equipment and facilities such
as tennis. Netball was the most popular game for all girls but,
again, running and jumping (and traditional dancing) were more
popular in rural areas while tennis and swimming were chosen by
urban girls. Traditional games and sports were chosen very infrequently by children in both urban and rural areas and are
thought to have been displaced in many cases by imported versions.

253

1. Introduction

The study of play became the subject of serious scholarly
investigation during the late nineteenth century, beginning with
animal studies (Groos, 1898) and moving inevitably to investigations of human play (Groos, 1916). Since these early writings,
the subject of play (and the relatives, games and sport) has taken
on an important role in both anthropology and social psychology
and has been shown to provide valuable insights about the way that
culture develops (Huizinga, 1949). More recently, studies of play
have become a focal point of interest among physical educators for
whom play, games and sport are the foundation of curriculum design.
Sutton-Smith (1981) summarized the necessary pre-conditions for
play to exist in any given society: he divided these into three
major groupings.

First, play has biological antecedents. This implies that
play takes place only when certain biological conditions such as
physical protection and safety are met and also play serves some
biological function such as reduction of excess drive (Bruner,
1975). Second, play has psychological antecedents. These
contigencies involve the mastery of current environmental stimulus
conditions, the means for management of social power or influence
and the existence of communication signals that allow play to be
recognized as such. Thirdly, cultural antecedents to play exist
and these have been the focus of an extensive body of literature
reporting cross-cultural differences and similarities in play,
games, and sport.

Many authors investigating numerous cultures have established
that antecedent customs (e.g. ritual occasions) represent an
important feature of how play behaviour develops (Simri, 1966;
Salter, 1967; Frederickson, 1960). Also, cultural complexity
affects play behaviour. Roberts and Sutton-Smith (1966) and Ball
(1974) established that different types of games (physical skill,
chance, or strategy) predominate depending on the cultural values
present in the society playing them. The conclusions of many such
ethnographic studies (e.g. Whiting and Whiting, 1975) agree that
cultural complexity and cultural values are important factors in
determining play behaviour. Child rearing practices and family
structure have also been shown to be linked to play and games
behaviour of children (e.g. Glassford, 1970; Roberts and Sutton-
Smith, 1962).

Although cross-cultural studies of play, games, and, to a
lesser extent, sport, are numerous, investigations of cultures in
southern Africa are sparse. In this study, the play, games, and
sport preferences of school children in Botswana are reported.
This study was not undertaken specifically to elucidate, for
anthropological purposes the complex links between cultural
factors and play behaviour in Botswana. However, where cultural
factors clearly affect the study's results, these are discussed
as a contribution to the literature in cross-cultural trends in
play behaviour.

Botswana is an independent, democratic republic, bound in

land-locked fashion by South Africa, Namibia, Zambia, and Zimbabwe. Although gradually modernizing its economy, and experiencing rapid urbanization, rural life still dominates the country's social fabric with cattle being the major source of wealth. Some dry land farming (especially of maize and sorghum) does take place despite the overwhelming presence of the Kalahari "desert" that covers most of the country. In the industrial sense, it is one of the world's least developed countries. Educationally, increasing access to public education is resulting in old programmes being re-designed and new ones being developed. Physical education is one subject currently being readied for introduction into schools: this study was done to facilitate curriculum design for physical education in Botswana.

2. Methods

A simple anonymous questionnaire was administered to 1000 children between the ages of 8 and 15 throughout Botswana. Demographic information is shown in Table 1.

School	District	Classification	Boys(N=)	Girls(N=)
1	Gaborone	Urban	108	107
2	Selibe-Phikwe	Urban	41	54
3	North East	Rural	158	143
4	Kweneng	Rural	113	133
5	Ngamiland	Rural	22	13
6	Central	Rural	32	32
7	Chobe	Rural	21	20

Table 1: Demographic information concerning questionnaire respondents

Children were asked to respond to two separate questions as follows:
1. What are your three favourite activities when you have free time, that is, when you can do anything you want to do?
2. What are your three favourite games or sports?
Results were compiled for question 1 by grouping responses into the following categories:
a) physically active play, game, or sport (e.g. football, running)
b) sedentary play or game (e.g. traditional bound games)
c) sedentary non-play (e.g. reading)
d) active work (e.g. herding, gardening)
e) sedentary work (e.g. cooking, sewing)
For each category, the number of first, second, and third responses was determined and these were weighted in the calculation of a total response score by multiplying first choices by three, second choices by two, and third choices by one. A scaled response score was calculated by expressing the weighted response score for each category as a fraction of the total weighted response scores for all categories together. This was done to allow comparisons between urban/rural, boy/girl pairings where total responses of

groups were not equal.

Results from question 2 were determined by weighting scores for first, second, and third choices and calculating a weighted response score for each game or sport. A scaled response score was then calculated (as described for the results from question 1) by expressing each weighted response score as a fraction of the total weighted response score for all games or sports. This again allows for inter-group comparisons where sample sizes are not equal.

3. Results

The responses of children to the question asking for their choices of favourite free time activities are shown in Table 2. Data is grouped by gender and degree of urbanization where the children attend school. The larger the scaled response value for an activity category, the greater is the preference for that category of activity by the group under which the score appears. This being the case, Table 2 shows clearly the following trends:

1. Throughout Botswana, children did not choose play, games, or sport activities as favourite free time activities.
2. Urban boys and girls showed an overwhelming preference for spending free time in sedentary, non-playful activities.
3. Rural boys and girls often chose work tasks as favourite free time activities, primarily physically active work for boys and a combination of sedentary and physically active work for girls. A substantial component of sedentary, non-playful activity was also chosen by rural children.

Category of Activity	Urban Children		Rural Children	
	Boys	Girls	Boys	Girls
Physically Active Play	0.12	0.12	0.16	0.13
Sedentary Play	0.01	0.04	0.08	0.08
Sedentary Non-Play	0.85	0.76	0.20	0.22
Physically Active Work	0	0.02	0.49	0.32
Sedentary Work	0.02	0.06	0.07	0.24

Table 2: Scaled response scores for favourite free time activities of Tswana children.

Table 3 displays data for preferences for specific games and sports: groupings are, again, by gender and degree of urbanization of the children's lifestyle. As in Table 2, the higher the value of the scaled response score, the greater the preference of a particular group for a particular game or sport. The data in Table 3 indicated the following trends:

1. In both urban and rural areas, football was the clear first choice of boys. Less strikingly, but clearly nevertheless, netball was the first choice of both urban and rural girls.
2. Athletics (running and jumping activities) was more popular in rural areas than in urban ones.
3. Games of low organization (e.g. hide-and-seek, follow-the-leader)

showed substantial popularity in rural areas but not in urban ones. Conversely, games requiring specialized facilities and equipment (e.g. tennis) were most popular in urban areas.

Activity	Urban Children		Rural Children	
	Boys	Girls	Boys	Girls
Football	0.76	0.03	0.74	0.05
Netball/Bk' Ball	0.02	0.58	0.02	0.55
Athletics	0.04	0.01	0.10	0.09
Tennis	0.06	0.08	0	0.01
Low Org. Games	0.01	0.06	0.05	0.12
West Board Games	0.01	0.06	0	0.01
Trad. Games	0	0	0.02	0.04
Softball	0.02	0.03	0.01	0.01
Volleyball	0.02	0.02	0.01	0.01
Skipping	0	0.02	0.01	0.08
Table Tennis	0.01	0	0	0
Trad. Dance	0	0.01	0.01	0.02
Dodge Ball	0.01	0.01	0.01	0.02
Swimming	0.02	0.03	0	0
Martial Arts	0.01	0	0	0
Bicycle Riding	0	0	0.01	0
Donkey Riding	0	0	0.01	0
Other	0.01	0.06	0	0

Table 3: Scaled response scores for preference for various games and sports played by Tswana children.

4. Discussion

Although there is a long tradition of writing about Tswana custom and history (e.g. Duggan Cronin, 1929; Schapera, 1938), there is virtually no recent literature available on sociological aspects of post-independence Botswana. In the absence of relevant and up-to-date social analysis, it is difficult to draw conclusions about the causal relationships between play, games, and sport behaviour and the previously-mentioned cultural indices such as complexity, traditional ritual, and family organization common in the literature dealing with the anthropology of play. Therefore, the discussion here will limit itself to aspects of play behaviour in Botswana and what they predict (according to generalizations derived from studies of other cultures) social analysis will eventually find when modern-day Botswana is adequately investigated sociologically.

First, many children in rural areas make little distinction between "work" and "play" when choosing how they prefer to spend their free time. This is not due to a lack of awareness of games and sports since they are quite capable of listing preferences for specific playful activities when asked to do so. The results suggest that rural children have an awareness of the exigencies of daily living (drawing water, collecting firewood, gardening, stamping grain, herding animals) that places these activities in the foreground when contemplating what to do in free (i.e. out-of-

school) time. They frequently choose, not their favourite of all
possible activities, but their favourites from among those things
that need to be done. As a social phenomenon, leisure is clearly
not a well-developed concept for children in rural Botswana.

Second, games of chance are almost absent from lists of
preferred games and sports of boys and girls in both urban and
rural settings. Games of chance tend to exist in cultures where
the adaptive potentiation value of play is used to emphasize the
powerful control over life exerted by influences beyond man's
understanding or management (Roberts and Sutton-Smith, 1966).
This suggests that Tswana culture does not hold to such beliefs,
although, upon superficial analysis this is somewhat surprising,
given the harsh agricultural conditions and the dependence upon
the vagaries of sparse rainfall by subsistence level farming.
Nevertheless, the dominant preferences are for agonistic games of
physical exertion and mastery (Caillois, 1961) and, to a lesser
extent, games of strategy. This is not a recent phenomenon but
a long standing one within Tswana culture whose traditional games
and sports (e.g. morabaraba, a board game of strategy) emphasize
skill and mastery of the playing environment.

Thirdly, traditional games and sports have been largely
superceded by more modern, and imported, ones. The international
nature of football is emphasized by the data in this study: it
would be totally unexpected for any other finding to result in
Botswana (or probably any other African country). In rural areas,
games of low organization are often Tswana versions of ubiquitously
distributed children's favourites (e.g. koe = skipping; mantwane =
make believe; keto = jacks) but even here, Setswana-speaking
children often reported games in English (e.g. follow-the-leader;
hide-and-seek) suggesting that these may either not have a
traditional equivalent or that the traditional version has been
deposed by a "western" one. In the cities, games of low
organization (traditional or otherwise) are not popular, taking
on a low status when compared with more complex activities such as
tennis, swimming, martial arts, and volleyball. Interestingly,
despite a century-long British presence in Botswana cricket is not
a feature of its sport culture. Softball, on the other hand, is
quite well-established despite a considerably briefer American
influence. One might hypothesize that the attachment to cricket
of nearby South Africa has over the years, labelled the sport
unacceptable for political reasons and its analogy, softball, has
filled the gap. Alternatively, a difference in cross-cultural
interactions might be involved. British colonialism was
characterized by cultural separation that precluded sporting
interaction with Batswana, thereby limiting cricket's acceptance
locally.

From the point of view of the physical educator seeking
guidance in the design of a physical education curriculum for
Botswana, several points of interest arise. First, it is reassuring
to note that children do have an awareness of a wide variety of
sports and games. However, there might be a level of resistance to

258

voluntary participation in vigorous physical activity when others, sedentary and non-playful pursuits appear to be the free time preferences of many children. This result has been noted previously with young adults (Corlett, 1984) with women being particularly disinterested in physical exercise of any kind. Therefore, it is essential that curriculum design emphasize enjoyment as much as possible since the school experience in physical education will be crucial in attempting to reverse the present trend to favouring sedentary activities. Unenjoyable and poorly presented programmes that are viewed more as punishment than fun will not induce favourable attitudes toward physical activity (Dickinson and Corlett, 1982) and this should be the primary goal of any newly-introduced curriculum. Corlett (1985; in press) has described a variety of features of particular relevance to physical education programmes in developing countries and these might well serve as guidelines for Botswana whose physical educators could be facing an uphill battle, especially in urban schools, in fostering positive attitudes toward exercise and sport.

Second, as in any developing country, costs are a major consideration in the implementation of any educational programme. In this regard, the feasibility of introducing a successful physical education curriculum at minimal cost might be far greater in rural areas than urban ones. Children in rural areas are much more attuned to imaginative activities requiring little or nothing in the way of equipment or facilities than urban children who are used to many more specialized sports that are facility-dependent and/or expensive to play (e.g. tennis, swimming). Therefore, the introduction of an inexpensive and creativity-based curriculum modelled on movement education (e.g. Kirchner, 1980) might be more successfully received in rural schools than urban ones. This is not to advocate a dichotomous curriculum, one part for urban areas and one part for rural ones. However, those responsible for programme implementation should, perhaps, expect different responses to the new curriculum for schools in different areas.

Finally, the specific content of the curriculum represents a major challenge in view of the fact that most curriculum design materials that deal with specific aspects of programme components are not written for developing countries. For example, Whitehead and Hendry (1976) and Underwood (1983) have concluded that in U.K. secondary schools, activities are selected from six major groups: athletics, dance, games, gymnastics, swimming, and outdoor pursuits. Of these, some are inappropriate for schools in Botswana: for example, swimming (due to lack of facilities), gymnastics (due to lack of equipment), and outdoor pursuits (due to the harsh environment and cultural inappropriateness) are unsuitable candidates. This leaves the curriculum potential more limited than in the U.K., for example, and creates the need for the most creative use of the remaining categories, athletics, dance, and games. There may well be a tendency to take the path of least resistance which would be to let the boys play football and the girls, netball. This should be avoided, however, lest physical education be degraded to the level of elitist sport, dominated by a few, and failing to explore the complete range of play activities for each child.

The beginning phase of any project is exciting. Optimism is the order of the day and the impositions of day to day reality have not yet been faced. Such is the present case with physical education in Botswana. It is hoped that the results of this study will be of some use in organizing a plan for physical education that will benefit all children in Botswana.

References
1. Ball, D., 1974. Control versus complexity-continuities in the scaling of gaming. Pacific Sociological Review, 17, 167-184.
2. Bruner, J., 1975. Play is serious business. Psychology Today, 8, 81-73.
3. Caillois, R., 1961: Man, Play, and Games. Glencoe, Ill.: Free Press.
4. Corlett, J.T., 1984. Health-related physical fitness of young Tswana adults. Botswana Notes and Records, 16, 59-61.
5. Corlett, J.T., 1985. Physical education in developing countries. World Health Organization Forum, 6, 123-126.
6. Corlett, J.T., Physical education as a tool for social and intellectual enhancement in developing countries. Physical Education Review, in press.
7. Dickinson, J. & Corlett, J.T., 1982. The problem of the non-participant in sport. In E. Geron (Ed.), Introduction to Sports Psychology. Tel Aviv: Wingate Press.
8. Duggan-Cronin, A.M., 1929. The Bechuana. Cambridge: Cambridge University Press.
9. Frederickson, F., 1960. Sports and the cultures of man. In W. Johnson (Ed.), Science and Medicine of Exercise and Sport. New York: Harper.
10. Glassford, G., 1970. Organization of games and adaptive strategies of the Canadian Eskimo. In G. Luschen (Ed.), The Cross-Cultural Analysis of Sport and Games. Champaign, Ill.: Stipes.
11. Groos, K., 1898. The Play of Animals. New York: Appleton.
12. Groos, K., 1916. The Play of Man. New York: Appleton.
13. Huizinga, J., 1949. Homo Ludens: A Study of the Play Element in Culture. London: Rotledge and Kegan Paul.
14. Kirchner, G., 1980. Physical Education for Elementary School Children. Dubuque: Wm. C. Brown.
15. Roberts, J.M. & Sutton-Smith, B., 1962. Child training and game involvement. Ethnology, 19, 166-185.
16. Roberts, J.M. & Sutton-Smith, B., 1966. Cross-cultural correlates of games of chance. Behaviour Science Notes, 3. 131-144.
17. Salter, M.A., 1967. Games and Pastimes of the Australian Aboriginals. Edmonton: University of Alberta.
18. Schapera, I., 1938. A Handbook of Tswana Law and Custom. London: Cass.

19. Simri, U., 1966. The Religious and Magical Functions of Ball Games of Various Cultures. Morgantown: W. Virginia Univ.
20. Sutton-Smith, B., 1981. Psychology and anthropology of play and games. In G. Luschen and G. Sage (Eds.), Handbook of Social Science of Sport, Champaign, Ill.: Stipes.
21. Underwood, G., 1982. The Physical Education Curriculum in the Secondary School. Basingstoke: Falmer Press.
22. Whitehead, N. & Hendry, L., 1976. Teaching Physical Education in England - Description and Analysis. London: Lepus.

SPORTING WOMEN: THE SOCIAL NETWORK OF REASONS FOR PARTICIPATION .

J.L. TAIT   Department of Social Aspects,
                    Dunfermline college of Physical
                    Education.
R.E.DOBASH Department of Sociology,
                    University of Stirling.

Abstract
Since the cultural definition of sport is
basically masculine in nature, it may be related
to the participation of men and women quite
differently , with a positive orientation to men
participating and a more negative and less
supportive orientation to the participation of
women. Consequently it is thought that women and
men may take part in sport for very different
reasons. This paper reports on research which has
analysed women's involvement in sport in relation
to both cultural and institutional factors.
However, the major focus here will be upon women's
own reasons for taking part in sport in the
context of the social network which surrounds
them, namely the attitudes of a man whom they
nominated as significant in their lives and their
perceptions of the attitudes of men in general.
Key words:Women, Participation, Reasons.

Introduction
There has been considerable growth in the
participation of women in sport during the last
ten years, with many women experiencing for the
first time the rewards that participation can
bring. Relatively though the proportion of women
participating remains low and it is thought that
in general, women are not commited sports
participants. Consequently in this paper we will
look at women's reasons for taking part in sport.
In doing so it is important to note that the
information presented in this paper is part of a
wider study which undertook to examine the nature
and characteristics of women's participation in
sport and the many factors which may inhibit or
affect that participation.

While different aspects of women's
participation in sport have been studied from a
historical, physiological or psychological
perspective, almost without exception studies have
focussed upon those women who take part in a
narrowly defined competitive context. In
addition, often the prevailing treatment of
sporting women simply means that they are included
under the category of sportsmen. With such little
information on women much is based on the
assumption that sport for women is contradictory
and that those who take part are 'unnatural'
and/or deviant. For example there have been few
studies which look at the whole range and
characteristics of women's participation in sport
and the constraints which operate upon women
throughout the life-cycle to affect their ability
to take part. Consequently little is known about
women's participation in sport and the factors
which affect it, so a great deal may be
unwittingly based on myth and
heresay.

Characteristiscs of the sample
The study from which this paper is drawn sought to
provide further information and construct a more
comprehensive picture of women's involvement in
sport. For these reasons the information
presented is from a varied sample of 340 women
who take part in sport in Scotland, Central region
in particular. While most take part at the
following three levels, club competitor,
internationalist and governing body administrator,
the vast majority are not exceptional performers
in the sports world. Nor as is characteristic in
mny other studies, are these women all of the same
age or background in sport. All of them have
taken part in sport at differing levels of ability
and commitment. While this research found that
restrictions in mobility, resources, time and
energy directly affect women's participation in
sport and their commitment to it, such findings
are not the direct concern of this paper. Rather
it is to indicate women's own reasons for taking
part and their perceptions of why others did so.
    While many authors have sought to show that
women do not take part in sport to the same extent
as men, (Coakley,1978) few have enquired about the
reasons for participation (Hall,1977;
Brown,1982;). It would appear that sport

functions for men and women quite differently eg
historically the cultural origins of nineteenth
century British sport led many to view sport as a
male bastion, the antithesis of womenhood, for
games and sports helped men to acquire and
practice physical, moral and leadership qualities
essential for success in a male world and
functioned to reinforce feeling of identity and
solidarity with men as distinct from
women.(Bodnar,1980;).The number, character and
prestige of sports in which men have statistical
superiority over women helps to perpetuate the
image of the female non-participant (Dyer,1982).
Women's involvement in sport may be seen as a
masculine interest unless they participate in
sports which celebrate female qualities such as
grace, elegance, flexibility and then only for
fun, social interaction and exercise. It is
thought that by participating in sport with any
serious conviction there is the underlying fear
that women will lose their unique identity and be
encouraged away from their traditional, passive,
supportive family and domestic role as well as
perhaps alter the fabric of an exclusively male
preserve. We might therefore expect women and men
to take part in sport for different reasons.

Method
In order to examine this, the women were asked to
indicate their own reasons for taking part, and
their perceptions of why others did so. The other
groups included the man they nominated as the most
influential or significant to them (eg either
husband, boyfriend, close male friend, boyfriend)
and men in general. This was done in order to
create a picture of the social network which
surrounds these women. Respondents were asked to
rate a list of reasons for taking part in sport in
terms of their level of importance. The reasons
for participation are grouped into two main
categories: sports orientation and social and
personal orientation.

Sports Orientated Reasons.
Figures 1a-c show the Sports Orientated Reasons
for each of the three groups. Beginning with
respondents, the findings in table 1a show that
for most, reasons for participation of ,fitness,
skill improvement and competition are seen as
highly important. Fewer attach such importance to

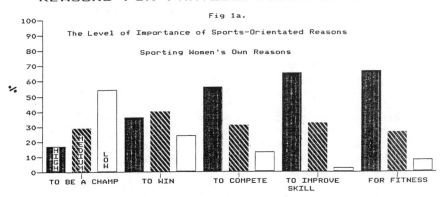

REASONS FOR PARTICIPATION IN SPORT

Fig 1a.

The Level of Importance of Sports-Orientated Reasons

Sporting Women's Own Reasons

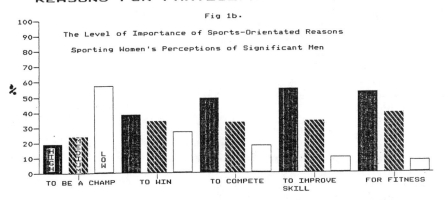

REASONS FOR PARTICIPATION IN SPORT

Fig 1b.

The Level of Importance of Sports-Orientated Reasons

Sporting Women's Perceptions of Significant Men

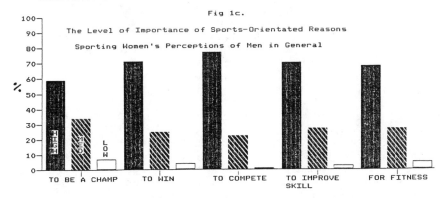

REASONS FOR PARTICIPATION IN SPORT

Fig 1c.

The Level of Importance of Sports-Orientated Reasons

Sporting Women's Perceptions of Men in General

265

winning or being a champion,although this is still
a fairly sizeable group. In this way, these women
may have internalised a traditional and
stereotypic orientation towards their role as a
woman in sport.

When the Sports Orientated Reasons of these
sportswomen are compared with their perceptions of
their 'significant man'(Figure 1b), an interesting
picture emerges. The patterns are remarkably
similar. This suggests that sportswomen see
themselves as like their select male in
motivations. Since sporting women have been found
to perceive a great deal of similarity of opinion
from the men closest to them, it may be unlikely
that these women will experience conflict related
to their sports orientated reasons for
participation. This pattern alters considerably
when we examine sportswomen's perceptions of why
'other men' take part in sport. The general trend
here indicates that they believe 'men in general'
to take part in sport for very different reasons.
Men are perceived to place great importance on all
Sports Orientated Reasons for participation. This
trend supports the suggestion that women
participants identify a different orientation or
attitude to sport amongst most men, one which is
compatitive and win orientated. It may also be
argued that since a great deal of sport is
organised and promoted by men these criteria will
predominate, with perhaps little reference to the
specific needs and attitudes of women, and this
may result in sport being seen as less attractive
to women.
Social and Personal Orientation
As has been argued the whole sport experince does
not consist solely of the benefits or costs of
competition, winning or 'being a champion ' . If
we look now at Figures 2a-c, it is possible to see
how respondents rated the importance of several
'social and personal' reasons for taking part in
sport. Beginning again with the participants
themselves, Figure 2a shows that sporting women
place a considerable importance on taking their
mind off their problems and to getting out of the
house. It may be that sport acts as a welcome
diversion from routine, whether that be domestic
or in relation to the demands of a career or wage
work. Sportig women view self-expression as
important and this may reflect an awareness of the
intrinsic benefits gained from sustained

REASONS FOR PARTICIPATION IN SPORT

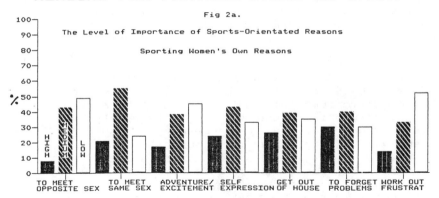

Fig 2a.

The Level of Importance of Sports-Orientated Reasons

Sporting Women's Own Reasons

REASONS FOR PARTICIPATION IN SPORT

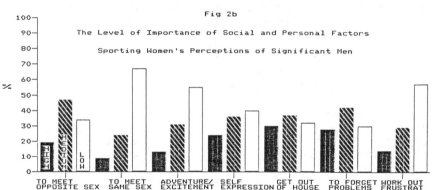

Fig 2b

The Level of Importance of Social and Personal Factors

Sporting Women's Perceptions of Significant Men

REASONS FOR PARTICIPATION IN SPORT

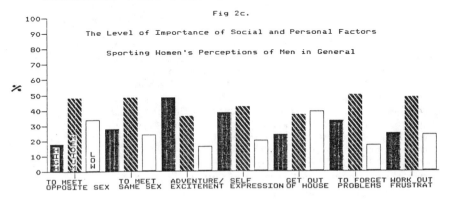

Fig 2c.

The Level of Importance of Social and Personal Factors

Sporting Women's Perceptions of Men in General

involvement in sport. Sport is also seen as a vehicle for meeting others, primarily members of the same sex . This may indicate that sportswomen see sport as a practical, physical and social activity.

Figure 2b shows how sporting women view the importance to their 'significant male' of social and personal reasons for taking part. As before they perceive that this man takes part for reasons most closely akin to their own. It is likely that this has not occurred by chance but that sporting women have consciously or unconsciously nominated or selected a male whose orientations are remarkably similar to their own. There is a slight difference in that they perceive the men to be slightly more orientated towards meeting others of the opposite sex and less towards meeeting members of the same sex. In general, the pattern demonstrated by these two groups regarding social and personal reasons for participation in sport are again very similar. This suggests that women who take part in sport perceive a very high degree fo support from their nominated or significant male.

Again these patterns change when looking at Figure 2c, women's perceptions of 'men in general'. Sportswomen perceive that 'adventure and excitement' and 'self-expression' are two very important reasons why men take part. They beleive that it is more impoartant for men to meet members of the opposite sex than it is for themselves but that the two groups are very similar in the impoartance they attach to meeting others of the same sex. Sport is an arena where adventure and excitement is readily accessible and acceptable and where meeting others of the same sex is facilitated. Certainly, it is well documented that sport can operate a unique 'cameraderie'or 'old-boy' network.

In conclusion, Figures 1-2 compare the importance attached to a variety of reasons for participation amongst sportswomen, the sporting women's significant male and men in general. Here they identify more with competition and skill improvement or the more ' Sports-Orientated Reasons'. For sportswomen,'being a champion', 'meeting members of the opposite sex','adventure and excitement' and 'working out frustrations' are of minor importance. Women in sport see themselves as attaching similar importance to reasons for participating as to their significant male. This suggests that they may have selected a man whose orientation is similar to their own or that one has adopted the orientation of the other. Either way, this similarity would seem to imply that they believe they have support for their participation from the man of importance to them. While there are numerous similarities between sportswomen, and the significant man, their perceptions of men in general differ markedly. It could be suggested that this is related to their view of the male stereotype in sport which emphasises competition, winning and the like. consequently, in differing from men in general, sportswomen may also be acknowledging that a female definition of involvment in sport exists.

References:

Hall, M.A. (1977) "The sociological perspective of females in sport" Pp37-51 in M.Adriane and J.Brame (eds) N.A.G.W.S. Research report, Vol 3 Washington American Alliance for Health, Physical Education and Recreation.
Bodnar, L.M. (1980) "The Historical role of Women in Sports" American Journal of Sports Medicine 8, 4: 290-92.
Brown,B.K. (1982) "Female Sport involvement:a preliminary conceptualisation." Pp 121-123 in A.D. Dunleavy,A.W.Miracle and C.R.Rees (eds) Studies in the Sociology of Sport. Fort Worth. Texas C.U. press.
Duquin,M (1982) "Social justice in Sport:The Norm of Expected inequity" Paper presented at the 3rd Annual N.A.S.S.meetings Toronto,Canada, 4-7 Nov.
Dyer,K (1982) Catching Up the Men: Women in Sport. London: Junction books.

THE LIFE PATH AND CAREER OF THE WOMEN IN LEADING POSITIONS IN FINNISH SPORTS ORGANIZATIONS

M-R. RAIVIO
The Sport Planning Institute, University of Jyväskylä, Finland

Abstract
Thirty to sixty percent of the members of Finnish sports organizations are women, whereas only 8% of leading and decision-making
positions are held by women. This study included women with a
university degree in physical education, who were employed in such
positions or elected to the governing bodies of the major sports
organizations in Finland.
A questionnaire was sent to all women in the positions mentioned;
ten women were selected for interview using the theme interview
method.
In childhood all respondents had mainly participated outdoor activities in groups consisting of both boys and girls. Most of the
respondents had also played with dolls but with less interest.
Fathers and mothers had had equally strong influence on these girls.
Their families had been both physically and organizationally more
active than Finnish families on the average. All respondents had
been physically very active already in childhood, and everybody had
belonged to at least one sport club. The choice of a career in
physical education had been obvious quite early, usually before the
senior high school level.
Key words: Life path, Career, Women's position, Sports organization,
Leading position, Decision-making, Socialization.

1. Introduction

In connection with the International Women's Year 1975 a project
entitled "Sport and Women in Finland" was carried out at the University of Jyväskylä. That study was based on available statistics
and public records. No deeper analysis was even planned (Heinilä,
1977). In 1981 a new project was started (Laitinen, 1983). Its
aim was to evaluate the position of women in the Finnish physical
culture, including history, competitive sports, organizational
activities, information etc. The approach was not only through
statistics but, mainly, through questionnaire and interview: how had
the women become involved in sports, how had they arrived at leading
and decision-making positions in sports, and how did they experience
the situation. Within this framework the aims of my study were:

1) To analyze the social background and the life path of women with organizational responsibilities in Finnish sports, 2) To find out which persons had influenced the respondents' interest and participation in physical activities on the personal and organizational level, 3) To evaluate the possible associations between personal physical activities and participation in sports organizations (Laakso, 1981, Raivio, 1982), and 4) To describe the career development of the respondents.

2. Methods

2.1. Subjects

At the first stage of this study, a questionnaire was sent to the women who were employed at leading or decision-making positions (N= 28) or elected to the governing bodies (councils, boards, committees) (N=147) of the major sports organizations in Finland, The Finnish Central Sports Federation (SVUL), Workers' Sports Federation (TUL), The Finnish Recreational Sports Association (SKUL) and The Workers' Association for Physical Fitness (TKL). The questionnaire was also sent to 80 men in the corresponding positions (Raivio, 1982, 1983 & 1985).

Ten of the female respondents with a university degree in physical education were selected to the second stage of the study. The size of this group was determined by the method used (=theme interview) and the number of women in these positions. The main criterion in the selection was the significance of the position in the organization. If there were more than one woman at the same level, the choice was made on the basis of other positions the person might have in sports organizations.

All four sports organizations were represented. Other characteristics were taken into account if possible: age, marital status, children, rural and urban background, international competitive sports backgruond etc. All ten women agreed to participate the second stage of this study.

2.2. Method

Theme interview was chosen as the method of this study. The main themes were (Laitinen et. al., 1983):

1, Childhood home and its enviroment
2, Human relations along the life path
3, Physical activities from childhood on
4, Other hobbies and activities
5, Career
6, Identity as a woman (idols, attitude to feminism etc.)
7, View of life (past, present, future)

Each subject was interviewed at least twice for a total of 4-9 hours. The interviews were taped and then analysed in a descriptive fashion. No generalizations beyond this group were made because of the small size of the sample. Such conclusions will be possible after the whole project is completed.

3.   Results

3.1. Description of the subjects
The women interviewed were 29-60 years old, mean age was 39,4 years.
Seven were married, two lived together with a man, and one alone.
Seven had 1-4 children. After their university degree, all ten had
continued their studies either at the university or at courses for
sport leaders organized   by the sports organizations.
     One was originally from Helsinki, four from other cities, the
rest were from the countryside. Home enviroment had in every case
been excellent for physical activities.

3.2. Plays and games
All respondents had preferred playing outdoors in bigger groups consisting of boys and girls, often more or only boys. Most popular
were different games of tag, hide-and-seek, ball games, climbing in
the trees etc., all mainly games which boys usually play also in
their own groups. All respondents had had dolls and eight had played
with them with girls, but these were not as popular.

3.3. Physical activities
All respondents had been interested in more than one sport already as
a child. Womens' gymnastics and cross-country skiing had been
practised by everyone, either in competitive or recreational form.
The following sports had been participated in by the respondents
during their lives:

     cross-country skiing (10)
     womens' gymnastics (10)
     Finnish baseball (8)
     swimming (7)
     skating (7)
     running (6)
     downhill skiing (4)
     gymnastics (4)
     basket ball (4)
     volley ball (3)
     high jump (3)
     long jump (3)
     jazz dance (3)
     tennis (3)
     shotput (3)
     walking (3)
     javelin (2)
     discus (2)
     bowling (2)
     ballet (2)
     bicycling (2)
     orienteering (2)

folkdance (2)
modern dance (2)

It was suprising that some comparatively new areas in physical
activities, such as aerobics, had not become more popular. On the
other hand, especially those respondents who had been or were competitors in some sport disclipine did not consider other sports as
their "hobbies". For example, most of the respondents had a bike,
and used it actively, but did not mention bicycling as a hobby. In
adulthood all but one had stopped competitions and changed into
recreational sports.

3.4. Stimulators to physical activities
All but one respondent had had a parent or a close relative to encourage to physical activities, and everyone had been free to participate. The mother was the main supporter for three respondents, the
father for two, and both parents for four.

Seven respondents had positive memories of their p.e.teachers,
but only two considered her as an idol or a model. Three did not
like their p.e.teacher   at all. Even these teachers had encouraged the respondents to sports and school competitions, but some
had been even nasty to pupils, who were less proficiant in sports.

All the men with whom the respondents were either married to or
lived together with supported these women in both personal and
organizational activities. One had experienced opposition, but was
determined to continue her activities, though she admitted that the
situation was difficult (Laakso, 1981).

3.5. Sport club and organizational activities
All had belonged to at least one sport club during their lives. The
parents had taken six respondents to the club; the others had gone
by themselves. All had found friends in the clubs, but usually they
met these friends only in the connection with these activities. If
the friend quit the sport, also the friendship waned gradually.

The women were usually treated equally with the men in these
clubs as far as training possibilities etc. were concerned. However,
in some clubs the men had better travel arrangements and other benefits compared to women.

The women were rather satisfied with their clubs. They believed
that in their clubs it was easy even for a woman to get onto the
board of the club. The main reason why there are only a few female
leaders in the clubs was ascribed to women themselves: they do not
appriciate a position on the board or they are too shy. On the other
hand the situation is different in the central sports organizations
according to these respondents: the attitudes in the councils, boards
and committees are against women. This attitude is common to both
men and women. A woman does not trust another woman in a leading or
a decision-making position. Women vote for men, even when there are
compitent female candidates.

The model for organizational activities for the respondents was
in their childhood homes: six fathers had been active in sport clubs
or organizations, four fathers in other organizations; two mothers

had been sport club members and four had belonged to other organizations. This is far above the Finnish average. Half of the respondents had a husband who belonged to a sport club or -organization.

3.5. Career development
All respondents had had some responsibilities at home but sport
activities came first. With one exception, the respondents could
skip home duties because of sport activities. All had also had
summer jobs during the school years. The choice of physical
education career was clear to half of the respondents already during
the junior highschool and to others in the beginning of senior high
school. All had also had other but less favoured alternatives (Lahikainen, 1984).

All the parents had been supportive, but had actually suggested
a career in p.e. to only half of the respondents. Other inducers
were p.e.teacher (1), trainer (2), boyfriend (2), friends (3) and a
close relative (2).

After graduation everybody had got a job as a p.e.teacher. From
that time to the interview each had had from two to six jobs; most
in junior and senior high schools, the others in other educational
institutions, communities, and sports organizations. Although none
were unemployed, six respondents had unsuccesfully applied for a job
and were, in their opinion, unfairly treated: in three cases the
reason had been sex and in three others politics.

Eight of ten respondents liked their present jobs. Problems
were few at school but in the sports organizations the bureaucracy
had been experienced as a big problem. Also the respondents considered the jobs in the sports organizations insecure.

4. Discussion

All respondents had excellent opporturnities for physical activities
in childhood. The home enviroment was good for sports and the people
at home had a positive attitude towards physical activities. The
model of the childhood home as well as the positive climate in the
adulthood home are important factors to the continuation of the
physical and also other activities outside home also according to
the previous studies (Martens, 1975, Greendorfer, 1977 & 1979b, Loy,
McPherson & Kenyon, 1978, Patriksson, 1979, Laakso, 1981).

According to this study, mother and father had equally important
roles as inducers to sports. In previous studies, either the mother
(Loy, McPherson & Kenyon, 1978, Greendorfer, 1979a, Patriksson 1979,
Laakso, 1981) or the father (Greendorfer, 1979b, Patriksson, 1979)
have been more significant in this respect.

The significance of the childhood home was dominant: even a less
popular p.e. teacher could not kill the interest in physical activities, which had started before school age (Greendorfer, 1977). Another problem is, how such teachers have affected children with less
inclination for p.e. and sports (Laakso, 1981).

Organizational activities also had their roots in childhood.
Firstly, most parents had belonged to sports or other organizations

(Loy, McPherson &Kenyon, 1978). Secondly, most respondents had preferred playing in groups with many boys and girls, which have provided role models for sports organizations (Ingham, Loy & Berryman, 1972, Loy, McPherson & Kenyon, 1978).

Even to day the leading positions on the councils, boards, and committees of sports organizations are occupied by men. The respondents gave mainly two reasons for this: men are afraid to get an equally or more competent woman to their side and women don't give support to another woman in elections, no matter her compitence. As mentioned before; it is impossible to make any generalizations based only on this study, but these attitudes are potentially so important that they must be further studied.

The choice of p.e. career has been clear very early to the respondents. Why are so few women employed by sports organizations? Why are so few interested in working for these organizations, although many are very active in the councils, boards and committees? The respondents thought that the sports organizations were very bureaucratic so that they might not get their ideas carried out. Some had thought of an organizational career but felt the school work "safer". These aspects will also be explored in the next phase of the study.

References

Greendorfer, S.L. (1977) Role of socializating agents in female sport involvement. Research Quarterly 48 (2), s. 304-310.
Greendorfer, S.L. (1979a) Childhood sport socialization influences of male and female track athletes. Arena Review, 3 (2), s. 39-53.
Greendorfer, S.L. (1979b) Differences in childhood socialization influences of women involved in sport and women not involved in sport. In Krotee, M.L. (ed.) The dimensions of sport sociology. West Point, NY: Leisure Press, s.59-72.
Heinilä, K. (ed.) (1977) Women in the Finnish Physical Culture. Jyväskylä, The Sport Planning Institute, studies nr 15.
Ingham, A.G., Loy, J.W. & Berryman, J.W. (1972) Socialization, Dialects and Sport. In Harris, D.V. (ed.) Women and Sport: a National Research Conference. The Pennsylvania State University: Penn State HPER Series No 2, s. 235-276.
Laakso, L. (1981) The enviroment of the childhood and adolescence explaining the physical activities of the adulthood: a retrospective study. Jyväskylä: University of Jyväskylä, Studies in Sport, Physical Education and Health 14.
Lahikainen, A-R. (1984) The choice of career as a result of the socialization process in the family. Helsinki: The department of social psychology of the University of Helsinki: studies.
Laitinen, A. (ed.) (1983) Physical Culture and Women in Finland. Jyväskylä: The Sport Planning Institute of the University of Jyväskylä.
Loy, J.W., McPherson, B.D. & Kenyon, G.S. (1978) Sport and social systems. A guide to the analysis, problems, and literature. Reading, Ma: Addison-Wesley Publishing Company.

Martens, R. (1975) Social psychology and physical activity. New York, NY: Harper & Row.

Patriksson, G. (1979) Socialization in involving in sport. Göteborg: Göteborg studies in educational sciences 31.

Raivio, M-R. (1982) The socialization of women in the leading and decision-making positions of the Finnish sports organizations. Jyväskylä: the University of Jyväskylä, The Sport Planning Institute.

Raivio, M-R. (1983) Women in the Finnish Physical Culture. In Laitinen, A. (ed.) Physical Culture and Women in Finland. Jyväskylä: The University of Jyväskylä, The Sport Planning Institute.

Raivio, M-R. (1985) Factors affecting the socialization of women in personal and organizational activities in sports. Liikunta ja tiede (=Sports and science- magazine) 2/85, s. 58-65.

Seppänen, P. (1981) Sport clubs and parents as socializing agents in sport. Liikunta ja tiede 1/81, s. 26-32.

SOCIALISATION INTO THE PHYSICAL EDUCATION PROFESSION: AN APPLICATION
OF HOLLAND'S THEORY OF VOCATIONAL CHOICE

M.J. REYNOLDS
Department of Physical Education and Recreation, Ballarat College of
Advanced Education

Abstract
This study applies Holland's theory of vocational choice to
investigate the socialisation experiences of prospective physical
education teachers during their high school and college education.
From Holland's research, physical education teachers are represented
by three personality types in descending order of importance:
(a) social, which involves informing, training or developing others;
(b) realistic, where they enjoy practical activities and generally
have good physical skills; (c) enterprising, where they prefer
organising and persuading others. The Vocational Preference
Inventory was administered to a group of physical education students
in their first and fourth years of training. It was predicted that
students' occupational profiles change over the three years in such a
way as to be similar to professional physical education teachers in
the workforce. An initial analysis found the first and fourth year
profiles to be significantly closer to the students' second subject
area environment than to the physical education environment. The
major analysis found that overall student profiles do not
significantly change over the first three years of professional
training although the social and enterprising orientations showed
some positive trends. Profiles indicated an intellectual component
which differed from studies conducted in America. This may be just a
cultural effect or it may reflect the high academic requirements for
students to enter Australian physical education courses.
Key words: Occupational socialisation, Physical education
socialisation, Teacher education, Vocational characteristics.

1. Introduction

A number of important studies during the last five years have
investigated factors associated with occupational socialisation into
the physical education career path (Johns, 1983; Lawson, 1983, 1985;
Templin, 1979). However, no real focus has been given to the
characteristics of the students who eventually begin the educational
process which leads to a physical education vocation.
    Regardless of the many factors which attract or influence an
individual towards a physical education career, academic success in

high school is the all important entry criterion into an Australian training programme. Although intellectual ability is required to undertake an academically oriented programme, there are other characteristics which are important for the actual job of teaching physical education. This idea was discussed by Lunn (1985) in association with the medical profession when he asked whether the brainiest doctors were the best doctors. In physical education it would appear that social and organisational skills are very important. Moreover, Holland's (1973) theory of vocational choice has shown that physical education teachers are represented by three main characteristics or personality types in descending order of importance: (a) social, which involves informing, training or developing others; (b) realistic, where they enjoy practical activities and generally have good physical skills; (c) enterprising, where they prefer organising and persuading others. Holland's theory is based on the assumption that an occupational environment can be defined by the personality type of its members. For example, the occupational environment of physical education teachers is made up of all other physical education teachers, and physical education teachers have similar characteristics. Therefore, the physical education environment is classified as predominantly social; other occupational environments can be either realistic, intellectual, conventional, enterprising or artistic. In addition, a person's relationship to his job environment can be assessed according to the degree of congruence between the individual's characteristics and the environment.

Only one recent study (Batesky, Malacos and Purcell, 1980) has actually applied Holland's vocational choice theory to physical education students. In this case, the study was primarily descriptive and then only job profiles were analysed.

This present study uses Holland's theory to assess the results of socialisation experiences during high school and college education. Occupational profiles are measured at the beginning of a physical education teacher training programme and then compared with profiles from those students remaining in the programme after three years. It is predicted that profiles change over the three years in such a way that students develop characteristics similar to those professionals out in the workforce.

2. Survey methods

2.1 Subjects
The Vocational Inventory (VPI) (Holland, 1978) was administered to all 60 students who entered the four year Bachelor of Education Post Primary Physical Education Degree Programme at Ballarat College of Advanced Education in 1983. After three years, the VPI was again administered to the 45 students still remaining in the course. These students were also asked to complete a brief questionnaire to assess their career intentions for 1987 after graduation in order to embellish the quantitative data.

2.2 Instruments

The VPI consists of a list of 160 job titles against which the respondent is required to check "yes" to those jobs which are interesting, "no" to those jobs considered uninteresting, and nothing to those jobs about which there is indecision. Each respondent's personality profile was therefore represented by a score (0-14) on each of the six Holland scales, realistic, intellectual, social, conventional, enterprising, and artistic.

Job congruency was determined by matching the respondent's VPI code with physical education and second subject job codes. The degree of job congruency was quantified by using the revised Compatability Index (CI) developed by Wiggins and Moody (1981). This is derived from the similarity between two Holland codes using a simple weighted order scale and ranges from 0-8. For example, a subject code ACI matched with the physical education job code SRE represents 0 for job congruency, IRS with SRE represents 4, while SRE with SRE is equivalent to 8.

With reference to reliability, the internal consistency of the VPI scales has shown that the content of the six job related scales is relatively homogeneous (Holland, 1972). Test-retest reliability coefficients for college students and older women demonstrated moderate to high reliability. The validity of the occupational classifications, developed from Holland's (1973) theory of vocational choice has received moderate support. Recent studies (Fabry, 1976; Gaffey and Walsh, 1976; Wiggins, Lederer, Salkowe, and Rys, 1983) have confirmed the theory in addition to the ninety investigations cited in Holland's (1973) Making Vocational Choices.

3. Results

3.1 Profile score comparisons

The six Holland code scores measured in 1983 were compared with the same six scores assessed from the sample in 1986. A Hotelling's T^2 procedure (Johnson and Wichern, 1982) was used to test the null hypothesis that the differences between the same variables at the two time periods, 1983 and 1986, were zero; that is:

Ho: $(\mu_1\ \mu_2\ \ldots\ \mu_6) = (0, 0, 0, 0, 0, 0)$.

The mean and standard deviations of the differences are shown in Table 1.

Table 1. Holland code differences between 1983 and 1986.

Holland codes	Cases	Mean	Standard deviation
Realistic	43	.0698	1.8438
Intellectual	43	-.6512	3.4009
Social	43	.4419	2.8810
Conventional	43	.0930	1.9000
Enterprising	43	.4419	2.8810
Artistic	43	-.1163	3.0175

The Hotelling's T^2 procedure resulted in an observed $T^2 = 6.733$ < $F_{6,37}$ (.05) = 16.07, and consequently Ho is not rejected at the 5% level of significance. Hence there was no overall significant difference between the 1983 and 1986 Holland code profiles for the sample of trainee physical education teachers.

3.2 Congruency score comparisons
Physical education and second subject congruency scores were assessed and compared for each student in 1983 and 1986 (see Table 2).

Table 2. Congruency scores.

Congruency	1983		1986	
	Mean	Standard deviation	Mean	Standard deviation
Physical education	3.7110	1.3919	4.1778	1.2665
Second subject	4.5778	1.6718	4.9111	1.7032

The difference between the physical education and second subject congruency scores for 1983 and 1986 were compared with t-tests. Both t-tests were significant; for 1983, t (2, 45) = 2.81, p <.05; for 1986, t (2, 45) = 2.32, p <.05.

3.3 Descriptive profile scores
The VPI profiles for the sample of students were compared between 1983 and 1986. The profiles show a summary of the top three personality orientations in rank order. The rankings were obtained by taking frequency counts of the number of times each code was ranked first, second, or third. Table 3 shows the rankings.

Table 3. Profile summaries

	R	I	S	C	E	A
1983						
First choice	3	12	14	0	8	8
Second choice	0	12	13	1	10	9
Third choice	6	8	11	2	11	7
Total	9	32	39	3	29	24
1986						
First choice	1	8	23	0	5	8
Second choice	7	13	7	0	12	6
Third choice	3	9	9	3	11	10
Total	11	30	39	3	28	24

The rankings from the 1983 profile summaries show the general vocational profile of the sample to be SIE. The same SIE pattern appears for 1986, but in this case, the profile is more definitive. In fact, 23 out of 45 students have a preference for a social type occupation which involves the training, informing or development of others.

4. Discussion

4.1 Profile score comparisons
For a sample of physical education students just beginning their final year of teacher training, there is no significant change in their occupational orientations. A few trends do, however, suggest some parallels with other studies. There is positive change in the social orientation which would be expected for prospective teachers. The enterprising characteristic, which Holland (1972) associates with ambition, dominance and self-confidence parallels the physical educator's personality as reviewed by Nettleton (1985). The apparent drop in the intellectual characteristic may reflect Bain's (1984) idea that a teacher education course focuses more on the method of teaching and less on the physical education subject matter.

With the non significant result above, Holland's theory of vocational choice and his VPI might be questioned. However, it should be noted that further important influences may still occur in the students' final year of training. In fact, all students will be taking part in two final rounds of teaching practice totalling eight weeks.

4.2 Congruency scores
From the congruency scores, it appears that the students on entry to the course are significantly more congruent with their second subject areas than with their major area of physical education. This may be explained by the number and exposure of subject area models in high school. Physical education is usually taught in Victorian high schools up to year 9 level only. For the final three years of secondary schooling, students would have less contact with physical education and much more exposure to other academic areas, especially to the academic area of most interest. However, this does not explain the reason for a continued significant difference after three years at the tertiary level.

4.3 Profile summaries
Profile summaries (Table 4) indicate that the overall Holland job code for the sample is SIE. This compares with SRE from Holland's (1973) research review and SER for a study by Batesky et al (1980), both of whom use American respondents. It shows that Australian physical education students may have a greater orientation towards analytical, intellectual and scientific pursuits (I) rather than towards the manipulation of objects, tools and machines (R). This

may reflect just a cultural difference. Alternatively, it may be a result of two other factors: (a) in academic entrance requirements, prospective physical education students rank only about fourth after medicine, law and physiotherapy students; (b) many Australian high schools now provide physical education as an academic subject area in years eleven and twelve.

Table 4. Comparison of profile summaries
```
--------------------------------------------------------------------
Current study          Holland (1973)          Batesky et al (1980)
--------------------------------------------------------------------
Social         S       Social         S        Social          S
Intellectual   I       Realistic      R        Enterprising    E
Enterprising   E       Enterprising   E        Realistic       R
--------------------------------------------------------------------
```

The different physical education job code suggests that any congruency computation should perhaps be derived from Australian physical education job codes rather than American. This would therefore question the actual difference found between physical education and second subject orientations in this study.

4.4 Professional perceptions

From a brief questionnaire given to the sample in early 1986, students were asked about their satisfaction with physical education as a career and what they hoped to do after graduation. The ten students who reported the least satisfaction with physical education as a profession, showed an average change in social orientation over three years to be -1.2 compared to +0.44 for the total sample. Furthermore, the only two students who wished to obtain a job outside of the physical education area had two of the three highest decreases in social orientation scores.

4.5 Future research

It may be beneficial to develop further study in this area on changes in the social orientation of physical education teachers in training. Such work could also show wider application to teachers in other subject areas. Furthermore, if job profiles were obtained from students at other Australian physical education colleges, this may provide a method for assessing the effects of high school academic physical education study on current physical education student teachers.

References

Bain, L. (1984) The hidden curriculum in teacher education, in
Physical Education Professional Preparation: Insights and
Foresights (ed. H.A. Hoffman and J.E. Rink), AAHPERD, Reston,
Virginia.
Batesky, J.A., Malacos, J.A. and Purcell, K.M. (1980) Comparison of
personality characteristics of physical education and recreation
majors, and factors which affect career choice. Perceptual and
Motor Skills, 51, 1291-1298.
Fabry, J.J. (1976) An investigation of Holland's vocational theory
across and within selected occupational groups. Journal of
Vocational Behavior, 8, 73-76.
Gaffey, R.L. and Walsh, W.B. (1974) Concurrent validity and
Holland's theory. Journal of Vocational Behavior, 5, 41-51.
Holland, J.L. (1972) Professional Manual for the Self-Directed
Search. Consulting Psychologists Press, Palo Alto, California.
Holland, J.L. (1973) Making Vocational Choices. Prentice Hall,
Englewood Cliffs, N.J.
Holland, J.L. (1978) Professional Manual for the Self-Directed
Search. Consulting Psychologists Press, Palo Alto, California.
Johns, D. (1983) Factors affecting students selection of
professional preparation in physical education. CAHPER Journal,
49, 16-19.
Johnson, R. and Wichern, D. (1982) Statistical Analysis. Prentice
Hall, Englewood Cliffs, N.J.
Lawson, H.A. (1983) Toward a model of teacher socialization in
physical education. Entry into schools, teachers' role
orientations and longevity in teaching, part 2. Journal of
Teaching in Physical Education, 3, 3-16.
Lawson, H.A. (1985) Knowledge to work in the physical education
profession. Sociology of Sport Journal, 2, 9-24.
Lunn, H. (1985, July 20-21) Are the brainiest the best doctors?
The Weekend Australian Magazine, p.6.
Nettleton, B. (1985) The Image of the Physical Education Teacher:
Fiction and Fact. ACHPER, Adelaide, South Australia.
Templin, T.J. (1979) Occupational socialization and the physical
education teacher. Research Quarterly, 60, 482-493.
Wiggins, J.D. and Moody, A. (1981) Compatability Index Description.
Training Associates, Dover, Del.
Wiggins, J.D., Lederer, D.A., Salkowe, A. and Rys, G.S. (1983) Job
satisfaction related to tested congruence and differentiation.
Journal of Vocational Behavior, 23, 112-121.

A COMPARISON OF MALE AND FEMALE SWIMMING PERFORMANCES IN AUSTRALIAN
PRIMARY SCHOOL AGED CHILDREN

N.D.O. HUNTER and P.A. DENHAM
Centre for Sports Studies, Canberra College of Advanced Education

Abstract
This project was conducted in response to an application of the
Australian Sex Discrimination Act 1984, regarding sporting competition at the primary school level. The objectives were to:
1) determine whether significant differences exist between the
performances of male and female swimmers (8-13 years); and 2)
ascertain predominant attitudes towards mixed sex-competition.

A survey and opinionaire were distributed to randomly chosen
Australian schools and swimming associations and 254 responses
were received. Times of the first four finishers in each age
group for 50 metre individual and 200 metre relay events for
their major 1984-85 swimming meet were requested. The opinionaire sought physical educators' attitudes towards mixed-sex
swimming competition.

Separate t-tests were conducted comparing the swimming times of
boys and girls for each age group for each stroke($\alpha=0.05$). These
male/female comparisons indicated: 1) no significant differences
between times in each of the four individual strokes amongst 8-11
year olds; 2) significant differences in each of the four individual strokes amongst 12-13 year olds; 3) significant differences
in relay times for all age groups. Responses to the opinionaire
were classified into 10 categories to determine predominant attitudes towards mixed-sex competition. The results indicated a
strong feeling against compulsory mixed-sex swimming races.
Key Words: Sex Discrimination, Swimming, Primary School Sport.

1. Introduction

Traditionally, there has been a dearth of sporting opportunities
for females in comparison to the many opportunities available for
males. However, in recent years females have begun to demand
sporting equality. The most significant gain for equal rights
in Australian sports has been the Sex Discrimination Act 1984,
which forbids discrimination on the basis of sex. In particular,
sports events for boys and girls under the age of 12 years must
henceforth be combined. In response to this legislation, the

Australian Federal Human Rights Commission sought research into Australian primary school sport to determine whether significant differences exist between the sporting performances of young boys and girls, and to ascertain the likely effects of mixed competition on the children. Swimming was the selected sport for this research as it is a widespread and popular activity in Australia and has long been a competitive sport for both sexes.

The objectives of this study were to: 1) determine whether a significant difference exists between the performances of male and female swimmers of primary school age (8-13 years, inclusive); and 2) ascertain the predominant attitudes of physical educators towards mixed-sex swimming competitions amongst primary school aged children.

2. Experimental methods

A combined survey and opinionaire was distributed to 100 randomly chosen primary schools in each of the 8 Australian states and territories and to 100 district swimming associations across the country. Each was asked to enter the times of the first four place getters in each age category for individual 50 metre freestyle, breaststroke, backstroke, butterfly and 4 x 50 metre team relay races for their major swimming meet in the 1984-85 swimming season.

Separate t-tests were conducted comparing the swimming times of boys and girls for each age group for each stroke(α=0.05). The percentage of schools in which boys recorded faster times than girls was also determined for each event, at each level of competition.

The opinionaire invited those physical educators who were directly involved with primary school age swimming, at the school and district levels, to state their attitudes on the likely effects of mixed competition on the children. It consisted of 3 questions that sought information on: 1) perceived differences between boys and girls in swimming capabilities; 2) possible effects on girls of mixed swimming competition; and 3) whether girls should be given the opportunity of competing in mixed competition. A fourth, open-ended question, invited the physical educators to make any additional personal comments on the matter.

3. Results

Responses were received from 254 schools and district associations across Australia. Unfortunately, 2 states gave no responses, owing to State Government disagreements. It was also found that many schools had not maintained proper records of their swimming meets, whilst other schools and districts had held races over different distances from those used in the survey, or had not catered to the specific age groups.

3.1 Survey

The results of the survey are summarized in Tables 1-5. In the individual freestyle, breaststroke and backstroke events there were no significant differences between girls' and boys' performances up to and including 11 years of age at the school and district levels. Amongst the 12-13 year olds, significant sex differences emerged in each of these strokes at the school and district levels and the percentage of schools and districts in which boys recorded the faster times became more pronounced (not subjected to statistical analysis). However, in the individual butterfly results the sex difference in performances at the school level in the 12-13 years age group did not reach a level of significance, despite boys recording faster times in this event in 71.1% of the surveys.

Significant differences in the performances of boys and girls emerged in all of the relay results at school and district levels, except for the 11 years age group at the school level. The results in this age group were affected by the small number of schools that held relays specifically for this group. In each of the relay events, boys recorded superior times to girls in no less than 80% of the surveys.

3.2 Opinionaire

In reply to the question concerning perceived differences between boys and girls in swimming capabilities, the majority of respondents felt that differences did exist between the swimming capabilities of boys and girls. On the rating scale, at school level 19% perceived great differences, 39.2% saw some differences, 25.3% felt that there was little difference, whilst only 3.8% perceived no difference. At the district level 2.5% perceived great differences, 15.0% felt there were some differences, 5.0% perceived little difference, with 0% believing there was no difference between boys and girls in swimming capabilities.

When asked what effect they thought mixed swimming might have on girls, most (54.4% at school level and 12.5% at district level) thought that it would have a detrimental effect, 21.5% at school level and 5.0% at district level thought there would be a neutral effect and 11.4% at school level and 5.0% at district level thought it would be constructive.

In reply to the question of whether girls should be given the opportunity of competing in mixed races, the majority of the physical educators felt that they should, but only in addition to all girl races (44.3% at school level and 12.5% at district level). 25.3% of respondents at school level and 7.5% at district level felt that girls should not be given the opportunity to compete in mixed races at all; whilst 12.7% at school level and 2.5% at district level thought that they should compete in mixed competition instead of all girl races.

286

Replies to the open-ended question are listed in Table 6, under the ten styles of comment that appeared. Many of the comments contained opinions supporting mixed-sex swimming and indeed some schools already practice it. However, most portrayed an opinion against mixed competition, stating, amongst other things, that it would put girls at a disadvantage and that girls would lose the respect of the boys.

3.3 Discussion

An assessment of differences between the performances of male and female children is highly complex. It is not clearly understood whether the differences are primarily biological/genetic in nature or environmental/cultural. However, evidence is now available to demonstrate that each of these areas is important and makes a significant contribution to the total differences observed (Wilmore 1979).

Studies on pre-pubescent childrens' sport have usually dwelt more on the similarities between sexes than discrepancies (Dyer 1982; Wilmore 1979; Adrian 1972). For example, Astrand & Rodahl (1977) found that girls and boys show no significant differences in VO_2 max values (a measurement of cardio-respiratory fitness) before puberty. Thereafter, the female's VO_2 max is, on average, 70-75% that of males. Wilmore (1979) suggests that the lack of an observed difference in VO_2 max at the younger ages may be due to similarities in maximal cardiac output and haemoglobin levels up to the age of puberty, at which point significant differences in performances start to appear.

Similarly, Adrian (1972) reported that there were no sex differences in the biomechanical techniques of young swimmers and, until age 11, there is little difference between height and weight of sexes. At ages 12-13, girls tend to become slightly heavier and taller.

Pate et al. (1982) noticed that performance matched groups of males and females display remarkably similar physiological profiles. Conversely, males and females with comparable physiological traits should be expected to perform at the same level. Accordingly, it is not surprising that some females outperform some males when the two sexes do participate in the same competitions, although there is some debate as to whether this is due to a general trend towards equality or just the efforts of a gifted few (Sharp 1984). Based strictly upon physiological research, neither sex appears to have any great advantage over the other prior to puberty. Because of the similarities, boys and girls in the 8-11 years age groups could compete in the same individual stroke events without a significant disadvantage to either sex. The small differences that do occur seem more than likely to relate to the cultural and social restrictions that are placed on girls from a very early age in the course of gender stereotyping (Dyer 1985; Dyer 1982). The improved standards and opportunities for competition provided by mixed-sex sports programmes may help in further diminishing the gap.

The small sex differences in the 8-11 years age groups were compounded in the relays, thereby producing significant differences in times.

The opinionaire shows that while some of the physical educators involved with children's swimming believe that moves toward mixed competition are desirable, many feel that sex integration could have detrimental effects, particularly on young female competitors. Indeed, the Michigan Swim Study (Mugno 1983) cited "too much pressure" as an important reason for young girls dropping out of competitive swimming. Increasing the pressure on young female swimmers, by making them compete against males, may deter many of them from competitive swimming in the long-term. In addition, Selby and Lewko (1976) found that boys who participate frequently in sporting activities may be those who are least in favour of having girls in the same sports classes. However, they propose that boys' indirect knowledge, or direct observation of girls participating in the same sports programmes, could lead to a more accepting attitude towards girls in their sporting activities.

3.4 Recommendations

The findings of this study recommend a course of action that provides: 1) optional mixed races for all age groups in primary school age swimming, in addition to separate sex events, in all individual strokes; and 2) sex differentiated relays for all age groups. This should give male and female children the widest possible opportunity for swimming competition without disadvantaging either sex.

TABLE 1: DIFFERENCES BETWEEN BOYS AND GIRLS IN FREESTYLE EVENTS
(* indicates significant difference)
(+ Sch B<G = % of schools/districts in which boys swam faster than girls)

			8 years (50m)	9 years (50m)	10 years (50m)	11 years (50m)	12 years (50m)	12-13 years (100m)
SCHOOL LEVEL		n	48	73	82	82	77	59
		$\bar{d}$	-2.388	-2.526	-1.427	-1.745	-3.471	-5.011
		s_d	15.780	11.753	7.999	7.209	4.926	11.976
		t	-0.741	-1.289	-1.142	-1.549	-4.372*	-2.272*
	+	% Sch B<G	58.3	58.9	63.4	59.8	72.7	64.4
		% Sch G<B	41.7	41.1	36.6	40.2	27.3	35.6
DISTRICT LEVEL		n	32	29	36	34	36	34
		$\bar{d}$	-0.648	-1.918	-0.774	-0.814	-2.103	-4.413
		s_d	6.210	6.002	3.287	2.979	2.559	5.343
		t	-0.417	-1.217	-0.999	-1.127	-3.487*	-3.405*
		% Dist B<G	56.3	65.5	69.4	58.8	81.9	82.4
		% Dist G<B	44.8	34.5	30.6	41.2	18.1	17.6

TABLE 2: DIFFERENCES BETWEEN BOYS AND GIRLS IN BREASTROKE EVENTS.

		10 years & under (50m)	11 years (50m)	12-13 years (50m)
SCHOOL LEVEL	n	69	27	71
	$\bar{d}$	-0.219	0.863	-3.321
	s_d	9.889	13.857	8.187
	t	-0.130	0.229	-2.417*
	% Sch B<G	55.1	48.1	59.2
	% Sch G<B	44.9	51.9	40.8
DISTRICT LEVEL	n	38	15	36
	$\bar{d}$	0.135	-0.109	-1.566
	s_d	6.376	6.343	3.136
	t	0.092	-0.047	-2.118*
	% Dist B<G	52.6	53.3	72.2
	% Dist G<B	47.4	46.7	27.8

TABLE 3: DIFFERENCES BETWEEN BOYS AND GIRLS IN BACKSTROKE EVENTS.

		10 years & under (50m)	11 years (50m)	12-13 years (50m)
SCHOOL LEVEL	n	73	28	74
	$\bar{d}$	-0.932	1.972	-2.317
	s_d	10.271	14.792	6.035
	t	-0.548	0.499	-2.335*
	% Sch B<G	53.4	42.9	67.6
	% Sch G<B	46.6	57.1	32.4
DISTRICT LEVEL	n	37	14	35
	$\bar{d}$	-0.218	-1.676	-2.334
	s_d	5.248	5.335	3.376
	t	-0.179	-0.831	-2.892*
	% Dist B<G	64.9	50	82.9
	% Dist G<B	35.1	50	17.1

TABLE 4: DIFFERENCES BETWEEN BOYS AND GIRLS IN BUTTERFLY EVENTS.

		10 years & under (50m)	11 years (50m)	12-13 years (50m)
SCHOOL LEVEL	n	33	8	45
	$\bar{d}$	-0.426	-4.108	-2.472
	s_d	15.288	15.541	9.831
	t	-0.113	-0.529	-1.193
	% Sch B<G	42.9	37.5	71.1
	% Sch G<B	57.6	62.5	28.9
DISTRICT LEVEL	n	30	11	33
	$\bar{d}$	0.519	-2.469	-4.661
	s_d	8.991	11.569	5.537
	t	0.224	-0.501	-3.420*
	% Dist B<G	56.7	54.5	93.9
	% Dist G<B	43.3	45.5	6.1

TABLE 5: DIFFERENCES BETWEEN BOYS AND GIRLS IN RELAY EVENTS.

		10 years & under (4 x 50m)	11 years (4 x 50m)	12-13 years (4 x 50m)
SCHOOL LEVEL	n	21	5	22
	$\bar{d}$	-11.401	-8.190	-11.431
	s_d	14.575	11.626	13.247
	t	-2.535*	-1.112	-2.862*
	% Sch B<G	85.7	80.0	86.4
	% Sch G<B	14.3	20.0	13.6
DISTRICT LEVEL	n	30	11	32
	$\bar{d}$	-9.493	-8.479	-9.818
	s_d	9.909	9.370	7.751
	t	-4.045*	-2.122*	-5.067*
	% Dist B<G	86.7	81.8	96.9
	% Dist G<B	13.3	18.2	3.1

TABLE 6: COMMENTS RECEIVED IN SECTION FOUR OF THE OPINIONAIRE.

No. Times Appeared.	COMMENT
22	"Girls would be disadvantaged by mixed races."
8	"Swimming at our school is more for enjoyment than competition, so is already mixed."
8	"Girls in our school/district are often superior to boys."
8	"Young girls' and boys' sport should be mixed, but social pressures have generally been against it in the past."
5	"Girls and boys should compete separately in sport."
4	"Boys are usually faster at our school/district."
3	"Girls would lose the respect of boys through sex integration."
3	"Children should be grouped in competition according to ability rather than sex."
2	"Optional mixed races should be provided."
2	"Mixed races provide stimulating competition."
189	Blank comment box.

References

Adrian, M. (1972) Sex differences in biomechanics, in Women and Sport: A National Research Conference (ed. D.V. Harris), Penn. State University, pp 389-97.

Dyer, K.F. (1982) Challenging the Men: The Social Biology of Female Sporting Achievement. University of Queensland Press, St. Lucia, Queensland.

Dyer, K.F. (1985) Making up the difference: some explanations for recent improvements in women's athletic performances. Search., 16, 264-69.

Mugno, D.A. (1983) The Michigan Swim Study: why are our young swimmers dropping out? Swimming World., 24, 27-30.

Pate, R.R., Barnes, C. and Miller W. (1982) A physiological comparison of performance-matched male and female distance runners. (Abstract) Medicine and Science in Sports and Exercise., 14, 139.

Selby, R. and Lewko, J.H. (1976) Children's attitudes towards females in sports: their relationship with sex, grade and sports participation. Research Quarterly., 47, 453-63.

Sex Discrimination Act 1984 (Com).

Sharp, C. (1984) Physiology and the woman athlete. New Scientist., 1415, 22-24.

Wilmore, J.H. (1979) The application of science to sport: physiological profiles of male and female athletes. Canadian Journal of Applied Sports Sciences., 4, 103-15.

TRAINING OF COMMONWEALTH AND IRISH TRACK AND FIELD ATHLETES IN U.S.
COLLEGES AND UNIVERSITIES

H. F. STIDWILL   416 Third Street West
                    Cornwall, Ontario
T. BEDECKI   CAHPER
                    Ottawa, Ontario

Abstract
The purpose of this paper is to chronicle the presence of many
Commonwealth and Irish track and field athletes being trained in U.S.
colleges and universities. References will be made to specific
recruiting pipelines, and the underlying motivations of these
athletes to attend U.S. schools. The primary motivation of foreign
athletes to attend U.S. universities is to compete and gain an
education at the same time. In most Commonwealth countries, athletic
scholarships are not available, intercollegiate competition is not
emphasized and entrance to national universities is difficult.
Consistent with the increased movement towards internationalism, this
trend will continue, with U.S. schools providing a training ground
for many Commonwealth athletes. Research techniques based on the
historical method of research will be utilized. Source material
will include interviews with selected coaches, newspaper and
magazine articles dealing with the subject of foreign track and
field athletes, and related books and journals.
Key words: Commonwealth athletes, track and field, NCAA.

Concurrent with the increased internationalization of sport in the
twentieth century has been the influx of track and field athletes
from the Commonwealth and Ireland to several American universities.
The presence of these athletes began with a small number of Canadians
competing for American schools at the turn of the century (Stidwill,
1981). Jamaican, Irish, English and Australian athletes also became
prominent at specific schools during the 1940's and 1950's.
"Pipelines", such as the one at Villanova for Irish athletes, soon
emerged. The successes of African track and field athletes in the
1968 and 1972 Olympic Games brought about a substantial recruitment
of African athletes, particularly from Kenya and Tanzania, with
several going to Washington State University and the University of
Texas at El Paso (Stidwill, 1984).

    This relocation of athletes represents a contemporary trend in
the evolution of sport and is worthy of study. This paper will,
accordingly, chronicle the presence of many Irish and Commonwealth
athletes being trained in U.S. colleges and universities. References
will be made to specific recruiting pipelines, and the underlying
motivations of these athletes to attend U.S. schools.

Canadian Athletes

Due to geographical proximity, Canadian athletes were the first foreign athletes to attend colleges and universities in the U.S. and to represent them at Olympic competition. Representing the University of Pennsylvania in 1900,George Orton, won a gold medal in the 2500 metre steeplechase. Two other Canadians also represented American universities at these Games. (Canada did not officially participate in these games.) (Stidwill, 1981)

Additional medal winners receiving training at U.S. schools have included: Earl Thompson, 1920; Duncan McNaughton, 1932; Alex Wilson, 1932; Phil Edwards, 1932 and 1936; Harry Jerome, 1964; and Greg Joy, 1976 (Stidwill, 1981).

Jamaican Athletes

The first prominent Jamaican athletes competing for American universities in the late 1940's and 1950's were Olympic medallists Herb McKinley and George Rhoden (Moore, 1983). Other prominent Olympians from Jamaica have included: George Kerr, 1960; Lennox Miller, 1968 and 1972; Donald Quarrie, 1976 and 1980; and Bert Cameron, 1984 (Moore).

The vast majority of the Jamaican athletes have been sprinters. This fact is, in large part, due to the early successes of athletes like McKinley and Rhoden both of whom helped establish a strong sprinting tradition. In addition to this tradition, Jamaican athletes often have lacked the athletic equipment and competent coaching in their own country with which to train for the more technical field events. The warm weather in the Caribbean region also precludes long distance training.

Irish, Australian, and British Athletes

During the early successes of the Jamaican athletes, Coach Jumbo Elliot of Villanova opened his so-called "Irish Pipeline" with Irish Olympian Jimmy Reardon in 1948. This was followed by a succession of Irish Olympians, including Ron Delany, who won the 1956 Olympic 1500-meter event for Ireland and four NCAA titles for Villanova; Noel Carrol, 1968; Frank Murphy, 1972; and Eamon Coughlan, two-time Olympian and 1983 World Cup Champion (Track & Field News, June 1974: 26)

Athletes from Australia as well as England have competed for American universities. In the late 1950's the cross-country team from the University of Houston was built around a nucleus of Australians, including Olympian and two-time NCAA cross-country champion Al Laurence. The University of Houston won the NCAA cross-country championship with an all foreign athlete squad whose average age was 26 (Manners, 1974). Idaho won the first Pacific Coast Cross-Country Championship in 1957 with an all-British team (Track and Field News, Nov. 1975: 3)

African Athletes

The presence of runners from several African nations has been a relatively recent but significant phenomenon. Prior to 1960, no African
athlete had won an Olympic gold medal. However, with the successes
of Kenyan runners in the 1968 and 1972 Olympic Games, came a corresponding interest by American coaches to recruit African athletes.
Among prominent African record holders recruited by American
universities have been Kenyan Henry Rono by Washington State and
Tanzanian Filbert Bayi by the University of Texas at El Paso (UTEP).

Patterns of Recruitment

The recruitment patterns of the national groupings are somewhat
diverse. The Canadian athletes appear to have attended several
United States schools in small numbers, with no distinct "pipelines"
being apparent. Among these universities were the University of
Oregon, Washington State, Michigan, East Michigan, several schools
in Ohio (such as Ohio State, University of Ohio, Miami University),
Southern Illinois, Stanford, Villanova, Nebraska, and UTEP.
(Stidwill, 1984).

Much of the Jamaican recruitment pattern shows specific pipeline
effects, with Jamaicans tending to compete at UTEP, Texas, Nebraska,
Idaho, Idaho State, and Florida (Hendershott, 1955-1984). It is
estimated that presently Jamaican athletes win ten to fifteen
scholarships a year (Moore). Athletes from Barbadoes and Trinidad
have gone to UTEP, Idaho, Seton Hall, Maryland State, East Michigan,
and Florida.

The English and Irish athletes tend to be more broadly dispersed
than the Jamaican athletes. Primary schools of attendance include
Villanova, Providence, Iowa State, Arkansas, Murray State, Western
Kentucky, Boston University, East Tennessee State, and Southern
Illinois (Hendershott).

Most African athletes come from Kenya, Tanzania, and Nigeria with
somewhat distinct pipelines being apparent. In the late 1960's and
early 1970's, several Kenyan runners attended Richmond and North
Carolina Central. Since the early 1970's, Kenyans have been heavily
recruited by UTEP, Washington State, and New Mexico. Recently, Iowa
State began recruiting Kenyans. Many prominent Tanzanian athletes,
including 30-year-old Filbert Bayi, are attending UTEP. Several
Nigerians attend the University of Missouri (Teel, 1984).

The mass exodus of African athletes concerns many Kenyan officials, who see it as a loss and a detriment to their athletic system (Tufa, 1983). Tanzania, on the other hand, fully supports its
athletes' going to the United States to the extent that virtually
the whole Tanzanian national team trains at UTEP (USA Today, Sept.
1983: 9).

Motivation of Athletes to Attend U.S. Universities

The primary motivation of these athletes to attend American universities are to train and compete, as well as gain an education.

294

Canadian track and field athletes initially were motivated to attend U.S. colleges because of the availability of athletic scholarships. They wanted to compete and gain an education at the same time. Until recently, Canada did not offer athletic scholarships. While the Canadian government now offers partial scholarships to certain elite or carded athletes, many of Canada's track and field athletes still come to the United States (Stidwill, 1984).

The availability of athletic scholarships to American colleges has also encouraged Jamaican athletes to come to the United States to compete. In 1981, Jamaica had a per capital income of approximately $1300 and an unemployment rate of 30 percent. In the Caribbean, the University of West Indies is the only major institution of higher education, and in accordance with British tradition, puts very little emphasis on competitive sports. Thus, the way for a Jamaican youth to develop as an athlete and a way out of a subsistence life are the same--an athletic scholarship to an American college (Moore, 1983:98). Also, the Jamaican athlete is exposed to superior training and competitive advantages in an American college which are not available to him in Jamaica.

Like other nationalities, the Irish and English athletes have been motivated to attend American colleges on scholarship in order to train and compete, as well as gain an education. Intercollegiate competition is not emphasized in the United Kingdom, because it is seen as a distraction from academic studies. Competition exists primarily at a somewhat less formal club system (McFadden & Ferrara, 1983:33). Admittance to higher education institutions in Ireland and England is restricted. Accepting an athletic scholarship to a college in the United States is an attractive alternative to working or going to trade school. Accordingly, many recruits from the United Kingdom often have higher scholastic standing than the average American student. Coach Del Hessel (1984) of New Mexico stated he particularly recruited English-speaking athletes because they performed well academically. Coaches John McDonnell (1984) of Arkansas and Dick Lee (1984) of Iowa State said that the British and Irish athletes were more dedicated and motivated both academically and athletically.

The African athlete, like the Jamaican or other Caribbean athletes, often suffers from a lack of adequate facilities, equipment, and coaching. For this reason, field events are virtually nonexistent in Africa. The University of Nairobi is the only university in Kenya, so the Kenyan athlete often views an athletic scholarship to the United States as a vehicle to a better life. As Kip Keino said about Kenyan athletes: "They all work for U.S. track scholarships. They have to be worried for their future employment and security and that is a difficult thing in Kenya right now" (Bentsen, April 1983:66). Similarly, Fred Hardy, head track coach at Richmond where many Kenyans attend, noted: "The motivation for many African runners is clear. When Western-educated graduates return home they can expect rapid advancement in government, private business or education."

Larry Heidebrecht (1984) of the University of Texas at El Paso said that the African runner was highly motivated in the classroom because to go home without a degree was a "disgrace." Running was, therefore, a vehicle to get a degree. Motivation in track and motivation in the classroom carried over into one another (Heidebrecht, 1984). Coach Bob Teel (1984) of Missouri echoed these sentiments, saying that most foreign athletes were highly motivated and that for them "athletics and academics go hand-in-hand." Coach Teel said that for his Nigerian athletes, "this combination is a key to a better life. Athletics and academics are a two-way street."

Coach John Chaplin (1984) of Washington State University said that most of his African athletes were more motivated in the sense that they had made a initial decision or commitment to come a long distance in the first place and, therefore, were very committed. He said that gaining an education was a prime concern particularly for the African athlete and that running provided that opportunity.

However, while athletics and education may go "hand-in-hand," several coaches said that student-athletes from Africa and the Caribbean, though highly motivated to do well academically, have problems. Coach Teel (1984) said that many of his Nigerian athletes had a difficult time reading English but they all graduated. Ted McLaughlin (1984) of Southern Methodist University stated that the African athlete was motivated but had to struggle due to having a poor educational background. Gary Pepin made similar comments regarding his Jamaican athletes.

Patriotic feelings may motivate athletes, particularly those from small or developing countries, to perform. Bert Cameron, an Olympian and two-time NCAA and World Cup 400-meter champion, stated that he tried to maintain the standards of the previous Jamiacan runners and that his love of Jamaica motivated him to run well (Track and Field, June 1983:49). Irish athletes, like those from Jamaica, have great expectations placed upon them. As Villanova graduate Eamon Coughlan stated: "The Irish people build me up all the time. They need someone to look up to, they need a morale booster" (Track and Field, July 1983:57).

Conclusion

Athletes from Ireland and the Commonwealth have been competing for American universities since the turn of the century. Indeed, many medal winners from these nations have received their training at American universities.

It is apparent that the primary motivation of these athletes to attend American colleges is to compete and gain an education at the same time. In these countries, athletic scholarships are not available, intercollegiate competition is not emphasized, and entrance to national universities is difficult. In the case of athletes from developing countries, their competing for American colleges offers them educational opportunities, which, in turn, avails them economic opportunities later on. The desire for a better quality of life, combined with patriotic feelings, provides a strong motivational basis for athletes of developing countries to compete in United States intercollegiate track and field.

It is suggested that future research examine the social and cultural effects of U.S. collegiate training on these athletes. Implicit in such a direction will be the need to marshall the social sciences and humanities to assess the intercultural significance of these experiences (Zeigler, 1985). In this fashion, sport will be seen to assume a rightful role in the forging of international links in the Commonwealth and the world-at-large.

References

Bentsen, C.(1983). Kenya. The Runner. March and April.

Chronicle of Higher Education, (1984), April 18, pp. 27-28.

Hendershott, J. (1955-1983). Where are they going? Track and Field News.

Henderson, J. (1969). Emerging nations share glory. Track and Field News. December, p. 16.

Manners, J. (1974). Foreign invasion. Sports Illustrated, June 24, pp. 34-35, 38.

McFadden, J. & Ferrara, D. (1983). Americans versus Europeans. Runner's World, August, p. 83.

Moore, K. (1983). Land of sprinters and dreamers. Sports Illustrated, February 14, pp. 94-110.

Stidwill H. (1981). The History of the Canadian Olympic Association. Unpublished master's thesis, University of Ottawa.

Stidwill, H. (1984). Motives toward track and field competition of foreign and domestic grant-in-aid student athletes in NCAA Division I colleges and universities. Unpublished doctoral dissertation, Oregan State University.

Track and Field News, 1956-1984.

Tufa, D.J. (1983). The African invasion. Runner's World, November, pp. 66-67, 110.

U.S.A. Today, (1983), March 2.

Zeigler, E. (1985). Marshelling the social sciences and humanities to assess the intercultural significance of physical education and sport. Comparative Physical Education and Sport, Fall.

SOCIO-DEMOGRAPHIC CHARACTERISTICS OF ELITE AUSTRALIAN ATHLETES: AN
EXPLORATORY CASE STUDY

J. McKAY, K. PEARSON[1]
University of Queensland
G. TAIT,
University of York

Abstract
This study examines the conventional wisdoms that Australian sport is
an egalitarian and meritocratic institution. Analysis of the
socio-demographic traits of Australian athletes participating in the
1982 Commonwealth Games revealed that : (1) they mainly came from
advantaged backgrounds; and (2) females were underrepresented. These
findings were explained in terms of the underlying structures of
inequality that are characteristic of Australian society in general.
It was concluded that current government policy toward sport actually
reproduces social inequalities by assisting athletes who come from
the predominantly privileged sectors of Australian society.
Key words: Social Inequality, Elite Athletes, Underrepresentation,
Opportunity-Set, Life Chances, Socialisation

1. Introduction
The common sense idea that social inequalities are the "natural"
outcome of meritocratic competition among individuals is an important
linchpin of liberal-conservative ideologies in Western capitalist
societies. This is especially true of sport, which embodies
masculine, bourgeoise and Anglocentric ideologies of "survival of the
fittest", impartial evaluation of "performance" by neutral referees,
competitive individualism and equality of opportunity to participate
(Clarke and Clarke 1982; Guttmann 1978; Hargreaves 1982a, 1982b;
Willis 1982). In everyday life, sporting metaphors often are used to
describe politics, education, the economy and social life in general
as "games", "contests", or "races" involving "dark horses",
"heavyweights", "marathon men", "thoroughbreds", and "also-rans"
(Balbus 1972; McKay 1986).
     This meritocratic ideology is particularly prevalent in
Australia, a society that is often claimed to be: (1) "sports-drunk"
(Polsky 1972); and (2) egalitarian (Connell 1974). For instance,
Daly (1985: 15) declares that, "Australian sport has always catered
for the masses. Community sport is available to anybody and
everybody." According to Pavia and Jaques (1978: 88), "Sport in
Australia has been regarded as a great 'equalizer' in that it is
available to everybody and affluence or poverty is of little or no
importance". In this paper we provide some insights into the
allegedly meritocratic nature of Australian sport, by analysing some
relationships among socioeconomic status, gender and opportunity set

298

in a sample of elite amateur athletes.

2. Methodology
The subjects used in this study came from a sample of Australian
athletes participating in the XII Commonwealth Games held in Brisbane
during September, 1982. Information was elicited from a self-
administered questionnaire containing questions about various socio-
demographic characteristics. The investigators were restricted by the
fact that Commonwealth Games officials would only approve a single
page questionnaire for distribution. Given this limitation, it was
decided to obtain a general socio-demographic profile of the
athletes. Details of the completion rates of the questionnaires for
each sport appear in Table 1.

Table 1. Response Rates to Questionnaire by Each Sport

| | No. of Team Members | | | No.Questionnaires | Response |
	Male	Female	Persons	Returned	Rate
AQUATICS	30	24	54	39	63%
ARCHERY	3	3	6	6	100
ATHLETICS	43	30	73	64	88
BADMINTON	5	5	10	10	100
BOWLS	6	6	12	12	100
BOXING	11	0	11	8	73
CYCLING	15	0	15	14	93
SHOOTING	15	1	16	13	81
WEIGHTLIFTING	10	0	10	9	90
WRESTLING	11	0	11	11	100
TOTAL	149	69	218	186	85

3. Results and Discussion

3.1 Socioeconomic Status and Opportunity Set
It can be seen from Table 2 that athletes were overrepresented in the
high socioeconomic stratum in comparison to the Australian
population. In explaining the overrepresentation of athletes with
high socioeconomic backgrounds, several interrelated factors can be
posited. First, despite the common sense idea that sport is an "open
system", it takes appreciable amounts of time, money and parental
encouragement for athletes to become and remain involved in sport.
Moreover, as is the case with education, some groups have
disproportionate shares of this these resources and thus are more
advantaged than others in terms of: (1) the range of sports to which
they are initially exposed; and (2) the ability to select a sport(s)
in which they subsequently will receive financial and emotional
support from their parents. For example, track and field, wrestling,
boxing and weightlifting require little financial outlay for
participants and are often run or subsidised by a public, charitable
or religious organisation. On the other hand, equipment for cycling,
archery and shooting is relatively expensive, and a considerable

Table 2. SES of Elite Athletes Compared with National Figures

SES*	Males		Females		Persons	
	Athletes (N=120)	National Figures	Athletes (N=52)	National Figures	Athletes (N=172)	National ** Figures
Low[1]	41%	65	21	33	35	53
High[2]	59	35	79	67	65	47

* Fifty-one respondents who were students were coded according to their father's occupation.
** National figures taken from Year Book Australia (1982)
[1] Includes professional, technical, executive, clerical and sales workers.
[2] Includes manual and service workers.

amount of discretionary time is generally required for parents to transport children to and from swimming lessons. In both these respects - time and money - middle class families are in a more advantageous position than working class ones.

For instance, it can be observed from Table 3 that the family was perceived to be the most important group by far in influencing the respondents to become involved in sport both generally and at the elite level. This pattern was slightly more pronounced in the high than in the low socioeconomic category. Respondents with a low socioeconomic status were marginally more likely than those with a high one to report being influenced by their peers. Table 4 shows that high SES athletes indicated they played more sport-type games during childhood than low SES athletes. Furthermore, it can be seen from Table 5 that male athletes from low SES backgrounds were overrepresented in contact/strength sports. In summary, our data suggest that compared to high SES athletes, low SES athletes: (1) have less exposure to sports during childhood; (2) receive less reinforcement for playing sport from their family; and (3) are exposed more to contact/strength sports.

Table 3. Individuals and Groups Perceived to be Influential in Athletes Initial Involvement in Sport by SES

Influential Individual or Group	SES			
	Low	High	Low	High
	Sport in General		Elite Sport	
Family	51%	61	47	50
Peers	29	22	20	14
Coach	11	5	22	21
Schoolteacher	2	5	3	8
Other	7	7	8	7
N =	46	99	42	94

Table 4. Number of Sport-Type Games Played During Childhood by SES

Number of Games	SES	
Played	Low	Hi
0-3	46%	19
4 or more	54	81
N =	65	110
Q =	.568	

Table 5. Type of Event by SES of Male Athletes

	SES	
	Lo	Hi
Contact/Strength	30%	16
Other	70	84
N =	54	70
Q =	.386	

4.2 Gender and Opportunity Set

Females constituted less than one-third of the Australian team (see Table 1) and diving was the only event in which there were more females (N = 3) than males (N = 2). Women were excluded from the combative/strength sports of boxing, weight lifting and wrestling, and were also barred from cycling, pole-vaulting, hammer-throwing and some endurance track events. Although women had equal or near equal representation in "mixed" sports like archery, bowls, badminton, track and field and swimming, they were vastly underrepresented in shooting. Table 6 indicates that there were differences between males and females regarding their perceptions of who encouraged them to become involved in sport. Females were slightly more likely than males to perceive their family as being influential and much less likely to perceive their peers as having influenced them. This finding suggests that females may experience conflicts with other females in attempting to be an athlete and a woman. On the other hand, females reported playing more games during childhood than did males (see Table 7).

Table 6. Individuals and Groups Perceived to be Influential in Athletes Initial Involvement in Sport by Gender

Influential Individual or Group	Sport in General		Elite Sport	
	Male	Female	Male	Female
Family	55%	61	46	55
Peers	26	16	21	7
Coach	9	3	20	22
Schoolteacher	7	9	6	7
Others	3	11	7	7
N =	106	52	97	50

Table 7. Number of Sport-Type Games Played During Childhood by Gender

Number of Games		Gender	
Played		Males	Females
0 to 3		34%	17
4 or more		66	83
	N =	128	58
	Q =	.416	

Table 2 demonstrates that there is a "double exclusion" effect for athletes who are female <u>and</u> from a low SES background, as respondents with these socio-demographic traits were the most underrepresented in the sample. This pattern is consistent with previous studies of elite athletes in Canada (Gruneau 1975) and the Federal Republic of Germany (Luschen 1969).

4. Summary and Conclusions

There are some obvious limitations to this study. In the first place the research lies totally within the "stratigraphic" tradition of survey research and only gives us a simplistic, static glimpse of some <u>distributional</u> aspects of social inequality in sport. We are keenly aware of the need for research in this area to extend the conventional distributional approach into <u>relational</u> and <u>normative</u> dimensions of social inequality. This, in turn, requires: (1) much more qualitative research based on ethnographies, and intensive interviews that would permit a closer analysis of context and subjective interpretations of life chances; and (2) historical and investigations of social inequality in Australian sport.

Also, we contend that the entire area of socialisation and social inequality in sport should be shifted away from its functionalist preoccupation with "roles" and its "society as entity" perspective. Both topics need to be located in a wider critical social theory of power in which the normative-symbolic aspects of socialisation are dialectically related to ideological hegemony, and relations of domination. Values, meanings, norms, beliefs and symbols <u>are</u> important for students of cultural studies. But some people's values, norms and beliefs <u>count more</u> than others, and these symbols and meanings must be theorised in a way that explains how they are used as modes of manipulation, persuasion and coercion in sustaining relations of domination/subordination. Although we have reservations about equally static "correspondence" theories, we are impressed by some of the recent work on social and cultural reproduction, "cultural capital", the state and schooling. Much of the research in this area is strikingly similar to the literature on sport regarding attempts by dominant groups to selectively legitimise specific educational values and practices and defend them from challenges by subordinate groups (Bourdieu, 1978).

These limitations notwithstanding, we would affirm that our findings are valuable in two ways. Firstly, they add to the demythologising of powerful common sense beliefs about the democratic nature of Australian sport. Contrary to conventional wisdom, sport

302

in Australia is not a meritocratic arena in which all "competitors" receive a "fair go". It more closely resembles a situation in which some groups are systematically given "flying starts", while others are always "handicapped". Overall, the findings support: (1) feminist critiques that Australian sport has a pronounced masculine bias (Australia 1985; Bryson 1983; Coles 1978, 1980a, 1980b; Darlison 1984; King 1979; McKay 1983, 1984; Walker 1985; Williams, Lawrence and Rowe 1986); (2) other studies of elite athletes and the general population that have shown that participation in Australian sport is structured by factors such as age, race, gender, education, income and marital status (Broome 1980; Crawford 1977; Lowe, Hill and Roberts 1975; McKay 1983, 1984; Pavia 1973; Pavia and Jaques 1978). It should also be noted that these patterns of social inequality in sport complement a larger body of historical and sociological research in Australian society, which has demonstrated that gender, age, race, ethnic background, income and wealth are decisive in systematically reproducing unequal access to and control of education, health and welfare services, housing and the occupational structure. In Berry's (1977: 43) words:

> By analogy, a meritocracy is like a fairly contested race in which all competitors start together and run over the same track with victory and the spoils going to the quickest. The Australian situation, in contrast, more closely resembles the case where a few competitors start one metre from the finishing line, a few more fifty metres back up the track, a larger group are further back hammering in their starting blocks, others are still changing in a crowded dressing room, while the remainder are at home under the impression that the race starts tomorrow.

Secondly, the study also underlines the contradictory nature of the Australian government's "assistance" to amateur sport. Presently, the overwhelming portion of funds and resources the Australian Department of Sport, Tourism and Recreation is allocated to elite sport and the Australian Institute of Sport in particular. This sort of social policy actually reinforces social inequalities in sport by providing monetary, administrative and coaching support to athletes from advantaged, even the most advantaged sectors of society. Concomitantly, little or nothing is done to address, let alone redress, the underlying structures of inequality that are so crucial in influencing what groups of males and females are systematically privileged and disadvantaged in terms of access to and participation in Australian sport.

Notes

1. The late Dr. Kent Pearson was mainly responsible for designing the questionnaire used for this study and assisted in collecting some of the data. We would like to thank John Ross, who also collected some of the data.
2. For details of the socio-demographic variables see Tait (1985).

References

Australia (1982) Yearbook of Australia. Canberra: Australian
   Government Publishing Service.
Australia (1985) Women, Sport and the Media; A Report to the Federal
   Government from the Working Group on Women in Sport. Canberra:
   Australian Government Publishing Service.
Balbus, I. (1975) Politics as Sports: The Political Ascendency of the
   Sport Metaphor in America. Monthly Review. 26(10), 26-39.
Berry, M. (1977) Inequality, in Australian Society: A Sociological
   Introduction (ed. A. Davies, S. Encel and M. Berry), Melbourne:
   Longman.
Bourdieu, P. (1978) Sport and Social Class. Social Science
   Information, 17, 819-840.
Broome, R. (1980) Aboriginal Boxers and Social Control in Australia
   1930-1979. Aboriginal History 4, 1, 48-71.
Bryson, L. (1983) Sport and the Oppression of Women. Australian and
   New Zealand Journal of Sociology, 19, 413-424.
Clarke, A. and Clarke, J. (1982) Highlights and Action Replays, in
   Sport, Culture and Ideology, (ed. J. Hargreaves). London:
   Routledge and Kegan Paul.
Coles, L. (1978) Sport and Cultural Hegemony: A Socio-Historical
   Analysis. Paper presented at SAANZ Conference, University of
   Queensland, May 24-27.
Coles, L. (1980a) Women and Leisure - A Critical Perspective, in
   Recreation and Social Change in Urban Australia, (eds. D. Mercer
   and E. Hamilton-Smith). Malvern: Sorrett.
Coles, L. (1980b) Sport in Schools: The Participation of Girls.
   Sydney, New South Wales Department of Education.
Connell, R. (1974) Images of Australia, in Social Change in
   Australia. (ed. D. Edgar). Melbourne: Cheshire.
Crawford, S. (1977) Occupational Prestige Rankings and the New
   Zealand Olympic Athlete. International Review of Sport Sociology.
   12, 5-15.
Daly, J. (1985) Structure, in Australian Sport: A Profile. Canberra:
   Australian Government Printing Service.
Darlison, L. (1984) The Games and the Place of Women in Australian
   Sport and Society, in The 1982 Commonwealth Games: A Retrospect.
   (ed. P. Reynolds). University of Queensland: Australian Studies
   Centre.
Gruneau, R. (1975) Sport, Social Differentiation and Social
   Inequality, in Sport and Social Order. (eds. D. Ball and J. Loy).
   Reading: Addison-Wesley.
Guttmann, A. (1978) From Ritual to Record. New York: Columbia
   University Press.
Hargreaves, J. (1982a) Sport, Culture and Ideology, in Sport, Culture
   and Ideology. (ed. J. Hargreaves). London: Routledge and Kegan
   Paul.
Hargreaves, J. (1982b) Sport and Hegemony: Some Theoretical Problems,
   in Sport, Culture and the Modern State, (eds. H. Cantelon and R.
   Gruneau). Toronto: University of Toronto Press.

King, H. (1979) The Sexual Politics of Sport, in Sport in History, (eds. R. Cashman and M. McKernan). St. Lucia: University of Queensland Press.

Lowe, B., Hill, P. and Roberts, I. (1975) A Cross-Cultural Study of Athletes Representing Four Countries in the Commonwealth Games. The Australian Journal for Health, Physical Education and Recreation, 70, 22-25.

Luschen, G. (1969) Social Stratification and Social Mobility Among Young Sportsmen, in Sport, Culture and Society. (ed. J. Loy and G. Kenyon). Toronto: Macmillan, pp. 258-276.

McKay, J. (1986) Hegemony, The State and Australian Sport, in Power Play: Essays in the Sociology of Australian Sport, (eds. G. Lawrence and D. Rowe). Sydney: Hale and Ironmonger (in press).

McKay, J. (1983) The Democratization of Australian Sport: Some Preliminary Observations of a National Survey. International Review of Sport Sociology. 3(18), 92-111.

McKay, J. (1984) The Democratization of Australian Leisure: Fact or Fancy? Paper presented at the 1984 Olympic Scientific Conference, University of Oregon, Eugene, Oregon, July 19-26.

Pavia, G. (1973) An Analysis of the Social Class of the 1972 Australian Olympic Team. The Australian Journal of Physical Education, 61, 14-19.

Pavia, G. and Jaques, T. (1978) The Socioeconomic Origin, Academic Attainment, Occupational Mobility and Parental Background of Selected Australian Athletes, in Sociology of Sport, (eds. F. Landry and W. Orban). Miami: Symposia Specialists.

Polsky, N. (1977) Emerging Trends in Entertainment, in Entertainment and Sociology. (ed. G. Caldwell). Canberra: Australian Government Printing Service.

Tait, G. (1985) A Study Into the Socio-Demographic Characteristics of Australian Athletes Participating in the XII Commonwealth Games. M.H.M.S. thesis, Department of Human Movement Studies, University of Queensland.

Walker, J. (1985) Louts and Legends: Male Youth Culture in an Inner City School. Paper presented at SAANZ Conference, University of Queensland.

Williams, C., Lawrence, G. and Rowe, D. (1986) Women in Sport: A Lost Ideal, in Power Play: Essays in the Sociology of Australian Sport, (eds. G. Lawrence and D. Rowe). Sydney: Hale and Ironmonger (in press).

Willis, P. (1982) Women in Sport in Ideology in Sport, Culture and Ideology, (ed. J. Hargreaves). London: Routledge and Kegan Paul.

SPORTING PRACTICE AS AN ENDLESS PLAY OF SELF-RELATIVISING TASTES:
INSIGHTS FROM PIERRE BOURDIEU

F.C. KEW
Department of Applied and Community Studies, Bradford and Ilkley
Community College

Abstract
Bourdieu argues that sporting practice demonstrates and reinforces
class stratification. His thesis, however, is a significant advance
on the economic determinism of much cultural analysis. According to
Bourdieu, early socialising influences give rise to a matrix of
transposable tastes, dispositions, and preferences which together
form an agent's 'habitus' and its logic of practice. This influences
agent's perception of, and meanings ascribed to, different sports,
and explains how tastes are acquired for sports which are best conceived as 'universes of stylistic possibles'. Survey and ethnographic research informs this sociology of taste. Tastes are to be
understood as social breaks, as distinctive expressions of groups
differentially located in social space. It is necessary therefore
to go beyond the statistical distribution of sports amongst different
social groups, to focus on the ways in which certain sports and
styles of sporting practice are predisposed for use by social groups
identified by their 'class habitus'.
Key words: Class habitus, Distributional significance, Cultural
capital, Sporting taste.

The influence of Pierre Bourdieu upon Anglo-Saxon thought has been
relatively fragmentary and mainly restricted to the discipline of
anthropology and the sub-discipline of education. The translation
into English in 1985 of his magnus opus 'Distinction' allows for a
preliminary assessment of the ways in which Bourdieu's analysis of
cultural production and consumption informs an understanding of
sport. This redresses the neglect of sport by most sociologists of
class (e.g. Giddens, Parkin, Goldthorpe). Bourdieu, and his
colleagues at the Centre of European Sociology in Paris have undertaken extensive analyses of cultural practice to demonstrate how
such practices systematically reproduce and reinforce existing class
stratification.
    Bourdieu argues then that sporting practice, together with other
cultural activities, demonstrates and sustains the reproduction of
the prevailing system of class inequalities. However, a cursory
observation of existing sporting practice immediately seems to
undermine this thesis. There is plenty of evidence to show

306

successful interpenetration of different sports by different social groups. Many sports are not the exclusive preserve of an identifiable social class or class fraction. Bourdieu himself acknowledges that rugby in France, for example, enjoys 'dual membership'. Many sports are relatively accessible in terms of material cost for both participant and spectator. The well-documented observation that the statistical distribution of many sports is not starkly arranged along class lines has resulted, as Hodgkiss (1982) points out, to a devaluation of 'class' as an explanatory factor of sporting involvement. Class is considered as being just one amongst a plurality of other influences upon sporting participation. In contrast to art, which necessitates considerable early training, conditionings, and particular forms of what Bourdieu calls 'cultural competences', sports seems to be easily available - the popular 'art form' of the masses. 'Sport for All' - the Sports Council's initiative - seems to be an uncontroversial aim. In State Socialist countries, sports (unlike arts) are valued precisely because such practices transcend ethnic, geographical, sex, class barriers. Sports are not considered to be socially devisive. From other perspectives, both Ashworth (1971) and Hargreaves (1984) point out that the world of sport offers an ideal 'egalitarian communistic utopia' within which all pre-existing inequalities are meaningless. There is also evidence to suggest that consumption patterns in sport are organised along lines of shared interest rather than class membership.

The case against class being a key factor influencing sporting practice would seem to be a strong one. I want to suggest however that none of the above observations undermine Bourdieu's thesis that sports practice sustains class inequalities and herein therefore lies its challenge.

I have identified three key elements in Bourdieu's cultural analysis. Firstly arising from his Theory of Practice, he develops a conception of preferences and tastes in sport which originate in and are thus wholly relative to an agent's socially located position. Hence, quite apart from the actual statistical distribution of sports amongst different social groups, there is considerable variation in the perception of the immediate and deferred profits to be gained from different sports. Agents vary in their perception of the meaning and function of different sports, a variation to be explained as the product of conditionings associated with a particular class of conditions of existence.

Secondly, and as the title of Bourdieu's recent work suggests, the motor behind these patterns of taste is a pursuit of distinction (distinctiveness). Tastes are to be understood as distastes of others, as a mark of distinction from others, as a social break. Hence sporting practice is an 'endless play of mutually self-relativising tastes', tastes which are experienced as natural since they are tactitly inculcated.

Thirdly, sporting practices confront the agent as an 'objectively instituted field of stylistic possibles', and agents are aware of how sports are differentiallly distributed amongst other agents who are themselves distributed in social space. Sports therefore have a

significance dependent upon this differential distribution, a significance which effectively delimits the field of possibility.
Agents are therefore not solely motivated by the intrinsic benefits
believed to accrue from particular sporting practice.

The bedrock upon which this cultural analysis is founded is
Bourdieu's Theory of Practice. This represents the better known
elements of his work (1973, 1977, 1981) developed in his analysis
of education, and hence is only briefly covered here. By what
mechanism do individuals choose particular sports, given the
diversity of possible choices available? The mechanism for Bourdieu
is the habitus - a system of 'lasting transposable dispositions'
which functions as a 'matrix of perceptions, appreciations and
actions', not randomly but according to a coherent 'logic of
practice'. This logic of practice, since inculcated in early childhood is necessarily tacit, hence operates unconsciously and cannot
be supplanted by another logic of practice. Later experiences
might alter its structure but such alterations are made according
to the structural logic of the existing habitus. Moreover, the
habitus is not an individual phenomenon since it is internalised to
use in social interaction. Hence it is a family and especially a
class phenomenon - one's logic of practice is a structural variant
of class practice. This allows Bourdieu to talk of a 'class
habitus' - a 'practice unifying' and 'practice-generating' principle;
the internalised form of class condition and of the conditionings
it entails. Objective class then is conceived of as agents placed
in homogeneous conditions of existence which gives rise to a set of
homogeneous conditionings (the habitus) which in turn translates
into a homogeneous system of dispositions (the logic of practice).

This is the basis from which life-styles are generated. Relatively homogeneous system of dispositions are the basic conceptual
categories and action frames through which people respond to and act
in the social world. Hence sporting practices are only one dimension
or expression of the 'ethos' or life-style of different social
classes. The same system of dispositions, the same logic of practice, operates in all cultural fields of practice, e.g. media consumption, club membership, drinking habits, clothing, holidays,
sporting practice.

To understand sporting practice, sports need to be conceived as
'universes of stylistic possibles' with which agents are confronted.
But agents are subject to various constraints which define, for
them, the field of possibility. Material constraints effectively
deny participation in certain sports and certain venues (e.g. private
facilities) at which sports are practiced. Age, sex, demands of
employment, give other constraints. Collectively, these constraints
delimit the field of possibility for individuals. Given these,
Bourdieu asks how is the taste acquired for different sports and how
therefore is the demand produced? Bourdieu's key proposal is to
consider the whole range of sports as a supply (subject to the above
constraints) intended to meet a <u>social</u> demand. What, are the 'social
conditions of possibility' for different agents appropriating the
various sports?

To talk of the 'social conditions of possibility' reminds us that to understand the logic of sporting practice, sports must be placed within the whole universe of cultural practices bound up with them since their common origin in the matrix of tastes, preferences, and perceptions that is a 'class habitus'. Early socialisation practices effectively circumscribe access to particular sporting practices. Sports practice for Bourdieu is but one dimension of the 'ethos' or life-style of groups differentially located in social space. They are 'a realisation of an aesthetic and ethic in a practical state'.

The sceptic however might still argue that other factors (age, sex, personality, marital status, religion) functioning in various conbinations, filter or screen participants into or out of sporting practice. Moreover, the statistical relationship between many sporting practices and social class membership is not significant. But this does not do justice to Bourdieu's thesis. Agents position in social space (from the habitus and consequent logic of practice) influences not only what is practiced amongst the range of stylistic possibles within and between particular sports, but also accounts for the variation in agents evaluation and perception of the immediate and deferred profits accruing - profits which cannot be reduced to a consideration of their putative intrinsic benefits.

Space precludes an extended consideration of artistic taste upon which most of Bourdieu's extensive empirical research is focussed. However a brief summary is necessary. Taste patterns are indicative of the class habitus. Bourdieu identifies three "zones" of taste corresponding to educational level and social class origin which leads him to propose 'an aesthetic disposition' and an 'anti-Kantian aesthetic'. The key point is that deriving from the logic of practice of the habitus, different social groups perceive and value different objects, artifacts, practices in different ways. For brevity this can be summarised as follows:

Taste of Reason: Disinterested, Form, Euphemised, Gratuitous,
                 Distanciation
Taste of the Senses: Interested, Function, Instrumental,
                 Motivated, Involved.

Sporting practice, like art, is a realisation of an aesthetic in a practical state. Notions of disinterestedness, refinement, control, distanciation, says Bourdieu, typify bourgeois sport involvement, the priveleged classes tending to treat the body as an end in itself. The emphasis is on the intrinsic functioning of the body and on its appearance as a perceptiable configuration. Bourdieu's observation about 'jogging' and other strictly health-oriented practices are instructive here. Jogging is only meaningful in relation to a theoretical abstract knowledge of the effects of exercise. It presupposes a rational faith in deferred and intangible profits from such exercise and is opposed to the practical-oriented movements of everyday life. Bourdieu has much to say about the macro-biotic health cult as a example of the bourgeois aesthetic in practical action. In contrast, ideal-typical working class sporting involvement is typified by instrumentality, by function rather than form.

There is a tendency for the working class to express an instrumental relation to the body often choosing sports which require large investments of effort.

Certain sports then are predisposed for use by certain groups (identified by their class habitus), in that potentialities are objectively inscribed to their practice. One of the primary lines of fracture discussed by Bourdieu in 'Distinction' is that between individual sports and team sports (which for Bourdieu encapsulate pure and barbarous taste). Many popular team sports only require bodily and cultural competences that are fairly equally distributed between classes and are therefore relatively accessible. Their accessibility and consequent lack of distinction tends to discredit them in the eyes of priveleged groups. They

> ... combine all the features which repel the·dominant class:
> not only the social composition of their public, which redoubles
> their commonness but also the values and virtues demanded,
> strength, endurance, violence, sacrifice, docility and
> submission to collective discipline - so contrary to bourgeois
> 'role distance' - and the exaltation of competition.(1985)

In contrast to team sports, individual sports display all the features which appeal to the 'dominant' taste. They are more free in that they are (often) practised in exclusive places at times one chooses, and with chosen partners. They require relatively low physical exertion (or at least such exertion is freely determined) but need a relatively high investment of time and (early) learning. These sports age well, i.e. are (relatively) independent of variations in bodily capital. They give rise to highly ritualised competitions governed by canons of acceptable behaviour (fair play) beyond the codified rules. "The sporting exchange takes on the air of a highly controlled social exchange excluding all physical or verbal violence, all anomic use of the body (shouting, wild gestures) and all forms of direct contact between the opponents".

Bourdieu's general proposition here is that a sport is more likely tobe adopted or appropriated by a particular social class if it does not contradict that class's relation to the body at its deepest and most tacit level - the 'body schema which is the depository of a whole world view'. This extended discussion of team and individual sports does not do justice to the subtlely of Bourdieu's thesis. He also considers opposition either within sports (e.g. expensive/cheap ways of participating), between sports (e.g. expensive v. cheap individual sports), and oppositions between 'mainly high energy sports', 'introverted self-expressive sports' and 'cybernetic sports'. Of especial interest is the homology he discusses between the 'new' and 'already established' fractions of the dominant class and their respective participation in new and traditional or classic sports. Consider also sporting participation amongst those richest in economic capital in contrast to those richest in cultural capital.

This series of oppositions relates to another dimension of Bourdieu's analysis of the motor behind cultural practice and consumption, a dimension which illustrates Bourdieu's commitment to a conception of cultural practices which cannot be reduced to either a passive materialism nor to the idealism of 'cognitive' or inter-active perspectives. Agents, points out Bourdieu, are presented with an objectively instituted universe of sporting practice, each of which have their own rules, traditions, equipment, symbols and codes of conduct. Moreover, agents are also aware of the distribution of these sports amongst other agents who are themselves distributed in social space. Sports then have a "distributional significance in the meaning they derive from their distribution amongst agents who are themselves distributed in social classes. This significance cuts across any intrinsic benefits sports might possess. It is instruc-tive therefore to consider two sports offering similar intrinsic benefits (e.g. golf and bowls or hockey and football) yet which attract a different spectrum of participants. Bourdieu writes: 'economic constraints define the field of possibility and inpossi-bility without determining within it an agents positive orientation towards this or that form of practice'.

Hence economic barriers and amount of spare time (which is a transformed form of economic capital) are not sufficient to explain the class distribution of sports. Their distributional significance is a key determinant of practice. Different sports have different images (note the use of different sports in the advertising industry) Such images might be perpetuated long after a relative change in their accessibility in purely material terms. Moreover, recalling Bourdieu's notions of cultural capital and cultural competence, some sports have a considerable number of hidden entry requirements deriving from the habitus (early training, obligatory manner, tech-niques of sociability) which tend to keep them effectively closed to the working lcass. In short, there is more to social exclusivity than economic cost.

I have tried then to identify the key themes in Bourdieu's social critique of taste in sports. Agents vary in their perception of, and meaning ascribed to different sports. Sports are more likely to be appropriated if they do not contradict that class's relation to the body. The distributional significance of sports and their con-commitant image is a key factor influencing choice. Different sports require different types of cultural capital. Dispositions, deriving from the habitus, are transposalbe; are operative in all forms of consumerism as well as sporting practice, e.g. mass media, house decor, cars, drinks, clothes, food, holidays. Each of these:

> provides the small number of distinctive features which, functioning as a system of differences, differential deviation, allows the most fundamental social differences to be expressed ... and offers well-nigh inexhaustible possibilities for the pursuit of distinction. (1985)

Discussion and Observations

(a) Anti-essentialism

Bourdieu's conception of sports as a supply intended to meet a social demand stands in sharp contrast to those idealist writings about sport's special formal characteristics (e.g. Novak, Arnold, Huizinga). Essentialist explanations giving an exclusive focus upon the intrinsic benefits of sporting practice are inadequate and are illustrative of an "occupational ideology" of sports professionals. They are relatively autonomous practices but are part of the social world.

(b) The illusion of cultural democratisation. To conceive of sporting practice as an endless play of self-relativising taste is to indicate that any notion of cultural democracy is illusory - the 'pursuit of chimeras' to borrow from Wittgenstein. Hence he charges many cultural critics with exaggerated radicalism. A recognition of the social dynamics of the fields of sporting consumption and the unending pursuit of distinction is a considerable advance on the relatively uncritical observation of cultural diffusion, i.e. the dissemination of former elite sports/practices to other social groups. According to Bourdieu, the colonisation of sports by certain groups leads to desertion by others in search of distinctive 'virgin' spaces. What then is meant by the Sports Council's 'Sport for All' campaign - which sports? For whom? How do changes in the supply of sports affect the social demand? What assumptions about sporting practice and about clients are implicit in strategies of sports policy-makers?

(c) Cultural Specificity. All Bourdieu's empirical research focusses on French (Parisian) cultural life. Future research must establish its saliency for other national and regional contexts; Douglas criticises Bourdieu's occupational classification as being specific to France. In addition, most of Bourdieu's empirical research focusses upon artistic practice. A straightforward transposition to sport may be problematic. Do the same aesthetic categories of taste apply to the evaluation and perception of sports?

(d) Methods of Research. Bourdieu proposes an answer to the question - according to what principles do agents choose between different sporting practices which, at a given time are offered as being possible? This necessitates utilisation of different research methods. As Murdock (1977) points out, surveys can map the general distribution of cultural preferences and involvements, but qualitative research methods (in-depth interviewing, participant-observation) are more appropriate to discover the dynamics of choice and the complexity of meanings, evaluations, perceptions underlying these choices. These latter interpretive methods have been under utilised in research into sporting practice to date.

Sporting practice in Time

There is no stasis in sporting practice, either in supply or demand. Consequently the universe of sporting stylistic possible is constantly evolving. At the level of supply there are changes in the nature and extent of sporting provision through public, private, commercial, institutional, voluntary sectors. Through technological

advances, new sports are invented and enter the field. With respect
to demand, there are changes in material constraints, in spare time,
and in the relative accessibility of different sports. In consequence the distributional significance of sports might alter with a
consequent effect on agents dispositions towards particular sporting
practice and the images those sports might hold.

Bourdieu suggests then that class habitus and the resultant logic
of practice is a key factor to understanding not just the statistical
distribution of sporting practice but the perception of, and dispositions towards sports by agents differentially located in social
space. The larger issue is whether sports, understood as relatively
autonomous fields of cultural practice, erode or perpetuate the
existing class structure. In short, how is cultural production and
consumption related to social reproduction. With respect to sports
the explanatory power of Bourdieu's thesis for different cultural
contexts awaits empirical verification.

References

Hodgkiss, P. (1982) Culture and Class: some theoretical issues in
    the Sociology of Leisure. University of Salford.
Murdock, G. (1977) 'Class stratification and cultural consumption:
    some motifs in the work of Pierre Bourdieu' in Leisure and Urban
    Society. M.A. Smith (ed) Leisure Studies Assoc. 1977
Ashworth, C. (1971) 'Sport as symbolic dialogue' Ch. 3 in The
    Sociology of Sport, E. Dunning (ed) Frank Cass, London.
Bourdieu, P. (1985) Distinction: a social critique of the
    judgement of taste. R.K.P. London

A STRUCTURAL SYMBOLIC INTERACTIONIST APPROACH TO INVOLVEMENT IN PHYSICAL ACTIVITY

C.ROGER REES
Department of Physical Education, Recreation, and Human Performance Science, Adelphi University

Abstract

In a recent review McPherson (1986) has called for a "new wave" of research into socialization theory which will integrate the structuralist position, (concerned with the effect of the social system on the individual), with the symbolic interactionist position, (concerned with the process by which the individual interacts with the environment). This paper draws on developments in identity theory to construct a "structural symbolic interactionist" theory of involvement in physical activity. According to Gecas (1979) roles provide a major link between the social system and the individual since they are part of the social environment and "embedded in cultural systems", yet at the same time are interpreted individually. The interactionist perspective is developed via the concept of role making rather than role taking through which the individuals perceive self-efficacy, the feeling that they "cause" their behavior (Gecas and Schwalbe, 1983; Stryker and Serpe, 1982; Turner, 1978). From this perspective commitment (to physical activity), "the degree to which the person's relationship to specified sets of others depends upon his or her being a particular kind of person" (Stryker and Serpe,1982, p 207), and positive evaluation (the degree to which behavior is perceived as self-efficacious) affects identity salience (a hierarchical organization of identities constituting the self), which in turn affects role related behavior (participation in physical activity).

Key words: Physical activity, Commitment, Identity salience, Self-efficacy.

1. Introduction

While the physiological and psychological benifits of regular physical activity have been well documented (Morgan, 1984), it is also true that life-long involvement in physical activity is the exception rather than the rule. McPherson (1982) has reviewed studies that show disengagement closely related to age in several different cultures, and, in a more recent review of the determinants of physical activity and exercise, Dishman, Sallis, and Orenstein (1985) point out that the higher the health risks the lower the chances of involvement. In other words, most people who could benefit from physical activity do not, and those that could benefit the most participate the least.

In the research efforts to unlock the secret of why some people participate in physical activity through the life cycle and others do not the concept of commitment has figured prominently. Commitment has been conceptualized as a psychological trait (Dishman, Ickes and Morgan, 1980), as actual behavior (Rees, Andres, and Howell, 1986), and as a combination of both (Carmack and Martens, 1979). In this paper the functionalist and the symbolic interactionist view of commitment are combined and a structural symbolic interactionist approach developed which closely follows the work of sociologist Sheldon Stryker (1979, 1980, Stryker and Serpe, 1982). The implications of this approach for the study of involvement in physical activity are discussed .

2. A functionalist view of involvement in physical activity

Although sociologists of sport have tended to eschew theory their domain assumptions have tended to follow a functionalist perspective (Kenyon, 1986). This is particularly true in past research on socialization (see McPherson, 1986) where the emphasis has been on how the social structure has influenced involvement in sport via the selection process or how the social system of sport changes the individual once he or she becomes involved. From the functionalist approach socialization is seen as a one-way process (Bush and Simmons, 1979) by which individuals adapt and adjust to the constraints placed on them by society. Thus the key to involvement in physical activity, sport, or any other leisure persuit, is found in the early socialization experiences in youth and adolescence. Socialization into sport is based upon early family, peer group and school experiences (Snyder and Spreitzer, 1976; McPherson, 1981). Continued involvement has been conceptualized in a social Darwinism, "survival of the fittest" manner in which adolescent and young adult experiences in sport serve to seperate the best from the rest, or, until recently, the men from the boys. Seen in this way involvement in sport is characterized by a high drop-out rate as age increases leaving only those with high physical ability and competitive and aggressive characteristics (McPherson, 1983; Snyder and Spreitzer, 1979). When dealing with socialization through the life cycle the functionalist perspective is maintained by emphasizing the way in which social norms and definitions influence behavior. For example, age related norms, or ageism, is seen as the major reason why the reduction of physical activity is so pervasive as age increases (McPherson, 1983; Ostrow, 1984).

From the functionalist perspective continued involvement through the life cycle would be related to high involvement in sport and physical activity during childhood and adolescence. However, the evidence to support this hypothesis is inconsistent. In their review Dishman, Sallis, and Orenstein (1985) note that , although there is a "relatively strong" relationship between involvement in organized sport in youth and involvement as an adult, the relationship does not extend to recreational sport activity or adherence to fitness programs. A recent study of the antecedents of involvement in recreational running found that previous sport involvement had no effect either upon commitment to or skill in running (Rees, Andres, and Howell, 1986). Dishman, Sallis, and Orenstein also cite evidence which shows that, in middle age, former athletes are less likely to be physically active than non-athletes.

The functionalist equivalence to the concern with social structure in sociology has been the "trait" approach in psychology. From this perspective commitment to physical activity is perceived as a psychological trait developed by the individual during early socialization. In both approaches the emphasis is on forces influencing the individual, the one from the outside (social structure), the other from within (the psychological trait). Perhaps the best example of the trait approach has been Dishman's work with self-motivation. This trait is suggested as a generalized tendency in people to follow through with behavioral decisions. Dishman has shown that self-motivation combined with the physical characteristics of body weight and body composition can predict adherence to fitness programs (Dishman, 1982; Dishman and Ickes, 1981), but does not predict daily participation in physical activity (Dishman, Sallis, and

Orenstein, 1985, p 165).

While acknowledging the importance of traits, Dishman notes that regular participation in physical activity and exercise is a _dynamic_ process which involves individual traits, environmental forces, biological factors, and personal capabilities and intentions (Dishman, 1984). A theory including all these factors would have to place the individual in an active rather than a passive role in relation to the environment. Such a view of the individual is basic to the symbolic interactionist perspective.

3. Involvement in physical activity - a symbolic interactionist perspective

According to Fine (1986, p 159), following Blumer, the symbolic interaction perspective rests upon 3 basic assumptions; that individuals act towards things on the basis of meanings that these things have for them, that these meanings develop out of social interaction, and that these meanings are always in a state of change. A fourth assumption, Fine suggests, is that the cause of behavior is social and conscious rather than biological and unconscious. Recent developments in symbolic interaction theory have moved away from the Blumer position and incorporated the social structure (see Stryker, 1980), but this will be delt with in the next section.

Within the area of socialization the symbolic interactionist emphasis has been on how the individual has interpreted the environment as affecting the "self". In fact, according to Stryker (1979) the shaping of the self and self-concept change is the heart of the problem of socialization from the symbolic interactionist standpoint. The individual may re-define social roles and obligations instead of just accepting the constraints imposed by the social structure. The key to this process lies in the motive to protect and maintain self-esteem (Gecas, 1982; Rosenberg, 1979). This is a dynamic process wich includes an impressive array of mechanisms such as selective interaction, selective causal attribution, selective interpretation, and selective comparisons. These defense mechanisms are used to interpret reality "in such a way that both we and other people see ourselves as we would wish to be seen" (Rosenberg, 1979, p 276).

Symbolic interaction approaches have been applied to intercollegiate athletics (Adler and Adler, 1985; Snyder, 1986), and the culture of little league baseball (Fine, 1979), but rarely to the idea of involvement in physical activity (see Snyder, 1983 for an exception). The concept of self-esteem protection can help to explain why people who think they have poor health may not become involved or maintain involvement in exercise programs, even though they realize that such programs may help improve their health (Dishman, Sallis, and Orenstein, 1985). It may also be used to explain why large numbers of children drop out of organized sport during adolescence. If, as McPherson (1983, p 171) suggests, many children have unpleasant experiences in sport because adult expectations are too high, because they experience failure, or because they get negative feedback from the coach, one way to solve the problem is to withdraw from the activity. Provided our self-esteem is protected or enhanced in some other area, the failure in sport will not be perceived as crucial to the protection of the self.

The above interpretation underscores the point made by Rosenberg and others (see Gecas, 1982, p 10) that we have many different selves, and the importance we attach to these selves can shift in response to perceived reactions from others. In order to extend this idea it is necessary to develop a model to explain how these hierarchical orderings of selves change. For some symbolic interactionists the answer is found in the concepts of role, identity, and identity salience. Since these are elements of the social structure (Gecas, 1982, p 14) the emphasis moves from Bulmer's perception of the self continually changing, that is, a concern only with the social process, to a synthesis of the social structure and the social process.

3. Towards a synthesis – structural symbolic interactionism

The decision about how to order the hierarchy of roles which make up the self is pereceived as a process of negotiation. It is this negotiation which provides the middle ground between the structuralist and the interactionalist position. Specifically, the structuralist can offer the interactionalist the general concept of role, by which behavioral consistency across situations is explained, and the interactionalist can offer the structuralist a systematic analysis of the mechanics of the interaction process (see Heiss, 1979). In this way roles provide a major link between the social structure and the individual since they are part of the social environment and yet are modified by the individual (Gecas, 1979, p 168).

   The result of this merger is structural symbolic interaction which combines the concept of "situation" and the concept of "role" (Gecas, 1982, p 13). Stryker suggests that individuals choose particular roles from a variety available to them. These roles make up their identities and are themselves organized into "salience hierarchies" (Stryker and Serpe, 1982, p 206). The salience of a role in the hierarchy is affected by commitment, the degree to which one is involved in social relationships dependent upon that identity. As Gecas (1982, p 14) notes, this conception of commitment emphasises the relational aspect of role identities and the importance of social networks which represent the social structure, and ultimately, "society's relevance for interaction" (Stryker, 1979, p 25). As commitment increases so does the identity salience (Hoetler, 1983; Stryker and Serpe, 1982).

   Identity salience is also influenced by the evaluation of one's performance. This evaluation is made by the members of our social networks, or more precisely, comprises our interpretation of these perceptions (Gecas and Schwalbe, 1983). Hoetler (1983) has shown that identity salience increases as the evaluation of one's performance within the role giving rise to the identity becomes more positive.

   In a recent 4 year participant observation study of an intercollegiate basketball team Adler and Adler (1986) show how both commitment and evaluation cause the reconstruction of the identity salience of the academic roles. The players' initial commitment to academic roles was reduced through their association with other athletes. These other athletes formed their main social network because the mode of housing (jock dorm) limited interaction with other social groups. The athletes academic roles received mainly negative evaluation since they generally received poor grades. This lack of positive reinforcement led the athletes to diminish the identity salience of the academic roles.

4. Commitment to physical activity from a structural symbolic interaction perspective

Structural symbolic interaction is seen as a major advance in social psychology because, by stressing the importance of the social structure, it develops a more sociologically adequate social psychology and advances beyond "individual and interpersonal reductionism" (Gecas and Schwalbe, 1983, see also Ickes and Knowles, 1982). At the same time it keeps the individual in the picture through the idea of self-definition and the protection of self-esteem. One major strategy that the individual uses for self-esteem protection and enhancement is the development of self-efficacy, that is, the belief that he or she is the causal agent in the environment (see Gecas and Schwalbe, 1983). It follows that commitment to roles ,and hence identity salience will be greatest in situations in which perceptions of self-efficacious behavior are high.

Hypotheses such as these have yet to be tested in sociology, and the theory is still being developed. However, even at this early stage, there are advantages to conceptualizing involvement in physical activity from the perspective of structural symbolic interactionism. McPherson (1986) emphasises the need for theories of socialization to integrate previously separate theoetical positions. Since socialization is a combination of social structure and social process a theory which accounts for both is valuable. Some implications for the study of participation in physical activity follow:

a. If roles are indeed part of the social environment then physical activity as a role will originate in the social structure. For example, the social structure provides models that help us define our athletic role and how one should behave as an athlete. There is some tentative evidence that thinking of oneself "as an athlete" may be an important aspect of identity salience which helps to put participation high on our hierarchy of leisure-time roles (Rees, Andres, and Howell, 1986; Snyder and Spreitzer, 1984).

b. The structural symbolic interactionalists (Gecas and Schwalbe,1982; Stryker, 1980; Stryker and Serpe, 1982) have suggested that roles vary in their concreteness so that sometimes individuals have autonomy in how they act and sometimes they do not. In the context of sport and physical activity there is great variation in the potential for role making. A high school or college athlete has little leeway for role making since the most common perception (and probably the reality) is one of obedience to the directions of the coach. However in recreational physical activity the opportunities for role making are greater, and the perceptions of efficacious behavior consequently increase.

c. If commitment depends upon the make-up of social networks, commitment to physical activity will be greater in social networks which are most supportive of that activity. From a functionalist perspective, re-socializing individuals into physical activity would be most successful if emphasis is placed on the socialization contexts. These should be structured in intense small-group situations in a closed environment with a high socialization ratio (see Gecas, 1979, p 191-4).

d. From the perspective of the social process the key to involvement in physical activity is the perception of efficacious action, that is, the idea that individuals feel responsible for their own actions. The perception of self-efficacy has interesting implications for conceptualizing involvement in physical activity. It allows the interpretation of identity salience and consequently role behavior as changable (Snyder, 1983), and from a practical point of view offers the possibility that ways can be found to help people include physical activity as salient in their identities and adopt this as life-long activity (see Rees, 1986). This approach also has significant implications for athletics and physical education (see Rees, 1986), and has been applied to coaching by Roberts (1984). Among his suggestion are to reduce performance comparisons across individuals and encourage performance comparisons within individuals (e.g. how did I do relative to my past performance?). This type of comparison is easier in recreational physical than in competetive sport, although it is interesting that the recent televising of the 1986 "Ironman" triathlon focused more on the personal struggles of the individual runners than on who actually won the race.

5. Summary

In their recent review of the determinants of physical activity and exercise Dishman and his colleagues (1985) noted that most studies are guided by applied concerns rather than theory. This paper has made an initial attempt to develop a theory of involvement in physical activity incorporating the social structure and the individual's interpretation of reality. Both social forces are necessary to adequately conceptualize the process of socialization in general and involvement in physical activity in particular.

References

Adler, P. and Adler, P.A. (1985) From idealism to pragmatic detachment: the academic performance of college athletes. Soc. Educ., 58, 241-250.
Adler, P. and Adler, P.A. (1986) Role conflict and identity salience: college athletes and the academic role. Unpub.
Busch, D.M. and Simmons, R.G. (1979) Socialization processes over the life course, in Social Psychology: Sociological Perspectives (ed M. Rosenberg and R.H. Turner), Basic Books, NY, pp 133-164.
Carmack, M.A. and Martens, R. (1979) Measuring commitment to running: a survey of runners' attitudes and mental states. J. Sport Psychol., 1, 25-42.
Dishman, R.K. (1982) Compliance/adherence in health-related exercise. Health Psychol., 1, 237-267.
Dishman, R.K. (1984) Motivation and exercise adherence, in Psychological Foundations of Sport (ed. J. Silva and R. Weinberg), Human Kinetics, Champaign, IL, pp 416-430.
Dishman, R.K. and Ickes, W. (1981) Self-motivation and adherence to therapeutic exercise. J. Behav. Med., 4, 421-438.
Dishman, R.K., Ickes, W. and Morgan, W.P. (1980) Self-motivation and adherence to habitual physical activity. J. Appl. Soc. Psychol., 10, 115-132.
Dishman, R.K., Sallis, J.F., and Orenstein, D.R. (1985) The determinants of physical activity and exercise. Pub. Health Reports, 100, 158-171.
Fine, G.A. (1979) Small group culture creation: the idioculture of little league baseball teams. Am. Soc. Rev., 44, 733-745.
Fine, G.A. (1986) Small groups and sport: a symbolic interaction perspective, in Sport and Social Theory (ed. C.R. Rees and A.W. Miracle), Human Kinetics, Champaign, IL, pp 159-169.
Gecas, V. (1979) Contexts of socialization, in Social Psychology: Sociological Perspectives (ed. M. Rosenberg and R.H. Turner), Basic Books, NY, pp 165-199.
Gecas, V. (1982) The self concept. Ann. Rev. Sociol., 8, 1-33.
Gecas, V. and Schwalbe, M.L. (1983) Beyond the looking-glass self: social structure and efficacy-based self-esteem. Soc. Psychol. Quart., 46, 77-88.
Heiss, J. (1979) Social roles. in Social Psychology: Sociological Perspectives (ed. M. Rosenberg and R. H. Turner), Basic Books, NY, pp 94-129.
Hoetler, J.W. (1983) The effects of role evaluation and commitment on identity salience. Soc. Psychol. Quart., 46, 140-147.
Ickes, W. and Knowles, E.S. (1982) Personality, Roles, and Social Behavior. Springer-Verlag, NY.
Kenyon, G.S. (1986) The significance of social theory in the development of sport sociology, in Sport and Social Theory (ed. C.R. Rees and A.W. Miracle), Human Kinetics, Champaign, IL, pp 3-22.
McPherson, B.D. (1981) Socialization in and through sport, in Handbook of Social Science of Sport (ed. G. Luschen and G. Sage), Sipes, Chicago, pp 246-273.
McPherson, B.D. (1982) Leisure life-styles and physical activity in the later years of the life-cycle. Rec. Research Rev., 9, 5-15.

McPherson, B.D. (1983) Aging as a Social Process, Butterworths, Toronto.

McPherson, B.D. (1986) Socialization theory and research: toward a "new wave" of scholarly inquiry in a sport context, in Sport and Social Theory (ed. C.R.Rees and A.W.Miracle), Human Kinetics, Champaign, IL, pp 111-134.

Morgan, W.P. (1984) Physical activity and mental health, in Exercise and Health: American Academy of Physical Education Papers, No 17. (ed. H.M. Eckert and H.J. Montoye), Human Kinetics, Champaign, IL, pp 132-145.

Ostrow, A.C. (1984) Physical Activity and the Older Adult. Princeton Book Co. Princeton, NJ.

Rees, C.R., Andres, F.F. and Howell, F.M. (1986) On the trail of the "turkey trotters": the effect of previous sport involvement and attitudes on commitment to and skill in running. Soc. Sport J., 3, in press.

Rees, C.R. (1986) The social role of the physical education teacher viewed from the perspective of social psychology, Unpub.

Roberts, G.C. (1984) Towards a new theory of achievement motivation, in Psychological Foundations of Sport (ed. J. Silva and R. Weinberg), Human Kinetics, Champaign, IL.

Rosenberg, M. (1979) Conceiving the Self, Basic Books, NY.

Snyder, E.E. (1983) Identity, commitment, and type of sport roles. Quest, 35, 97-106.

Snyder, E.E. (1986) Athletics and higher education: a symbolic interaction perspective, in Sport and Social Theory (ed. C.R. Rees and A.W. Miracle), Human Kinetics, Champaign, IL, pp 211-226.

Snyder, E.E. and Spreitzer, E.A. (1976) Family influences and involvement in sports. Res. Quart., 44, pp 249-255.

Snyder, E.E. and Spreitzer, E.A. (1979) Lifelong involvement in sport as a leisure persuit: aspects of role construction. Quest, 31, 57-70.

Snyder, E.E. and Spreitzer, E.A. (1984) Patterns of adherence to a physical conditioning program. Soc. Sport J., 1, 103-116.

Stryker, S. (1979) Symbolic interactionism: themes and variations, in Social Psychology: Sociological Perspectives (ed. M. Rosenberg and R.H. Turner), Basic Books, NY, pp 3-29.

Stryker, S. (1980) Symbolic Interactionism: A Social Structural Version. Benjamin/Cummings, Melno Park, CA.

Stryker, S. and Serpe, R.T. (1982) Commitment, identity salience, and role behavior: theory and research example, in Personality, Roles, and Social Behavior (ed. W. Ickes and E.S. Knowles), Springer-Yerlag, NY.

Turner, R.H. (1978) The role and the person. Am. J. Soc., 84, 1-23.

SOME RELATIONSHIPS BETWEEN LEADERSHIP CAPTAINCY, MANAGEMENT AND
PLAYING POSITIONS IN THE ENGLISH FOOTBALL LEAGUE

W.J. MURPHY and S. PARKER
Department of Sport and Recreation Studies, Liverpool Polytechnic

Abstract
The study investigated relationships between playing position,
captaincy and recruitment to management in the Football League of
England and Wales. Centrality theory was considered together with
a structural model of leadership function based on the parameters
of propinquity and task dependence. The model suggested the
hypothesis that captains are found in central defensive
positions. It was further hypothesised that managers had played in
similar positions during their playing career. Survey methods were
utilised to obtain information related to all ninety two Football
League clubs. Chi Square tests were applied to the results and
statistical support was found for the first hypothesis only. No
correlation was found between playing position and recruitment to
manager.

Introduction

Within the organisation of a Football Club there are a number of
leaders who may be identified, two of whom are the Captain and the
Manager. The Captain is a 'sub-leader' to the Manager, who, in
turn, is subordinate to the Board of Directors.
    A major role for the Captain is that of team leader during the
game situation, when there may be a need for one individual to
direct, control and co-ordinate the efforts of the team. The
Captain may need to fill a number of roles. For example, he may
need to be a source of inspiration, be capable of dictating the
play and controlling the behaviour of the rest of the team. To do
this he must be able to communicate easily with all team members.
    The role of the Manager as a leader is not so much dependent on
example, as on his style of leadership. There is no standard
method of team management and many widely different styles have
been employed, with differing degrees of success. Thus the Manager
has to adopt many different roles related to the great variety of
situations he encounters. In some respects the roles of the
Captain and the Manager are similar, yet they differ in others.
Differences are apparent in the type of power each has, and the
leadership styles they have to adopt, but the facility to
communicate readily and efficiently in formally structured and
spontaneous situations is a required characteristic of both roles.

Leadership in Sports Organisations

Some leadership theories are sceptical about inherited traits as causal factors in ascendency to positions of leadership. In some laboratory experiments it has been found that "individuals occupying the most central position within a group are most frequently chosen as leaders" (Carron 1980). One possible explanation is that this individual becomes focal point for the communication and interaction of the members. Within a game situation therefore, players in positions demanding a high degree of interaction, that is having a central playing position, are more liable to be chosen as the Leader or Captain.

According to this theory therefore, on a Soccer field, the ideal position for the Captain would be the centre of midfield.

A second factor, however which may be considered is that of individual visibility, that is, how easy it is for the other group members to see the leader. Compliance with this proposal would seem to support the positioning of the Captain in the centre of the attack, here he would almost always be in view of the remaining team members. However, there would be problems with communication due to the peripheral nature of the position.

An alternative view suggests that observability is the most important factor, that is, the width of vision allowed by a position. (Chelladurai and Carron, 1977). An extreme interpretation of this theory would favour the goalkeeper as the most suitable position for the Captain as play will always be in front of him. Again, it is likely that there would be problems with communication. In their research of American Football, Baseball and Basketball, Chelladurai and Carron found that players at the rear of the game are often chosen as leaders. Their model considers both observability and visibility within the two parameters of 1. Propinquity - observability and visibility and 2. Task Dependence. These factors may be placed on the axes of a graph, using a continuum ranging from low to high, where all positions may be represented. For example the graph for soccer may be developed as follows.

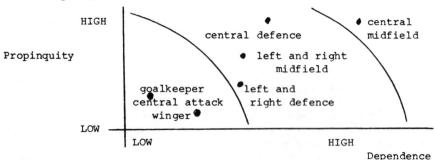

Fig. 1   Categorisation of Association Football positions on the basis of the interaction of Propinquity and Task Dependence, after Chelladurai and Carron, 1977.

The higher the level of propinquity, the greater the degree of observability and visibility, thus the individual may gain greater authority and prestige. It may be important therefore, for the captain to be near the play, but also to be in a position where he can easily see and be seen.

Thus a position in the centre of defence may well be the most advantageous compromise.

Wingers are not a very common feature in modern soccer and, like the goalkeeper and centre forward, occupy peripheral positions on the field of play. The centre of defence and midfield are closer to the centre of play, and their positions are thus highly dependent. This emphasises the fact that the more peripheral positions such as goalkeeper should be ranked lower than more propinquitous positions such as the centre of midfield.

Grusky (1963) also studied the relationships between playing position and recruitment to management in professional Baseball. His results showed that players in positions of high interaction and centrality are more likely to become managers. If this were true for soccer, then managers may be expected to have played in central defensive and midfield positions during their playing careers.

The theories of observability and visibility, seem to be impractical for soccer at the extreme level of application, instead a compromise may be needed between the two. The communication theory suggests a centrality approach for the positioning of the Captain in conjunction with or modified observability/visibility perspective. Thus discussion suggests two hypotheses

1. that captains will generally occupy positions in the centre of defence
2. that managers will have occupied similar positions during their playing careers.

The current paper owes much to the investigation of Lee et al (1983) into the influence of team structure in determining leadership function in association football. Their sample consisted of twenty two captains of professional teams and twenty school team captains. In this paper correlations were sought between playing positions and the roles of captain and manager in all English Football League clubs.

Data Collection

Information was obtained using a survey questionnaire which was circulated to all of the 92 clubs in the English Football League. A secondary source of information was the Football League Information Office in London, which proved helpful for filling in gaps.

Questions related to the Captains asked for playing position and lateral preference, age and number of years in office. Questions related to the Managers asked for playing position and lateral preference, age, number of years in office, professional status and highest standard played.

It was possible to obtain the required information from only 91 clubs because one club was without a Manager at the time. Other Managers have vacated their posts since the research was conducted and so the results are based on information which was correct when the questionnaires were completed in March 1984.

Data Analysis

This was divided into three sections:-

1. The number of responses to each question were counted and the results noted for each division.
2. From these values, the percentages were calculated for each response, as well as the total percentages for each division.
3. These figures were then analysed statistically utilising Chi Square Tests.

In some cases, the total number of responses pertainig to position played is greater than the number of clubs. This was due to some respondents choosing more than one answer.

Results

Playing Position of the Captain

The initial results for the captain's playing position displayed in tables 1 and 2, show that a large proportion of the sample play in either defence or midfield, and occupy a central position.
However, when these figures were subjected to statistical analysis by Chi Square, using the three most popular playing formations for the outfield players the values were not significant.

In the 4-2-4 formation, there were very few individual values significant $(P > 0.05)$. In Division 1, it was found that the number of captains occupying a midfield position was significant $(P < 0.001)$. As there were no captains in attack, this value was also significant $(P < 0.01)$. With respect to the lateral position of the captain, none of the values were significant $(P > 0.05)$.

In the 4-3-3 formation, few individual values were found to be significant, however, the values for each division were; the first and third division $(P < 0.01)$, the fourth division $(P < 0.05)$. Despite the lack of significance of individual values, the result for the whole league was significant $(P < 0.001)$.

The values for lateral position using the 4-3-3 formation in the first division show a significantly high number of captains occupying central positions, results being significant for the whole league $(P < 0.01)$.

Values for the 4-4-2 formation were generally not significant with respect to both longitudinal and lateral positions. Exceptions were found in the values for the whole of league and in the high number of captains occupying central positions in the First Division $(P < 0.01)$. One notable factor was the lack of goalkeepers as captains, apart from two in the fourth division.

	Goalkeeper	Defence	Midfield	Attack	
Division 1	0 0%	11 50%	11 50%	0 0%	22
Division 2	0 0%	13 59.1%	6 27.3%	3 13.6%	22
Division 3	0 0%	15 65.2%	7 30.4%	1 4.4%	23
Division 4	2 7.4%	15 55.6%	9 33.3%	1 3.7%	27
Totals for whole league	2 2.1%	54 57.4%	33 35.1%	5 5.3%	

Table 1. Captains by division and longitudinal playing position.

	Right	Central	Left	
Division 1	2 8.8%	18 78.3%	3 13%	23
Division 2	3 12%	16 64%	6 24%	25
Division 3	4 16%	15 60%	6 24%	25
Division 4	6 23.1%	16 61.5%	4 15.4%	26
Totals for whole league	15 15.2%	65 65.7%	19 19.2%	

Table 2. Captains by division and lateral playing position.

Playing Position of Managers

From table 3, it can be seen that a large proportion of the managers had played in either midfield or defensive positions. However, in each division, there was a significant number of managers who had been attacking players. Here, despite a general

325

lack of significance within the divisions findings related to the whole league were found to be significant (P < 0.01).

When considering the lateral position occupied by managers during their playing careers there was a much wider distribution through the three categories, as a result, none of these values proved to be significant. Once again, it was notable that there is a lack of goalkeepers ascending to positions of power or authority.

	Goalkeeper	Defence	Midfield	Attack	
Division 1	0 0%	9 42.6%	7 33.3%	5 23.8%	21
Division 2	1 4.5%	12 54.5%	4 18.2%	5 22.7%	22
Division 3	0 0%	8 33.3%	12 50%	4 16.7%	24
Division 4	0 0%	12 46.2%	8 30.8%	6 23%	26
Totals for whole league	1 1.1%	41 44.1%	31 33.3%	20 21.5%	

Table 3. Managers by division and previous longitudinal playing position.

	Right	Central	Left	
Division 1	9 41%	9 41%	4 18%	22
Division 2	5 23.8%	10 47.6%	6 28.6%	21
Division 3	8 33.3%	12 50%	4 16.6%	24
Division 4	9 31%	14 48.3%	6 20.7%	29
Totals for whole league	31 32.3%	45 46.9%	20 20.8%	

Table 4. Managers by division and previous lateral playing position.

Discussion

The results related to the captain's positin show that the majority play in central defensive positions in all four divisions. (Table 5). However, this may not be due to centre back being the most advantageous position for the captain. It could be partially explained by the fact that within the three formations used there will always be four players in defence as opposed to only two or three in midfield, therefore there is a greater probability of the captain playing in defence.

The Centrality Theory would favour the positioning of the captain in the centre of midfield, however it has been observed that "....leadership efficiency based upon centrality in a communicaiton system is inadequate for explaining efficient leadership function in sports where the influence of the captain has an important bearing upon team performance" (Lee, Coburn and Partridge 1983 p.65).

The observability/visibility theory also has disadvantages. An extreme interpretation of the two proposals require the captain to be positioned at opposite ends of the pitch, and as such they cannot be used together to analyse leader position. The goalkeeper and attacking players are peripheral positions and as such, in theory would be impractical for captaincy due to problems of communication. The results indicate that there are only two goalkeepers and five attacking players who are captains, none of whom are in the First Division. It seems that the higher the standard of football, the captain's role is less likely to be spread among the four playing categories.

The positions the manager used to play, show a much greater spread with respect to both longitudinal and lateral positions. (Table 5). Again there is a notable lack of goalkeepers ascending to positions of power. This may be because goalkeeping is a specialised peripheral position, and the players may be considered to be less knowledgeable about the game as a whole. Another reason may be that when selecting an individual for the post of manager, the club may be interested not only in his management abilities, but also how well known he was as a player. This could be a dangerous strategy since successful players need not necessarily have the qualities required for good management.

Summary and Conclusions

As hypothesised, there are patterns within the results to indicate that captains in English Football League teams occupy central and defensive positions in terms of both laterality and longitudinality. However, these trends were not generally significant when subjected to Chi Square analysis.

The sample used however showed no apparent correlation between playing position and recruitment to management, apart from an obvious lack of goalkeepers. In this respect therefore the second hypothesis was rejected.

Longitudinal Positions

	Goalkeeper	Defence	M/Field	Attack
Captains	2.1%	57.4%	35.1%	5.3%
Managers	1.1%	44.1%	33.3%	21.5%

Lateral Positions

	Right	Centre	Left
Captains	15.2%	65.7%	19.2%
Managers	32.3%	46.9%	20.8%

Table 5. Captains and Managers by longitudinal and lateral playing
positions for the whole league.

References

Carron, A.V. (1980) Social Psychology of Sport, Mouvement
    Publications, Ontario.
Chellandurai, P. and Carron, A.V. (1977) "A Reanalysis of Formal
    Structure in Sport" Canadian Journal of Applied Sport Science
    Vol. 2.
Grusky, O. (1963) "The Effects of Formal Structure on Managerial
    Recruitment: A Study of Baseball Organisation". Sociometry,
    Vol. 26.
Lee, M.J., Coburn, T. and Partidge, R. (1983) "The Influence of
    Team Structure in Determing Leadership Function in Association
    Football". Journal of Sport Behaviour, Vol. 6, No. 2, July.

SOME ASPECTS OF NORMATIVE SYSTEMS AS THE BASES OF CONTRACTUAL
COMMITMENT IN COMPETITIVE CONTEST

A.G.L. VENTRE
Faculty of Physical Activity Studies, University of Regina

Abstract
Sport as sub-culture, law, moral law and mores are identified as
normative systems relevant to the contractual process in competitive
contest. Changing values, conventional and unconventional values,
heroism, counter culture and anti-culture, and ambivalence and
ambiquity (dualism) are selected as some aspects of these normative
systems which are examined in the context of forging the contract to
compete.
Key words: Normative System, Normative Instructions, Rules, Laws,
Mores, Moral Law, Customs, Codes, Conventions, Common Practice,
Contract, Values, Culture, Counter-culture, Anti-culture.

1. Introduction

Attorneys general speak: who listens? Parents speak: who listens?
The teacher speaks: who listens? When the coach speaks: who
listens? In our society, positions taken by 'significant others'
create 'noise' in the form of messages.* These significant others†

---

* For an explanation of message and persuasion in normative systems
see Antony Allot, The Limits of Law, Butterworths London, 1980, pp.
121-160.

† The notion of the 'significant other' has been used in the literature of sociometry for several decades. The person accorded special
status is located at the 'centre of the socius.' In a variety of
ways it is used by such authors as Moreno 1939 in Who Will Survive?
in the context of the 'Great Man' influential in the social group,
and since then authors, such as, Northway (1958), and McPherson
(1979). Importantly, Fred Inglis in the Promise of Happiness, (1981,
p. 83) explains that moral structures are shaped by 'significant
others', by society formed of institutions and by society in the
material form of cultural experience influencing the person in
action. Values and our support of them are built into the normative
system. Try as we may to be free of their influences sometimes, we
must learn to live with them, generally.

represent a variety of normative systems and when they speak their messages carry normative instructions. From within these normative systems are proposed and promoted laws, rules, norms, customs and codes which are intended to shape behavior. We receive their messages giving preference to some and choosing to be influenced less by others.

In a traditional society, customs are clear and competing messages less of a problem. In modern society, the conurban* structure makes the system of norm transmission somewhat inaccessible, and there is a tendency to operate highly specialized roles as a part of a 'professionalizing process' wherein agents and agencies transmit loud and frequent messages in an attempt to reach the 'receiver', usually in some sub-cultural context. The elements of 'noise' and 'persuasion' are evident all around us. Indeed, in modern society, messages and persuasions are significantly part of the matrix of normative systems.

2. Normative Systems

Sport as sub-culture is a normative system. Other normative systems which are relevant to the contractual process in sport include morality, mores and law. The person committed in the sub-culture of sport is the recipient of normative messages. Often, these normative messages will be of different types and sometimes the legal message or the moral message is in competition with the normative instructions emanating from, say, community mores or the sub-cultural mores of sport. When such conflict happens problems may arise for the person required to discriminate between these messages. Furthermore, the norm-giver in such circumstances may elect to engage persuasion in an effort to influence the recipient; and to some extent persuasion invites allegiance to a particular normative system, inevitable. While the systems which I have identified are separable to some extent for the purpose of analysis, let me emphasize that really they are part of one system, if only because that which is common practice must ultimately be reconciled with that which is legal, quasi-legal and moral, if society is not to be in conflict with itself.

---

* For an explanation of the long term shift in the civilizing process see Norbert Elias, Ueber Den Prozess Der Zivilisation, 2nd Edition, Basle, 1939 and translated from the German in 1978 by Jephcote. His use of the term civilized is not one which I favour. Instead, I use the term conurban society. Whichever term is used what is meant is an advanced state of social development in urban areas subject to by-laws. The conurban society is based in industrial, commercial and technical specialisms which confine a person's role and make reciprocal functioning essential. The more the system demands competence in a role, the less the person performing it can exist independent of the competencies of other specialists. This is what Elias calls 'functional bonding': a phenomenon of the civilizing process.

2.1 Sport as Sub-culture

In the context of the development of sport as a prominent part of culture, different peoples have contributed to the code of conduct in games. But persisting throughout history until the second half of this century, one concept of sporting conduct has evolved, namely, that of 'gentlemanly' conduct. In Ancient Greece the free citizen had the time, money and education to play, the slave did not! In the Italian City States, courtiers of the Renaissance enjoyed education, wealth and leisure such that sporting pastimes were their prerogative. In the British Isles, during the nineteenth century, the English gentleman was similarly in a privileged class and practised sports within a code of conduct derived directly from the value system of his social class and historically from cultures, such as, the Ancient Greeks and the Renaissance Italians of similar class. The concept of amateur, lover of sport, is intimately entwined with gentlemanly conduct in games and is historically derived from the values of persons who were in a privileged class. As Inglis (1977) said, the idea of gentleman is "...an ethic in which display and courtesy and magnificence lay close together in the moral positives of society." (p.66) The idea of sportsman is an ethic based in the concepts of Greek freeman, Renaissance Courtier, English gentleman, in which courtesy, loyalty, honour, dignity and 'fair play' were composed as a moral stereotype. Only in recent times with the influence of the United States of America, followed by the totalitarian states and now the Third World countries, each using sport to compete with other forms of nationalism, has this value system been found to be inadequate.

In Western countries there has been the extensive effect of television, of professionalization of sport, and of the mass of people seeking to be involved in the development of sport administratively, organizationally, technically, tactically and aesthetically. The effect of television has been such that the styles of action of highly regarded performers have been copied regardless of their worth technically, tactically, strategically or ethically. The needs of professional sport have been sufficiently different from amateur sport to require that a professional model of sport be built, part of which became a restructuring of the code of playing conduct so that exclusively playing to win could be condoned, ethically. The effect of mass involvement has been to replace the value system of the privileged class with a value system which attempts to be classless.

Effectively, the code of game conduct which has developed can be said;

i) to be an imitation of the style and behaviour of professional athletes without examination,

ii) to have been justified by the practice of situtional ethics, and

iii) to reflect a value system which because it is classless is vulnerable, i.e., open to influence by temporary, divergent extravagances, and answerable to no one, since to be classless is to be identity 'tagless'.

Sportsmanship is a style of games action. For some, it is a form of gallantry, a frame of mind, a characteristic spirit of the community of sportsmen and women, and a climate of the heart. Admittedly, 'sportsmanship' was derived from an exclusive social stratum and it was not always real, but in its accommodation of altruistic principles in a competitive milieu, it did work! 'Gamesmanship', if not self-centered, is competition centered and the egoism it fosters is far from altruism. The farther from a principled, responsible frame of action we deviate in the name of self-centered conduct the more strain is placed upon the idea of sport as it is conventionally understood.

Today, sport in most forms and in most cultures, is practised in a model of sport developed essentially in North America in which:

i)   is developed a genuine love of sport, very meaningful to the participants,

ii)   is distinguished the difference between amateur and professional by criteria, such as, the amount of time spent in training, level of skill, dedication to the pursuit of excellence, quality of organizations and administration, quality of officiating, spectator appeal, intensity of preparation for the game and the intention to win above all else. In effect, sport groups attempt to be as 'professional' as possible in operation. (The criteria of financial remuneration for playing has been a non-issue for a very long time, except in relation to participating in the Olympic Games and Games of a lower order which articulate with the Olympic Games),

iii) is emphasized the written rule as the only way in which all those involved can operate in an orderly, accountable system,

iv)   is accepted that a rule which is open to interpretation should be exploited until such time as an amendment to the rule can be introduced,

v)   is recognized the role of organizers, administrators and coaches as the initiators of rule changes, policy and philosophy, even with their 'professional' bias or vested interest,

vi)   is encouraged a concept of competition which requires the athlete to pursue victory aggressively,

vii) the game is analyzed statistically along with the performances of players both statistically and technically through video-tape play back for the purpose of eliminating error and weakness,

viii) is practised the analysis of weakness of opponents as a preparation for the contest,

ix)   is emphasized more and more formal sanctions and penalties to ensure that all concerned operate within the rules set,

x)   is expected that players decide without ethical concern, whether or not to act illegally to prevent a score,

xi)   is accelerated the rate of change in sport by all means possible in the search for athletic superiority with little regard of the effect upon the person, the group and the sport subculture,

xii) is sought the identity of all of the factors in performance so that they might be submitted to scrutiny by specialists in the sciences, and

xiii) is expected the support of government, socio-politically and socio-economically.

In the model of sport which has become redundant philosophically and administratively, there was a clear policy of participation and achievement by natural, individual effort and personal, unsponsored resources as Heinila (1966, p. 36) observed. Within such a model of sport three concepts were identified:

i)   the concept of amateur meant a gentle, casual, incidental involvement in a sport for the joy of participating and aesthetic sensation therein derived,

ii)   the concept of sportsmanlike conduct meant the practice of a code of ethics befitting a gentleman, a disciplined response in competition within the bounds of 'proper' athletic conduct, and a willingness to promote altruistic rather than egoistic values, even at the expense of losing the contest, and

iii) the concept of good will meant reconciling rivalry with the hand of friendship and offering hospitality in the manner of the best host.

The effect of the present model on the development of sport has been very rapid progress on all fronts, admirably portrayed in superb athletic artistry. The pace of development has been such that 'frills' have been discarded! Within the contemporary model of sport we live with not one but at least three moralities. It is reasonable to say that the morality historically derived from aristocratic class systems has been reconciled within a morality which if not classless is fairly reflective of the values of competitive society. Democratic control of sport among other factors led to the clash of these two moralities. The effect was a kind of professionalization and empirically the facts are clear enough for us to deduce the statement that:

The 'professionalization' of sport contributes to higher levels of performance and emphasises a value system situationally and ethically prejudiced to support 'aggressive athleticism' and de-emphasises a value system supporting friendly, hospitable relationships and ethical conduct in all circumstances.

However, we are in the early stages of a new style of professional control of sport by trained administrators and coaches from which will develop a new clash of moralities. It remains to be seen whether the new development will become a morality of autocracy or of a professional aristocracy.

2.2 Law
Law, in its legislated form, is a collection of statutes specifying the legal imperatives of conduct. Society and the civilizing process are dependent on laws and by-laws as the basis of order. Of course, in the day to day process of living law is a socio-political process, also. Elliott (1978, p. 18), discussing the public regulation of sport as private activity, points out that the legal system is reactive to changes of social climate, especially in relation to practices and norms. Let me take hockey as an example:

333

In Canada, arising from actions in hockey in 1975 - 1976, more than thirty persons, players, coaches and spectators were charged with a variety of offences from creating a disturbance to assault causing bodily harm. All of the cases ended with convictions or pleas of guilty. One resulted in a prison sentence and the other cases in fines, suspended sentences, probation and absolute discharges. The prison sentence was one of ten days (and $100 fine) imposed on a seventeen year old coach for assault on a sixteen year old referee in Sudbury, Ontario on December 17th, 1975.

In this period of one year, the number of cases was approximately four times that charged in each of the two previous seasons. It can be assumed that these increases in law enforcement were the result of the energetic attempt by the Ministry of Community and Social Services through an inquiry by W.R. McMurtry (1974) to make hockey players realize their accountability in law.

As Smith (1978) puts it in a prelude to his summary of nine major cases or developments related to violence in hockey in Canada, "...beginning in the late '60's, a series of dramatic events pushed hockey violence onto the front stage, making visible what for so long had been taken for granted." (p. 92)

On December 12th, 1977 in Cleveland, Montreal Canadiens defeated the Barons by 5 goals to 1. In the second period with the score of 3-1 Stewart (Barons) knocked Tremblay (Canadiens) into the boards behind the Cleveland net and this act provoked both teams to "clear their benches", whereafter play was halted for 11 minutes. Stewart and Ahern (Barons) and Lupien and Risebrough (Canadiens) were assessed 112 minutes of penalties as the principals. That day in New York, John Ziegler, National Hockey League President, in a luncheon speech said, "I do not find it unacceptable, in a game where frustration is constant, for men to drop their sticks and gloves and take swings at each other. I think that kind of outlet is important for players in our games." Speaking of violence in the game he said also, "A lot is made of it that doesn't need to be. We have a violent sport." He went on to explain that skating at speed, using the body to impact opponents, using the boards as a weapon and the intensity of competition are elements contributing to the violent form of the sport and quite acceptable in his view. He was careful to single out as unacceptable, "any use of the stick to injure or attempt to injure someone intentionally." (Leader Post, 1977, p. 11)

A clear value judgement reflected in the President's statement is that:

i) hockey is a game for men,
ii) skating at speed and the use of the body to check opponents impactfully combine to make the game a celebration of speed, physical toughness and courage,
iii) the use of the boards to establish physical and strategic dominance is an essential feature of the game,
iv) intensity of competition is important especially as it contributes to the violent form of the game,
v) fist fighting is a reasonable response to highly charged, perhaps frustrating, competitive circumstance, and

vi) only use of the stick as a weapon with intent to injure an opponent is "violent".

This macho-aesthetic distinguishes illegal acts of aggression and violence by rules and sanctions and yet condones them in a competitive morality pronounced as trite dogma by the governors of the sport, supported extensively and intensely in the sport's infrastructure by parents, players, policemen, priests...Further, the professional model pervades the subculture of the game and is most impressed upon young children (Smith, 1978, pp. 104-5). From this model, the competitive morality which is learned incidentally by them does not involve moderation and self restraint or the practice of fairness and reasonableness. How should the legal system react to this social climate?

2.3 Moral Law

Morality, at least for those who practice the Judeo-Christian system of ethics, is a code of conduct based in imperatives. These imperatives of action may be imposed by some moral authority, such as, God, or may be imposed from within the person in the form of conscience. Presumably, that which comes from within the person can be said to have arisen as a consequence of moral education. In our society, moral messages pervade society massively. In the education of children we seek to establish and reinforce conventional moral values in the expectation that each person will grow to moral maturity in some post-conventional stage of personal development. Our society functions best (and our education system functions best) when the legal messages, the moral messages and mores, at least complement each other as one compatible primary message system.* It may be that we try too hard to use sport to promote a moral profile, viz., fairness, effort, work, perseverance, loyalty, obedience, conformity... Certainly, (Dunning, 1971, pp. 47-48) would agree as he points out that sociologists have been slow to recognize the importance of sport for pleasure and enjoyment and too willing to see sport as a solution to social problems, such as, aggression, crime, war, an agent of socialization and education... Essentially I agree with him.

Grisez and Shaw (1974) offer an important perspective when they recognize a difference between movement and action. Their position has become, and indeed they have become quite famous for it, that for a movement to be defined as action, it must be directed to do or attempt to do some good or avoid some evil - an action which is 'wrong' is done by a moral person in pursuit of some objective which seems 'good' to him. For Grisez and Shaw, to place action in a moral frame, it must impinge upon elements important in humanity, such as, life itself, communicable knowledge or friendship. Action which places humanity at risk is immoral. Action which does not impinge upon elements important in humanity and is neither directed to do nor attempts to do some good or avoid some evil, may be reclassified as

---

* For an explanation of the primary message system see Hall (1959).

movement. Movement is outside the sphere of morals.

By this argument, much of what we do athletically in a game or contest is outside the sphere of morals and some of what we do can be included. Competing in sport, we set out to achieve technical objectives which are relative to a given competitive situation. As such, these objectives are mere products of our movements and in no sense are they categorical imperatives of action.

The distinctions between movement and action need further elaboration: Most of what we do in sport is governed by cause and effect and the person in the circumstances of action is rarely free of the bonds of the subculture or the pressure of the competitive movement. Even within these constraints, when they choose athletes can be free to act autonomously as well as bound teleologically.* They do so by crossing a threshold between cognitive and habitual intention, or as Kant puts it crossing from the intelligible to the sensible world. When athletes cross this threshold for determining intention which leads to action and move from a cognitive mode to an habitual mode, they depend to a considerable extend upon experience. In the latter mode they do what is necessary and sacrifice intellectual autonomy to a considerable extent, although they can opt out, cross the threshold and regain autonomy at will. Submerging cognitive awareness in an habitual frame is easy for an athlete, or for anyone who is trained to do so! The process of habit is very convenient to athletic action. It is a form of neural programming which enables the person to 'act' fluently without full cognitive awareness of all the aspects of the action and it is an example of the person sublimating intention and therefore freedom of thought and will. The 'habit box of action' is indispensable to quality performance in sport (but it is also an illustration of man's inclination to be a creature of habit, to escape from conscious examination of what he does culturally and constitutionally).

2.4 Mores

Mores, particularly the customs, practices, attitudes, values and style of action distinguish sub-culture. This normative system may be conventional or unconventional but is more likely to be a mix of both.

The participants in sport, players and non-players ranging from administrators to spectators committed in the sub-culture, have a choice of acting morally or otherwise in some degree. If the participants are mature, rational persons they will display their rationality by functioning morally and autonomously. Their 'morality of principle't which they are bound to obey if they remain rational and therefore loyal to it, is the product of their own intention (will). If they concede a morality of principle for a 'morality of loyalty't then they concede their autonomy and may concede their

---

* Teleology is the doctrine of final causes: developments are due to the purpose or design that is served by them.

t The terms 'morality of principle' and 'morality of loyalty' are borrowed from Bredemier and Stephenson (1962, p. 17).

principles. In doing so they become a means or agent of some other person's intention. For example, the 'macho' tradition of dropping the gloves in responding to insult in ice hockey is accepted in Canadian society (Smith, 1974, 1975, 1977 and Faulkner, 1974) so long as the fight is 'fair' and not so violent as to attract the attention of the law (McMurtry, 1974). In such circumstances, institutionalized order does not make violence more or less moral. Clearly, the institutionalized mores of the sport of hockey and of Canadian society in relation to hockey are less concerned with a 'morality of principle' (in which everyone is treated alike according to derived 'universal' principles) and are more concerned with a 'morality of loyalty' in which hockey players and the sport of hockey are treated differently because of the place the game has in society.

Sport takes on material and institutional form being continually redefined as the participants respond to the conflicting demands which they create for themselves in the system. It is characterized by:

i)   the form of sport, as rules and content,
ii)   the framework of values, which give meaning to both the form of it and the roles performed by the participants, and
iii)   the fronts or props as posture, gesture, dress and manner of movement which create impressions and make role playing colourful.

Ingham and Loy (1972, pp. 3-23) present this humanistic model of sport to explain the evolution of sport from play. Forms, frames and fronts are the elements which they separate and distinguish for the purpose of analysis of the social process and the social fact of sport. They warn that sport, like any social institution, is dependent upon the devotees of it for both process and reality; so long as participants accept the consequences of its reality, it can be a virile institution - and it does seem that sport is distinguished by participants who enjoy its reality and ensure its virility. It may be that the 'reality' and 'virility' of sport are achieved by the use of mores conventionally and unconventionally.

3.   The Contract To Compete

The contract to compete is forged in each person distinctly. It must be so for each person practises a constant set of values or inclination to action based partly in genetic inheritance and partly in that which is derived from the interpretation placed on and the force of attraction to particular normative values. It is impossible to identify elements of contract except illustratively. Probably, some elements of contract are common, such as, the athlete agrees to attend training regularly, support the team, be loyal to the coach, dress in a particular way, behave in a particular style...however, the focus of this presentation is not to make a long list of things which the athlete, the team, the coach or the administrator agree to do explicitly or implicitly, but rather is one of examining some aspects of the different normative systems which shape the content of the contract to compete.

Presumably, contracting to compete in a game requires acceptance of the written and unwritten rules, laws, mores, codes, customs and practices expected within a particular athletic discipline. Athletes go into competition sensing excitement, anticipating action and assuming that what they are about to do is somehow eminently special, pure and proper. One of the attractions of the athletic contest is that it is an engagement by proponent and opponent wherein is real life suspended so that what occurs may take place in some simplified matrix of action not subject to the usual moral and legal scrutiny because it is simply not necessary to do so. For the most part, athletes commit in contest intent upon honoring the contract. For some athletes, the contract to compete means very little and they may well commit in contest being willing both to break the rules of the game, thereby cheating to gain an advantage unearned, and to violate the laws of morality and society in some violent act.

4. Some Aspects of The Normative System Which Affect The Contract To Compete

4.1 Changing Values
Actions, behaviour and qualities which are approved of are gathered "within a single field of moral force" according to Inglis (1981, p. 51) and as such are given public and private meaning as values. Values change with time, place and cultural experience, though some persist to a degree regardless of culture, time and place.

As a boy I became intoxicated by the heady moral fumes given off in sport and from boyhood literature. It may have been the same for you. Courage and fairness were values I understood, or I thought I did! The moral idealism which pervaded my education, and pervaded the ethos of sport and the stories I read, is not quite in tune with the values of the day! The values of moral idealism which I absorbed arose historically from an upper class nobility, and subsequently were reinforced by a class conscious system of education* which identified, for example, the notion of sportsmanship. The changes which have surfaced in contemporary society have come about as a consequence of incidental and calculated dissidence. Calculated dissidence is seen best in literature, the electronic media, in the leadership and oratory of 'significant others' and through the various activities of the human and civil rights groups, for example. Incidental dissidence is seen best in the shift in society from a concern for humanity to a concern for self, the shift in sport from playing fairly to playing to win at a cost to be calculated, and the shift in patriotism from being prepared to honour the flag and die in war to dodging the draft, at least for one war.

---

* For his treatment of the influence of an upper class nobility on the normative value system of sport see Peter McIntosh. He has referred to this influence in so much of his writing on the history of physical education that a general review of his published work is recommended. However, highly recommended is his most recent book, Fair Play, Ethics in Sport and Education, 1979.

For Inglis (1981, p. 58) this moral idealism was the means of clearing an 'ethical space' wherein could flourish values associated with patriotism, nationalism and athletic idealism, for example. It was promoted by all agents and agencies with a stake in the moral climate. These agents and agencies have had to adjust to the changing moral climate. For young athletes the fumes may be just as intoxicating but the moral idealism that they appreciate is not that which I knew in childhood.

4.2 Conventional and Unconventional Values

A team, club or similar unit of a sport, through its appointed representatives, interacts with the governing body of its sport, the larger sub-culture of sport, and the society in which the sub-culture is a part. At different times, it may represent the views of its members to the governing body of its sport or represent its sport form to the sub-culture of sport or to the larger society. In these formal moments, it operates a conventional value system as a set of standards acceptable to its sport, the sub-culture of sport and the larger society, and represents it outwardly to 'outsiders' and inwardly to 'insiders'*. In addition, it supports implicitly an unconventional value system operated from within by 'insiders' for 'insiders'. Essentially, it does so in order that the appointed representatives may claim themselves to be 'insiders' and also that it may cheat surreptitiously on the institutionalized values in order to promote its own well being, say, in attempting to be successful in competition with other teams. As Sutton Smith and Roberts (1970) have suggested, games are models of power and, "an opportunity to learn all those necessary arts of trickery, deception, harassment, decimation and foul play..." (p. 7).

Cheating on the institutionalized values is of two sorts, according to Eitzen (1979, p. 81). It is to do that which is contrary to the rules and values but which is condoned, overlooked or accepted as common enough practice (institutionalized cheating) or to break rules which other similar institutions will not condone and which incur heavy penalty (deviant cheating). Notably, 'deviant cheating' is offences against the rules and regulations of the institution of that sport and the sub-culture of sport, such as, using illegal equipment, allowing the use of drugs, or using an ineligible player, whereas, 'institutionalized cheating is looking for and exploiting a loophole in regulations, dishonouring the spirit of the rules and teaching or encouraging illegal techniques and tactics, for example. Usually, institutionalized cheating involves either less likelihood of being caught or doing things which other teams do and get away with. Attempts to justify such deviancy often involve inconsistent ethical argument.

Apart from the institutionalized values, the deviant values of the 'insiders' are operated not by the formally appointed representatives

---

* Legitimate deviance is explained by Becker (1963, p. 12) and Taylor (1979, pp. 15-18). Taylor is recommended also for his outstanding treatment of the effect of class in the normative system, especially sport.

but by the authority of peer group leaders and in accordance with the infrastructural values of the group established by practice common during the history of the group. In a male fraternity, these deviant values are largely counter-conventional as,

   i) profane conversation, songs, jokes, teasing, insult, gesture and posture, and
   ii) 'macho' values in fighting, risk taking, tolerating pain and injury, being competitively aggressive, appearing to enjoy aggressive and even violent impact without flinching, and 'standing up' under pressure to face adversity with determination. In fact, though these values are formally counter-conventional to values of the society at large and of the sport, they are quite standard in many male groups regardless of subculture and are a recognized part of the sub-culture of sport. For the most part, they are understood and condoned by the society at large so long as they do not result in conduct which, when displayed publicly, causes affront. Listiak (1976, p. 420) suggests that certain forms of deviance receive social approval and are toler-ated even in highly visible form at certain times, effectively as delinquency in festival. My own view is that 'legitimate deviance' is a part of the infra-structure of society generally and occurs in a variety of forms throughout sub-culture heightened in moments of festivity, no doubt. However, it must also be said that the society which condones 'legitimate deviance' is one which reflects middle class values. The 'legitimate deviance' of groups of low socio-economic males is tolerated much less readily either because of class prejudice or because such groups display their deviance openly and in a style which itself is judged to be unacceptably deviant.

4.3 The Notion of Heroism
Heroism is linked with adulthood. Usually, in childhood the notion of heroism is implanted as a romantic ideal. In boyhood, the princi-pal forms of the romantic ideal are seen in the context of war and sport. Achievement, superiority, dominance and superhuman qualities are emphasized vicariously in literature, sport and other forms of art. As part of the mix, altruism, patriotism, leadership, power, authority and success are blended in the worlds of work, leisure, fact and fantasy.
   Heroism is beyond boredom and anxiety. It involves adventure, excitement, drama, challenge, mastery, insight, intellect and the capacity to make the right judgements in life and death circum-stances! It involves the primacy of duty and loyalty and the notions of self-sarcifice, honour, moral integrity, courage in adversity, displaying strength of character, the calculated acceptance of risk, the willingness to tolerate pain and the notions of nobility and comradeship of men in groups and probably of women in groups, also.

4.4 Counter-Culture and Anti-Culture
Willis (1978) tells us that culture is not art or humanity but a shared material experience: "It is in relation to the commonplace, to trivia and the slow accumulation of concrete lessons that individ-uals in groups come to recognize their subjectivity" (p. 2). By this Willis suggests that the dominant 'establishment' values and skills

of society, imposed in an unreal world of education, mean little to those who are not interested in adopting them. For such persons, the alternative to conventional learning is street learning by random and dialectical relationships. Without the benefit of an established cultural form, they must create one of their own. What begins as random experience without consciousness or purpose and in unforeseen circumstances, often dominated by the trivial, emerges as meaningful elements of a culture for those involved! Beyond this stage, the social group, which by now had adopted cultural items which come to resemble what they seek to be, refines and develops its culture form creatively and dialectically. The course of such cultural development is largely unspecified and unintended, yet the things which are central to the emerging culture relate to the position of the social group within the structure or society. In some cases, the frustrations, contradictions, feelings, emotions, attitudes, opinions and beliefs blend in a profane culture. At this point, the supporters of a profane culture in which they have consciously or unconsciously, intentionally or unintentionally shared in its creation, treat the established system with irreverance or disregard. Moral principle as the basis of humanity is far removed from it.

In a school programme of physical activity, as any broadly experienced teacher of physical education in western society will affirm, participation in physical education classes is difficult to sustain. Two problem groups are apparent, apart from students who simply dislike physical education, namely, girls who have opted out of the system in order to practice the 'props' and 'fronts' of a feminine stereo-type and boys with a particular interpretation of the masculine stereotype. They are reluctant participants because they have committed to cultures creatively variant from the athletic sub-culture. Depending upon the social class in which their parents are located, boys and girls separately in groups, or mixed in groups, commit to the influence of the market place of trivia and of revolution. They set out not to establish a culture, for intuitively they see no purpose in establishing something which they will outgrow, but to create an anti-culture which does not need to be secured or established (the advantage of an anti-culture is that it leaves no lasting effect as a created culture and therefore does not need to be challenged by others). In fact, they create cultures in spite of themselves! For boys, the form of their anti-culture is to be against the motives of physical well being, athletic excellence, locker and shower room discipline, and standards of dress and cleanliness. For girls, it is to be for the motives of posture, gesture, dress, language, manner of movement and music which are in conflict with the physical culture to such an extent that they feel disloyal to the feminine stereotype by taking part in physical activity. For both boys and girls wearing a clean uniform or any kind of conformity to dress standards in physical activity would be seen as disloyalty to their anti-cultures. To take part, other than to make fun of the system and to disrupt the conventions and mores, would be to allow the physical culture to exert some influence upon them. Whether what they create is culture or anti-culture, often it is profanely anti-establishment!

4.5 Ambivalence and Ambiguity

The literature about sport is festooned with antithetical proposi-
tions. The distinction between athletics and sport, sport and
recreation, professional and amateur, work and play, expressive and
functional, serious and fun, utilitarian and purely wasteful, real
and unreal, is more than semantic argument, it is an indication that
persons have difficulty in dealing with both ambiguity and
ambivalence in the art form activities which give them pleasure and
enjoyment. Ambivalence and ambiguity persist because the reification
of sport (and of other forms of art) have not occurred in society.
We would find concurrence from Ingham and Loy (1971), "...a
successful game consists of a ludic encounter having a certain
outcome, a relatively high degree of sociability and permitting
participants the maximum display of relevant skills and attributes."
(p. 45), from Turner (1974, p. 90) who sees sport art and work as
having taken over the flow function* in culture from ritual and
religious drama, because in them meaningful challenge to the
individual enables engagement of a state of flow and from Ardrey
(1966, p. 333) who sees identity, stimulation and security as the
needs of man. In games, participants pursue a personae and a group
identity, enjoying excitement and challenge, secure within a cultural
game form in which a competitive contract is understood. Anonymity,
boredom and anxiety, the cultural opposites of Ardrey's needs of
mankind, are set aside naturally in the pleasure and enjoyment of
playing games.

Illustrative of the many forms of ambivalence and ambiguity in
sport are:

i)   Competition is morally and legally ambiguous, for within its
players consent to suspend the morality normally recognized as the
basis of action and put in its place a competitive contract which
permits contest, rivalry, aggression and stylized animosity, even to
the extent of inflicting physical injury upon an opponent.

ii) Sport is a thoroughly familiar phenomenon, and playing in a
game whether as sport or recreation† is seen to be a harmless enough
pastime (even when it is serious endeavour). In such ambivalence is
the moral ambiguity rationalized. The experience of sport can
neither harm the player nor the observer of his play. Sporting man
is impervious to evil! It is only a game, even when the mores of the
sub-culture are in violation of both the competitive contract and
sometimes common and criminal law or, as occurs very frequently in

---

* Flow function refers to Csikszartmihalyi's (1975) autotelic
experience, that is, experience satisfying in itself and in which the
person can merge awareness of self within the action, becoming a part
of it.

† Sport and recreation do not exist on a continuum except as a
normative exercise. What is sport to one is recreation to another.
What is vocational to one is often avocational to that person, also.
What is physically demanding work athletically in one context is
autotelically pleasurable in another, to the same person.

many different kinds of games, when a player by calculated protagon-
ism or emotionally responsive antagonism, breaks the conventional
contract.

iii) The ideal of modesty, if not of sportsmanship, in relation to
achievement, is in contrast with the inclination to create legend,
myth, hero and history from the sporting achievements of super
(human) performance. It is the style of the devoted follower of a
sport to create heroes and special memories as monuments. These are
not retained in their social and physical reality but gilded in
myth. The hero is typically self assured, physically well propor-
tioned, attractive of features, balanced and lithe of movement,
virile, astute in tactical and strategical judgements, superbly
skillful in action with a power to weight ratio that sets him apart
in his athleticism (not quite "bionic" but nearly so,) and a leader
not a follower! The special moment in performance is exaggerated and
dramatized to make a good story to be recounted to others or recalled
in personal reminiscence. Modesty is set aside in myth and legend.

iv) Some sports are classified as "contact" but are really
"impact", some are "non-contact" but in them players use contact and
impact surreptitiously, others are "individual participation"
contests in which the intimidation of an opponent is technically
unnecessary in order to compete...not only is there ambiguity within
classifications, but the players and other devoted participants of a
game ambivalently enjoy the courage, manliness and aggressive
competitiveness displayed by their team members, even when it is
delinquent, profane, illegal and contrary to the rules and spirit of
the rules of their game. Privately, transgressions are enjoyed:
"insiders" know that football of all kinds is impact sport and they
take special masculine pride in the status of the added dimension of
contact; "insiders" know that (non-contact) basketball is not for the
fainthearted, especially in action under the basket when being made
of the "right stuff" counts; "insiders" know that psychological
intimidation is not part of the athletic ideal yet they approve of it
in secret as a way of gaining competitive advantage in almost every
sport.

v) Boxers fight with fists clad in gloves for the protection of
the contestants. Contests are rigidly controlled, lest the activity
loses its right to be classified as a sport. For the spectator of
it, the fascination is enveloped in ambivalence and ambiguity. The
prospect of one boxer reducing another to a defenceless state by
inflicting physical blows to the "target" of head and body is an
unpleasant human activity. The physical reality is plain to see, yet
the fantasy is maintained that what is being enacted is a contest in
the noble art of self defence. The notion that the sport is not
physically damaging to the participants is frequently expressed by
those who would defend it. In this aesthetic, which has been created
by the devotees of boxing, what is essentially repugnant in humani-
tarian terms is seen as noble, sporting, manly and as a form of art.

vi) Athletes fight illegally during a game. Usually, the circumstances in which a fight occurs involves provocation which leads to
loss of control by either protagonist or antagonist. Such a trans-
gression is understood though not condoned within the rules or the
conventional morality which the participants display in most games.

What is not displayed clearly is the ambivalence felt by the administrators who sustain an affinity with players, to maintain status as
"insider" by retaining some of the unconventional, quasi-delinquent
underworld of values to which they were once privileged! Also, what
is not readily visible is the ambivalence of players who are required
to honour the core of conventional sporting conduct and also to obey
the mores of the peer group, especially in displaying competitive
aggression towards winning and being made of the "right stuff" in
response to provocation or intimidation. As for spectators, they may
disapprove of fighting in principle yet be fascinated ambivalently by
the drama of it in practice. In hockey, the moral ambiguity in the
game is profound. The game officially prohibits fighting. Even so,
the mores of the hockey subculture condone the act of fighting as a
necessary characteristic of its ethos, which is in itself a remarkable example of ambivalence.

vii) When players consent to take part in a game they commit to a
competitive contract in which they concede fairly and reasonably to
take part accordingly to the laws, rules, practices, norms and codes
which are commonly understood. Thus, a person contracting in an
impact/contact sport accepts a measure of physical assault. However,
they do not have the right to inflict harm upon another or consent
and submit to harm upon self judged to be criminal. A person who
assaults an opponent in a game may not claim the consent of his
opponent as a defence of his action: assaulting a person by his
permission is a contradiction in terms and unacceptable in law.
Duelling provides an historical example of an activity in which a
person was expected to respond to a challenge as part of a code of
honour in which it was cowardly to refuse. Minors may commit in
impact sports for a similar reason for the tyranny of a macho-
aesthetic is well known and supported by adults in the mistaken
belief that it is necessary to encourage manliness as a characteristic in a young male. Compulsive public opinion is involved in
sports, such as, hockey, and football and in other cultures,
rugby... While a challenge in these activities is issued and accepted
differently in each, the social force pattern behind the challenge is
not so different. It is not so much that minors should not be coerc-
ed to play such games. Rather is it important to know that culture
is a tyranny of a sort and we should understand both the coerciveness
of what we do within the sub-culture of sport and the extent to which
the person consents, confined and bound by the culture.

viii) A person in action may have regard for others as a
principle of action and this we would describe as altruism. Neither
individuals nor society can survive without it. Altruistic conduct
is the mechanism that keeps society positively arranged, planning,
building and dreaming for the future. Humanity is at its best when
altruism pervades society. Of course, altruism is not heavy handed
principle, killing joy, happiness and hope, nor is it in conflict
with individuality and freedom. Rather is it merely a personal
accountability on the part of each of us to recognize that what we do
must not intrude, restrict or affect others adversely. Competition
and rivalry in which we compete for some prize which is exclusive,
and in the process seek to defeat another, is in conflict with
altruism, unless we can agree that for the purpose of play such

principles can be set aside temporarily in favour of another code of conduct, designed to replace the code of altruistic conduct.

ix) Culture is fashioned when the participants perceive, attend, intend and act in support of it. Because a culture requires conformity for its presence, it is restrictive upon its supporters. Only certain modes of conduct are encouraged and others are directly discouraged and thus remain undeveloped: both the unit of group organization and the persons within it sacrifice some potential. Sport becomes a subculture because the conformity required to sustain and practice it is different from that required in other cultural affiliation. In that sense, it divides, taking away the person from other cultural forms and also denying individuality of the person. Sometimes, the conflict which it introduces requires the person to make a choice of little consequence but sometimes the conflict, say, with family or educational priorities, may make the choice of considerable significance. Culture is always a gilded invitation to be a part of something rather than something else and usually it requires the participant to submerge personal identity and assume a "persona". As Tiger (1970, p. 58) points out, any culture encourages individuality only within the confines of its expectations.

Finally, some aspects of the normative systems which affect the contract to compete have become many aspects. Yet, there is much more that could be said, except that, to turn back to where I began, unlike "when E.F. Hutton speaks...", when Peter Ventre speaks: who listens?

References

Becker, Howard S. Outsiders: Studies in the Sociology of Deviance. Glencoe: The Free Press, 1963.

Clarke, John et all. "Subcultures, Cultures and Class" Working Papers in Cultural Studies (Centre for Contemporary Cultural Studies, University of Birmingham), 7 & 8, 1975, 9-74.

Eitzen, D. Stanley. Sport in Contemporary Society. New York: St. Martin's Press, 1979.

Elliot, M.J. "Law and Sport: The Public Regulation of Private Activity." In Sport and the Law. eds. J. Neville Turner and Charles Jenkins. Proceedings of a Conference held at the University of Birmingham, July, 1978.

Grisez, G. and R. Shaw. Beyond the New Morality: The Responsibilities of Freedom. University of Notre Dame Press, Notre Dame, Illinois, 1974.

Hall, Edward T. The Silent Language. Garden City: New York: Doubleday and Co. Inc., 1959.

Ingham, Alan G. and John W. Loy Jr. "The Structure of Ludic Action". A paper presented at The Third Symposium on the Sociology of Sport, University of Waterloo, Ontario, Canada, August 22-28, 1971.

Inglis, Fred. The Name of the Game: Sport and Society London: Heinemann, 1977.

Inglis, Fred. The Promise of Happiness. Cambridge University Press, Cambridge, 1981.

Leader Post, Regina, Saskatchewan, December 13th, 1977, p. 11.

Listiak, Alan. "'Legitimate Deviance' and Social Class: Bar Behavior During Grey Cup Week." In Canadian Sport: Sociological Prospectives. eds. Richard S. Gouneau and John G. Albinson. Don Mills, Ontario: Addison Wesley (Canada) Ltd., 1976.

McIntosh, Peter. Fair Play: Ethics in Sport and Education. London: Heinemann, 1979.

McMurtry, William R. Investigations and Inquiry into Violence in Amateur Hockey: Report to the Honourable Rene Brunelle, Ontario Minister of Community and Social Services. Toronto: Ontario Government Bookstore, 1974.

Smith, Michael D. "Social Learning of Violence in Minor Hockey" in Psychological Perspectives in Youth Sports Frank L. Small and Ronald E. Smith. Toronto: John Wiley and Sons, 1978.

Sutton Smith, Brian and John M. Roberts. "The Cross Cultural and Psychological Study of Games" in The Cross Cultural Analysis of Sport and Games ed. Gunther Luschen. Champaign, Illinois: Stipes Publishing co., 1970.

Taylor, Ian. "Class Violence and Sport: The Case for Soccer Hooliganism in Britain". A paper presented at the International Symposium on Sport, Culture and the Modern State" at Queen's University, Kingston, Ontario, Canada, October 20th, 1979.

Tiger, Lionel. Men in Groups London: Thomas Nelson and Sons Ltd., 1969.

Turner, Victor. "Luminal to Luminoid in Play Flow and Ritual," Rice University Studies, 10, No. 3 (1974) 53-92.

Willis, Paul, Profane Culture London: Routledge Kegan Paul Ltd., 1978.

Index

This index is compiled from the 'key words' assigned to papers by their authors. The page numbers refer to the first page of the paper in which the reference is to be found.